SEAFOOD OF SOUTH-EAST ASIA

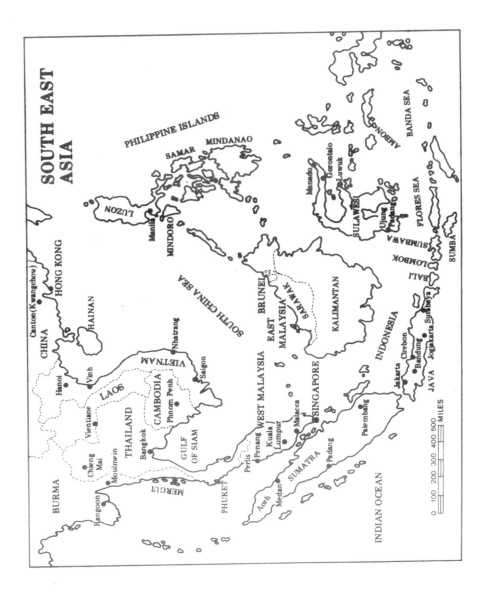

Seafood of South-East Asia

A Comprehensive Guide with Recipes

2nd Edition

Alan Davidson

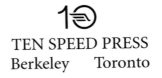

TEN SPEED PRESS
Berkeley   Toronto

Published by Ten Speed Press, in association with Prospect Books UK.

Ten Speed Press
P.O. Box 7123,
Berkeley, California 94707
www. tenspeed.com

Distributed in Australia by Simon & Schuster Australia, in Canada by Ten Speed Press Canada, in New Zealand by Southern Publishers Group, and in South Africa by Real Books.

Set in Minion by Emma Glaisher
Manufactured in Great Britain

Library of Congress Cataloging-in-Publication Data

Davidson, Alan, 1924-
Seafood of South-East Asia : comprehensive guide with recipes /
by Alan Davidson.-- 2nd ed.
p. cm.
ISBN 1-58008-452-4
1. Cookery (Seafood) 2. Cookery, Southeast Asian. 3. Fishes--Asia, Southeastern. 4. Shellfish--Asia, Southeastern.
I. Title.

TX747 .D278 2003
641.6'92'0959--dc21

2003014545

1 2 3 4 5 6 7 8 9 10 — 07 06 05 04 03

Contents

'Owing to its reproductive powers, in China the fish is a symbol of regeneration. As fish are reputed to swim in pairs, so a pair of fish is emblematic of connubial bliss. As in water fish move easily in any direction they signify freedom from all restraints, so in the Buddha-state the fully emancipated know no restraints or obstructions. Their scaly armour makes them a symbol of martial attributes, bringing strength and courage; and swimming against the current provides an emblem of perseverance. The fish is a symbol of abundance or wealth and prosperity, because they are so plentiful in the seas and rivers. . .' (Read, *Chinese Materia Medica*)

Acknowledgements

My first thanks go to the Food and Agriculture Organisation of the United Nations (FAO), who – happily for me – produced their admirable Species Identification Sheets for fish of the region at the very time when I was starting to write this book and who encouraged me to make full use of their work in mine. I am particularly grateful to the editor of the Identification Sheets, Dr Walter Fischer; and to the various FAO experts working in the area, notably Dr Domingo Tapiador and Dr Einar Kvaran, who generously gave me their advice.

The other institutions and individuals who have helped me to compile my catalogues of species include:

in Burma, Professor Ko Ko Gyi at the University of Rangoon, U Tint Hlaing at the Department of Fisheries and U Kenneth Bau Tint, Director of the People's Pearl and Fisheries Corporation;

in Thailand, the Department of Fisheries at Bangkok, where Mr Thosaporn Wongratana tendered much useful advice; the Marine Biological Research Centre at Phuket, where the then Director, Dr Vagn Hansen, assisted me most lavishly, as did the Thai marine biologists working with him; Dr Supap Monkolprasit of the Fisheries Department of Kasetsart University; Mrs Ti Garden and Mr Thep Thavonsouk;

in Cambodia, the University of Phnom Penh and the Department of Fisheries (as they were in 1974);

in Vietnam, the Department of Fisheries and the University of Agriculture at Saigon (again, 1974 version); the University of Cantho (Faculty of Agriculture); officials of the fishing industry who kindly received me at Haiphong; and the Director and staff of the National Library at Hanoi, who placed special facilities at my disposal for research in their institution;

at Kwangchow (Canton), Mr Li Wei-Liang and the Director of the Permanent Exhibition of Marine Products of Kwangtung Province;

at Hong Kong, Mr E. H. Nichols, Director of the Department of Agriculture and Fisheries, and Dr William Chan at the Fisheries Research Station at Aberdeen;

in the Philippines, Professor Inocencio Ronquillo, Director of the Fisheries Research Division of the Bureau of Fisheries and Aquatic Resources at Intramuros, Manila, and Dr A. F. Umali, doyen of Filipino ichthyologists, who kindly let me consult him in his retirement;

in Indonesia, Mr M. Unar, Director of the Marine Fisheries Research Institute, and his staff; Mr V. Susanto, Director of Resources in the Ministry dealing with Fisheries; Mr Sutik Muaadi, Chief of the Fisheries Service, for help at the wholesale fish market; and Mr Subagjo Soemodiharjo, Head of the Molluscs Division of the Institute of Marine Research;

in Brunei, the Fisheries Department and the Hassanal Bolkiah Aquarium at Bandar Seri Begawan;

in Singapore, the staffs of the main wholesale fish market and of the South East Asia Fisheries Development Center (SEAFDEC) at Changi Point;

in Malaysia, Dr Chua Tia Eng of the Universiti Sains Malaysia at Penang, who took great pains to help at a time when he was busy on his own forthcoming books, *A Handbook of the Common Coastal Fishes of West Sabah* (with Dr H. C. Lai) and *A Handbook of the Common Food Fishes of Malaysia and Singapore*; and the Department of Fisheries at Kuala Lumpur;

in London, Dr Peter Whitehead, Dr Ray Ingle, Dr Anthony Fincham and Mrs Solene Whybrow at the British Museum (Natural History); and the Tropical Products Institute.

In between the scientific and culinary acknowledgements I offer with my love one bouquet to my wife Jane for her constant encouragement and help, and for her company on almost all my research journeys; and another to my daughter Caroline for undertaking one such journey, to West Malaysia and Singapore, in my stead and for the valuable contribution which she thereby made to both halves of the book; and a third to my daughter Jennifer for her careful compilation of the index.

I also trumpet one thank-you of a general character. My colleagues in the British Diplomatic Service and their wives, throughout the region, were extremely kind in paving ways and providing facilities for me. If I do not list them it is only because the roll-call would be so long that it might lend to the book an official aura which it should not have. But my thanks to them, and to members of the Development Division at the British Embassy in Bangkok, are heartfelt.

In making my collection of recipes I have profited greatly from the help of numerous experts and enthusiasts. Most of them are named in the recipe section, and it goes without saying that my thanks are due to all of them as well as to the authors of the cookery books listed in the Bibliography. I add here, for general help on Indonesian cuisine, the names of Mrs Sudharto and Mrs Saptodewo, and that of Mr Tony Hunt.

For the second time in twelve months I have Janet Lovelock to thank for preparing a book of mine for the printers. On the present occasion, when the whole work of editing the book and superintending its composition fell to her, I have done so by means of the dedication. Here I thank Maria Jebb for her diligent collation and preparation of the illustrations. The illustrations themselves are acknowledged in the Introduction to the Catalogues.

Finally, I record my warm gratitude to Mr One Sy and his staff at the Imprimerie Nationale in Vientiane (especially the chief compositor, Mr Somlit Norasingh) for composing the book with rapidity and care, despite many distractions.

ACKNOWLEDGEMENTS FOR THE NEW EDITION

My principal and warmest thanks for this new edition go to Helen Saberi who joined me in the further research which underlies the very numerous corrections and improvements in the book, and who has been largely responsible for implementing them: six months' diligent work. She and I hope that the spirit and flavour of the original book have been fully preserved throughout this period of change.

On this occasion we have received invaluable help from: Fuchsia Dunlop for an arduous and highly beneficial review of Chinese names throughout the book; the late Professor Doreen Fernandez for many improvements to passages pertaining to the Philippines; and Philip Iddison for much help with ichthyological and nomenclatural information from the Gulf. I am grateful to Emma Glaisher who achieved the type setting with her usual diligence, and to my wife Jane for proof reading the Cookery Section. Last but not least, warmest thanks must also go to my publishers, Aaron Wehner and his colleagues at Ten Speed Press in Berkeley and Tom Jaine of Prospect Books in Devon, for the enthusiasm and care with which they have handled this edition.

Introduction to the First Edition

This book is intended to help English-speaking readers in South-East Asia to enjoy the seafood of that region.

There is no great problem in identifying meat and poultry. A pig is a pig the world over; and a chicken is a chicken. But fish are another matter. There are thousands and thousands of species of edible fish. Although some, such as the bluefin tuna, are found in all the oceans, and although many species of the North Atlantic have close relations in the Indo-Pacific region, it is no easy task to relate the fish in the markets at, say, Bangkok or Singapore to those on sale at Aberdeen, Concarneau or Boston.

The problem is confounded by the loose way in which English names have been applied to Indo-Pacific species on the basis of a resemblance, real or fancied, to North Atlantic species. And even the local names in the languages of the South-East Asian countries present a disconcerting tangle. Precision can only be achieved by using the system of scientific names which ichthyologists employ and by relating the various popular names to these. This is what is done in the catalogue which constitutes the first part of the book, and which is intended to help the reader identify the various fish and other sea creatures. One is at a disadvantage if one does not know what one is cooking, eating or asking the waiter to bring.

The catalogue is complemented by a collection of recipes from the region. These show how the fish of South-East Asia are prepared locally. The results are often very different from the seafood dishes of, say, the Mediterranean. But these differences are not a function of differences between the respective fish populations (such differences being negligible from the cook's point of view) but of the differences between the other available ingredients and spices and the indigenous techniques of cooking. There is nothing about the fish of South-East Asia which makes them apt for being steamed in banana leaves or prepared with ginger or lemon grass; nor is there anything about them which should deter the cook from using olive oil or thyme or making a chowder. Thus, although the recipe section itself is strictly South-East Asian, the general advice offered in the catalogue on how to cook the various species transcends local practice and is intended to encourage a more varied use of the seafood of the region.

I must finish my introduction by saying clearly that the book, in this first edition, contains more omissions and errors than a book should. Of this I am sure. However, I am also sure that it is already considerably better than nothing at all, which is what anyone looking for such a book so far would have found. And it is my hope that readers who fill in gaps or mistakes in their own copies will have the kindness to share their amendments with me (care of the publishers) so that any subsequent editions may benefit from their knowledge.

ALAN DAVIDSON

Vientiane, Laos
The World's End, London
September, 1973 – December, 1975

Introduction to the Revised Edition

What I said in 1975 about omissions and errors in this book resulted in various individuals and institutions helping me to plug gaps and make corrections. Now, while acknowledging that there must be some omissions and errors still present, I can say that they are far fewer. This improvement reflects not only the helpful advice which I have received from others in correspondence and while visiting the region but also a radical change for the better in the amount of published source materials available.

In this connection I would like to put a spotlight, not for the first time, on the enormously impressive and beneficial work of the Food and Agriculture Organisation (FAO) of the United Nations, and in particular the Fisheries Division and the Publications Division. For nearly half a century their work has underpinned or encapsulated just about all serious studies of fish and fisheries, but it is in the last quarter of a century that this work has, so to speak, fully flowered, especially with regard to the Indo-Pacific. For South-East Asia I have found it quite indispensable. Volumes such as those edited by Kent Carpenter and Volker Niem, covering in comprehensive detail all the forms of seafood in the Western Central Pacific, together with the more finely focussed work such as that by De Bruin, Russell and Bogusch on the Marine Fishery Resources of Sri Lanka and the excellent book by Gabriella Bianchi on the Commercial Marine and Brackish-water Species of Pakistan, provide a bedrock of carefully researched and brilliantly illustrated information without which an amateur like myself could not hope to produce books like the present one.

In this connection, I must refer also to what I always think of as 'the orange volumes' – studies published by the FAO, in an orange paperback format, of particular families of fish, treated on a worldwide basis. The volumes cited in the bibliography under Heemstra and Randall (*Groupers of the World*), and Allen (*Snappers of the World*) are fine examples as is one of the first books in the series, that on *Shrimps and Prawns of the World* by my friend, Professor Holthuis, but there are many others.

However, while emphasizing the debt I owe to the FAO (and the multitudinous experts and artists and editors who have collaborated in their publications) I can still claim credit myself for something, to wit providing the only book which covers both seafood and seafood cookery for the region. There was no other such book when my work was first published in 1976,* and to the best of my knowledge there is still nothing else of comparable scope. So this book, in its new and improved version, can continue to fill the niche in the literature which it has occupied for a quarter of a century. And I will continue to think of it as a sort of thank-you present to the peoples of South-East Asia whose hospitality and help, in every country of the region, we enjoyed when we lived there in the 1970s.

---

* Readers who purchased the very first, limited edition of the book in 1976 will be well aware that all revenues from that edition went to the Christopher Ewart-Biggs Memorial Fund, commemorating the life of this friend of mine who was murdered in July 1976 just after taking up his appointment as British Ambassador to Ireland. However, they will not know how successful this charitable edition was. I am happy to record here that it raised nearly £2000 for the fund, the largest contribution by an individual to it. The work of the fund has continued ever since, striving to promote peace in Ireland, an aim especially dear to my heart because I was born in Londonderry in the north and my mother was brought up in Dublin in the south.

Catalogues

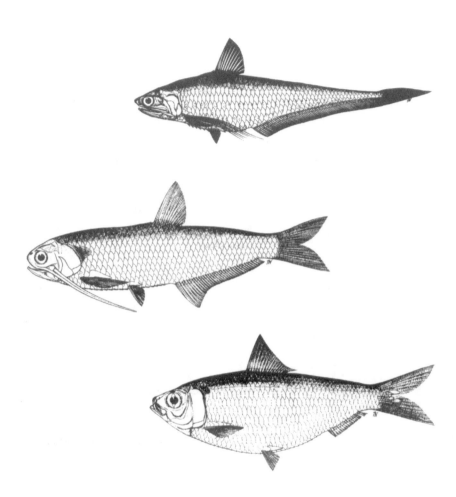

This page of drawings by Mr Thosaporn Wongratana is a pleasing decoration, but serves also as a reminder of the great importance and variety of the clupeoid fish in S. E. Asia. The uppermost fish is *Coilia dussumieri* Cuvier and Valenciennes, one of the hairtail anchovies. In the centre *Thryssa setirostris* (Broussonet), most whiskered of the 'whiskered' anchovies, displays its remarkably long maxillaries. At the bottom is *Sardinella brachysoma* Bleeker, that deep bodied, prosperous-looking magnate of the sardine tribe.

Explanation of the Catalogues

The catalogues which follow are intended to include the most common and the most interesting of the species of fish and other seafood in the region of S. E. Asia which are likely to be met in markets or restaurants.

S. E. Asia is taken to include Burma, Thailand, Cambodia, Vietnam, the southern coast of China and Hong Kong, the Philippines, Brunei, Indonesia and Malaysia. This is as much a political as a geographical definition. But, although human beings may be familiar with national boundaries, fish pay no heed to them and distribute themselves in the oceans and seas on quite other principles.

Moreover, the Indian and Pacific Oceans and their subsidiary seas constitute between them a single, vast area of fish populations. It is common for a species to be distributed right across the whole area; and many species are described as Indo-Pacific in indication of this.

Thus a book which deals with the fish of S. E. Asia is relevant also for cooks in Bangladesh, India, Pakistan, Sri Lanka and even the Red Sea, the Persian Gulf and East Africa. Again, although a broad distinction may be made between the species of tropical or near-tropical waters and those of the colder waters to the north or south, there is no clear division; many species found in S. E. Asian waters are also known in Japan, for example. So, while the focus of the book is S. E. Asia, the field of view is necessarily much wider and the catalogues reflect this circumstance.

I should add that, although I have not followed exclusively any one authority, I have aligned my own catalogue of fish closely with the admirable volumes produced by the Food and Agricultural Organisation (FAO) of the United Nations (see page 10 for details), which incorporate the latest work of ichthyologists on the fish of the region. I take the opportunity to salute once more the achievements of the FAO in this and other fields of activity.

A LITTLE SCIENCE

In the catalogues the name of each species is given first in a Latinized form. This is the scientific name. It usually consists of two words, the first indicating the genus and the second the species within the genus. Some species are shown with more than one Latin name. The explanation is that different naturalists have given them different names and that more than one is in current use.

The first scientific name given is the preferred name and is followed by the name of the naturalist who bestowed it on the species in question. Sometimes the naturalist appears in brackets, sometimes not. The brackets are used to show that the specific name given by the naturalist has been retained, but that the generic name has been changed, since the species is now assigned to a different genus. (This business with the brackets is the correct and established way of conveying information on this point, although it risks giving the layman an impression of erratic punctuation or haphazard type-setting.)

Where a generic name is followed by the useful abbreviation 'spp.', this means that reference is being made to a number of species in the genus together. This device is employed when it would be tedious and unrewarding to list the species separately.

A species belongs to a genus, which belongs to a family, which belongs to an order, which belongs to a class. The introductory passages to the various sections of the catalogue will enable the reader to keep track of the broader categories if he wishes to do so, while each catalogue entry shows the species, genus and family of its subject.

THE LANGUAGES

I give the common names of the species in the principal languages of the region. These languages vary in the extent to which they possess specific common names for fish, and in the extent to which these have been recorded and published. There has also been some variation in the extent to which I have been able to do research on the spot in the different countries. The lists are therefore incomplete, but still have the merit of being fuller than any previously published for the region as a whole.

In some countries the problem is not that there is no specific common name for a given species, but that there are too many, whether of different languages (as in the Philippines and Indonesia) or different dialects (as in Thailand). I have not hesitated to cite more than one name when this seems appropriate, but have not even attempted to give them all when they are numerous. I have followed the principle of preferring the main dialects or languages (for example Tagalog in the Philippines and Bahasa Indonesia in Indonesia) and supplementing these with others only when the additional names seem to have wide currency or to be of particular interest.

The transliteration of Burmese, Thai, Cambodian and Chinese names is a problem with which I have done my best, while well aware that my practice will strike experts as being incorrect, inconsistent, or both.

Where I show a name in brackets, this is to indicate either that it is rather a general name or that it belongs to a closely related species rather than to the species being described or that there is something else not quite right about it.

THE DRAWINGS

Mr Banjong Mianmanus, working at the Phuket Marine Biological Centre, did those on pages 18 (lower), 19, 38, 64 (lower), 72, 82 (upper), 96 (lower), 97, 123 (upper), 138, 142, 144, 149 (upper), 150, 152, 153, 154, 155, 156, 157, 158 (upper and lower), 160, 161, 162, 164, 165, 166, 167, 168 (lower), 170 (upper), 171, 172, 173, 174, 176, 179, 191 and 192.

Mr Thosaporn Wongratana is responsible for the drawings of clupeoid fish on pages 12, 25 (lower) and 30 (upper). These are taken, by kind permission, from the thesis which Mr Wongratana prepared for the Imperial College of Science and Technology in London on 'The systematics of the clupeoid fishes of South East

Asia'. Mr Wongratana was also good enough to provide some simpler drawings where they were needed elsewhere in the book.

The Laotian artist **Soun Vannithone**, with his colleagues **Elian Prasit Souvannavong** and **Singha**, did the drawings on pages 32 (upper), 35 (upper), 102, 169, 203, 206, 207, 208, 210, 211, 212, 213, 214 (except for the soy bean plant), 215, 216, 217, 218, 282 and for the Weights and Measures at the very end of the book.

The drawings on pages 24, 33, 34 (lower), 40, 41, 44, 45, 51, 58 (upper), 59, 62, 63 (upper), 65 (upper), 68, 69, 70, 71, 76, 79, 80, 81, 82 (lower), 83, 88, 90, 91 (upper), 92, 103, 108, 109, 113, 114, 118, 119, 120 and 121 are reproduced from the **FAO Species Identification Sheets**, to which I have referred in my Acknowledgements.

Other drawings reproduced by kind permission of the FAO from the volumes mentioned on page 10: those on pages 22, 23 (lower), 24 (lower), 25, 26, 27, 28, 29, 30 (lower), 32 (lower), 35 (lower), 36, 37, 42, 43, 46 48, 49, 50, 52, 54, 55, 56, 57, 58 (lower), 60, 63 (lower), 65 (lower), 66, 67, 74, 75, 77, 78, 84, 85, 86, 87, 90 (lower), 91 (lower), 94, 95, 96 (upper), 98, 100, 101, 105, 110 (lower), 112, 115, 116, 122, 124, 125, 127, 133, 139, 140, 141, 145, 147, 154 (middle), 158 (lower), 163, 170 (lower), 175, 184, 187, 188, 193.

The drawings of prawns on pages 135 to 137 are reproduced from Dr Hall's book of *Observations on the Taxonomy and Biology of some Indo-West Pacific Penaeidae (Crustacea Decapoda)*, by kind permission of the Overseas Development Ministry in London.

The drawings of cephalopods on pages 180 to 185 (except for 184) are reproduced by kind permission of the Hong Kong Government from *Cephalopods of Hong Kong* by Doctors Voss and Williamson.

The drawings on pages 20, 34 (upper), 50 (lower), 101 (lower), 106, 110 (upper), 111, 115 (lower), 123 (lower) and 168 (upper) come from *Common Food Fishes of Taiwan*, by kind permission of the Fisheries Division of the Joint Commission on Rural Reconstruction in Taipei. These drawings are by Mr Yang.

The crabs shown on pages 146, 148 and 149 (lower) come from the publication by the Academia Sinica cited in the Bibliography. The drawing of *Caulerpa lentillifera* on page 197 comes from *An Illustrated Seaweed Flora of Calatagan, Batangas, Philippines* by Gavino C. Trono, Jr. and Edna T. Ganzon-Fortes.

REMARKS

For each species I have shown the maximum length, which is measured thus:
  fish: from the snout to where the tail begins;
  lobsters, prawns etc: from the front of the head to the end of the tail;
  crabs: from one side of the shell to the other at the point of greatest width;
  single shells: from one end to the other;
  bivalves: the greatest diameter of the shell;
  cephalopods: from the front of the head to the end of the tentacles.

I have also shown for many species the common or market length, which is often much less than the maximum length, especially when the fish have been caught before they are fully grown.

Information about colour is also given. Apart from shape (shown in the drawings) and size, this feature is most likely to strike the layman. But the colours of many fish vary according to their habitat and may change when they are taken out of the water. Surer clues to identification are provided by features such as the number and position of fins. The simple drawing below explains the few technical terms which have been used to enable the reader to take advantage of these clues.

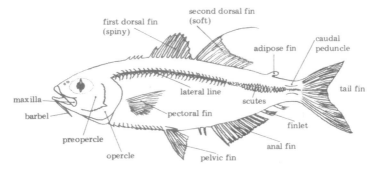

USING THE CATALOGUES

In each catalogue entry the reader will find, under the heading Cuisine, a summary indication of how the fish or other sea creatures can best be prepared for the table. In many of the catalogue entries there are additional signposts to recipes in the Recipe Section of the book which are specifically suitable.

ABBREVIATIONS

Besides conventional abbreviations which need no explanation I have used the following for foreign names:

UAE	United Arab Emirates	PH	Philippines
BE	Bengal	CA	Cambodia
TA	Tamil	VI	Vietnam
SI	Singhalese	HK	Hong Kong
BU	Burma	CH	China
TH	Thailand	TAI	Taiwan
MA	Malaysia	JA	Japan
IN	Indonesia		

In the context of abbreviations I should mention that I have in a number of places used the term Malaya (for example in historical allusions) as a convenient equivalent for the correct modern name West Malaysia.

Catalogue of Fish

Herring-like Fish, Big and Small

The first section of the catalogue covers fish of the Order *Clupeiforms*. These are, in S. E. Asia as well as in other parts of the world, of great economic importance. Taken together they easily surpass in numbers any comparable group of fish in the sea.

Characteristics of these fish include a single, non-spiny dorsal fin; a more or less elongated and streamlined shape; and well-developed scales (often deciduous, which is to say that they are shed quite easily, for example when the fish are handled) on the body. Indeed Chinese authors quoted by Read say that fish of the genus **Ilisha** are so proud of the scales that they do not struggle, for fear of damaging the scales, when taken in a net; and that these same scales, after being soaked in lime and dried and removed layer by layer, are used in making head ornaments for women.

I have one more observation about the herring family. They are a deplorably bony family. But if they are properly cooked the flesh can be separated from the bones without too much trouble; and the flavour is generally so good that this trouble is worth taking.

It is anyway possible to derive some marginal benefits from the boniness of these fish. Thus, readers in possession of musk-melons which fail to become ripe at the appropriate time may like to know that if they pierce the peduncles of the refractory fruit with a bone of **Ilisha elongata** (page 26) the fruit will then ripen overnight. This is the advice of a Chinese sage.

TEN-POUNDER, LADYFISH

Family *Elopidae*

Elops machnata (Forskål)

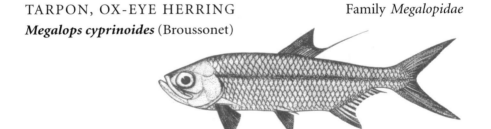

REMARKS Maximum length 90 cm. Market length 40–50 cm, sometimes referred to as 'giant herring'. The back is olive, the sides and belly silvery. In general appearance, the ten-pounder (which can, by the way, weigh as much as 10 kilos) is similar to the milkfish, with which it is sometimes confused. It is a pelagic fish, found in coastal waters.

Distribution: from East Africa and the Red Sea across to the West Pacific.

There is a close relation, of similar size, in the central western Pacific: *E. hawaiensis*, the Hawaiian ladyfish.

TA: manna
SI: ranava
BU: ah-shin-pote
TH: pla ta lüak
MA: bandang, menangin
IN: bandeng lelaki
PH: bid-bid
VI: cá mòi diròng
HK: yuk sor

CUISINE Not very popular because the flesh is full of small bones, but with an acceptable flavour.

TARPON, OX-EYE HERRING

Family *Megalopidae*

Megalops cyprinoides (Broussonet)

REMARKS Maximum length over 50 cm. Common length 25 to 30 cm. The back is olive, the sides and belly silvery. The last dorsal ray, which is prolonged into a filament, is a good recognition point.

Distribution: Indo-Pacific, from South Africa and the Red Sea, north to southern Korea, south to New South Wales to Tahiti.

TA: marua
SI: illeya
BU: ka-law-leh
TH: pla ta lüak
MA/IN: bulan-bulan
PH: buan-buan
VI: cá cháo
HK: yuk sor
CH: da hai lian
JA: hairen

CUISINE A disappointing fish. The flesh is poor and bony. I record, however, one more favourable opinion. Maxwell wrote that 'from an edible standpoint' (I see what he means, but the phrase is a startling one) this fish ranks very highly and that its flesh is firm and well-flavoured.

BONEFISH, BANANA FISH
Albula vulpes (Linnaeus)

Family *Albulidae*

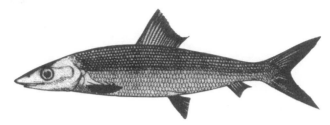

REMARKS Maximum length about 1 metre. It is a swift, wary fish, hard to catch and not often seen in the markets. However, it may be met in Malaysia, the Philippines, Thailand, Indonesia, Burma and Japan. If you do meet it, by all means eat it.

CUISINE The flesh is good and may be prepared in any of the standard ways, for example by grilling or baking. The problems arise at table rather than in the kitchen, but can be overcome by patient dissection.

SI: vauva, miya
BU: nga-kway-seip
TH: pla luk kluey ngern
MA: pisang-pisang
IN: bandeng cecurut, banang
PH: bid-bid
TAI: hu tou wen
JA: sotoiwashi

MILKFISH
Chanos chanos (Forskål)

Family *Chanidae*

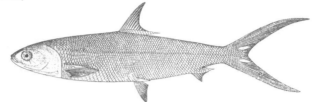

REMARKS Maximum length 1 metre 80. Market length anything up to 1 metre.

Greenish-grey above, with silvery sides.

Adults are hard to catch. They decline bait and leap over nets. However, a supply for the markets can be assured by catching the fry at sea and then rearing them in fish-ponds as is done in Indonesia and the Philippines, where 100,000 tons or more are brought to market annually. They feed eagerly on a kind of sea moss, and grow rapidly. Maxwell quotes an interesting old account of their being raised in the region of Manila.

'The eggs are deposited in the sea. The young appear during the months of April, May, June and July. They are to be found in great numbers along the beaches and are captured by the natives and placed in large earthen jars full of water called palyok. They are then conveyed to the fish ponds, frequently a hundred miles distant.

'One of the jars contains about 2,500 young Bangos. About 60,000 are used to stock one pond of 1 hektare. As the fish grow they are thinned out by transfers to other ponds. Thirty-three per cent should reach marketable size and a yearling should measure half a metre.'

Distribution: the range of the milkfish extends to the Red Sea, East Africa, Japan and Australia, and the species is abundant on the Pacific coast of the United States.

TA: pal meen
SI: vaikka
BU: nga-tain
TH: pla thu nam jüt,
    pla nuan chan
    thaleh*, pla hai ling
MA: bangus, pisang-
    pisang
IN: bandeng
PH: bangos
VI: cá măng
HK: yuk sor
CH: zhe mu yu
JA: sabahii

* nuan chan means soft sandalwood

CUISINE What to do with the milkfish is an important question in the Philippines, where it is a dominant species in the markets. The main problem which it presents to the cook is that it has a dismayingly large number of fine small bones.

One solution is to learn how to debone these fish by the professional technique. Patricia Arroyo (in her serious and charming book on *The Science of Philippine Foods*, pp. 137–8) explains fully what to do. You need a knife, scissors, clinical forceps, clean water and a chopping board. You also need twenty minutes for each fish, even after you have had some practice.

An alternative is to buy milkfish which have been cooked under pressure so that the bones become soft and edible, like the bones of tinned sardines. I have break-fasted off such fish, and found them easy to eat although slightly disappointing in taste and texture.

Of course, it is also possible to pressure-cook these fish with other ingredients, to ensure an interesting flavour. Nora V. Daza quotes an interesting recipe attributed to Arsenio Lacson, which I have not tried but which should certainly have flavourful results. Buy a kilo of small bangos, two dozen to the kilo. Gut, do not scale them. Then cook them for an hour in a 4-quart pressure cooker with 4 hot chilli peppers (siling pasiti); ½ cup each of green olives and sweet mixed pickles; 2 cups of olive oil; ½ cup soy sauce; ¾ cup of cooking brandy; a bay leaf; 1 teaspoonful each of salt and whole peppercorns.

Do not neglect the skin of the milkfish. I met an antique dealer in Manila who had had bangos for lunch. 'The skin!' he said, 'it's so delicious that we were practically fighting for it over the table.'

There is certainly no lack of recipes for the milkfish, and I have only been able to include a small section in the recipe section, where the reader will find:

DORAB, WOLF HERRING
Chirocentrus dorab (Forskål)

Family *Chirocentridae*

REMARKS Specimens of 2 metres or more have been reported in other parts of the world; but for S. E. Asia, the FAO give the maximum length as 1 metre only and the common length as 30 to 50 cm.

The back is bluish-green and the sides silvery, but the colours change after death.

Note the large upturned mouth, in which there are strong teeth, and the deeply forked tail fin. The dorsal fin is edged with black, which distinguishes this species from its near twin, **C. nudus** Swainson, the White-fin wolf herring.

Maxwell gives a pleasant vignette of Singapore in 1917. 'Passengers by steamers proceeding through the Eastern entrance to Singapore roads will see a large number of small canoes in the deep water channel and will hear the noise of rattles, which each Malay fisherman wields unceasingly. These rattles do not attract the fish, but keep the hand occupied and the fisherman on the 'qui vive'. The Parang-parang is not a greedy biter and does not stay in one place. He is a rapid swimming precacious fish who has no time for more than a snap as he darts through the water. Bites are usually few and far between and an inexpert or somnolent fisherman would catch nothing. With an ever moving hand engaged with a rattle the fish is struck and hooked almost at the instant he bites.'

Distribution: from the Red Sea and East Africa to the Pacific Islands, north to southern Japan and south to northern Australia.

TA: mullu valai
BU: nga-site-tho
TH: pla dap lao, pla fak pra
MA/IN: parang-parang
PH: parang-parang
CA: trey srom dao mara
VI: cá bình thiên
HK: po do
TAI: bao dao yu
JA: oki-iwashi

CUISINE Everyone agrees that this is a deplorably bony fish but many regard this disadvantage as outweighed by the good taste of the flesh. One solution, favoured at Hong Kong, is to use it for fish balls.

See also the recipe from Brunei on page 317.

THE FAMILY *CLUPEIDAE*

Having dealt with the larger species, we now come to the smaller ones, the fish which can loosely be described as sprats, herring, shad, sardines and anchovies.

These smaller species have one characteristic which distinguishes them from their larger brethren. With few exceptions (notably the species catalogued on this page) they have scutes (that is to say, little bony plates) along their bellies. These may be seen in the drawings.

Except for the anchovies (family *Engraulidae*) all these smaller species belong to the mighty and populous family *Clupeidae*. Indeed, it is so mighty that it has been found convenient to split it into sub-families. The catalogue entries which follow show to which sub-family each species belongs.

I should, however, mention that these shoals of little fish have always posed problems for the taxonomist. Although recent studies, notably that of Dr Whitehead (see the Bibliography) on **Sardinella** spp., have done much to clarify the situation, it is likely that further work will suggest further changes in the classification of the species, some of which have already had as many as a dozen different scientific names bestowed on them by successive ichthyologists. However, these problems need not affect our buying and cooking any of the numerous species. For the consumer, there is little to choose between them.

RAINBOW SARDINE   Sub-family *Dussumierinae*
Dussumieria acuta Valenciennes

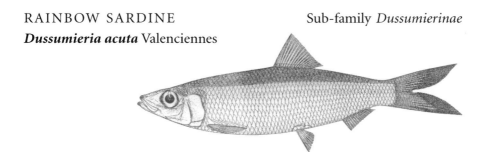

REMARKS Maximum length 20 cm, common length 12 cm. These little fish are dark green above and silvery below, with a golden band along each side. The belly is rounded and without scutes.

Great shoals of this species occur in shallow coastal waters. The English names 'sprat' and 'round herring' have occasionally been applied to this fish, and to **Spratelloides delicatulus** Bleeker, known as anak tamban jepoh in Malaya, which is usually dried before being marketed.

TA: tondai
BU: nga-kyaw-nyo
TH: pla ok rak kluay,
   pla ku lae kluay
MA/IN: tamban bulat/
   buluh, janggul
PH: tulis
VI: cá lầm
HK: hoi ho
TAI: jian du shi wen
JA: gin'iwashi

Distribution: warmer waters of Indo-Pacific, from the 'Gulf' east to India, Malaysia to Indonesia and the Philippines.

CUISINE An important food fish, e.g. in Malaysia. The flesh is tasty and may be grilled or fried. These fish are marketed both fresh and dried.

SARDINE, FRINGE-SCALE SARDINELLA   Sub-family *Clupeinae*
Sardinella fimbriata (Valenciennes)

REMARKS Maximum length 13 cm, average market size a little smaller.

This sardine has the typical blue-green back and silvery sides and belly, but also a yellow lateral stripe. Another distinguishing feature consists in the scales, which have a fringed edge.

The Filipinos have a special name, siliniasi, for young ones.

Distribution: from southern India and the Bay of Bengal to the Philippines and the eastern tip of Papua New Guinea.

CUISINE Fresh sardines are excellent fare when grilled. They may also be fried, although their flesh is already rich in fat. Deep-frying is to be preferred to pan-frying.

UAE: ooma (general name)
BE: hoira, khaira
TA: sandai, salai, saudai
BU: nga-baw-ngan, bown-jay
TH: pla kureh
MA: tamban lopek / sisek
IN: tembang
PH: tunsoy
VI: cá trích
HK: ching luen
TAI: hei sha ding

Another possibility is to behead and gut them, open them out and remove the backbones, then marinate them for a while in lime juice. This is a good technique for small specimens. The lime juice (or, of course, lemon juice or calamansi juice) has an effect on them which is in some respects the same as that produced by cooking.

Sardinella brachysoma Bleeker has an even deeper body, and is known as the Short-bodied sardine. It is abundant in the Bangkok markets. It is not shown on this page, since there is a fine drawing of it on page 12.

Sardinella gibbosa (Bleeker), one of the most abundant Sardinella species in the Indo-West Pacific region, has a thin yellow line along its side, separating the blue-green back from the silvery flanks.

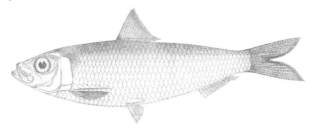

Sardinella longiceps Valenciennes has a very wide distribution. In the Indo-Pacific area it ranges from the Red Sea to the Philippines and Taiwan; but it is also present in the Atlantic. It is abundant at Hong Kong in the summer.

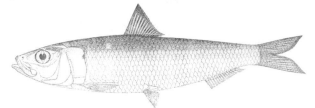

Sardinella melanura (Cuvier) has black tips to its tail. It is tandipa in Indonesia, tamban sisek in Malaysia and painneh-rape in Burma. It ranges from Mauritius to Taiwan.

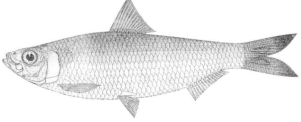

SPOTTED SARDINELLA   Sub-family *Clupeinae*
Amblygaster sirm (Walbaum)

REMARKS Maximum length 23 cm.

This is one of three species which are classified in the sub-genus **Amblygaster**. They may be distinguished from the preceding species by various subtle means, but for the layman it is perhaps most interesting to note the simple difference that they are bigger. **A. sirm** is easily recognized by the row of up to 15 dark spots which run along each side. The fins are pale yellow; the dorsal and caudal fins are dusky, at least at the edges, and the other fins hyaline.

Large quantities are caught off the east coast of Malaysia.

Distribution: from East Africa to the western Pacific, and from southern Japan and northern Australia.

UAE: ooma
TA: keerimeen chalai
TH: pla lang khieo
MA: tamban beluru
IN: sardin
PH: tambang bato
VI: cá lâm
TAI: se mu sha ding
JA: hoshi-yamato-mizun

Shad and Bengal

Shad occur all round the world. They are anadromous, going up rivers to spawn but at other times being found in the sea or estuarine waters. In Europe and N. America there are only a few species, but in the Indo-Pacific there are scores, often difficult to tell apart. One authority, referring to the genus **Ilisha**, remarks that: 'Many of the Indo-Pacific species were seriously confused until fundamental differences in the swimbladder were found between superficially very similar species.' No attempt has been made here to go into such minutiae or to give anything like a comprehensive coverage; only a few of the more important species are catalogued.

However, this is where I should mention the exceptional importance of shad in Bengal. Only some of the S.E. Asian species occur there, but those that do, especially the famous hilsa of India (see next page) enjoy remarkably high esteem. Whitehead observes that in Sanskrit and Bengali literature this fish is described as matsyaraja (the king of fishes) and that according to one saying it is finer than nectar. This may seem strange, given the numerous small bones which for many people are the dominant characteristic of all shad, but a measure of explanation was provided by Roberts (1998) when he explained that both boniness and smelliness are acceptable features of fish in Bengal. He writes that: 'eating them is comparable to walking through a minefield because of the profusion of tiny bones which appear to be randomly distributed. The ability to eat a *hilsa* fish gracefully, removing the fish from the needlelike bones inside one's mouth, then placing the clean bones on the side of the *thali*, is seen as proof of a good upbringing.'

SLENDER SHAD   Sub-family *Pristigasterinae*

Ilisha elongata (Bennett)

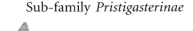

REMARKS Maximum length 40 cm; common length 30 cm. The fish of this genus all have blue/green backs and bright silvery flanks. The scales are large and rub off easily.

Distribution: mainly in the Java Sea (Singapore) and the East China Sea (as far north as southern Japan).

BE: dhala
TA: puvali
MA/IN: beliak mata
VI: cá be
HK: tso pak, lak yue
TAI: chang qi le
JA: hira

CUISINE As noted above, shad are notorious for having small bones, which puts some cooks off completely. But for those who can cope with the boniness the best plan is to fry, bake or steam. The species dealt with here is said to be at its best when steamed or baked. It commands a good price at Hong Kong in salted form.

TOLI SHAD
Tenualosa toli (Valenciennes)

Sub-family *Alosinae*

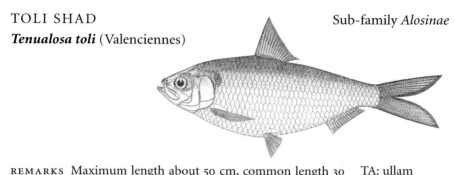

REMARKS Maximum length about 50 cm, common length 30 to 40 cm. The body is silvery, with a darker back, which may be greenish-grey or lead-coloured. Distribution: mainly the Indian sub-continent and Indonesia.

    T. macrura (Bleeker) is a shad with a longer tail (for which reason it has been called the Longtail shad).

    T. ilisha is the well known Hilsa shad mentioned on page 26.

TA: ullam
BE: chadan-ilish
TH: pla talum
    phuk
MA/IN: terubuk
VI: (cá cháy)
HK: cho paak

CUISINE The flesh of *T. toli*, like that of other shad, is moderately oily and rich. The roe is highly prized by the Malays and Chinese as an ingredient in cookery (in which it plays the same sort of role as Blachan – see page 205).

    Given what was said on the preceding page about *T. ilisha*, the hilsa, it is interesting to read what Roberts says about its preparation in Bengal. Having observed that the classic way of eating it (*Ilish bhaja*) is coated with turmeric, chili powder and salt and fried, he proceeds to describe seven other hilsa dishes, including *ilish maaccher paturi* (hilsa with mustard and chili paste smoked in banana leaves) and *doi ilish maacch* (steamed *hilsa* coated with a yoghurt and ginger sauce).

    See page 26 and also the recipes on pages 220 and 226.

KELEE SHAD
Hilsa kelee (Cuvier)

Sub-family *Alosinae*

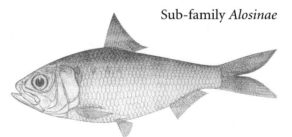

REMARKS Maximum length 25 cm, common length 15 cm. The back is light yellow, the sides and belly silvery. Note the (4 to 7) blotches, which accounts for a name occasionally met: five-spot herring. The dorsal fin is yellow with a black tip; the tail yellow.

    Distribution: widespread from East Africa to Hong Kong and Papua New Guinea.

BU: nga-thalauk
TH: maak pang
MA/IN: tiram, terubok
PH: law-law
CA: trey koun
VI: cá mòi dâu
HK: cho paak
TAI: zhong guo shi

INDIAN PELLONA
Pellona ditchela Valenciennes

Sub-family *Pristigasterinae*

REMARKS Maximum length 20 cm or a little more; common length 15 cm. A silvery fish with a blue/brown back and colourless fins. It is often found at river mouths, although primarily a marine fish.

Distribution: East Africa to Papua New Guinea and north-western Australia.

MA: puput
IN: mata besar
PH: tuabak, silag-
    habato, kundilat
VI: cá be
HK: cho paak
TAI: bi long le

CUISINE See page 26. These fish are perhaps more likely to be met in East African markets than in S. E. Asian ones. They have a good flavour.

GIZZARD SHAD
Nematalosa nasus (Bloch)

Sub-family *Dorosomatinae*

REMARKS Maximum length about 20 cm. A deep-bodied silvery fish with yellow fins and a dark patch on each shoulder. Note the filamentous extension of the last ray of the dorsal fin.

A smaller species, with an even deeper body, *Anodontostoma chacunda* (Hamilton-Buchanan), is the Chacunda gizzard shad. Known as kabasi in the Philippines, it has considerable economic importance.

The gizzard shads are so-called because they have thick muscular stomachs like the gizzard of a fowl. They are said to eat mud and to use these strong stomachs for milling tiny particles of food therefrom.

BU: nga-wun-pa-kyettaw
TH: pla khok, pla tapi-en
    namkhem
MA: kebasi
IN: selangat belau
PH: kabasi
CA: trey trachéak kmao
VI: cá mòi
HK: wong yue
TAI: gao bi shui hua

CUISINE A bony little fish of inferior flavour, but plentiful and cheap. Bake, fry or steam. May often be had dried and salted.

ANCHOVY, SHORTHEAD ANCHOVY
Encrasicholina heteroloba (Rüppell)

Family *Engraulidae*

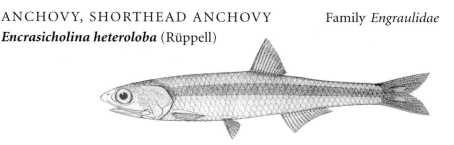

REMARKS Maximum length 12 cm.

The body is pale, with a silvery stripe along the flank.

Encrasicholina heteroloba may be the most abundant species of anchovy in the region. (I say 'may' because there are few people capable of distinguishing, or indeed seeking to distinguish, between the species in this genus.) Another is *Stolephorus indicus* (van Hasselt), the Indian anchovy, which may reach a length of 17 cm and which is shown in the lower drawing. Yet another is *S. commersonii* Lacepède (maximum length 15 cm). A general Japanese name for anchovy is katakuchi iwashi.

UAE: gashr (general name)
BU: yay-kyin-ngair, nga-nan-gyaung
TH: pla bai pai, pla hua awn, pla katak
MA: bilis
IN: teri, bilis
PH: gurayan (Visayan)
CA: (cá cum)
VI: cá com
HK: kung yue

CUISINE Although some species of anchovy, including this one, may more often be used for fish sauce, as bait, or sold in dried form, than cooked fresh, this is the place to make general remarks about cooking anchovies.

Anchovies may be grilled fresh. The marinating technique suggested on page 23 for sardines may also be applied to them with good results.

Very small specimens are sometimes presented (not incorrectly) as 'whitebait'.

In Malaya anchovies are served in a sambal with curries (or put up in bottles as 'Macassar red fish').

It is not advisable to boil fresh anchovies.

Recipes for anchovy are given on pages 242, 259, 289 and 303.

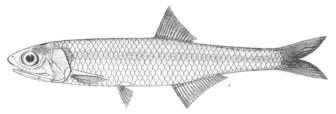

ADDITIONAL NOTE I have not made a catalogue entry for anchovies of the genus *Coilia*, which seem to be of minor importance. However, they are found in the markets and it seems worth while to mention them here. Their characteristic shape is well shown in the drawing which appears on page 12 of *Coilia dussumieri* Valenciennes, the Goldspotted grenadier anchovy, with a row of pearly spots along its flanks.

ANCHOVY, HAIRFIN ANCHOVY
Setipinna taty (Valenciennes)

Family *Engraulidae*

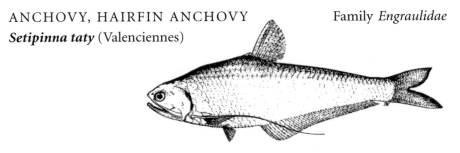

REMARKS Maximum length 20 cm, common length 16 cm. This fish has a brown or blue back and silvery flanks. The FAO English name for it, 'scaly hairfin anchovy', refers to the fact that it, alone in its family, has scales on its dorsal and anal fins. A small spine just before the dorsal fin is a feature of the species of this genus.

    S. melanochir (Bleeker) is another common species in it. Its pectoral fins are black; and it is often found in brackish or fresh water (for example, far upstream in Thai rivers).

    The range of **S. taty** extends from the east coast of India to Malaysia and Java.

BU: nga-pashar
TH: pla maeo (hu
   yao or hu dam)
MA/IN: kasai janggut
PH: dilis, lagunlong
VI: cá lep
HK: wong gu
CH: huang ji
TAI: si chi ji

ANCHOVY, MOUSTACHED ANCHOVY
Thryssa mystax (Schneider)

Family *Engraulidae*

REMARKS Maximum length 20 cm, common length about 17 cm. A silvery fish with a dark back. The lower part of the head is powdered with black. The long rear-ward extensions of the upper jaw (maxillary) are thought to resemble a moustache or the whiskers of a cat. Maeo in the Thai name means cat.

    Distribution: the Indian Ocean, Burma south to Pinang, to Indonesia and south to Java.

    There are half a dozen other species in this genus. Some of them have even longer maxillaries. And one of them, **T. scratchleyi** (Ramsay and Ogilby), which has a very limited distribution in and near Papua New Guinea is much the largest of all known anchovies, reaching a maximum length of 37 cm.

BU: (nga-pa),
  (nga-thapya)
TH: pla maeo
MA: kasai minyak,
  bakok daun
IN: bulu ayam, pirang
PH: tigi
VI: cá lep hai quai
HK: wong gu
TAI: xu jian ji

A Mixed Bag: Catfish, Eels, Lizard Fish, Garfish, Half-beaks and Flying Fish

The second section of the catalogue covers fish belonging to several orders. They are interesting as fish, but lack lustre in the cook's eye.

The catfish eel and sea catfish are representatives of a very large group of fish which belong mainly to fresh waters, where the best of them are to be found, including the best of all, the fabulous but real **Pangasianodon gigas**, a giant catfish of the Mekong, which has never been seen in the sea but is such a mysterious creature (see my *Fish and Fish Dishes of Laos*) that one cannot be quite sure.

Eels are disappointing in S. E. Asia. There are moray eels in the region and I dare say that if one could buy them one would find them to be as good as those of the Mediterranean. But in practice the silver conger is the only marine eel brought to market and it has nowhere aroused great enthusiasm. The common (freshwater, although born in the sea) eel is appreciated in Japan, less so elsewhere.

Nor are the lizard fish of great merit. Their relation, the flabby bummalow, enjoys the advantage of being famous in its dried form as 'Bombay duck', an odd name which may add zest to a first taste.

The names bummalow and Bombay duck are both unusual. On the former, Hobson-Jobson comments that it may be derived from the Mahratti bombil. This became bambulim in Portuguese, which was perhaps a factor in producing the large number of alternative spellings (or transcriptions): e.g. bumbelow, bumbaloe, bummelo, and even bobil. The 'Bombay' in Bombay duck is easily explained. These dried fish were exported on a large scale from Bombay. But why 'duck'? Hobson-Jobson draws an analogy with the name Digby chicks, applied in the past to certain small fish of the herring family which were cured in a special way at Digby in Lincolnshire.

The section closes with the various beaked or half-beaked fish, which have some importance as food, and the flying fish which is a palatable curiosity, appreciated by shipwrecked sailors on whose rafts it inadvertently lands but rarely sought by fishermen.

CATFISH EEL, EEL-CATFISH

Family *Plotosidae*

Plotosus canius Hamilton

REMARKS Maximum length well over 1 metre, but a good market length is 50 cm. This species is dark grey or brown-grey above (so sometimes called 'grey eel-catfish') and buff below. It is found in estuaries and the lower courses of rivers as well as in the sea. It and other catfish eels are dangerous; their serrated dorsal and pectoral spines can inflict painful wounds on incautious bathers or fishermen.

Distribution: west and south coasts of India, eastwards to Cambodia through the Indo-Australian archipelago and to the Philippines and as far as Papua New Guinea.

BE: kaun magur
TA: irung-kelletee,
   keduthal
BU: nga-nu
TH: pla duk thaleh
MA/IN: sembilang
   (karang, gemang)
PH: (kanduli)
CA: trey andèng koy
VI: cá ngát

CUISINE Despite its unattractive appearance the catfish eel is good to eat. It may be steamed or prepared in a curry.

SOLDIER CATFISH

Family *Ariidae*

Osteogeneiosus militaris (Linnaeus)

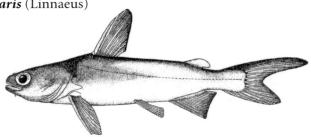

REMARKS Maximum length 35 cm, common length 20 to 25 cm. The back is dark blue, the sides silvery with faint grey dots. The fins are whiteish, some tipped with dark blue. There is only one pair of barbels, which are stiff and bony.

The second Thai name and the Vietnamese name apparently refer to the sound ('uck') made by the fish.

Distribution: from India across to East Malaysia.

BU: nga-yaung
TH: pla kot, pla uk
MA/IN: songop, duri
   monchong
CA: trey kaok
VI: cá úc thép

CUISINE Despised in Thailand, where it is one of the cheapest fish in the market. However, it is edible.

GIANT SEA CATFISH

Family *Ariidae*

Arius thalassina (Rüppell)

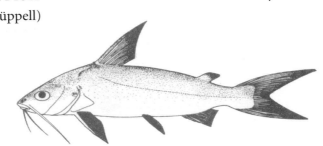

REMARKS Maximum length may be as much as 1½ metres, although the common length is only 25 to 70 cm. This species is one of the largest of a numerous family. (Well over 50 species are found in S. E. Asian waters.)

BU: nga-yaung
TH: pla kot thaleh
MA/IN: duri
PH: kanduli, arahan
CA: (trey andeng)
VI: cá thiêu
HK: (chek yue)
CH: hai nian

It has a reddish brown back, shading to whiteish below, all with a bronze or silvery lustre.

These catfish have proper tails, unlike the catfish eels (see preceding entry), but they are likewise dangerous, and equipped with barbels for scavenging on the bottom.

One of the most abundant species in the family is the smooth-headed sea catfish *Arius leiotetocephalus* Bleeker (pla thu kang in Thailand, pedukang in Malaya – the names are doubtless connected – and bongoan in the Philippines, where it is regarded as the best sea catfish). Another is the Spotted sea catfish *A. thunbergi* Lacepède, which often ascends rivers. Its eggs are marketed at Chantabun in Thailand, where it bears vernacular names such as pla kot na nu (the last two words meaning mouse-face, a curious epithet for a creature whose appearance is supposed to be cat-like).

Distribution: from the Indian sub-continent in the west to the Indo-Australian archipelago in the east.

CUISINE This is a better fish than its appearance and habits would suggest. Steaks may be fried successfully. Steaming is another possibility, or a fish curry.

Recipes are given on pages 223 and 224.

CONGER PIKE [PIKE CONGER]   Family *Muraenesocidae*
Muraenesox cinereus (Forskål)

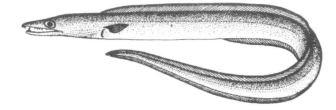

REMARKS Maximum length just over 2 metres, common length about 1 metre 50.

A silvery fish with a grey or yellow sheen, which inhabits estuaries and enters fresh water.

The Thai name means dragon fish, in allusion to its fierce array of teeth (see small drawing below), and the epithet 'daggertooth' is sometimes added to the English names.

Distribution: from India to Hong Kong. **M. bagio** (Hamilton), the 'common pike conger', which is similar, ranges wider, to East Africa and Australia and Samoa.

TA: kadal vilangu
BU: (nga hauk),
    (nga-shwe)
TH: pla mangkor
MA: malong
IN: pucok nipah
PH: pindanga
CA: trey kchung
VI: cá lat bac
HK: moon sin
CH: hai man
JA: hamo

CUISINE Excellent eating, says Munro in a rare comment; but this fish is most often used for making fish balls. Chinese authors have recommended the flesh of this marine eel, like that of freshwater eels, as an aphrodisiac (yes, yet another!) and also say that if it is boiled with Chinese 'five spices' it makes an excellent general tonic.

Another eel-like fish of S. E. Asian waters is **Pisodonophis boro** (Hamilton), which may be almost a metre long and is a popular food fish in some places. In Thailand, where the usual practice is to cut it into sections and cook it with curry, it is called pla lai; in Malaysia belin; and in Vietnam con lich. In English it may be referred to as 'rice paddy eel'.

Some recipes for which conger pike is suitable are given on pages 220, 223 and 302.

LIZARDFISH, GREATER LIZARDFISH   Family *Synodontidae*
Saurida tumbil (Bloch)

REMARKS Maximum length about 55 cm, market length up to about 30 cm. The head, which resembles that of a lizard, and body are pale in colour, reddish brown above and silvery below. A ferocious bottom fish.

   S. undosquamis (Richardson), the Brushtooth lizardfish, is a close relation. *Trachinocephalus myops* (Forster), the Snakefish, is a smaller lizard fish, often seen in Malaysian markets under the names conor or mudin.

   Distribution: from East Africa to S. E. Asia and Australia.

TA: oolooway, thumbil
BU: nga palway
TH: pla pak khom
MA/IN: mengkarong, buntut kerbo
PH: uting bondo
VI: cá môi
HK: kau kwun
CH: duo chi she zi

CUISINE Lizardfish are fairly good, but have rather dry flesh. Thus it is best not to grill them. In Thailand, where *S. undosquamis* is the preferred species, they are usually boiled, made into fish balls, or canned.

BUMMALOW, BOMBAY DUCK (when dried)   Family *Harpadontidae*
Harpadon nehereus Hamilton

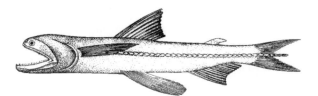

REMARKS Maximum length about 40 cm. The body is pale in colour, almost translucent when the fish is alive. The flesh is soft and flaccid, but the bummalow is a predatory fish and its teeth are hard and needlelike. It hunts in shoals, which hoover up small crustaceans from the seabed; but which are themselves preyed on by the great golden-mouthed corvina, known as ghôl in India.

   Distribution: widespread in the Indo-West Pacific.

CUISINE This fish is a delicacy in India, where it is eaten both fresh and dried when it is known as Bombay duck, which becomes bombeidakku in Japanese.

BE: loitta
BU: nga-hnat, barega
TH: pla pak khom nam jut
MA: lumi-lumi
IN: luli
PH: kalasao
CA: trey kà chen
VI: cá khoai
HK: kau kwun
TAI: xiao qi lian chi yu

HALF-BEAK
Hemirhamphus far (Forskål)

Family *Hemirhamphidae*

REMARKS Maximum length 45 cm. There are dark blotches on the sides, which accounts for the name 'spotted half-beak', used in some places.

This is the largest of a whole tribe of half-beaks, all of which have the distinctive bony projection from the lower jaw, equipped with a sensitive fringe so that it serves for the detection of food. (Umali, in his book on *Edible Fishes of Manila*, mentions that this tissue at the tip of the half-beak is either red or green and that Tagalog fishermen in the Philippines call fish with a red chin buguing and those with a green chin kansusuit.) The half-beaks are capable of sustained gliding above the surface of the water. This may account for the Thai name, which means water beetle fish.

H. marginatus (Forskål) is a related but smaller species, known as the Yellowtip half-beak.

Distribution of *H. far* extends from East Africa to the Ryukyu Islands and northern Australia.

CUISINE The flesh is delicate but bony. It may be baked, fried or poached.

TA: mural
BU: (nga-taung-myin)
TH: pla kathung heo
MA: jolong-jolong
IN: kacang kacang
PH: kansusuwit
CA: (trey phtong kley)
VI: cá kìm, cá gioi
HK: ching chum
TAI: hei zhen
JA: hoshi-zayori

NEEDLEFISH, GARFISH

Family *Belonidae*

Tylosurus crocodilus crocodilus (Péron and Lesueur)

REMARKS Maximum length over 1 metre.

This is among the largest of several garfish which are all common in the Indo-West Pacific region and easily recognized by their elongated jaws. This one has a forked tail. *Strongylura strongylura* (van Hasselt), the Spottail needlefish is much smaller and has a rounded tail. It is batalay in the Philippines. *S. leiura* (Bleeker) reaches a length of 1 metre 20 and has a square tail. Both these species are loncong or kajang in Indonesia. I should also mention *Ablennes hians* (Valenciennes), a garfish with a very strongly compressed body, which is kambabalo in the Philippines.

These are pelagic fish, but are willing to enter estuaries. They swim at high speed, near or even partly above the surface of the water. Umali relates that some unlucky people, who have inadvertently been in their path, have been pierced by their beaks and killed.

Munro, in his excellent book of 1955 on the fishes of Ceylon (now Sri Lanka) gives the useful drawing below to illustrate the difference between the jaws of garfish (*Belonidae*) and half-beaks (*Hemirhamphidae*).

CUISINE These are good fish. It is unfortunate that many people abstain from eating them because they have green bones. The flesh, when cooked, is reassuringly white and has a good flavour, but tends to be somewhat dry; so a sauce or dressing should be added.

UAE: hagoul
  (general name)
TA: koliya mural
BU: sa-lone-kyaut
TH: pla kathung heo
  hu dam
IN: kacangan
PH: haba, doal
CA: (trey phtong
  veng)
VI: cá nhái
TAI: e xing he zhen
JA: okizayori

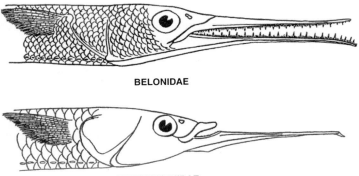

BELONIDAE

HEMIRHAMPHIDAE

FLYING FISH
Cypselurus oligolepis (Bleeker)

Family *Exocoetidae*

REMARKS Maximum length may be over 25 cm, common length under 20 cm.

Distribution: from East Africa to southern China to Solomon Islands and Queensland, Australia.

The flying fishes (for there are various species, difficult to distinguish, of which this is only one, sometimes distinguished by the name 'large-scaled flying fish') are blue to blue-black above, and silvery below. Their wings, which are greatly enlarged pectoral fins, are multi-coloured and pretty. Do they fly? 'It is not quite correct', says Scott, 'to talk about these fish as (flying) as they merely glide, their wings remaining fairly rigid while they are in the air, ... In order to become airborne the fish attains a maximum swimming speed of about 15 m.p.h. and then shoots out of the water until, with head lifted and pectoral fins fully extended but not expanded, only the lower lobe of the tail remains in the waters. The tail is then vibrated rapidly from side to side, accelerating the fish from swimming speed to about 40 m.p.h. in as little as one second. Having attained flying speed the fish then takes off, gliding along about a foot above the surface of the sea until the speed drops to about 25 m.p.h. when the fish plops back into the water or, with another burst of sculling with its tail, accelerates to flying speed again.'

A more recent observer was Michael Sullivan of BBC television, who found himself after the fall of Saigon perched on the prow of an evacuation vessel bound for the Philippines. Looking down at the sea sixty feet below he had a perfect view of numerous flying fish and used his knowledge of aeronautics and his stopwatch to record precisely their performance. The longest flight was of 30 seconds, punctuated perhaps by several dips of the tail in the water. Flying speed was as Scott said.

TA: paravai-kola
TH: pla nok krachok (sparrow fish)
MA: terbang, belalang
IN: torani, ikan terbang
PH: bolador
CA: (trey hoh)
VI: cá chuồn
HK: fay yue
CH: xiao lin yan yao yu

CUISINE The flying fish are not in great demand as food in most of S. E. Asia, but they are popular in the Philippines, where at least one regional recipe (Bolador with Ubod, page 290) is devoted to them. The flesh is similar to that of the half-beaks.

Barracuda, Grey Mullet and Threadfin

These three families of fish fall in the Order *Mugiliformes*. They all have two dorsal fins, and are mostly elongate in shape. The order also includes the family *Atherinidae*, the Silversides (renyau or paku in Malaya); but these are not at present of commercial importance in S. E. Asia (although Maxwell drew attention long ago to their potential value) and are not included in the catalogue.

At the end of this section of the catalogue I have included the Soldier fish from a family which falls in the Order *Beryciformes*.

The barracuda are well known as fierce fish. I prefer to contemplate the inoffensive grey mullet, and have particularly enjoyed the description given by Maxwell of how the fishing for them took place near the mouth of the Trengganu river on the east coast of Malaya. At the end of the year the rivers are in full spate and bear down to the sea quantities of yellowish foam and scum which attract the anding, as the grey mullet were called.

'A day of steady incessant tropical rain during the N.E. monsoon is the day above all others to which all Trengganu Malays, male and female, look forward. When the rivers are in full flood, the sun obscured, the N.E. monsoon blowing half a gale, the surf thundering on the beach and full of yellow yeasty foam, then you will see all the Malay ladies trooping out in their best silk coats and sarongs, and all the old blades and young bloods are in attendance.

'They are all out for the day to enjoy themselves and to catch mullet and the more it rains and blows the better they like it, the ladies, perhaps, because their vivid silken raiment looks best when it is wet, or may be it fits their figures better so, and the men, perhaps, because they will catch more mullet!'

Maxwell goes on to describe the actual fishing. 'Keeping far back on the sandy beach, the men follow the shore line until mullet (Anding) are seen, and, to the novice, it is a difficult matter to see them. But there they are, and when you know what to look for, in the smother and foam, you will notice little black heads, in hundreds, between the breakers. Now these Anding are the shyest fish that swim. A wave of the hand and they have disappeared to pop up again at a distance further seawards, where no man can hope to reach them.

'This, then, is the manner of their capture. There will come a moment when a great wave like a wall hurls itself on the beach. In fact these waves do it all the time! However, there is a measure of two or three moments and no more when that wave stands like a wall between you and the fish, and the fish forget your existence. In that brief time your caster of the mullet net sprints down to the very verge of the breaking wave and up to or over his knees in the water; the net truly held and truly swung, with a long pendulum swing, clears the crest of the approaching wave and falls fairly on the group of mullet concealed in the hollow beyond, and in this way perhaps he may be fortunate enough to take one or two hundred fish in one cast. But you will serve a long apprenticeship, and will, when learning, throw half a hundred times and have no mullet.'

BARRACUDA, GIANT SEA PIKE
Sphyraena jello (Cuvier)

Family *Sphyraenidae*

REMARKS Maximum length may be as much as 1 metre 75; common length 50 cm to 1 metre.

Dark brownish above, whiteish below, with about 20 short dark vertical bars (which disappear with age). All fins except the pelvic fins are black. The inside of the mouth is dark grey.

Note the large jaws and fearsome array of teeth. Scott opines that many victims of 'shark attacks' were really the prey of a barracuda, described as being among the most savage creatures on earth. What a contrast with their relations, the timid grey mullet!

S. barracuda (Walbaum), the Great barracuda, for which **S. picuda** (Bloch and Schneider) is a synonym, is of equal size and ferocity, but has a bluish back. Both the pectoral and pelvic fins are white. It is kutjul in Indonesia.

Distribution: widespread in S. E. Asian waters plus northern Australia and various Pacific islands.

UAE: jid, ghaili
(general names)
BE: darkoota
TA: jeela
BU: pinle-
ngamwehto
TH: pla nam dok
mai, pla sak dam
MA: alu-alu*
IN: alu-alu, tenok
PH: asogon
CA: trey ang ré yeak
VI: cá nhồng cồ
HK: chuk tsim
TAI: zhu zhen yu
JA: kamasu (for
S. japonicus)

CUISINE The flesh is very good. It may be steamed or fried. See also the recipe on page 223.

---

* Malay names for barracuda tend to go by size rather than species. Thus kacang kacang (up to 60 cm), alu alu (of medium size) and tenak or tenok (the largest).

STRIPED SEA PIKE / BARRACUDA
Sphyraena obtusata Cuvier

Family *Sphyraenidae*

REMARKS Maximum length about 45 cm, common length 25 cm. Because of its smaller size this species has sometimes been referred to as 'pygmy barracuda'.

Green-grey or yellowish green above, with darker markings, white below. An olive yellow longitudinal band runs along below the lateral line; and the fins nearly all have a yellowish colour or tinge. The inside of the mouth is yellow.

Here is another, subtle recognition point; the edge of the pre-operculum forms a right angle, not a curve.

This barracuda is a coastal species, which enters estuaries. Its distribution is much the same as that of **S. jello**.

There is another fairly small barracuda, **S. forsteri** Cuvier, the Bigeye barracuda; black above, silvery below, dorsal and tail fins black, pelvic and pectoral and anal fins white.

BU: pinle-ngamwehto
TH: pla nam dok mai
MA: kacang kacang
IN: alu alu, taneak
PH: tursilyo
CA: trey ang ré kanlath
VI: cá nhồng
HK: chuk jim
CH: dun yu
TAI: da mo jin jin suo yu

CUISINE See the preceding entry. The smaller barracuda may be similarly treated.

GREENBACK (GREY) MULLET, GREY MULLET

Family *Mugilidae*

Liza subviridis (Valenciennes)

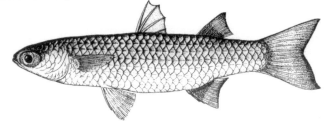

REMARKS Maximum length 40 cm, common length 25 cm.

This grey mullet usually has 3 to 7 dark stripes along the scale rows, and a greenish back.

All the grey mullets share one peculiarity, that they have no lateral line. They are also conspicuously well-behaved fish. As I have related elsewhere, the Greek poet Oppian, who was inclined to praise or blame fish according to their behaviour rather than judge them by their taste, had great admiration and sympathy for the grey mullet. Among all the nurslings of the sea, he believed, they had the most gentle and just disposition, harming neither each other nor any other creatures, never staining their lips with blood but in holy fashion feeding always on the green seaweed or mere mud. Oppian also believed that their exemplary behaviour brought its meet reward, in that baby grey mullet were not eaten by other fish.

L. subviridis is one of the most common species in the region, with a range extending right across it and including northern Australia, but there are quite a few others, of which two are shown on the next page. The largest of all is *Mugil cephalus* (Linnaeus), the Flathead mullet, a species found all round the world (although it is more common in the Indian Ocean and in Chinese and Japanese waters than in the central parts of the S. E. Asian region). It may attain 80 cm. It is nga-kin-pan in Burma, trey kbak sâr in Cambodia, gerita or belanak in Indonesia, and bora in Japan.

BU: nga-kin-kyin
TH: pla kabawk, pla
   luk moh (young)
MA: anding, belanak
IN: belanak, gereh
PH: banak, bilugan*
CA: trey kbak prak
VI: cá đối
HK: hin chai

CUISINE Grey mullet which have been living and feeding in clean waters make very good eating, and are relatively free of tiresome small bones. They may be grilled; or pieces may be fried. But I think that the larger specimens are best suited to recipes for baked or stuffed fish.

Two specific recipes are given on pages 251 and 273.

*These two names are applied to all grey mullet in the Philippines.

DIAMOND-SCALE / SQUARE-TAIL MULLET

Family *Mugilidae*

Liza vaigiensis (Quoy and Gaimard)

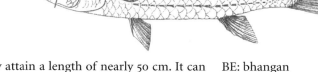

REMARKS May attain a length of nearly 50 cm. It can be recognized by the large diamond pattern of its scales, as shown in the drawing. It has dark fins.

L. macrolepsis (Smith), the Borneo mullet, is a similar species with a wide distribution. *L. tade* (Forskål) has a green-brown back and is relatively large; it may reach a length of 75 cm or more. It bears the Malay name jampal, and is belanak sipit in Java.

Distribution: *L. vaigiensis* has an extensive range, from South Africa to all parts of S. E. Asia, Japan and northern Australia.

BE: bhangan
BU: kabaloo, nga-kan-byaing
TH: pla kabawk tai
MA: belanak
IN: (belanak jumpul)
PH: banak
VI: cá dôi
HK: hin chai
TAI: fo ji zi

CUISINE See the preceding entry.

BLUE-SPOT MULLET

Family *Mugilidae*

Valamugil seheli (Forskål)

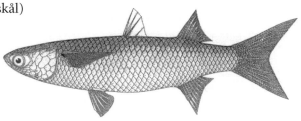

REMARKS Maximum length 45 cm, common length 25 cm. The blue spot is noticeable on the side, where the yellow pectoral fin joins the body. The back is blue too.

This species is one of several in the genus ***Valamugil*** (all of which, for those who like to wield magnifying glasses, have digitated rear edges to their scales) and has a range extending from the Red Sea to the Pacific Islands.

UAE: be-yah (general)
BU: kabaloo, bee-nyo
TH: pla kabawk hang see yao
MA: belanak, angin
IN: belanak, gereh
PH: banak, bilugan
VI: cá dôi côi
HK: hin chai

CUISINE See the preceding page.

THREADFIN, INDIAN THREADFIN / TASSEL FISH
Family *Polynemidae*

Polydactylus indicus (Shaw)

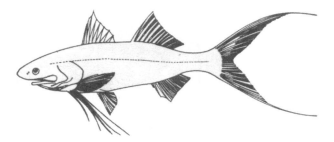

REMARKS Maximum length 1 metre 20.

This fish has a golden body, darker above, and yellow fins. The long thread-like rays which extend from the lower part of the pectoral fins are used as feelers to explore the sea bottom.

The threadfin is found in coastal waters and rivers and is common on the west coast of Malaya.

Polynemus paradisius Linnaeus is the Tupsi fish of India and the Mango fish (nga-pon-na) of Burma: it is regarded as a great delicacy in both countries, but is quite small (just over 20 cm). In Thailand it is pla nuat phram, meaning the fish with a Brahmin moustache.

BE: goojwali
TA: polun-kalah
BU: nga-let-khwa
TH: pla kurau hang yau
MA: kurau, serangin
IN: kuro
PH: mamal
CA: trey carao
VI: cá chét con
HK: ma yau
TAI: yin du ma ba

CUISINE A fish of excellent quality. Highly esteemed in Malaysia. I enjoyed a fillet, grilled and served with garlic butter, in Pinang. The flesh is large-flaked.

Recipes are given on pages 328 and 329.

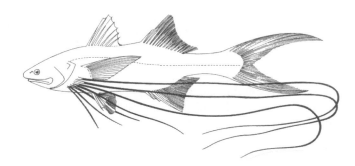

THREADFIN, FOUR FINGER THREADFIN

Family *Polynemidae*

Eleutheronema tetradactylum (Shaw)

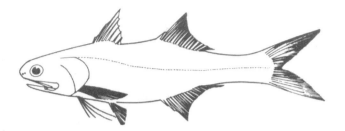

REMARKS Maximum length over 1 metre 75; normal length much less. Silvery green above, creamy below. The name **tetradactylum** refers to the four threads on each pectoral fin. Some related species have six or seven. However, the best is **E. tridactylon** (Bleeker) which has three and is yellow in colour, with black tips to the dorsal fins and green tassels.

Distribution: from the west coast of India through all S. E. Asian waters to Queensland, Australia.

CUISINE This fish is highly esteemed in Thailand – to be fried, boiled, roasted, steamed, dried or pickled. It is also good for rice soup. However **E. tridactylon** costs more and is considered to be quite the best species for certain fishy soups.

TA: kalemeen
BU: nga-kat-tha
TH: pla kurau nuat
   see saen
MA: senangin, kurau
   janggut
IN: kurau, senangin
   (Sumatra)
PH: mamali
CA: trey chao
VI: cá chét bôn râu
HK: ma yau
CH: si zhi ma ba*

*This means four-fingered horse fish

SOLDIERFISH, PINECONE/RED SOLDIERFISH
Family *Holocentridae*

Myripristis murdjan (Forskål)

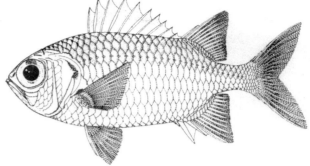

REMARKS Maximum length 30 cm.

This soldierfish has an almost oblong, thin body, dark red in colour and marked by dusky longitudinal bands. It and its relations all present a spiny appearance and frequent shallow coastal waters. It is widespread from the Red Sea across to the Philippines.

Sargocentron rubrum (Forskål) is one of the numerous species in the family of soldierfish, squirrel fish etc. It is rather small but may be met in the markets. It is shown in the drawing at the bottom of the page.

CUISINE The soldierfish are only moderately good to eat. They are so bony that in Malaysia, for example, they are hardly eaten at all.

TA: parullam, punakanni
TH: pla khao mao nam luk khrip dam*
MA: lolong batu, sebekah karang, logu
IN: murjan
PH: baga-baga, suga-suga (general name)
VI: cá son
HK: cheung kwun gaap
CH: bai bian ju lin yu
TAI: chi song qiu
JA: yogore-matsukasa

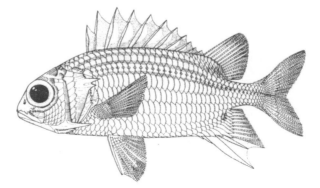

*What a long name! The last word means black-tipped. The fourth and fifth words mean deep water. The second and third mean 'green' rice.

Some Perch-like Fish,
including the Barramundi and Tripletail

The Order *Perciformes*, to which we now come, is of outstanding importance and accounts for over half of the catalogue of fish. It is so big that it has been divided into sub-orders, for example the sub-order *Percoidei*, which comes first and which embraces what one might call the most perch-like of the perch-like fishes.

To say this invites the question: what does 'perch-like' mean? The answer is that the fish of this Order all have some spiny fins. Some of the leading rays of the dorsal and anal fins are always thickened, unjointed and (in most instances) sharp. The pelvic fins usually have one spiny ray each, and are well forward on the fish, beneath the pectoral fins. The pectoral fins themselves are high up on the body (whereas the more primitive bony fishes have low-slung pectorals).

There are other characteristics too, but the above indications are the easiest for the layman to follow. There are of course very wide variations in other regards among the 8000 or so species of perch-like fish, including variations in edibility. However, this next little section of the catalogue includes some delicious species such as **Lates calcarifer**, the best of the species which are called in Thailand pla kaphong (a name dear to fishmongers who sell fish to foreigners, since many such carry this one fish name in their heads as the name of an indisputably good fish, not realising that the name applies to a number of species of varying quality).

I should mention here one good sea perch, **Psammoperca waigiensis** (Cuvier), which is highly appreciated in Thailand, although it is rare in the markets and has not therefore been catalogued. It has a maximum length of about 35 cm, and is reddish-brown above, silvery below. The fins are also reddish-brown. The Thai names are pla kaphong sam and pla kaphong ta maeo. The last words in the second Thai name meants cat's eye. The Khmer name is trey spong; and the Indonesian name rongan.

BARRAMUNDI, SILVER/GIANT SEA PERCH
Family *Centropomidae*

Lates calcarifer (Bloch)

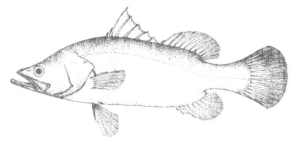

REMARKS Maximum length not far short of 2 metres, usual length up to about 1 metre 20.

The fish is golden-brown above and silvery below. The fins are all brown (the upper ones dark, the lower ones paler). The eyes are noticeably small.*

This is one of the great game fishes of the region. It is famous in Bengal in particular; and Europeans living in India bestowed on it the rather startling name cock-up. The name barramundi used in Queensland and Western Australia is the aboriginal one.

The dried air bladder of this species fetches a high price.

Distribution: from the eastern edge of the Arabian Gulf through to northern Australia, Taiwan and southern Japan.

BE: bhetki
TA: painee-meen, koduva
BU: nga-ka-kadit
TH: pla kaphong khao
MA: siakap, kapah (puteh)
IN: kakap, kanja
PH: apahap
CA: trey spong yeak
VI: cá chēm
HK: maan cho
CH: jian wen lu
TAI: bian hong yan lu
JA: akame

CUISINE A fish of excellent quality, highly esteemed at Hong Kong, in Malaysia and in Thailand. Bake, grill, steam, fry or use in fish soups.

Writing of the barramundi in Australia, Roughley notes that it was 'a favourite food of the aborigines, who wrapped it in the leaves of the wild ginger plant and baked it in hot ashes', and that people who have tried it thus in modern times declare this treatment to be unsurpassed by any other.

A specific recipe is given on page 225.

* In fact the Hong Kong Chinese name maan cho (or mang ts'o) means blind seabass.

TRIPLE-TAIL, BROWN / DUSKY TRIPLE-TAIL

Family *Lobotidae*

Lobotes surinamensis (Bloch)

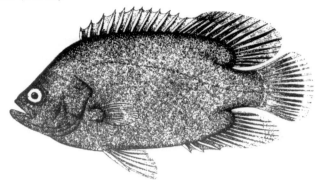

REMARKS Maximum length just over 1 metre, common length about 45 cm. The back is dark brown or olive, and the fish is silvery below. Dusky lines and faint spots may appear on the body.

This species has a more or less global distribution, extending to the West Indies, as the scientific name implies.

CUISINE A fish of excellent quality. Steam, fry, bake; or grill the smaller specimens whole.

BE: samudra koi
BU: pinle-ngapyama
TH: pla lepo, pla
    kaphong dam, pla
    kaphong khee sao*
MA: pechah periok
IN: kakap-batu; bekuku
    (Java)
PH: kakap-bato
VI: cá huong vên
HK: tid-laap
TAI: song diao
JA: matsudai

*the sluggish snapper!

CRESCENT PERCH, GRUNTER
Terapon jarbua (Forskål)

Family *Terapontidae*

REMARKS Maximum length 30 cm, common length 15 to 20 cm. Brownish above, silvery below. Note the dark brown crescent bands and the distinctive colour pattern on the tail fin. Its distinctive appearance has resulted in this fish being called crescent-banded grunter/tiger-fish in some places in the west Pacific.

Distribution: from the Red Sea and East Africa to Samoa, north to southern Japan and south to Australia.

Terapon theraps (Cuvier), the Large-scaled terapon, is a close relation, rather smaller, but with larger scales. It is called kerong-kerong or kerong-kerong gendang in Malaysia.

TA: palin-keetchan
BU: nga-khone-kyar
TH: pla khang taphao
MA/IN: kerong-kerong
PH: bagaong
VI: cá căng
HK: waan-mun-dang-kung
CH: xi lin la
JA: kotohiki

CUISINE A fish of moderately good quality; but it is difficult to scale and the skin is tough.

BIGEYE, PURPLE-SPOTTED BIGEYE
Priacanthus tayenus Richardson

Family *Priacanthidae*

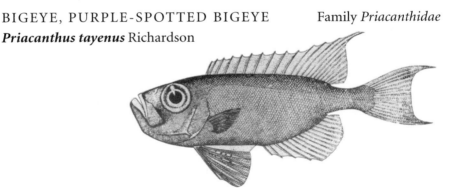

REMARKS Maximum length 30 cm, common length 25 cm. Reddish above, silvery below. The pelvic fin bears distinct blackish-red spots. A close relation, *P. macracanthus* Cuvier, Red bigeye, has yellow-brown spots on its fins.

Distribution: from the Persian Gulf to the western Pacific, including northern Queensland, Australia.

BU: myet-lone-gyi
TH: pla ta phawong, pla ta van, pla ta to
MA: ikan temenggong
IN: serinding tembakau
PH: mata hari
VI: cá son thóc

CUISINE This fish is abundant at Hong Kong, but not very popular. 'The rather unpleasant brilliant crimson-red colour, the tough skin with firm and rough scales, and the unusually large eyes are probably the cause of its unpopularity. However, it is of excellent edible quality. It can be roasted, baked or steamed. When it is ready for the table, the skin is very easily peeled off, and the flesh is extremely palatable.' (Chan)

HK: muk min
CH: chang wei da yan diao
TAI: ye si da yan diao

SILVER SILLAGO / WHITING
Sillago sihama (Forskål)

Family *Sillaginidae*

REMARKS Maximum length 30 cm.

Light grey or olive above, silvery below.

The range of this species is from the Red Sea to Japan and Polynesia. It is found in coastal waters, estuaries and trawling banks. A closely related species, **S. maculata** Quoy and Gaimard, is also widely distributed; it is the Trumpeter whiting of Queensland and New South Wales.

Maxwell, writing of both species, observed that:

'They frequent shallow water and sandy bottoms where they feed on small crustaceans, worms, sand hoppers, etc. There is probably no cleaner feeding fish than the Whiting, a fact which perhaps accounts in some measure for its delicate flavour and wholesomeness.

'Both our varieties, whether adult or young, are very shy and instantly bury themselves in the sand on the appearance of any danger. Even a passing dark cloud leads to their immediate disappearance into the sand whence they emerge a few moments later.'

BE: shoondra
   (general name)
TA: kilaken
BU: nga-palway
TH: pla sai, pla burut
MA: bulus-bulus,
   putung damar
IN: rejung
PH: asohos
VI: cá duc
HK: sa chuen
CH: duo lin xi
TAI: sha suo
JA: kisu

CUISINE Excellent fish, with white flesh, easily digestible and with a characteristic and agreeable flavour.

FALSE TREVALLY, MILKFISH, WHITEFISH

Family *Lactariidae*

Lactarius lactarius (Bloch and Schneider)

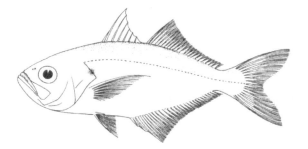

REMARKS Maximum length about 35 cm, market length 20 to 25 cm.

Light grey or blue-grey above, silvery below, with a black spot on the shoulder. The tail fin has a dusky black border and the other fins are pale yellowish. The 'milk' theme, reflecting the colour of the fish, recurs in a number of common names, including milk trevally. An alternative Indonesian name is ikan santan, meaning 'coconut-milk fish'.

Distribution: throughout S. E. Asian waters and south to northern Australia.

A schooling fish of coastal waters and trawling grounds. It is caught all the year round by trawl and bamboo stake traps in the Gulf of Thailand. The catching has been carried out with such enthusiasm in West Malaysia that the species had become virtually extinct by the early '70s.

TA: sudumbu
BU: (hin-cho-ma)
TH: pla (sab) khanun, pla yuan
MA: kelapa-kelapa (coconut)
IN: ikan susu, lemahan
PH: pelyan
CA: trey yuon
VI: cá liêt lô
HK: hoi lin
TAI: ru qing
JA: akuta-uo

CUISINE Opinions differ. This is the third most expensive sea fish in Thailand, and is esteemed in India. Excellent flesh, but spoils quickly, so buy very fresh. So advise the FAO experts. Yet it is disdained at Hong Kong and not popular in Malaysia. It may be had salted.

Fry or boil.

Groupers and Seabass:
The Family Serranidae

This family is well-known in tropical waters, and some temperate waters too, right round the world. Its members are almost all good to eat, some of them outstandingly so. The mérou, a Mediterranean grouper, was my favourite fare when I lived on the North African coast; but only a few species are found there, whereas the waters of S. E. Asia harbour several dozen.

The name grouper, which is best applied exclusively or mainly to fish of the genus *Epinephelus*, is of uncertain origin. Scott gives three accounts, of which I prefer the last. ' "Grouper" is said to originate, from the fact that, although normally leading a solitary existence, at breeding times the fish congregate at certain spots from miles around and at such times the fish are caught in immense quantities by the fishermen who known when and where to find them. Another theory is that the name should be "Groper" after the manner in which the fish noses its way into holes and crannies in the reefs. Yet another suggestion is that both these names are merely corruptions of the native names which in the Philippines, Borneo and India all bear a striking resemblance to the Malay name "Kerapu".'

Some species of grouper are found in deep water and some in estuaries, but most of them inhabit the coral reefs. Hence such names as Reef cod or Coral cod, which have unfittingly been given to them. (They do share with the cod a certain thick-lippedness and a burliness of body, but there are more points of difference than of resemblance.)

However, although the genus *Epinephelus* is the most important in the family it is not the only one. Besides the groupers there are various seabass which rival them in quality and match them closely in appearance.

The species which I catalogue in the following pages are a representative selection of those which are common in the region. But there are many more, especially of the smaller species, and local names are confusing. It is well to keep in mind the general names used for fish of this family, as follows:

Burma:	Kyauk-nga
Thailand:	Pla karang
Cambodia:	Trey tukké
Vietnam:	Cá mú
Hong Kong:	names ending in -paan
Philippines:	Korapo
Indonesia:	Kerapu
Malaysia:	Kerapu
China:	Shi ban yu

A final warning: Australians use the name Groper for certain wrasses and parrotfishes, and Rock cod or Coral cod (the very names which I have deplored above) for the groupers.

Recipes for which groupers are recommended appear on pages 236, 251, 257, 273 and 291.

HUMPBACK / POLKA-DOT GROUPER

Cromileptes altivelis (Valenciennes)

Family *Serranidae*

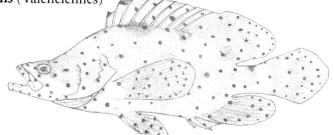

REMARKS Maximum length about 60 cm. This is a pale brown or lilac/brown fish noticeably marked with a profusion of black spots all over, for which polka dots is exactly the right description.

The back has a humped appearance which is thought to resemble the featherback (a common fresh water fish of S. E. Asia) and accounts for the Malay name. It is also the reason for the local Chinese name in Hong Kong, which means rat grouper.

Distribution: from the eastern Indian Ocean to southern Japan, Pacific islands and Australia.

CUISINE A superb fish and the most expensive of all food fishes at Hong Kong.

BU: nga-tauk-tu
TH: pla karang na ngawn*
MA: kerapu belida
IN: kerapu tikus
PH: lapu-lapung señorita
CA: trey tukké korm
VI: cá mú heo
HK: lo sue baan
TAI: min yu
JA: sarasa-hata

* the last two words mean gracefully curved like an elephant's tusk.

CHOCOLATE HIND, BROWN CORAL COD

Cephalopholis boenak (Bloch)

Family *Serranidae*

REMARKS Maximum length nearly 30 cm. This fish is brown, marked with indistinct darker vertical strips. Schroeder remarks that its rather subdued chocolate-like colouring has made the species less popular for the aquarium than its more colourful relations, of which a couple of mentioned below.

C. argus Bloch and Schneider, the Peacock grouper,

TA: verri-kaleva
TH: pla karang
MA: kerapu tenggarong
IN: kerapu batu
PH: lapu-lapu
CA: trey tukké kuoch
VI: cá mú

presents a dramatic appearance, the body being reddish-brown or purplish-black and covered all over
with light bluish grey dots. It is a larger fish (up to
45 cm). *C. leopardus* (Lacepède) is the Leopard
grouper (or Leopard hind), names which reflect its light reddish-brown colour
and numerous small round or oval red spots. It may reach a length of 40 cm and,
like so many groupers, is called lapu-lapu in the Philippines. *Aethaloperca rogaa*
(Forskål) is larger still (up to 60 cm) and of a uniform dark brown or blackish
colour, which has earned it the name 'dusky rock-cod'. It is noticeably deep-
bodied.

HK: woo-sze
TAI: hei kuai
JA: aosujihata, yamihata

Distribution (of *Cephalopholis boenak*): from India throughout S. E. Asian
waters to Australia and many islands of the Pacific.

CUISINE Fry, bake or use for fish soups. The larger species yield steaks for grilling.

GREASY GROUPER   Family *Serranidae*
Epinephelus tauvina (Forskål)

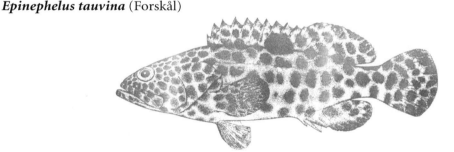

REMARKS Maximum length over 1 metre, but this is
unusual; the common length is around 60 cm.

Young specimens are brown with darker markings
and red-brown spots as shown; old ones are uniformly
brown.

Distribution: wide, from the Red Sea to South Africa,
and including all S. E. Asian waters, much of Australia,
some Pacific islands and north to Japan.

Chan remarks that this is one of the most abundant
groupers in the Hong Kong market, and adds the following interesting comments: 'Giant specimens have a
very bulky head and comparatively short and low fins.
Scales are extremely adherent to the skin, and bones are
very tough. When a giant specimen is caught, it is
always tied to the side of the boat instead of being placed on the deck. It is
believed that the flesh deteriorates very quickly on contact with wood.'

BE: bhol (general name
    for *Epinephelus*)
TA: punni-callawah
BU: nga-tauk-tu
TH: pla karang
MA: kerapu, kertang
IN: kerapu lumpur
PH: lapu-lapu
VI: cá mú ruði
HK: fah-paan
CH: ju shi ban yu
TAI: lu hua si ban
JA: hitomihata

CUISINE A fish of good quality. In Thailand it is fried or used in rice soup.

LONGFIN GROUPER

Family *Serranidae*

Epinephelus quoyanus (Valenciennes)

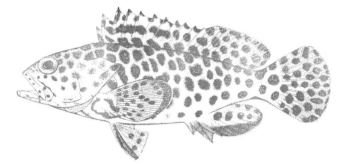

REMARKS Maximum length only about 30 cm; a 'sedentary little grouper' say Heemstra and Randall.

This fish is almost completely covered by large hexagonal patches of dark reddish-brown colour, in a sort of honeycomb pattern, perhaps more accurately referred to as 'reticulated'.

Distribution: a western Pacific species ranging from southern Japan to Australia and the easterly parts of S. E. Asia, but not the Indian Ocean.

TH: pla karang
MA: kerapu
IN: kerapu tutul
PH: lapo-lapong liglig
CA: trey tukké khmoun
HK: gum-chin-paan
JA: mayôhata

E. merra (Bloch), known as the Honeycomb grouper is of similar length but has shorter pectoral fins. It is pla karang dok in Thailand, kyauk-nga or nga-tauk-tu in Burma; cá mú chấm in Vietnam; and kerapu balong in Indonesia. This species has a wide distribution in the Indo-Pacific, from South Africa to French Polynesia, and seems to favour the waters surrounding islands and over coral reefs.

E. areolatus (Forskål), shown below, is similar in size and shape, but its spots form a pattern described as 'areolated' and it has a square-ended (truncate) tail. An Australian name is 'yellow-spotted rock cod'. It is relatively common in Malaysian waters.

Another species, *E. coioides*, has a range extending westwards to the Gulf, where groupers are called hamoor and this is the most highly prized in the genus.

CUISINE These are all good fish. See the preceding entries.

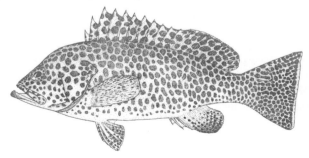

BROWN-MARBLED GROUPER
Epinephelus fuscoguttatus (Forskål)

Family *Serranidae*

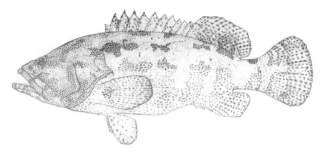

REMARKS Maximum length almost 1 metre (although 1 metre 20 has been reported from the Philippines). Common length 60 to 70 cm.

BU: kyauk-nga, nga-tauk-tu
TH: pla karang lai
MA: kerapu hitam
IN: kerapu bebek
PH: garopa
CA: trey tukké och
VI: cá mú
HK: hung dim paan
CH: zong dian shi ban yu
JA: akamadarahata

The colouration is brown, with darker blotches grouped in about 5 vertical bands. There is a distinctive dark blotch on the base of the tail. All the fins have brown spots.

This is a solitary grouper, found in rocky areas, occurring widely in the Indo-Pacific region from East Africa to many islands in the Pacific.

I mention here another relatively large grouper of a generally brown aspect. This is *E. bruneus* Bloch, known as Longtooth grouper and also Mud grouper. It is sometimes as much as 1 metre in length. It is marked by dark bands which disappear in older specimens. The species is known at Hong Kong (as ching-paan when small, lai-paan when full-grown) and in northern Vietnam but does not penetrate further south; so its claim to be classed as a S. E. Asian fish is not very strong.

This was no doubt one of the groupers which Guilbert (*La Pêche dans le Golfe du Tonkin*) had in mind when he remarked that the fish which were most often served at European tables in Tonkin, during colonial times, were wrasses and groupers; and that they were collectively termed 'vieilles' (a familiar French name which should, however, have been applied to the wrasses only, mérou being the French for grouper).

E. bleekeri (Vaillant), the Duskytail grouper, is an excellent grouper, well worth buying. It is pale brown with numerous orange-yellow spots. The tail fin is extraordinary. The upper part of it bears these same orange-yellow spots, but the lower part is uniformly purplish brown. Maximum total length about 75 cm, common length 50 cm. The name in Hong Kong is sheung-sik-mei-hung-paan, or just hung-paan.

CUISINE *E. fuscoguttatus* is another species which the Thai fry or use in soup. This one is highly rated, so is *E. bruneus* at Hong Kong. *E. bleekeri* is another excellent fish, but not abundant.

YELLOW GROUPER
Epinephelus awoara (Temminck and Schlegel)

Family *Serranidae*

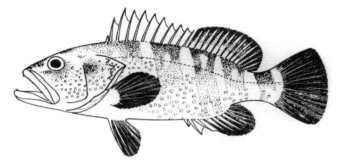

REMARKS Maximum length 60 cm, common length around 30 cm.

PH: lapu-lapu
VI: cá song den
HK: wong paan (large), wong dang (small)
CH: qing shi ban yu
JA: aohata

This grouper belongs to the coasts of China and Japan, but rates inclusion in the catalogue because it is well-known at Hong Kong and in northern Vietnam; and also because of its striking colours. Adults are yellow below and pale brown/grey above, with yellow spots and yellow margins to the dorsal, anal and tail fins; younger specimens are marked by 6 dark-brown near-vertical bands.

The Hong Kong grouper, *E. akaara* (Temminck and Schlegel), also known as the Red or Redspotted grouper, is also a species of China and Japan. It has the distinction of being the most expensive grouper marketed at Hong Kong, where it is known as hung-paan. Chan explains that it is so valuable that it is frequently kept alive in order to bring the maximum price. 'To do this, local fishermen always make a puncture at the vent. This puncture releases the excessive pressure inside the fish, and allows it to acquire its normal swimming position. The fish is later cleansed with a piece of cloth soaked in fresh water. After this treatment it is kept in a live tank, which is a standard feature of a "grouper hand-liner". Specimens thus treated can survive for a considerable length of time in captivity.' The Red grouper (aka means red in Japanese) is in fact a brownish fish with orange to red spots and often marked by irregular dark brown bands; see drawing below.

CUISINE The Yellow grouper is of excellent quality, and the Red, as noted above, is even more highly esteemed at Hong Kong.

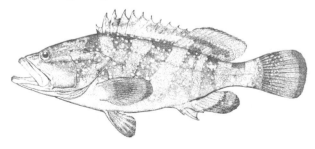

GIANT SEABASS   Family *Serranidae*

Epinephelus lanceolatus (Bloch)
(formerly *Promicrops lanceolatus*)

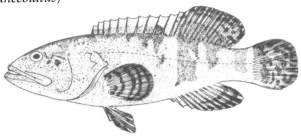

REMARKS Maximum length over 3 metres. The giant of the family. Specimens of 25 to 50 kg are not uncommon, and weights of 400 kg, or even more, have been reported.

Young specimens have dark brown backs and light yellow undersides, with greyish yellow sides marked with brown. Adults become uniformly dark brown in colour and may finish up almost black.

This grouper is reputed to attack men, rushing from its hiding place in terrifying fashion; and there are many stories of struggles between it and fishermen. Maxwell recalls that he and a Malay caught one which was estimated to weigh 400 kg, and that they had to sink their boat in order to get it aboard.

BU: kyauk-nga,
    nga-tauk-tu
TH: pla maw thaleh
MA: pertang
IN: kerapu lumpur,
    kerapu bebek
PH: lapu-lapu
VI: cá mú song
JA: tamakai

Distribution: *E. lanceolatus* is the most widely distributed grouper in the world from the Red Sea down to South Africa and eastward to Hawaii, north to Japan and south to Australia.

CUISINE I have found no reports of how the really big ones taste; nor do I know whether anyone has attempted to cook such a monster whole. Those of moderate size can be dealt with normally, and are reputedly of good quality.

The knowledgeable French writer 'le Nestour' vouched for the esteem in which they were held in the south of Vietnam (and added two interesting notes: that the maximum girth of this huge fish is the same as its length; and that the thick skin, which could itself weigh more than 20 kg after being dried, was also an article of commerce).

LEOPARD CORAL-GROUPER, BLUE-SPOTTED CORAL TROUT
Plectropomus leopardus (Lacepède)

Family *Serranidae*

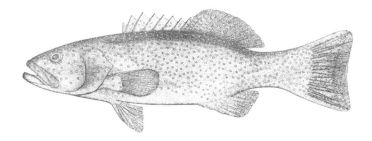

REMARKS Maximum length 1 metre 20, common length 70 to 80 cm.

This species has a range from Japan to Australia and right across the Indo-Pacific area. It has a variable but always striking colouration – the body is light red (even orange) or brown, and largely covered with dark-edged blue spots. It may be distinguished from all other serranid species in the region, including the generally similar *P. maculatus* (Bloch) by the shape of its tail (for which the technical term is emarginate).

There is another species which has a somewhat similar colour scheme (little blue specks all over a purplish body) and a distinctive tail (crescent-shaped – see the lower drawing). This is the Moon-tailed coral-trout, *Variola louti* (Forskål), a widely distributed species which is known as lapo-lapong señorita in the Philippines and cheung-may-paan at Hong Kong. Many of the common names refer to its distinctive tail, variously described as moon-shaped, lunar, or (the FAO official English name) yellow-edged lyre tail.

BU: kyauk-nga, nga-tauk-tu
TH: pla kaang daeng jutfa
MA: kerapu bara
IN: lodi, kerapu lodi
PH: lapo-lapo
CA: pla karang
VI: cá mú cham
HK: tsut-sing-paan
CH: sai ji lu
TAI: bao kuai
JA: suji-ara

CUISINE An excellent and expensive fish.

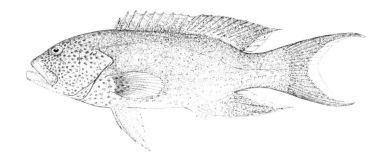

The Carangid Fish, the Runner and the Moonfish

The family *Carangidae* is a large one, and the classification of species within it has not yet reached a satisfactory conclusion. There is, moreover, considerable confusion over the English names which may be applied to these fish. The names Jack, Trevally, Scad, Horse mackerel and Cavalla are all used in a general way; and the day still seems distant when ichthyologists from the various English-speaking countries will be able to agree on a rational system of nomenclature. Never mind; this must rank low among the problems of the world and does not constitute a practical difficulty in Asia, where the indigenous languages do on the whole succeed in distinguishing clearly between the most important species.

The carangid fish fall into two groups, those which have no scutes along the lateral line and those which do. The next four catalogue entries describe the principal scuteless species; thereafter, for many pages, I review the ones which have scutes.

Many of the carangid fish have highly compressed bodies, which is to say that they are built on lean lines and have rather little flesh in proportion to their length and depth. Even so, some of them are well worth the cook's attention. I have tried to indicate in this part of the catalogue which are the best to buy among those which are regularly brought to market; but must remind the reader that there are many more species than I have room to describe, and that all are of at least moderately good quality.

In general, the carangid fish are many times more important in S. E. Asia than are the scad and horse mackerel of European waters. But it is worth remembering that there are some good European recipes for horse mackerel which can be applied to the abundance of similar species in S. E. Asia, for example the French dish Sévéreaux aux petits pois, which involves cooking cleaned pieces of the fish in a casserole with tender young peas. Some of the carangid species are known as jash in the Gulf and this treatment would suit them too.

One member of the family, **Parastromateus niger**, the Black pomfret, was until recently counted as a member of the family *Formionidae* and in this catalogue has stayed in the place which it had under the old classification. This is convenient because it remains adjacent to the White pomfret, which it resembles, see pages 100–101.

This section of the catalogue concludes with entries for the Cobia and Moonfish, which are both highly commendable fish but differ from each other markedly in appearance and habits, illustrating yet again the very wide variety of forms which are embraced in the Order *Perciformes*.

QUEENFISH, TALANG QUEENFISH   Family *Carangidae*
Scomberoides commersoniannus (Lacepède)

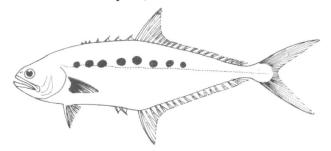

REMARKS Maximum length about 1 metre 20, common length 50 or 60 cm.

The back is blue-green, the sides and belly golden-yellow. But the golden colour may fade, patchily, to silver after death. There are 6 to 8 dark blotches like thumbprints above the lateral line. The fins are yellowish.

This queenfish is widespread in the coastal waters of the Indo-West Pacific area, as are several close relations.

S. tol (Cuvier), the Needle-scaled queenfish, has a maximum length of only 60 cm. It also has spots, along the lateral line. It is talang-padi in Malaysia and daun bambu in Indonesia. **S. tala** (Cuvier), Barred queenfish, is about the same length but deeper in the body.

S. lysan (Forskål), Doublespotted queenfish, has a double row of spots on each side.

TA: toal-parah
BU: nga-letwa
TH: pla chaliap
MA: talang
IN: talang-talang, lima jari
PH: dorado
CA: trey sampan
VI: cá chầng ngòi
HK: talang, wong cheung
CH: chang he chun shen
JA: okuchi-ikekatsuo

CUISINE These are fish of moderate quality. Since the flesh tends to be rather dry, it is usually best to fry (after cutting into steaks). The skin is tough – hence the names 'leather jacket' and 'leatherskin', occasionally met in e.g. the Philippines. These fish are sometimes marketed in salted and dried form, e.g. in Hong Kong, where their reputation is not high.

The remarkable little treatise by 'le Nestour', on the fisheries of Cochinchina contains an enthusiastic passage about cá chang – presumably **Scomberoides** sp. – in which the author remarks how easily the firm flesh may be separated from the backbone and states that he used to preserve it in orange wine or pineapple wine for as long as two or three years.

Singaporeans have mixed attitudes towards the queenfish. Tham Ah Kow (writing in *Animal Life and Nature in Singapore*, listed under Chuang in the Bibliography) says that:

'These fish are known to local Chinese consumers as tuah peh kong hu because of the five black marks on each side of the fish. It is believed in certain quarters that the god of the sea has reserved this fish for himself by placing his fingerprints on the fish and the Chinese therefore do not usually eat it, but it is eaten by members of the other communities.'

RAINBOW RUNNER
Family *Carangidae*

Elagatis bipinnulata (Quoy and Gaimard)

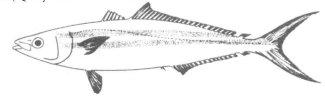

REMARKS Maximum length may be as much as 1 metre 80, common length around 60 cm.

A pelagic fish. It is slimmer than the preceding species, and has a different arrangement of dorsal fins. The colours are vivid, but fade soon after death. The back is greenish-blue; and each side bears horizontal bands of sky-blue, yellow and sky-blue again.

Distribution is worldwide.

CUISINE A fish of good quality; but it fetches a low price in Bangkok because it is little known.

TA: kulkul
TH: pla kluay kaw, pla leüang phrong
MA: pisang-pisang
IN: sunglir
PH: salmon
VI: cá soc muop, cá õng vải
HK: wang mun chun
CH: fang chui sui
TAI: shuang dai shen
JA: tsumuburi

AMBERJACK, BLACKBANDED TREVALLY/KINGFISH
Family *Carangidae*

Seriolina nigrofasciata (Rüppell)

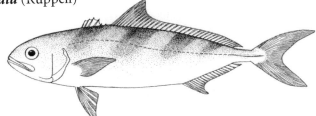

REMARKS Maximum length 70 cm, common length 40 cm. Dusky olive brown or dusky grey above, silvery grey below. Young species bear black oblique bands.

Names in Francophone areas introduce the theme of love in connection with these fish; for example, l'amoureuse petite in Reunion and seriole amourez in Djibouti.

Seriola dumerili Risso is considerably larger. The back is purplish red and the belly silvery white. A yellow horizontal band runs from eye to tail.

Distribution: from the Red Sea, East Africa and South Africa to Japan and Australia.

BU: hin-cho-khup
TH: pla sam lee
MA: pisang-pisang, aji-aji, kekek
HK: cheung-kung
TAI: xiao gan shen
JA: aiburi

CUISINE A good fish, which may be had fresh or salted. *S. dumerili* is less esteemed, anyway at Hong Kong, where it is usually salted.

POMPANO, SNUBNOSE POMPANO/DART

Trachinotus blochii (Lacepède)

Family *Carangidae*

REMARKS Maximum length about 1 metre, common length 45 to 60 cm. In the market this fish is gold in colour, and a beautiful sight.

T. baillonii (Lacepède), Smallspotted dart, has a greenish back and silvery body with 3 to 5 black spots along the lateral line. It is smaller.

Distribution: Indo-Pacific from the Red Sea and East Africa to the Pacific (Samoa), north to southern Japan, south to Australia through Micronesia.

CUISINE Moderately good. Steam or fry.
See also the recipe on page 285.

SI: kutili
BU: myet-lone-gyi
TH: pla ang sa, (pla nua awn)
MA: nyior-nyior
IN: lowang, borung
PH: talakitok
VI: cá sòng trúng
HK: wong laap chong
JA: marukoban

SCAD, INDIAN SCAD, MACKEREL SCAD

Family *Carangidae*

Decapterus russelli (Rüppell)

REMARKS Maximum length 45 cm, market length 30 cm. Dark or greeny blue above, silvery below. The fins are yellowish or reddish. This species is abundant in the Philippines, as is *D. macrosoma* (Bleeker), the Shortfin scad. The fishery for the two species together is now the most important single fishery in the Philippines.

Distribution: East Africa to Japan and Australia.

CUISINE These are popular fish in Malaysia and the Philippines. Frying or steaming is recommended.

TA: moon-dakun-kilichi
BU: pan-zin, nga-gyi-gan
TH: pla thu khaek
MA: selayang, cerut (cigar), curut-curut
IN: lajang, lajeng, layang
PH: galunggong
VI: cá nuc
HK: tsee-yue
TAI: hong gua shen
JA: oaka-muro

HARDTAIL/TORPEDO SCAD
Family *Carangidae*
Megalaspis cordyla (Linnaeus)

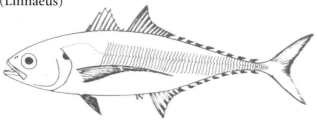

REMARKS Maximum length 40 cm, market size about 30 cm. Bluish green above and silvery below; most of the fins are dusky grey. The species is easily recognized by its torpedo-like body, numerous finlets and stiff thin tail.

Distribution: East Africa to Japan and Australia.

CUISINE Of medium quality. The fishery authorities at Hong Kong declare it to be 'a tasty fish when fried or steamed', but it may also be grilled or cooked in a court-bouillon.

TA: vangadi, komara-parah
BU: pan-zin
TH: pla hang kheang
MA: cencaru
IN: selar tengkek
PH: oriles, pak-an
CA: trey kantuy rung
VI: cá sòng
HK: kap-tse
JA: oni-aji

TREVALLY, CREVALLY
Family *Carangidae*
Atropus atropus (Bloch and Schneider)

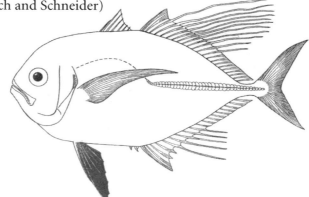

REMARKS Maximum length 35 cm, common length 20 cm. Blue-green above, silvery below. Note the black ventral fins. The other fins are pale or light yellow. An unusual feature of this fish is a groove along the belly into which the long pelvic fin fits when depressed: hence a new official name for it, Cleftbelly trevally.

CUISINE One of the preferred marine fishes in Thailand and Cambodia. It is used in soup, or fried. It may also be had salted and dried.

TA: kunni-parah
TH: pla paen
MA: rambai
IN: cipa-cipa
PH: salay-salay
CA: trey slek bas
VI: cá nóc bâu
HK: tsau-pai

GOLDEN TREVALLY
Gnathanodon speciosus (Forskål)

Family *Carangidae*

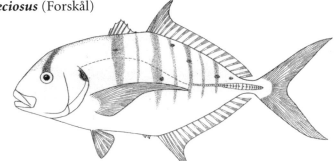

REMARKS Maximum length just over 1 metre, common length 50 cm. The body is golden-yellow, with 8 to 10 vertical blackish stripes, alternately broad and narrow; but the larger specimens are paler in colour, with black patches and faint cross-bars on the sides.

Distribution: from the Gulf through the Indo-Pacific to the Americas.

CUISINE A good food fish, which is highly regarded in Thailand and Cambodia. Steam, boil, fry, use in soup.

UAE: zredi
TA: pathi-para
BU: kalagnu
TH: pla taklawng leüang
MA: gerong-gerong, daing belang
IN: badong (Javanese)
PH: malapandong dilau, talakitok
CA: trey kam kuoch
VI: cá bè cam
HK: wong sui tsun

AFRICAN POMPANO, THREADFIN TREVALLY
Family *Carangidae*

Alectis ciliaris (Bloch)

REMARKS Maximum length well over 1 metre; common length of adults around 40 cm. The colour is basically an iridescent silver, with a blue back. Young specimens may bear indistinct vertical bands.

Distributed worldwide in tropical seas.

CUISINE One of the best food fishes of the family, but not common. Steam or fry.

BU: nga-dama
TH: pla chom ngam, pla jum, pla phon nang (ladies' hair fish)
MA: cermin, rambai landeh
IN: kwee rombeh, lowang
PH: trakitilyo
CA: trey chen chah
VI: cá lão nhót
HK: paak-so-kung

YELLOWSTRIPE SCAD/TREVALLY
Selaroides leptolepis (Cuvier)

Family *Carangidae*

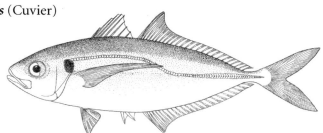

REMARKS Maximum length 20 cm, common length 15 cm. This fish has a greenish back, a silver belly and a broad golden lateral band. (The Thai name means yellow side.) Note the black opercular spot. The scales are small but conspicuous.

Distribution: Indo-West Pacific. Persian Gulf eastwards to the Philippines, north to Okinawa and the Ryukyu Islands and south to Australia.

CUISINE The Malays dry and export this fish, which is plentiful off their east coast, in large quantities. Its quality is good, although its small size restricts the culinary possibilities.

TA: choo parai
BU: zar-kyan
TH: pla khang leüang
MA: selar kuning
IN: salar kuning
PH: salay-salay batang
CA: trey chhnot loeung
VI: cá liêt ngân
HK: wong mun ha chee
TAI: mu ye shen
JA: hosohira-aji

YELLOWTAIL SCAD
Atule mate (Cuvier)

Family *Carangidae*

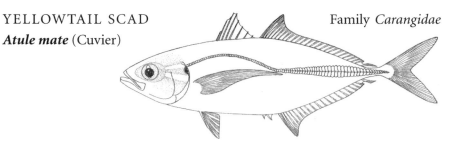

REMARKS Maximum length 30 cm.

Grey-blue above, silvery below. Other species in this genus of small carangid fish include *Alepes djedaba* (Forskål) which is salay-salay lalaki in the Philippines. They all occur in large schools.

Distribution: from the Red Sea and East Africa to Hawaii and Samoa and northern Australia.

CUISINE This scad is abundant all the year round in the Gulf of Thailand, and is prized as a food fish by the Thai and the Khmer.

Boil, steam, fry. May be had salted and dried.

UAE: dardaman
TA: warri-parah
BU: nga-kyikan
TH: pla seekun, pla hang kang
MA: selar gelek, pelata
IN: selar como
PH: salay-salay
CA: trey kantuy rea
VI: cá trác
HK: lay kay ching gay
TAI: shou ping shen
JA: mate-aji

BIG-EYE SCAD
Selar crumenophthalmus (Bloch)

Family *Carangidae*

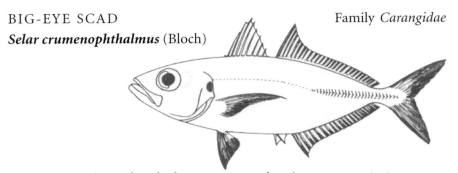

REMARKS Maximum length about 60 cm, market size between 20 and 30 cm. Bluish-silver above, silvery below.

The specific name **crumenophthalmus** refers to the large eyes of this fish. **S. boops** (Cuvier) also has large eyes (**boops** means ox-eyed) and is known in Burma (nga-kyi-kan), Thailand (pla seekun khang luad), Malaysia (selar kuning) and the Philippines (mataan dagat).

The big-eye scad enjoys worldwide distribution in tropical and sub-tropical waters. It prefers clear oceanic waters around islands.

CUISINE Of moderate quality. Thai cooks usually boil it.

BU: nga-kyikan
TH: pla seekun thawng
MA: selar pucat
IN: selar bentong
PH: matang-baka
VI: cá trác
HK: dai ngan tse
CH: zhi yan ao jian shen
TAI: bai shen
JA: meaji

BLACKFIN SCAD
Alepes melanoptera Swainson

Family *Carangidae*

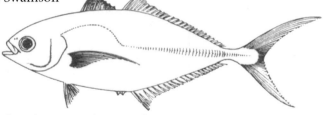

REMARKS Maximum length 30 cm (or more), common length 20 cm.

Dark green or brownish above, silvery below. There are 6 to 9 vertical bands on the upper part of each side, which fade in adults, and the spinous dorsal fin is distinctively black.

Distribution: a wide range in the Indo-Pacific area.

CUISINE This fish is highly esteemed in Thailand and Cambodia. Fry, steam or bake. It may also be had salted and dried.

BU: hin-cho-khup
TH: pla seekun, pla hang kiu
MA: betong, songsong arus, selar papan
IN: selar ubur-ubur
PH: salay-salay (general name)
CA: trey kantuy rung
VI: cá ngâm bôt
HK: lay kay ching gay
JA: seguro-mabuta-aji

BIGEYE TREVALLY   Family *Carangidae*
Caranx sexfasciatus Quoy and Gaimard

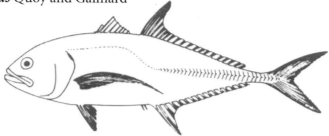

REMARKS Maximum length over 1 metre, common length 50 cm. A silvery fish with a blue sheen, grey above and lighter below, sometimes with a yellow tinge. The younger specimens bear six vertical dark bands, which account for the name *sexfasciatus*. This is one of the largest fish in the genus, and is regarded by anglers as a good sporting fish.

BU: zar-kyan
TH: pla seekun
MA: putih, cupak
IN: selar
PH: talakitok*, pinkit
CA: trey kantuy rea
VI: cá bè dâu
HK: sui tsun
CH: liu dai shen
JA: gingame-aji

However, *C. ignobilis* (Forskål), the Giant trevally, is even larger (it is said to have a total length of 1 metre 70 and to weigh as much as 80 kg). See the lower drawing.

The Filipinos, who call it maliputo, hold this species in very high esteem, particularly the specimens taken in the volcanic Lake Taal, whose flesh is said to be delicately flavoured by the sulphur in the lava rocks. The Thai name is pla seekun phuak. These fish have a dusky back and are silvery below. Adults have fine black dots sprinkled over head and body.

Distribution: the Bigeye trevally has a very wide range from the Red Sea and East Africa to southern Japan, Australia and Mexico.

CUISINE This species is of considerable commercial value. It may be fried or steamed. Grilling is also possible, and it is used for soup in Cambodia. Also sold in dried and salted form.

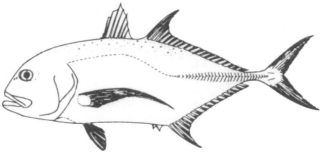

*A generic name for *Caranx* sp. There are lots of others, e.g. babadlong, bulubukto, kalap-ato, malimango.

TREVALLY, MALABAR TREVALLY

Carangoides malabaricus
(Bloch and Schneider)

Family *Carangidae*

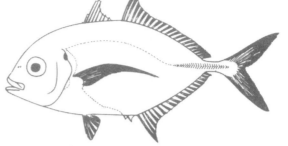

REMARKS Maximum length 60 cm, common length 30 cm. A silvery fish with a blue-green hue above and almost white below.

The shape of the fish, and a certain amount of imagination, must account for the second Thai name, in which chalapao means a sort of steamed pork and vegetable Thai hamburger.

Distribution: East Africa to Japan and Australia.

CUISINE As for the other carangid species.

UAE: jash (general name)
BU: nga-kyi-kan
TH: pla paan, pla
  chalapao
MA: chupak, rambai
IN: kuweh
PH: malapando, sebo
VI: cá viên
HK: dai yue tsai
JA: taiwan-yoroi-aji

LONGFIN TREVALLY

Carangoides armatus (Rüppell)

Family *Carangidae*

REMARKS Maximum length 60 cm, common length 30 cm. Blue-green above, silvery below. Young specimens bear half a dozen vertical stripes. The tail fin is yellow, and the others are either pale or yellowish. The elongate dorsal and anal fins may be regarded either as armour (hence ***armatus*** in the scientific name) or as resembling eyelashes (which gave rise to a former name, ***ciliarius***).

BU: nga-dama
TH: pla takrong khao
MA: chermin, betek, rambai
IN: kuweh, putihan
PH: talakitok (general name)
CA: trey kantuy rea
VI: cá bè dao
HK: dai yue tsai

This species, which has a wide distribution, is known as Kingfish in South Africa.

CUISINE Highly esteemed in Thailand and Cambodia. Steam, fry.

COBIA, RUNNER, BLACK KINGFISH   Family *Rachycentridae*
Rachycentron canadum (Linnaeus)

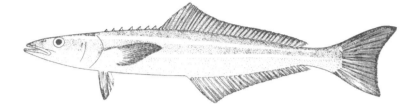

REMARKS Maximum length 2 metres, market length 60 cm to 1 metre.

Backs and flanks are dark brown, the belly paler. The fins are brownish. Two silvery stripes run along each side, enclosing a brown band. Older fish may have only one silvery stripe. Umali, remarking that the fish is sometimes known as the Sergeant fish, attributes the name to these stripes; but all the sergeants who barked at me in my youth wore three stripes, not two or one.

Whatever its putative military rank, the cobia is a fine game fish, swift and voracious. In general appearance it looks like a member of the mackerel family, and large specimens brought to market may be confused with Spanish mackerel or tuna.

The shape of the tail varies with the age of the fish; it gradually assumes an increasingly pronounced crescent form.

Distribution: worldwide in tropical and subtropical waters except the eastern Pacific.

UAE: sichil
TA: kedal viral
BU: pinleh-ngayanh
TH: pla chawn thaleh,
    pla takrong khao
MA: aruan tasek
IN: gabus laut,
    mondoh
PH: dalag-dagat
CA: trey phtuok samot
VI: cá bôp
HK: mone chung
TAI: hai li
JA: sugi

CUISINE A fish of good quality, which does not enjoy everywhere the popularity which it deserves. It may be treated like Spanish mackerel. The flesh is white, firm and of a good flavour, although a little coarser than that of the Spanish mackerel. A correspondent in the UAE reports steaming this fish (gutted and beheaded) in a fish kettle, with very good results.

MOONFISH

Family *Menidae*

Mene maculata (Bloch and Schneider)

REMARKS Maximum length 30 cm.

A fish of engaging appearance, for which the late Walt Disney might have created a suitable personality. The back is bluish, the sides and belly silver; and there are 2 to 4 irregular series of grey spots above and below the lateral line.

This is an oceanic fish, ubiquitous in the warm waters of the Indo-Pacific area, but nowhere common. It comes inshore and enters estuaries.

CUISINE A delicious fish. Grill, steam or fry. I recall seeing in a Manila restaurant a large bowl full of small specimens which had been fried and looked like stacks of silver cardboard cut-outs.

TA: ambattankathi
BU: nga-auk-thadama
TH: pla eepaeh, pla phrachan*, pla baipho **
MA: kekek gedabang, gedabang
IN: peperek kodi, golok kasut
PH: sapatero, tabas
CA: trey taing tor
VI: cá luõi búa
HK: chu dough
TAI: yan kuang yu
JA: ginkagami

*moon
** banyan leaf

Snappers

Scott introduces the family *Lutjanidae* thus: 'One of the most important groups of the local food fishes ... The family includes some of the best-known of the Malayan fishes, several species being known collectively as "Ikan merah", that highly-esteemed, almost essential part of any important dinner or "Chinese makan". The different species ... exhibit a wide range of colours ... but most have a fairly characteristic body-shape in common and, as a group, they are easily recognised. They are small- to medium-sized fishes, most of them with a fairly straight vertical profile and an arched dorsal profile with a pointed snout and large well-toothed mouth, the snapping of which, when they are caught, giving them their common name. They are for the most part brightly coloured, the larger species in general deep red, the smaller predominantly yellow or silvery, usually with coloured lines or spots.'

The snappers, almost without exception, make very good eating. The one which is sub-standard, with rather coarse flesh of inferior flavour, is **Lutjanus bohar**. The best of all are the large red ones, especially **L. malabaricus**. One word of caution: several of the species are said to have occasioned what is called ciguatera poisoning (due to the presence of certain neurotoxins sometimes harboured by some tropical fish), so buy only from a reputable and knowledgeable source.

An illustrated catalogue of all the snappers would make an attractive small book. Here, however, they must be fitted into half a dozen pages. I have therefore given only a selection, preferring those which are found throughout the region and often seen in the markets. The reader should, however, bear in mind that my baker's dozen of such species are easily outnumbered by those I have neglected to mention; and the reader in Hong Kong should particularly note that there are several excellent species which are taken there and even further south but are not found throughout S. E. Asian waters. I have in mind **Aphareus rutilans** Cuvier, the Silvery-gilled snapper or Rusty jobfish (length up to 110 cm, local name ngun soi gor lay), which is definitely a fish to seek in the market.

In most of the S. E. Asian countries there are general names for snapper, for example nga pahni (Burma), pla kaphong (Thailand), cá hồng and cá róc (Vietnam), maya-maya (Philippines), and ikan merah (for the red ones) in both Indonesia and Malaysia. In the UAE three general names are in use: hamra, naiser and aglaah.

Recipes for snapper will be found on pages 234, 235, 270 (smoked snapper), 306, 323, 324 (ikan masak molek, a great favourite of mine).

MANGROVE RED SNAPPER   Family *Lutjanidae*
Lutjanus argentimaculatus (Forskål)

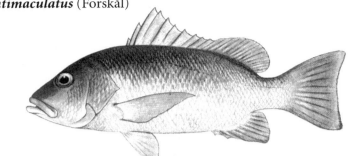

REMARKS Maximum length 120 cm, common length 50 to 80 cm.

This snapper is grey to pink above, shading to a silvery red below. There is sometimes a silvery patch in the centre of each scale. The body turns a darker red after death. Juveniles present quite a different appearance, as shown in the second drawing, lower left. The third drawing, lower right, shows a sub-adult specimen of **L. sebae**, one of the species described on the next page.

The species is widespread in the warm waters of the Indo-Pacific area. In Natal it is known as rock salmon, with no more taxonomic but slightly more gastronomic justification than could be claimed by British fishmongers who used to bestow the same name on dogfish.

The name mangrove red snapper is given because mangrove swamps are a favourite haunt of this species.

Distribution: widespread from East Africa to as far as the East China Sea and Samoa and south to Australia.

TA: ad allu
BU: nga-pahni
TH: pla kaphong si thao
MA: jenehak, siakap merah*
IN: kakap merah
PH: iso, aliso, also
CA: trey ankeuy prak
VI: cá huong vàng
HK: hung yau
TAI: yin wen di diao
JA: goma-fuedai

CUISINE An excellent fish. Steaks may be grilled or fried. Specimens of moderate size may be steamed or baked whole.

* The explanation of this name is that the Malay people see a resemblance between this fish and the siakap (page 48).

CRIMSON SNAPPER
Lutjanus erythropterus Bloch

Family *Lutjanidae*

REMARKS Maximum length about 60 cm, common length 40 to 45 cm. Juvenile specimens have a large black spot where the tail fin joins the body, but this and other markings have disappeared in adults.

This snapper has a wide range from the north of the Indian Ocean to northern Australia, and the southern tip of Japan.

CUISINE An excellent food fish, as is the Emperor red snapper (below).

BU: kyauk-ngawet
TH: pla kaphong
    daeng, pla sisawan
MA: ikan merah pucat
IN: bambangan
PH: maya-maya
CA: trey krâhâm
VI: cá hồng
HK: hung yue
CH: hong qi di diao
JA: yoko-fuedai

EMPEROR RED SNAPPER, GOVERNMENT BREAM
Lutjanus sebae (Cuvier)

Family *Lutjanidae*

REMARKS Maximum length 1 metre. A silvery reddish fish. Each scale always bears a pearly white dot.

The amusing name Government bream was given to the fish in Malaysia, either because of the broad arrow formed by the dusky red stripes on sub-adult specimens (see drawing on preceding page, bottom right), reminiscent of the symbol for government property or perhaps because the same stripes give the impression that the fish is entangled in red tape. Whatever the explanation, Malaysians think very highly of this fish.

Distribution: from East Africa to southern Japan and Australia.

TA: nai-kerruchi
BU: nga pahni
TH: pla kaphong daeng
MA: ikan merah boreng
IN: gajah
PH: maya-maya
CA: trey 'Sergent'
VI: cá hồng lang
HK: paak dim hung yue
CH: qian nian di diao
JA: sen-nendai

Lutjanus malabaricus (Bloch and Schneider), the Malabar red snapper, is perhaps the finest of all. Its red hue is relieved by narrow yellow streaks along the scale rows; and by a dark blotch at the base of the tail fin, preceded by a pearly spot. Maximum length 100 cm, common length 45 cm. Specific local names: pla kaphong daeng (Thai), ikan merah (Malaysia).

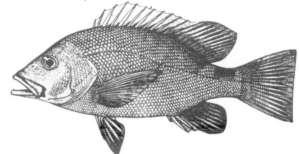

Lutjanus bohar (Forskål), the Two-spot or White-spotted red snapper. Maximum length 90 cm and common length 50 cm. It is red or purplish red in colour, and each scale usually has a silvery centre. The younger fish of this species, and some adults, may also be recognized by a pair of silvery spots on each side above the lateral line. Local names: pla kaphong daeng paan khau (Thai), mailah (Indonesia).

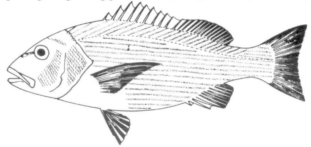

Lutjanus johnii (Bloch) has a maximum length of 70 cm and a common length of 50 cm. It is known as John's snapper or the Moses perch. Other specific common names include tambangan or jenaha (Indonesia), cá huong cham (Vietnam) and ngar dim (Hong Kong). The body colour may be bronze red, gold, olive or silvery green. Each scale has a distinct dark spot on it, giving the effect of dark streaks along the scale rows. There is often a black blotch above the lateral line just below the junction of the spiny and soft parts of the dorsal fin.

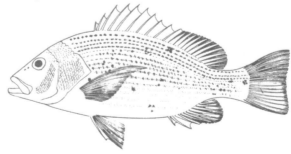

Lutjanus gibbus (Forskål), the Humpback red snapper. Maximum length 50 cm and common length 40 cm. Colour deep red. Note the 'hump' and the characteristic arrangement of the scale rows. Specific local names include hoi lei (Hong Kong), pla kaphong daeng hang mon (Thai), jenaha (Indonesia) and himai-fuedai (Japan).

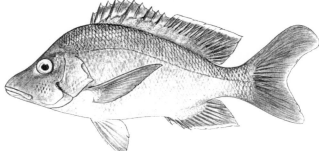

Lutjanus fulvus (Forster), the Blacktail (or Flametail) snapper. Maximum length about 40 cm, common length 25 cm. This is a good snapper, known as pla kaphong nam tam daeng (Thai), cá huong roc (Vietnam), bambangin, pargo (Philippines) and oki-fuedai (Japan).

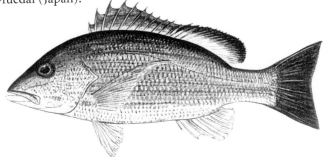

Lutjanus fulviflamma (Forskål), the Blackspot snapper (known as Dory snapper in South Africa), may be as long as 35 cm, but is usually around the 25 cm mark. It is yellow or greenish yellow above and silvery pink below, sometimes with golden longitudinal stripes. Note the black blotch (sometimes surrounded by a pearly border) on the lateral line, and the pattern of the scale rows. Specific common names include ikan tanda-tanda or jenaha (Indonesia). **Lutjanus russellii** (Bleeker), not illustrated, is generally similar but a little larger to 50 cm, market length 25–30 cm.

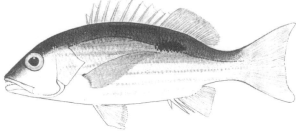

Lutjanus lutjanus (Rüppell), the Bigeye snapper, has also been known as **L. lineolatus and L. erythropterus**. Maximum length nearly 40 cm. It is purplish red on the back and golden yellow below, with a dark brown band running fore and aft at the level of the lateral line. It is cá huong móm in Vietnam, kunyit-kunyit in Malaysia and hung wa may in Hong Kong.

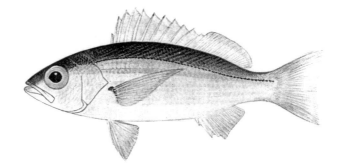

Lutjanus vitta (Quoy and Gaimard), has a maximum length of 40 cm and is known as the Brownstripe red snapper, having a very noticeable stripe of this colour running from eye to tail fin in a straight line. The body is pale red/yellow above, with thin brown stripes along the scale rows, and silvery below. It is dayang-dayang in the Philippines.

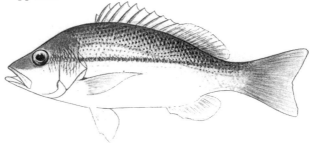

Lutjanus kasmira (Forskål), the Common bluestripe snapper, is easily identified: a yellow snapper marked with thin blue lines as shown in the drawing. It has a wide range from the Red Sea to the Pacific. It is common and popular in both Malaysia and Thailand. Local names nga-wet-panni (Burma), lam sin wa may (Hong Kong) and yosuji-fuedai (Japan).

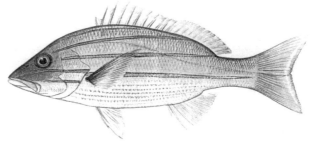

GREEN JOBFISH

Family *Lutjanidae*

Aprion virescens Valenciennes

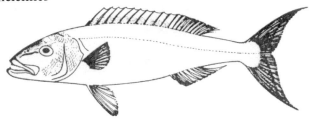

REMARKS Maximum length just over 1 metre, common length 65 cm.

This is a dark green or blue-green fish. Note the groove in front of the eye and the short rounded pectoral fins.

Distribution: East Africa to the Hawaiian Islands, north to southern Japan, south to Australia.

CUISINE As for the other snappers. This species is popular in Singapore, where it is known as ikan kerisi China (the China Sea bream). It is highly rated in Hawaii (as uku), where frying (of fillets) is recommended by local authors.

TA: dhiula
BU: nga-kyaw-sein
TH: pla kaphong
    khieo
MA: kerisi basi
HK: hoi nam chai
CH: lu duan qi yu
JA: aochibiki

SHARPTOOTH JOBFISH/SNAPPER

Family *Lutjanidae*

Pristipomoides typus Bleeker

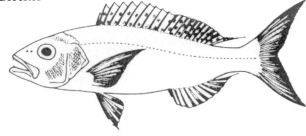

REMARKS Maximum length about 70 cm, market length 40 to 60 cm.

A pink fish, shading to silvery below, with noticeable filaments at the rear of the dorsal and anal fins. It may bear longitudinal yellow bands.

Distribution: eastern Indian Ocean to western Pacific and northern Australia.

CUISINE A popular but inexpensive fish in Thailand. (I am told that it is also a common food fish in Portuguese East Africa.)

TA: lomia
BU: nga-pahni
TH: pla kaphong
    khieo
MA: kerisi bali
PH: matangal
HK: kor lee
CH: zi yu
TAI: chang qi ji
    diao
JA: bara-himedai

FUSILIER, REDBELLY YELLOWTAIL FUSILIER

Family *Caesionidae*

Caesio cuning Bloch

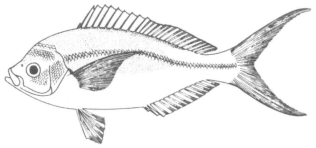

REMARKS Maximum length to about 50 cm.

The fusiliers are all fairly small fish, metallic blue above and silvery pink below with some golden or yellow colouring as well. This one has a yellow tail fin without markings, and the rear part of the back is yellow too.

Two other species have yellow bands along the lateral line. One is **C. caerulaurea** Lacepède, Blue and gold fusilier, which bears a broad black band on each lobe of its tail fin. It is pisang-pisang in Indonesia and trey sputnik in Cambodia. **Pterocaesio chrysozona** Cuvier, Goldband fusilier, has a black tip to each lobe of the tail fin. It is dalagang bukid in the Philippines, this being a general name for fusiliers, and pisang-pisang in Indonesia (another general name).

TA: cul kilchi,
   vairpara
TH: pla hang lueng
MA: pisang-pisang,
   delah
IN: ekor kuning
PH: dalagang-bukid
   lapad
CA: (trey sputnik)
VI: cá chàm bi
HK: wong may
JA: yume-umeiro

These are among the few economically important fish of the coral reefs. 'They are taken by an exciting operation involving the positioning of a net by the reef and the driving of the fish into it by a team of swimming men, each holding a long string weighted at the bottom and flagged at intervals in its length with pieces of white cloth. These strings are jerked up and down and the moving flags scare the fish and drive them into the net. This strenous mode of fishing is of Japanese origin and is still called by its Japanese name "muro ami".'(Tweedie and Harrison)

The distribution of **Caesio cuning** is from Sri Lanka to southern Japan, northern Australia and some islands in the West Pacific.

CUISINE Of medium quality, although Maxwell declared that one species of the genus, known in Malaysia as ikan merah china, is a real delicacy. I wish that I knew which he meant.

The fusiliers are usually steamed or used in fish soups. The Chinese make fish balls with them. See also the recipes on pages 284 and 298.

Bream, Mojarras and Grunts

We now come to some other families of perch-like fish, which are generally less interesting than the snappers but which still include some good species. Many of them belong to the group of fish known as bream (American porgy). These are carnivorous fish, which abound among coastal reefs. Like the snappers, they have strong teeth, and are often red in colour. The Threadfin bream also tend to have a yellow/red colour scheme, and the best of them are well worth eating. The remaining species catalogued in this section are of less gastronomic interest but are found in the markets often enough to require notice.

It is noteworthy that the emperors (family *Lethrinidae*) constitute an important part of the catch in the Gulf. At least four species appear regularly in the UAE markets, where they bear several names: shaeri, suli, shekhaili.

BLACK PORGY, BLACK SEA-BREAM   Family *Sparidae*
Acanthopagrus berda (Forskål)

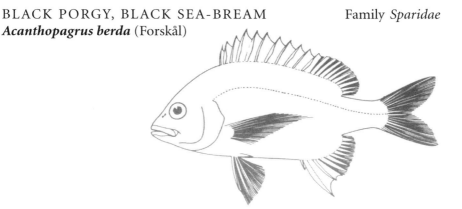

REMARKS Maximum length 90 cm, common length 30 to 50 cm. Range from Africa to Japan and northern Australia. Sometimes called picnic (sea) bream.

The colour is dark grey/silver, or olive/brown with a black spot at the base of most scales and silvery or brassy reflections. I have yet to see an explanation of the use of the word 'picnic' in various common names (not just English). Another name, 'river bream', is more explicable – this fish enters the lower reaches of rivers e.g. in South Africa and Zimbabwe.

Argyrops spinifer (Forskål), the King soldierbream, is a slightly shorter fish with a deeper, reddish body and with the dorsal fin prolonged into filaments. It is mahuwana in the Philippines, abat in Indonesia, and pla kaphong taiwan in Thailand. In the Gulf it has the name merjan.

TA: cooree
BU: nga-ba-yin
TH: pla eekhut
MA: kapas-kapas, bekukong
IN: katombal (Javanese)
PH: bakokong moro, gaud-gaud
CA: kranh phok
VI: cá hanh
HK: hak lap
JA: nanyôchinu

CUISINE The best of the family. Steam, grill, fry. See also the recipes on pages 251 and 256.

SPANGLED EMPEROR   Family *Lethrinidae*
Lethrinus nebulosus (Forskål)

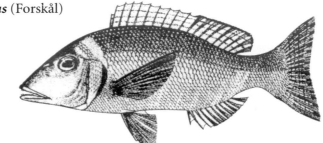

REMARKS Maximum length 85 cm.

An olive fish with irregular dark stripes and pale orange fins. The inside of the mouth is orange.

The long and scale-less snout of fish in the family *Lethrinidae* is the reason for the name pigface being used in some places, and can be seen in the drawing of this species. ***L. miniatus*** (Forster), Trumpet emperor, has a longer snout (combined with a less deep body) and more clearly deserves the name. ***L. lentjan*** (Lacepède), the Pink ear emperor, is bukaual or kanuping in the Philippines.

Distribution: The Spangled emperor ranges from the Red Sea, the Gulf and East Africa to southern Japan and Samoa.

UAE: shaeri, suli, shekhaili
TA: pulli vella meen
BU: (kyauk-nga)
TH: pla mu see kaem daeng
MA: pelandok
IN: lencam
PH: bitilya (general name)
CA: trey ankeuy
VI: cá sao, cà hè
HK: lin tsim, lentjan
CH: xing ban guan jia diao
TAI: qing zui long zhan
JA: hama-fuefuki

CUISINE Of medium quality. Moderately popular in Cambodia, where it is usually presented fresh and boiled, but not in great demand in Malaysia.

GREY LARGE-EYE BREAM,   Family *Lethrinidae*
GINKGO FISH

Gymnocranius griseus
(Temminck and Schlegel)

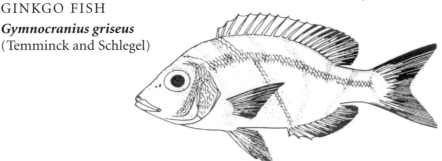

REMARKS Maximum length 35 cm (but larger specimens have been reported). A silvery-brown fish with a dark band running fore and aft at eye level and with three violet-blue bars on the head. This, the true

BU: kyauk-nga
TH: pla eekhut bang
MA: mempasir
IN: kapas-kapas laut

Ginkgo fish, is matched by the false ginkgo fish, **Wattsia mossambica**, known at Hong Kong as sha tsut paak gwor and reputedly an excellent food fish.

The true ginkgo fish belongs to the Indo-West Pacific region, possibly including India and extending north to southern Japan. The false ginkgo fish has been reported in widely scattered locations, from Mozambique to Papua New Guinea and north to southern Japan.

VI: cá hè xám
HK: pak kwo
TAI: hui guan ding diao
JA: meichi-dai

CUISINE Steam or fry. Of good quality.

THREADFIN BREAM
Nemipterus japonicus (Bloch)

Family *Nemipteridae*

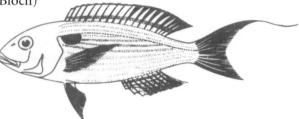

REMARKS Maximum length 32 cm, common length 12 to 25 cm.

The body bears longitudinal stripes and is generally pink above and yellow below.

This species has a filament extending from its tail fin as well as from the ventral fin. It is well-known at Hong Kong, as is **N. bathybius** Snyder, called Wong to or Yellow belly (threadfin bream). However, the threadfin which is landed in the largest quantity at Hong Kong is **N. virgatus** (Houttuyn), called Hung sam or Golden thread or Golden threadfin bream. This is the most abundant food fish at Hong Kong, and the largest of the threadfin breams.

TA: changarah, thullunkendai
BU: shwe-nga
TH: pla sai daeng
MA: kerisi
IN: kerisi, gurisi
PH: bisugo, bisugong bututan
VI: cá dông (winter fish)
HK: kwa sam (melon coat)
CH: ri ben jin xian yu
JA: nihon-itoyori

Although the species in the family *Nemipteridae* are often referred to collectively as threadfin breams, they do not all have the filaments which justify the epithet threadfin. **N. hexodon** (Quoy and Gaimard), the Ornate threadfin bream, is one common species which has no filaments.

Distribution for **N. japonicus**: Indo-Pacific region, western limit uncertain.

CUISINE Although these fish are small, they have white and tender flesh, well worth eating. In the Philippines it is said to be especially valuable in a convalescent diet. The Thai, who think well of the threadfin breams, steam or fry them, or use them for fish balls. They may also be had in salted and dried form.

MONOCLE BREAM, WHITE-CHEEKED MONOCLE BREAM

Scolopsis vosmeri (Bloch)

Family *Nemipteridae*

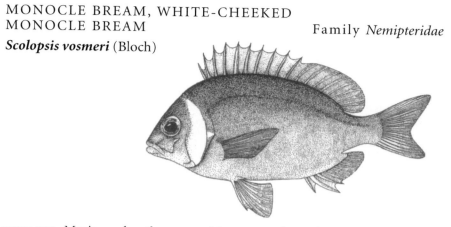

REMARKS Maximum length 25 cm and it ranges as far south as Durban and as far east as northern Australia.

There are many other related species, all colourful, with large scales and with a characteristic backward-facing spine below each eye.

The largest of the monocle breams is **S. taeniopterus** (Cuvier), the Lattice monocle bream or Red-spot monocle bream, with a maximum length of 30 cm; market size around 15 to 20 cm. In life this fish is brightly marked with blue and yellow.

S. lineatus (Quoy and Gaimard), the Striped monocle bream, abounds in the Gulf of Thailand, and is big enough to have some value as food.

TA: andiyan, pal muta
TH: pla sai khao
MA: pasir-pasir, kerisi
IN: pasir pasir
PH: tagisang lawin
CA: (pla sai khao)
VI: cá tráo
HK: (paak gang lo ah)
TAI: bai jing chi wei
    dong
JA: taiwan-taamagashira

CUISINE The monocle breams are usually regarded as unexciting fare, but **S. taeniopterus** arouses some enthusiasm in Thailand, where it is usually steamed or made into fish balls. And Maxwell, while acknowledging that these fish are often rather small, wrote: ' ... I have taken them up to a pound or more in 30 fathoms near Thioman Island. Kerisi fishing ... used to be the favourite out-door sport of the Malay Princesses of Pahang, and during the SW Monsoon regular expeditions were made to the Kerisi grounds and the little fish would be hauled in until the boats were deep in the water and the Royal ladies exhausted. At the right season, there are few more delicately flavoured fish than the Kerisi and they remind one of really good Whiting. But they must be absolutely fresh and caught on the right ground; if out of season or stale, Kerisi have an unpleasant tang about them.'

SILVER BIDDY, MOJARRA (Spanish)   Family *Gerreidae*
Gerres filamentosus Cuvier

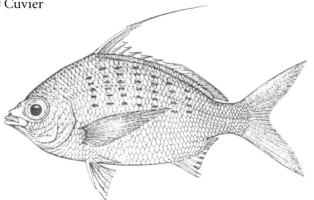

REMARKS Maximum length 35 cm, common length 15 to 20 cm.

The silver biddies are a clan of small silvery fish which belong to inshore waters and estuaries. This one has a series of bluish blotches on its sides which may almost coalesce into bars; and its second dorsal spine becomes longer and longer as it grows older (hence *filamentosus* and its FAO name Whipfin silverbiddy).

Distribution: East Africa to Japan and Australia.

There are numerous related species. The name ponyfish has sometimes been applied to them.

CUISINE Not especially good, but plentiful and cheap – and not to be despised when really fresh.

Steam, fry, boil with vegetables.

TA: udagam
BU: nga-din-ga
TH: pla dok mak
MA: kapas-kapas,
    kapas laut
IN: kapas besar
PH: malakapas
CA: trey doh angkor
VI: cá móm
HK: lin mai
CH: chang ji yin lu
TAI: ye si zuan zui yu
JA: itohikisagi

SILVER GRUNT, GRUNTER
Pomadasys argenteus (Forskål)

Family *Haemulidae*

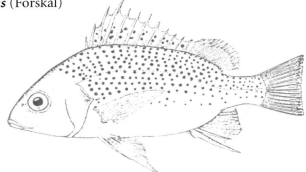

REMARKS Maximum length 80 cm, common length 35 to 45 cm.

A silver-grey fish with a yellow sheen and 4 or 5 interrupted dark grey bands along the sides.

It is an Indo-Pacific species, common in Hong Kong waters and elsewhere.

P. maculatum (Bloch), the Saddle grunt, is a smaller species which has large blotches on its sides and at the front of the dorsal fin. It is pla si-krud in Thailand, sikoy in the Philippines.

CUISINE 'Excellent eating' said Maxwell and Scott from their vantage point in Malaya. And the related species which is known as the Queensland trumpeter is highly esteemed in Australia. Yet in Thailand the silver grunt is regarded as being of medium quality only.

Steaming is recommended; or cook it in a court-bouillon.

A recipe is given on page 223.

TA: kithayu valayen
BU: nga-gone
TH: pla kaphong sam, pla krurt krat
IN: gerot-gerot, krot-krot
PH: aguot
CA: trey loc cop
VI: cá sao
HK: tai ki
CH: duan ban shi lu
TAI: xing ji yu

SWEETLIPS   Family *Haemulidae*

Plectorhinchus pictus (Thunberg)

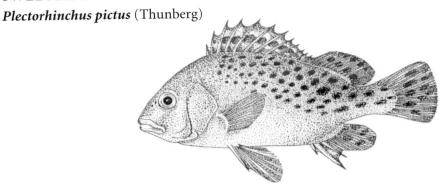

REMARKS Maximum length 75 cm, common length 45 cm. Like other fish in this family, the sweetlips may be called grunts because of the grunting noise they make by grinding their pharyngeal teeth together, amplifying this sound through the swim bladder.

UAE: farsh
BU: nga-gone
TH: pla khang ta pao
  (young), pla soi
  nok khao (adult)
MA/IN: kaci, kaci-
  kaci, gaji
PH: bakoko
CA: trey yeak lom
VI: cá kêm
HK: sai luen
CH: hu jiao diao
TAI: xi lin shi lu
JA: korodai

The young are orange with brown longitudinal markings. Adults are blue-grey above with dark brown or deep yellow spots and streaks along the sides. The markings, which account for the English name 'trout sweetlips' are less distinct on older fish. The fins are also spotted with brown or yellow. The lips are noticeably thick – a characteristic of the family.

Distribution: the Gulf to Sri Lanka and eastwards to China.

This family is a perplexing one. There are many species and, as Scott observes, the markings and colouration are so variable that taxonomists may have listed more species than really exist. One of these, the Painted sweetlips, is now classified as *Diagramma pictum* (Thunberg). It has a golden tinge to the body.

Besides 'sweetlips' , these fish have been called 'rubberlips' and 'hotlips'. The FAO have allocated to the species *Plectorhinchus gibbosus*, as its official English name, the striking combination 'Harry hotlips'.

CUISINE A common and popular fish in Malaysian markets, where it finds a ready sale. A correspondent in the Gulf tells me that the flesh reminds him of haddock.

PONYFISH, SILVER BELLY   Family *Leignathidae*
Leiognathus splendens (Cuvier)

REMARKS Maximum length 17 cm, common to 10 cm.
A silvery fish with black dots on the end of its snout. The
scales of the lateral line are bright yellow.

A common related species is **L. equulus** (Forskål), also
known as sapsap in the Philippines. It has indistinct
narrow vertical stripes on its back and a dark brown
'saddle' at the tail. It can be over 25 cm long, market
length 18 to 20 cm.

Ponyfish tend to shoal in estuaries and are quite ready
to enter freshwater. They have the unattractive characteristic of being coated with slime; and to make matters
worse they exude a lot of mucus after death. The names
Slimy and Soapy are given to them for these reasons.

The ponyfish have a very protractile mouth (which
accounts for another name, Slipmouth). This phenome-
non can be demonstrated by squeezing the head between thumb and forefinger,
when the mouth will shoot forward. If one applies this procedure to a closely
related species, **Gazza minuta** (Bloch), the Toothed ponyfish, one will find that it
has caniniform (dog-like) teeth.

Despite their small size the ponyfish have some economic importance. They
account for about 15 per cent of the trawl catches in the Gulf of Thailand, and are
used for feeding ducks and in the production of fish meal. Many of these ponyfish
are common in Pakistan (kaanteri in Sindi, mith in Baluchi).

Distribution: the Red Sea, Madagascar, along coasts of India and Sri Lanka and
east to Australia and Fiji.

TA: kulli-kare
BU: nga-oo-gyee
   (Arakan)
TH: pla pan yai
MA: pepetek, kekek
   labu
IN: bondol
PH: sapsap (general
   name)
CA: trey sambor
   loeung
VI: cá liêt
HK: fa chong
TAI: tai bi

CUISINE The Thai reckon that this is the best of the ponyfish. They fry it or serve
it in fish soup. It may also be had salted and dried.

Croakers

The croakers belong to the large Family *Sciaenidae*, and may also be referred to as Jewfish or Drums. Most of them are of small or medium size and relatively dull colouration. They often occur in dense shoals and are taken in great numbers, for example on the Malaysian coast. But, although they have some economic importance as food fish, they are not of the first quality. The flesh tends to be insipid.*

Scott provides the following note on the name croaker as applied to this group of fish. He explains that it 'comes from their ability to produce a loud, croaking sound, similar to that of a frog. The large swim-bladder is used as a sounding-box. The noise is not only heard when the fish has been pulled out of the water but is clearly audible by underwater listening devices and to the Malay "Jeru selam" who lowers himself under the water and listens for the noises made by shoals of fish from which he can deduce the size of the shoal, species of fish and their approximate position, after which he directs his fishermen to set the net to capture the fish. Even persons drifting in a small boat while fishing have been mystified by the loud "frogs' chorus" suddenly starting up all round them, the source of which remained unseen until they started to catch the still-croaking vocalists ...' According to Read (1977) who quotes ancient Chinese authors to this effect, the listening devices used by Chinese fishermen were long bamboo tubes lowered to the sea bottom, and it is in the fourth moon of every year that the croakers 'come in from the ocean in file several miles long, making a thundering noise'.

There are many croakers which really belong to more northerly waters, although they penetrate the S. E. Asian area in the vicinity of Hong Kong and South China. I have not catalogued any such species, but mention here that one of them, **Nibea albiflora** (Richardson), attains a length of 90 cm and is well-known at Hong Kong under the names White-flower croaker or baak fa. Its bladder is a delicacy and has this distinction, that it costs more than any other croaker bladder. Another species which is an important food fish in Chinese waters but rarely found further south is the Large yellow croaker, **Pseudosciaena crocea**.

*Gruvel makes the interesting general comment that fish of this family are much less sought after in Indochina than in France, where the ombrine, for example, is rated quite highly.

CROAKER, BLACKSPOTTED CROAKER
Protonibea diacanthus (Lacepède)

Family *Sciaenidae*

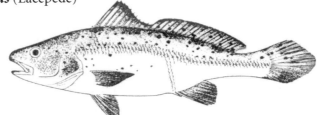

REMARKS Maximum length 1 metre 20, market length up to about 75 cm.

    The body is brown or grey above, silvery below. There are usually five dark blotches along the back and lots of small spots on the upper part of the body and the dorsal fin. Fins below the lateral line are black.

    Distribution: from East Africa and the east coast of India through S. E. Asian waters to northern Australia, north to Japan and various Pacific islands.

BU: nga-we-yaung
TH: pla mian
MA: ibu gelama
IN: ikan tambareh
CA: trey changkom
   bey
VI: cá sửu bong
HK: man yue, mo
   sheung

CUISINE This is one of the best croakers. Boil, steam, fry. See the recipe on page 272.

SOLDIER CROAKER
Nibea soldado (Lacepède)

Family *Sciaenidae*

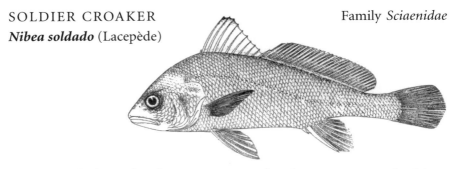

REMARKS Maximum length 60 cm, common length 20 to 40 cm.

    This species can be distinguished by its green back, which arches high above grey sides and a white belly.

    Distribution: from the eastern Indian Ocean through all S. E. Asian waters to northern Australia and various Pacific islands. It enters fresh water and is found in the Great Lakes of Cambodia and in the Mekong as far upstream as Luang Prabang (2000 km from the sea). In fact it seems to exist in a freshwater as well as a marine form.

BU: nga-poke-thin
TH: pla chuat thau
MA/IN: gelama
   bongkok, gelama
   papan, tengkerong
PH: abo
CA: trey pama
VI: cá sửu
HK: wak

CUISINE Of moderate quality. Steam, boil or bake.

WHISKERED/BEARDED CROAKER
Johnius dussumieri (Cuvier)

Family *Sciaenidae*

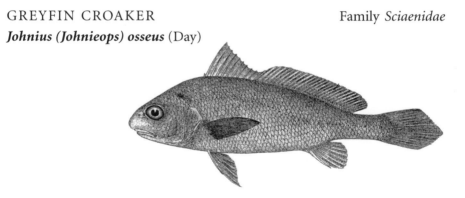

REMARKS Maximum length 25 cm, common length 15 cm.
The body is brown or greyish above, often with a metallic lustre which has been described as coppery. The fins are yellowish-brown. Note the line of the lower jaw; also the single barbel, which is characteristic of this genus and accounts for the name Whiskered or bearded croaker.

Distribution: from East Africa through S. E. Asian waters to some Pacific islands.

Fish of this species sometimes gather in what are said to be 'incredibly large shoals' in the Gulf of Thailand.

BU: nga-poke-thin
TH: pla chuat
MA: gelama kling
IN: gelama papan
PH: kabang, ibot
CA: trey pama
VI: cá uop
HK: shek wak
TAI: du shi you
    kou

CUISINE Edible but uninspiring. It is possible to grill or fry these small croakers, but it may be more satisfactory to use them for fish balls or soup.

GREYFIN CROAKER
Johnius (Johnieops) osseus (Day)

Family *Sciaenidae*

REMARKS Maximum length 25 cm, common length a little less.

Silvery-grey above, white below. The rear dorsal fin is greyish and the tail fin is tipped with grey; otherwise the fins are yellowish.

Distribution: the Greyfin croaker ranges from the Arabian Gulf east to Taiwan and south through the Philippines and Borneo to about the southern tip of Java.

CUISINE See the preceding entry.

TH: pla chuat
    hua to
MA/IN: gelama
PH: alakaak
CA: trey pama
VI: cá sửru
HK: gai daan
    wak

TIGER-TOOTHED CROAKER
Otolithes ruber (Bloch and Schneider)

Family *Sciaenidae*

REMARKS Maximum length 90 cm or more, common length around 40 cm.

The colour is brownish-red, shot with silver and sometimes golden below.

The range of this species is from South Africa to Japan and Australia. It has strong canine teeth and for this reason has been called Longtooth salmon in South Africa.

Whereas fish of the genus **Johnius** have pores on their chin, those of the genus **Otolithes** do not. The name **Otolithes** refers to the well-developed ear-stones found in these fish; they are large enough to be strung in necklaces.

BE: lal poa, poa
(general name)
BU: nga-poke-thin
MA: gelama jarang
gigi, tengkerong
IN: gelik, (grabak)
PH: abo, alakaak
VI: cá uóp thăng
HK: ngaa wak

CUISINE Maxwell declared that this fish was 'not bad' in curry. I agree. Without some such treatment to provide strong added flavours, the flesh is rather insipid. For this reason it is often sold salted and dried rather than fresh.

Isinglass made from the air bladders of this fish is of very good quality and is said to be capable of gelatinizing 26 times its weight of water.

Goatfish and Some Small Fish of the Coral Reefs

Visitors to the Mediterranean will recall how good are the red mullet (French rouget, Italian triglia, Spanish salmonete, Greek barboúni or koutsomoúra) which are to be had there. Such persons may be surprised to learn that the same family (*Mullidae*) is strongly represented in the Indo-Pacific region and that it is possible anywhere in S. E. Asia to re-create such dishes as Rougets à la Niçoise and Triglie alla Livornese. Indeed two of the Indo-Pacific species are among those found nowadays in the Mediterranean, the gradual lowering of the salinity in the Bitter Lakes having eventually permitted the inquisitive creatures to pass through the Suez Canal from the Red Sea to the Eastern Mediterranean, as I have explained elsewhere.*

Unfortunately, at least for the tidy-minded, the numerous species of goatfish in S. E. Asian waters are difficult to identify and classify, partly because their colouration is variable even in life and markedly so from life to death. The few species here catalogued are, so far as I can discover, among the most common in the markets; but there are many others.

After the goatfish, we come to whole shoals of other fish which are pretty and brightly-coloured, but rather small and of little interest as food. Many of them are fish of the coral reefs, with deep, thin bodies. The six which have been catalogued must serve as examples to cover the scores which are omitted. The families are:

Drepanidae:	Batfish or Sickle fish
Ephippidae:	Batfish, Spadefish, or Angel fish
Monodactylidae:	Silvery batfish
Scatophagidae:	Butterfish, which reputedly feed on excrement**
Pomacanthidae:	Angel or Coral fish
Chaetodontidae:	Butterfly or Coral fish
Pomacentridae:	Demoiselles, Pullers, Anemone fish
Labridae:	Wrasse or Rainbow fish
Scaridae:	Parrot fishes, with beak-like mouths

Some of these fish act as 'cleaners' for other fish. They take up stations by some well-defined object such as a patch of white sand. (It has been suggested that their bright colours also help their 'client' fish to find them.) The clients swim up and wait patiently for their turn. 'The cleaning process is very thorough and the cleaners even go inside the branchial cavities to remove parasites from the gills.' (Ommaney, *A Draught of Fishes*, in a brilliantly written passage which explains the mutual advantages of this procedure – 'the clients get cleaned and the cleaners get food' – and the conventions attending it.)

Mediterranean Seafood, Penguin 1972 and Prospect Books/Ten Speed Press 2002
** But they are eaten, e.g. in the Philippines, where they are known as litang. A specimen of **Scatophagus argus** tasted perfectly wholesome to me. It had been poached in vinegar with onions and garlic. This fish is now being cultivated in the Philippines.

GOATFISH, FRECKLED GOATFISH

Upeneus tragula Richardson

Family *Mullidae*

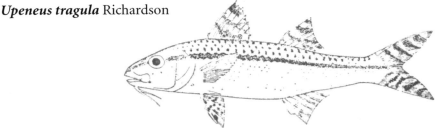

REMARKS Maximum length 30 cm, market length around 17 cm.

The back is usually reddish brown. Note the dark stripe running the whole length of the fish and the distinctive marking of the tail fin.

U. sulphureus Cuvier, the Yellow goatfish, has a maximum length of 23 cm. The back is greenish bronze or olive green, the lower sides and belly yellow. Two yellow or orange bands run along each side. The tail fin bears no marks; it is grey-green with a dusky rear edge. This species, which is shown in the drawing below, may be called kunir in Indonesia.

Distribution: the Freckled goatfish has a range from East Africa to southern Japan and Micronesia.

BU: kyo-wa
TH: pla pha, pla nuat rersi
MA: biji nangka, karang
IN: biji nangka
PH: babayao
CA: trey popé
VI: cá phèn
HK: saam so*
TAI: yang zuan qui gu yu
JA: yome-himeji

CUISINE The Chinese hold the goatfish in higher esteem than do, for example, the Thai. The usual practice in many S. E. Asian countries seems to be to steam or boil them, in complete contrast to the treatment of red mullet in the Mediterranean, where frying or grilling are usual and anything in the nature of 'boiling' proscribed. I recommend following the Mediterranean procedures.

*At Hong Kong the best-known goatfish is *U. moluccensis* (Bleeker), the Goldband goatfish, and is known there as hung sin (Red goatfish). The name saam so is a general one for goatfish; it means 'three beards', with reference to what are in fact only two barbels. It is these barbels, of course, which account for the name Goatfish and also for the Malayan names biji nangka or butir nangka (the jackfruit seed, whose filaments resemble the barbels) and ikan lebai (in reference to the beard of the pious Malay lebai).

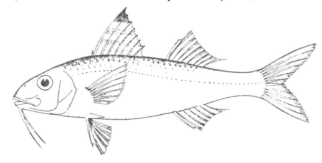

YELLOW-STRIPED GOATFISH

Family *Mullidae*

Upeneus vittatus (Forskål)

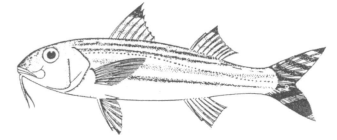

REMARKS Maximum length 28 cm, common length 15 to 20 cm.

This species has a wide range in the Indo-Pacific area from East Africa to Australia, some Pacific islands and Japan and its colouration seems to vary from one area to another. But it should always have 3 bronze and 2 yellow longitudinal stripes and characteristic markings on the tail fin.

Parupeneus indicus (Shaw), the Indian goatfish, is larger (up to 40 cm) and is marked by a broad purple band from eye to snout (below).

A representative of a further genus in the family deserves mention. *Mulloidichthys auriflamma*, now apparently *Parupeneus forsskali* (Fourmanoir & Guézé), is again fairly large (up to 28 cm) and has a reddish-brown back and pale sides marked by a bright yellow band from eye to tail. It is trey popé in Cambodia.

TA: manjelkithu nakharai
BU: kyo-wa
MA/IN: biji nangka
PH: amarilis, saging-saging
VI: cá phèn
JA: minami-himeji

CUISINE See under *Upeneus tragula*.

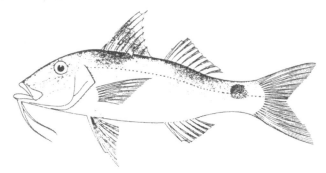

SPOTTED SICKLE FISH, BATFISH
Drepane punctata (Linnaeus)

Family *Drepanidae*

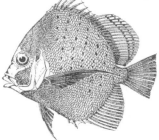

REMARKS Maximum length 50 cm, common length 20 to 30 cm.

The thin, silvery body is dotted with sepia spots. Note the long sickle-shaped pectoral fin. The general form of the body is considered in India to be moonlike: hence the Indian name chanda.

Distribution: Indo-West Pacific – temperate and tropical waters from India to northern Australia.

CUISINE The flesh is somewhat dry, but white and flaky, free from troublesome small bones, and good when steamed.

BE: roopee chanda
TA: painthi
BU: nga-paleh (pearl fish),
     sin-nah (elephant ear)
TH: pla m'leng po, pla hu chang
MA: daun baharu
IN: ketang-ketang
PH: mayang, kilyong
CA: trey trachéak damrey
VI: cá bảng
HK: kai lung chong
CH: ban dian ji long chang
JA: yûdachi sudaredai

BLUE-RINGED ANGEL FISH
Pomacanthus annularis (Bloch)

Family *Pomacanthidae*

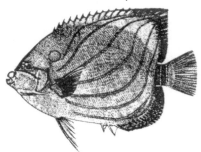

REMARKS Maximum length nearly 45 cm. The body is brown, with blue lines radiating from the pectoral fin and a blue, irregular ring on the shoulder.

Distribution: Indian Ocean and West Pacific – Mozambique to Sri Lanka, the Philippines and Australia.

CUISINE These angel fish are quite satisfactory food, e.g. in fish soups, but not especially popular.

TH: pla sin samut
MA: taring pelandok
IN: ikan kambing
CA: trey mé am bao
VI: cá thia dà
HK: ho pau yue
CH: jian huan ci gai yu

COPPERBAND BUTTERFLY FISH
Chelmon rostratus (Linnaeus)

Family *Chaetodontidae*

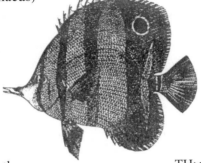

REMARKS Maximum length 22 cm.

One of a number of small brightly coloured fish. This species is marked by four or five bright orange bands. Note the distinctive snout, for prying into the crevices of coral; hence another name, 'beaked butterfly fish'.

Distribution: wide in the Indo-West Pacific.

CUISINE Not very good, but found in the markets.

TH: pla paeseva
MA: sumpit-sumpit
IN: kepe kepe sumpit
PH: para-parungdagat
CA: trey bophari
HK: ho pau yue
TAI: chang wen hei dai die yu

BATFISH
Platax orbicularis (Forskål)

Family *Ephippidae*

REMARKS Maximum length 50 cm, common length 35 cm. A grey or brown fish with vertical stripes on each side. Umali remarks that 'the young resembles a leaf in colour, and it sinks inertly on its side through the water'; this accounts for an English name some-times used, leaf-fish.

Distribution: from the Red Sea and East Africa to southern Japan and northern Australia.

CUISINE This fish is cheap in Thailand and favoured for use in fish soups.

TA: chellal
BU: nga-mote-kyi
TH: pla hu chang klom
MA: tudang periok
IN: gebel
PH: dahong gabi, bayang
CA: trey srey srok
VI: cá chim cò
TAI: jian chi yan yu
JA: tsubame-uo

FLORAL WRASSE
Cheilinus chlorourus (Bloch)

Family *Labridae*

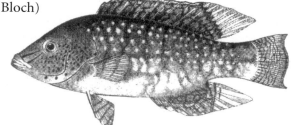

REMARKS Maximum length 30 cm.

This wrasse is one of dozens known in the region. It is olive-green in colour. It has numerous red spots on the head which may form lines and anastomosed figures (i.e. in a pattern like that of branches), which appear also on the greenish brown fins.

The range of the Floral wrasse is extensive, from E. Africa to the West Pacific (north to the Ryukyu Islands, south to northern Australia). Other wrasses, such as the so-called Blackspot tuskfish – *Choerodon schoenleinii* (Valenciennes) – range equally far and wide.

TA: kili meen
TH: pla nok khun
   thawng, see fa
MA/IN: bayan, batu
PH: maming, bungat
CA: trey damlong
VI: cá mó
HK: tsing (or ching) yi
TAI: qing yi han diao
JA: akaten-mochino-uo

CUISINE The wrasses do not have a good reputation as food fish, but this one is an expensive fish at Hong Kong, especially when sold alive. It is usually steamed.

BLUE-BARRED PARROTFISH
Scarus ghobban (Forskål)

Family *Scaridae*

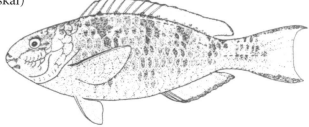

REMARKS There are lots and lots of parrotfish, some quite large. *Scarus ghobban*, a yellow fish with blue spots, reaches a length of 90 cm.

The teeth of parrotfish are fused into a beak which resembles that of a parrot and can administer a powerful bite.

This species has a very wide range: South and East Africa to Japan, the Gulf of California and Australia.

CUISINE Popular in Hong Kong restaurants; they are usually steamed.

BU: (nga-sein)
TH: pla nok kaew see plerng
MA: bayan
IN: kakatua biru
PH: loro, molmol (general)
VI: cá mó
HK: ying gor lie
CH: qing dian ying zui yu
JA: hibudai

A Miscellany of Other Perch-like Fish

The seven species catalogued in this section belong to six different sub-orders and have little in common except for their membership of the Order *Perciformes* and the fact that they are all interesting fish.

We begin with the Pomfrets, on which I cannot resist quoting Scott once more: 'The pomfrets are regarded by the Chinese as the choicest sea-fish of Malayan waters and the fish is the most important course of many a "Chinese makan". This esteem is reflected in the price in the market and the speed with which the fish are bought up. The quality being what it may, the fishes are regarded by the Malay fishermen as among the most stupid of all fishes. They follow each other like sheep and are attracted by anything floating in the water, traits which are exploited by the fishermen to make the capture of the "bawal" a comparatively simple matter once a shoal is located. The fish are surrounded by a net as it follows the boat and, when ready, the fishermen beat the water and make as much noise as possible whereupon the fish rush away from the disturbance into the net. An additional refinement is often introduced by casting a wooden spear with a flat white blade or a white tip into the water between the shoal and the bag of the net once the net is closed and just as the men start to splash the water. The fish, mistaking the white flash of the spear for one of themselves escaping from the uproar, rush towards the lure and into the bag of the net.'

The Goby and the Rabbit fish have peculiarities of structure which make them worth studying as well as worth eating. There have, by the way, been reports of rabbit fish and surgeonfish harbouring toxins in certain environments and/or circumstances; so they should be bought from a reputable source.

The Hairtail, the Flathead and the Dolphin fish all share one characteristic which is hard to explain; they are greatly prized in some places or by certain nationalities, while being despised or at least neglected in other places or by different ethnic groups. I had my first notice of this paradox when my wife and I were sailing in a Tunisian trawler many years ago. One trawl brought up some scabbard fish (as the Hairtail is known in the Mediterranean). The captain gave us one and kept the others for his wife, remarking that these fish were unsaleable in the market but among the best which one could hope to catch. As knowledge spreads and fishery resources are exploited more fully these puzzling differences of attitude may tend to disappear. Indeed this is already happening. In Tahiti, for example, no-one bothered to catch the dolphin fish (mahi-mahi) up to the time of the Second World War, but nowadays every available specimen is snapped up by the hotels and restaurants. However, until appreciation of these species becomes uniform those of us who know will be able to profit from the situation in places where they are unwanted and therefore cheap.

WHITE POMFRET, SILVER POMFRET   Family *Stromateidae*
Pampus argenteus (Euphrasen)

REMARKS Maximum length 60 cm, common length 20 to 30 cm.

The colour shades from steely grey above through silver to white below, with tiny black dots all over. The silvery scales are shed very easily. There are no pelvic fins. I am told that the Cantonese have another name, kou k'o shui yu, for this fish, and that it means drowsy dog fish. I suppose that there is a certain resemblance between the pomfret and certain species of lap dog, at least in the facial expression.

P. chinensis (Euphrasen), the Chinese silver pomfret, is a little smaller, brownish grey above and bearing brown spots, of which the larger have silver centres. It is zhong guo chang in Taiwan and bawal tambak in Malaysia. In Pakistan, this and the White pomfret share the Sindi names achopito and sufaid-poplet.

Distribution: Indo-West Pacific – the Persian Gulf east to Indonesia, northward to Hokkaido (Japan).

UAE: zubedi
BE: fali chanda
TA: vella vavel
BU: hsin-nga-hmok, nga-yuzana
TH: pla jara met khao
MA: bawal puteh
IN: bawal putih
PH: duhay, alumbeberas
CA: trey chap sar, trey pek chhieu
VI: cá chim trăng, cá chim mi
HK: pak cheong
CH: yin chang
TAI: bai chang
JA: managatsuo

CUISINE One of the most highly prized fish of the region. It has delicious flesh easily separable from the bones and well adapted to almost any kind of preparation. Grill, fry, steam, cook in a court-bouillon.

If you fry a pomfret, be sure to eat the soft lower fin and the tail, which are particularly delicious. This advice came from a Thai marine biologist and is worth passing on, since the morsels are readily overlooked by the uninitiated.

RECIPES
Nga-htoke-paung, page 228
Panggang ikan bawal Jawa, page 303
Rica-rica ikan, page 304

Ikan panggang kuali, page 322
Panggang ikan bawal, page 322

BLACK POMFRET

Parastromateus niger (Bloch)

Family *Carangidae*
(formerly *Formionidae* – see page 61)

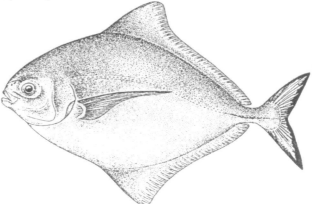

REMARKS Size much the same as the White pomfret.

The colour is brown-grey with blue reflections. The fins are grey/brown with darker edges. Note the absence of pelvic fins, and the scute-like scales of the lateral line at the tail.

This species, which belongs to a different family from the White pomfret, is more common in Indonesian waters and around the Philippines than the latter. It is also one of the few species to have been portrayed on a North Vietnamese postage stamp.

Its range is from East Africa to southern Japan and Australia. It may be found swimming on its side near the surface.

In the northern part of the South China Sea there are two other species akin to the pomfret but not in the same family. One is ***Psenopsis anomala*** (Temminck & Schlegel), the Melon seed, ci chang (spiny chang) in China and gua zi chang (melon-seed chang) in Taiwan. It is pale in colour and attains a length of 30 cm and is shown in the lower drawing. The other is ***Ariomma indica*** (Day), the Indian ariomma, known as cha mei or fork-tail at Hong Kong, a little fish which is worth frying.

TA: karuvaval
BU: kywe-ngamoke
TH: pla jara met dum
MA/IN: bawal hitam
PH: duhay
CA: trey chap khmao,
    trey or chhieu
VI: cá chim den
HK: hak chong
JA: kuroaji-modoki

CUISINE The Black pomfret is not quite so highly esteemed as the White pomfret, but is still an excellent fish and equally adapted to all standard methods of preparation.

It is available salted and dried.

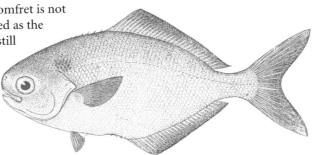

TANK GOBY   Family *Gobiidae*
Glossogobius giuris (Hamilton)

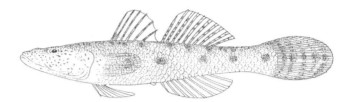

REMARKS Maximum length 50 cm, common length around 30 cm.

The colouration is variable, but is likely to be olive or buff or greenish above and lighter below, with spots on the head and blotches on the side.

This is a relatively large goby, and the only one regularly offered for sale in the region. (In the unlikely event of Turkish immigration into S. E. Asia the situation could change. The Turks eat smaller gobies with great enthusiasm and are indeed the world experts on this. Meanwhile the Filipinos are the most appreciative goby-eaters in S. E. Asia.)

BE: bele
TA: uluvai
BU: ka-tha-bo, nga-sha-po
MA: ikan ubi*
IN: ploso
PH: bia, biyang puti
CA: trey ksan
VI: cá bong cat
HK: lam go ue
CH: she xia hu yu
TAI: cha she xia hu yu

The gobies as a family have some interesting characteristics. The ventral fins are united to form a single roundish unit which they can use for clinging to rocks etc. This fused fin also enables the gobies to withstand currents which would be too strong for other fish. The large and mobile eyes on top of the head are another distinctive feature.

Gobies inhabit bays, rivers, swamps and lakes, but are never far from the shore. They are among the fish which can change colour in order to blend in with their surroundings, and often become almost invisible.

Distribution: Africa to Oceania.

CUISINE A Filipino recipe for this large goby is given on page 288, together with one suited to small gobies. As for the really tiny white gobies, the Filipinos make them into a friture with mung bean sprouts, using ground rice as the coating flour.

---

*meaning potato fish – there are also some general names for the gobies, such as belodok.

SURGEONFISH

Family *Acanthuridae*

Acanthurus mata Cuvier

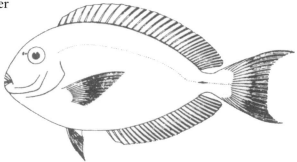

REMARKS Maximum length 50 cm, market length 30 cm.

These leathery-skinned fish swim around in schools not far from the shore, feeding on marine algae. This species has a brown or pale blue body marked with numerous longitudinal blue lines. It is the most common surgeon-fish in the markets.

Distribution: Red Sea to South Africa, also to Japan and to the Great Barrier Reef and Micronesia.

TH: pla khee tang bet lai
MA: debam, dengkis
IN: buntana
PH: labahita
CA: trey peth
HK: ngau maan
JA: osuji-kurohagi

CUISINE The flesh has a good flavour, although its texture is coarse.

RABBIT FISH, SPINEFOOT

Family *Siganidae*

Siganus canaliculatus (Park)

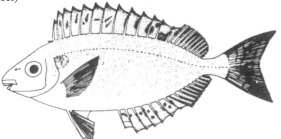

REMARKS Maximum length 30 cm.

Rabbit fish have oval, thin bodies. This one is olive above, lighter below, with lots of pearly spots (hence the name 'whitespotted spinefoot' which is sometimes used).

The front dorsal spines can inflict nasty stabs.

Distribution: from the Persian Gulf through S. E. Asian waters to southern China and Western Australia.

CUISINE The flesh is firm and palatable. The belly is better than the back. I enjoyed one which had been fried and was served on a bed of papaya pickle in Manila.

UAE: safy
BU: mae-daw-let-yweh
TH: pla salit
MA: dengkis
IN: beronang lada
PH: samaral
CA: trey knay moan
VI: cá dià vàng
HK: nai maan

HAIRTAIL, RIBBON FISH
Trichiurus lepturus Linnaeus

Family *Trichiuridae*

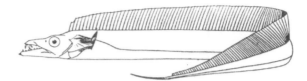

REMARKS Maximum length is reputed to be over 2 metres.

This is a long, thin, scaleless fish with a silver skin and a villainous head. (It is, I think, the combination of big eyes and ferocious teeth which give it this 'wicked Sir Jasper' aspect.) It has no tail fin.

Distribution: it has a very wide range throughout tropical and temperate waters of the world.

There are other closely related species in the area. ***Eupleurogrammus muticus*** Gray, the Smallhead hairtail, is tin-white in colour, which accounts for the emphatic Malay name timah-timah. ***Lepturacanthus savala*** (Cuvier) has a range from India to the Philippines and Australia.

An interesting alternative name for these fish in the Philippines in the Ilokano language is olungonas, meaning sugar-cane leaf.

BE: rupapatiya
    (general name)
TA: sonaka-wahlah
BU: nga-tagoon
TH: pla dab ngeon
MA: timah, selayar
IN: lajuru
PH: balila
CA: trey tua hu, trey
    kok
VI: cá hó
HK: ngar-taai
TAI: bai dai yu
JA: tachiuo

CUISINE Since these fish are so thin, there is not a great deal of flesh to be had from them. But it is of good quality, and quite convenient for the cook to handle if the fish is cut into sections of about 5 cm in length. The price is generally low and the fish a 'Good Buy', especially the larger specimens.

Fry, steam or use in soup. Sections of the fish may also be baked with added liquid and vegetables; but it is not advisable to grill them.

These fish are among the most important marine food fishes consumed in China, and are sought after by Chinese living abroad. Being long and thin, they are particularly suitable for drying and salting and are often so treated, for example in Cambodia.

A recipe is given on page 222.

FLATHEAD
Platycephalus indicus (Linnaeus)

Family *Platycephalidae*

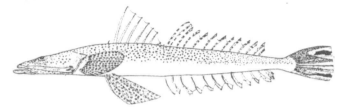

REMARKS Maximum length is said to be 1 metre, common length 30 cm.

The body is normally brownish above and white below. But this bottom-dwelling fish can change colour to match its surroundings. Note the large pectoral fins, which help it to move around on the bottom. The distinctive pattern on its tail has resulted in its being called 'bartail' flathead to distinguish it from other fish in the genus.

There are numerous species in this genus, all of the same general aspect. The Malay name refers to the wedge-shaped head.

'They live on the bottom, hidden in the sand as a rule, and as they depend on their protective colouring and spines to save them from possible enemies, they do not swim to any distance when disturbed but dart away for an instant and then lie motionless half buried in the sand. This peculiarity renders them particularly liable to be taken by trawls ...' (Maxwell)

Several dozen species of flathead are found in Australian waters, and many of them are important food fishes. The Tiger flathead of New South Wales and the Dusky flathead, the King flathead and the Grassy flathead of the south, and the Rock flathead of the north are all highly esteemed.

Distribution: at the western extremity of its wide range, occurs in the Red Sea and now also in the East Mediterranean. Present throughout S. E. Asian waters and northern Australia.

BE: mur bailla
TA: ulupathi
BU: saut-pwet, kywe-pa-done (Arakan)
TH: pla chang yiap, pla hang khwai
MA: baji-baji
IN: ikan anjing
PH: sunog
CA: trey kbal péach
HK: ngau chow
CH: yong yu
TAI: yin du niu wei yu
JA: kochi

CUISINE The flesh is good, although the fish has an unprepossessing appearance. Australians count it as good fare and the Chinese also like it, detecting a resemblance between its flesh and that of a chicken. One which I ate in the Philippines had been prepared in a stew with sili leaves; quite good, but it did not seem like a chicken to me.

DOLPHIN FISH
Coryphaena hippurus Linnaeus

Family *Coryphaenidae*

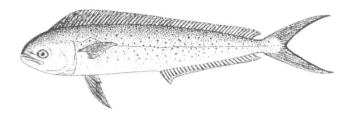

REMARKS Maximum length said to be about 2 metres, common length 60 cm.

A beautiful fish in life, but the iridescent blue, green, pink and gold fade quickly after death.

The dolphin fish (not, by the way, to be confused with the dolphin, which is not a fish but a marine mammal) is a fish of the seven seas, omnipresent but nowhere as plentiful as one would wish. Malta is one place where they are taken in fairly large quantities. And Japanese fishermen bring in enough to make the dolphin fish one of the most important food fishes in Japan. But in many of the great fish markets it is a rarity.

Distribution: world-wide in tropical and sub-tropical waters.

TA: ailai
BU: nga-ba-yin
   (kingfish)
TH: pla na mawn,
   pla eeto mawn
MA: belitong, golok
IN: lemadang
PH: dorado
VI: cá dũa, cá nuc
   heo
HK: ngau tau yue
CH: qi qiu
TAI: gui tou dau
JA: shiira

CUISINE Although this fish is not often seen in the markets, it is well worth buying when it does appear. It responds well to being baked, but may also be fried (fillets) or grilled (steaks) or made into a pie with vegetables, which is the favourite Maltese practice, see the recipe for lampuki pie in my *Mediterranean Seafood*.

When it is available in Hong Kong it costs less than its quality warrants. People there steam it and it is also available as dried fish.

Tahiti is well outside our region but there, as in Hawaii, the dolphin fish is highly regarded. The authors of *Poissons de Polynésie* (see under Bagnis in the Bibliography) recommend Darne de mahi-mahi. Slices of the flesh, about 2 cm thick and free of skin and bone, are floured and then dipped in a mixture of 2 beaten eggs, a liqueur-glassful of milk and salt and pepper. The mixture should be allowed to soak right in. The steaks are then put in a pan of very hot butter, turned once and allowed to finish cooking on a low flame (the blackened butter being taken out, if you wish, and replaced by fresh butter). Cooking time 10 minutes.

Mackerel, Tuna, Swordfish and Sailfish

Most of the fish in this section of the catalogue belong to the great family *Scombridae*, well-known everywhere in the world. These are pelagic fish, which swim at speed across the open waters of the oceans and seas. They are muscular for this reason, and their muscles are well supplied with blood; so they typically have flesh which is reddish as well as being highly compact. People who prefer meat to fish will find that fish of this family suit their taste. In fact mackerel and tunny are in strong demand as food and offer excellent and varied opportunities to the cook.

However, the larger tunny have to be caught by specialized fishing which is mainly carried out in the region by Japanese boats. Fresh tunny is not often available in India or the S. E. Asian markets except for the smaller species.

The genus best represented in the S. E. Asian markets are **Rastrelliger** and **Scomberomorus**. In the northern and north-eastern parts of the South China Sea two species of the genus **Scomber** are also taken in quantity. These are the Spotted chub mackerel, **Scomber australasicus** Cuvier, with a range from Australia northwards to Japan. It does not have a catalogue entry because its presence in S. E. Asian waters is rather limited. The other species **S. japonicus** Houttuyn, the Chub mackerel, has a range from Japan down to the Philippines only.

The general name for mackerel in Taiwan is qing. Thus *S. japonicus* is ri ben hua qing, meaning Japanese patterned mackerel. There is also a general name for tuna in Taiwan – jian. However, this last name is widely used in mainland China for members of the family – and can even be applied to the swordfish.

The section concludes with entries for certain pelagic fish which swim alone or in small numbers and which are of more interest to the game fisherman than to the professional. Two of these, the swordfish and the wahoo, are of exceptional quality. I mention here, additionally, **Makaira indica** (Cuvier), the Black marlin (which I have also seen referred to as Indian spearfish or Joo-hoo). It is quite close to the swordfish in general appearance, but may be distinguished easily by its possession of ventral fins and by its shorter 'spear' or 'sword'. The Indonesian name is setuhuk.

INDIAN MACKEREL, CHUB MACKEREL   Family *Scombridae*
Rastrelliger kanagurta (Cuvier)

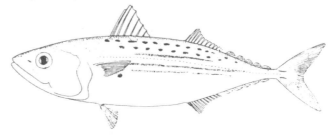

REMARKS Maximum length 35 cm.

The colour is an iridescent green above (with hints of blue) and silver below. About 16 blackish spots appear on the back along the base of the dorsal fins; and larger specimens have narrow dark longitudinal lines along their upper sides.

This fish and the following species provide the most important fishery in the Gulf of Thailand, where they are caught all the year round by purse seine and in bamboo stake traps. Scott notes that the main Malayan fishing grounds for these species are in the north-west, 'where fleets of boats from Kuala Kedah and Pulan Pangkor fish with purse seine nets on moonless nights, spotting the fish by the phosphorescence caused by the shoals when they are near the surface of the sea'.

Distribution: wide – from South Africa and the Red Sea in the west to northern Australia and Micronesia and north to Japan.

UAE: gurfa
TA: augalai, kumbala
SI: mahakara bolla
BU: nga-atpon, nga-gongree
TH: pla thu, pla lung
MA: kembong, temenong
IN: kembung lelaki, banjar
PH: alumahan
CA: trey kamong
VI: cá bac má
HK: fa kau
CH: yu sai tai
TAI: yin du qing
JA: gurukuma

CUISINE This is the favourite marine fish of the Thai people, and appreciated elsewhere in the region.

It may be boiled, steamed, fried, grilled or baked. Besides being sold fresh, it is available in salted and dried form, canned and in fish sauce.

RECIPES for this and other mackerel of moderate size include:

Nam prik num, page 236
Miang pla thu, page 238
Kaeng sai bua with pla thu nung, page 241
Jaew pla thu, page 242
Chhouchhi trey ton (stuffed mackerel), page 252
Dabu-dabu sesi, page 308
Laksa asam, page 318
Bapsetek ikan, page 323

SHORT/SHORT-BODIED MACKEREL

Rastrelliger brachysoma (Bleeker)

Family *Scombridae*

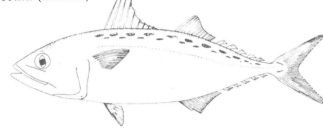

REMARKS Maximum length 35 cm, average length 20 cm.

The relatively great depth of the body is a good recognition point.

This mackerel is one of the most important food fishes in the Philippines, and also in Thailand.

Distribution: from the Andaman Sea, east to Thailand, Indonesia, Papua New Guinea, Philippines and Fiji.

Another and smaller species. *R. faughni* Matsui, the Island mackerel, has been found to be present in large numbers throughout S. E. Asian waters. Like the other two species of *Rastrelliger*, it has spots on its back. Its maximum length is only 20 cm. Essentially a species of S. E. Asia but found as far west as Madras.

HI: bangadi
BU: pa-la-tu
TH: pla thu, pla lung
MA: kembong
IN: kembung
    perempuan
PH: hasa-hasa
VI: cá bạc má
JA: agurukuma

CUISINE See the preceding entry. These are excellent fish, which may be prepared in all the conventional ways.

In the Philippines they are available salted and dried, or canned, or put up as Paksiw (see page 280). The species is important in Cambodia, where it is sold fresh, boiled (trey chamhoy), salted (trey prolok) and canned (as maquereau à l'huile).

FRIGATE TUNA / FRIGATE MACKEREL   Family *Scombridae*
Auxis thazard thazard (Lacepède)

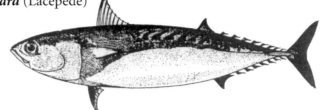

REMARKS Maximum length 65 cm, common length 25 to 40 cm.

Note the space between the two dorsal fins and the pattern of wavy lines on the back.

A cosmopolitan species, as is its brother, ***A. rochei rochei*** (Risso) which has a pattern of bars rather than wavy lines on its back. Between them they circle the globe. Both are present in Asian waters.

The relatively large species ***Sarda orientalis*** (length up to 1 metre) is something of a mystery fish, known from Japan and parts of Australia, Hawaii and the Pacific coast of the Americas, but only patchily reported in S. E. Asian waters. Its English name is Striped bonito, but it may be called Oriental bonito in Australia. It has a plenitude of names in Japan, notably hagatsua.

HI: choora
BU: nga-kyi-kan
TH: pla o
MA: kayau, baculan, tongol
IN: balaki
PH: bagoong tuligan
VI: cá bò
HK: faa gau
TAI: su jian
JA: many many names in Japan, including hirsôda, soda-gatsuo

CUISINE A fish of moderate quality.

SPOTTED SPANISH MACKEREL, KING MACKEREL
Family *Scombridae*
Scomberomorus guttatus (Bloch and Schneider)

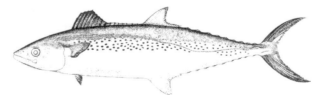

REMARKS Maximum length 75 cm, common length around 50 cm.

The back is dark and the sides silvery with three rows of roughly circular spots.

Distribution: from the Persian Gulf to Japan.

S. lineolatus (Cuvier), the Streaked seerfish, is a little larger (to 80 cm) and marked in the manner implied by this name. The streaks are four rows of

BE: nijram
TA: vanjiram, anjila
BU: nga-bu-zin
TH: pla in see jud, pla in see khao tok
MA: tenggiri papan, tohok langi
IN: tenggiri, ajong-ajong

brownish spots elongated so as almost to run into each other. This species is tenggiri musang in Malaysia, nga-bu-zin in Burma, trey béka chhot in Cambodia, and cá thu lòng in Vietnam.

CA: trey béka kroab
VI: cá thu chẩm
HK: chuk gau
CH: ban dian ma jiao
JA: taiwan-sawara

S. koreanus (Kishinouye), the Korean seerfish, is larger still (to 1 metre 50 cm) and has a similar distribution, but no further west than Bombay.

CUISINE An excellent species. See the following entry.

SPANISH MACKEREL, BARRED or NARROW-BARRED MACKEREL

Family *Scombridae*

Scomberomorus commerson Lacepède

REMARKS Maximum length over 2.40 metres, common length about 80 cm to 1 metre.

Distribution: from South Africa and Red Sea (even, recently, the eastern Mediterranean) in the west to Australia, Fiji and Japan in the east.

The back is dark blue or greenish, shading to silvery grey below. The sides are marked by wavy vertical grey stripes, more noticeable on the lower half of the body.

S. niphonius (Cuvier), the Japanese Spanish mackerel, is a related species of Chinese and Japanese waters. Maximum length 1 metre. It is sawara in Japan, lan dian ma jiao in China and ri ben chun in Taiwan. **S. sinensis** (Lacepède) the Chinese seerfish, is zhong hua chun in Taiwan and ushi-sawara in Japan. Its range extends from Japan to Cambodia and it also goes some distance up the River Mekong.

UAE: chanad
TA: arekula, konam
BU: nga-kyi-kan
TH: pla in see bung
MA: tenggiri batang
IN: tenggiri
PH: tangigi
CA: trey béka intri
VI: cá thu ào, cá thu dài
HK: kau yue
JA: yokoshi-masawara

CUISINE The Spanish mackerel is generally acclaimed as one of the finest food fishes of the region. The flesh is firm and of good flavour and the bones are not obstrusive. Steaks may be grilled, fried or baked with equally good results. Our favourite family recipe is for mackerel baked in a ginger sauce. It has not found a place in this book as it is not the pure Vietnamese version. But there are good recipes from Indonesia and elsewhere, on pages 257, 302, 307, 308, 325 and 326.

SKIPJACK, SKIPJACK TUNA
Katsuwonus pelamis (Linnaeus)

Family *Scombridae*

REMARKS Maximum length a shade over 1 metre, common length 40 to 80 cm.

The back is dark blue with indistinct light marks. The sides and belly are silvery with 4 to 6 dark longitudinal bands. This is a cosmopolitan species, known in almost all the tropical and warm waters of the world. The skipjack visit coastal waters in large schools, following the anchovies and other smaller fish on which they feed.

CUISINE The flesh is firm and compact. It is best grilled or baked. Steaks may be cooked en papillote, sealed up in aluminium foil with butter and herbs. Three recipes are given on pages 307 and 308.

BU: nga-me-lone,
tone-pyan
(rocket)
MA: kayu, tongkol
jepun
IN: cakalang
PH: gulyasan
VI: cá chầm
HK: doe chung
CH: jian
JA: katsuo

MACKEREL TUNA, KAWAKAWA
Euthynnus affinis (Cantor)

Family *Scombridae*

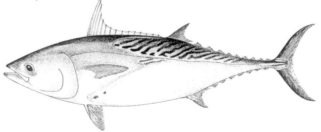

REMARKS Maximum length may be as much as 1 metre, common length 40 to 60 cm.

The back is dark blue, with the pattern of stripes shown in the drawing. The streamlined shape of the body accounts for an alternative name at Hong Kong, jar daan yue (bomb fish).

Distribution: widespread in the warm waters of the Indo-West Pacific.

CUISINE The flesh is red and best grilled.

BU: nga-mae-lone, tone-pyan
TH: pla o maw, pla o klaep
MA: tongkol, ambu-ambu
IN: tongkol, tongkol komo
PH: tulingan puti
VI: cá ngù
HK: doe chung
JA: hiragatsuo

NORTHERN BLUEFIN TUNA, LONGTAIL TUNA

Family *Scombridae*

Thunnus tonggol (Bleeker)

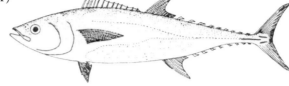

REMARKS Maximum length 1 metre 30, common length 40 to 70 cm.

The back is blue, even black, the lower part of the body silvery white with lots of colourless oval spots. Dorsal, pectoral, pelvic and tail fins are blackish. The anal fin is silvery.

This is a small tunny, which is better known in the S. E. Asian countries than its larger brethren.

Distribution: Indo-West Pacific from the Red Sea and Somalia to India and east to Japan, the Philippines and Australia.

CUISINE The flesh is pale in colour and delicious.

UAE: gubab
BU: nga-me-lone
TH: pla o maw
MA: tongkol hitam
IN: abu-abu
PH: tulingan (Visayan)
CA: trey chhéam khieu
VI: cá bò
HK: doe chung
CH: qing gan jin qiang yu
TAI: xiao huang qi wei
JA: koshinaga

BIGEYE TUNA

Family *Scombridae*

Thunnus obesus (Lowe)

REMARKS Maximum length 2.5 metres, common length 60 cm to 1 metre 75.

As the name indicates, this tuna has relatively big eyes. The back is dark metallic blue, the lower sides and belly whiteish. There is an iridescent blue band running along each side. Dorsal and anal fins are yellow. The species is present in open waters throughout the region, but is mainly taken by Japanese longliners.

Distribution: found in tropical and sub-tropical waters of the Atlantic, Indian and Pacific.

MA: tongkol, ayahitam, bakulan
IN: mata behar
PH: sobad, tulingan (both Visayan)
VI: cá bò, cá thu
CH: da yan jin qiang yu
TAI: duan wei
JA: mebachi

CUISINE The flesh is pink, compact and rather heavy. Fresh tuna is not readily available; but if you obtain some try braising it in white wine with shallots, tomatoes, garlic etc. It is too rich to be fried.

ALBACORE, LONGFIN TUNA
Thunnus alalunga (Bonnaterre)

Family *Scombridae*

REMARKS Maximum length 1 metre 40 cm, common length 40 cm to 1 metre.

This species is distinguished by its long pectoral fins. Its colouration is like that of the preceding species.

Distribution: cosmopolitan in all oceans in tropical and temperate waters.

MA: tongkol
PH: albakora
VI: cá ngir vây dài
TAI: chang qi wei
KO: nal-gae-da-
   raeng-i
JA: binnaga

CUISINE The flesh is fairly tender and mostly white or of a delicate pink colour. Some think it inferior to that of the preceding species. It is, however, used for canning.

YELLOWFIN TUNA
Thunnus albacares (Bonnaterre)

Family *Scombridae*

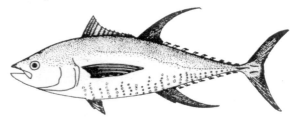

REMARKS Maximum length over 2.50 metres, common length 50 cm to 1 metre 50.

The fins of this species are all yellow, as one would expect from the English name. Note the exceptional length of the second dorsal fin and the anal fin.

Distribution: worldwide in tropical and sub-tropical waters (but not in the Mediterranean).

CUISINE A tuna of excellent quality. The flesh is particularly good in the summer months.

TA: kelavai, soccer
MA: tongkol, aya,
   bakulan
IN: gelang kawung
PH: tambakol, albakora,
   badla-an, buyo
VI: cá bò vàng
TAI: huang qi wei
JA: kihada

WAHOO

Family *Scombridae*

Acanthocybium solandri (Cuvier)

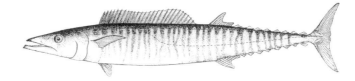

REMARKS Maximum length about 2.50 metres.

The back is a dark slaty blue, the belly a light silver grey.

This is one of the finest game fishes of the world. It is not common but occurs throughout the warm waters of the Indo-Pacific area and also in the West Indies and off the coast of Florida, and in the Mediterranean.

TA: savara
TH: pla in see lawt
IN: tenggiri selasih,
 tenggiri bahar
PH: peto, guachu
CH: ci ba

CUISINE As for the swordfish, see below.

SWORDFISH

Family *Xiphiidae*

Xiphias gladius Linnaeus

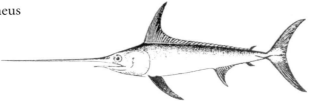

REMARKS Maximum length 4.50 metres (including the long sword).

The purpose of the sword is not to drive holes through the bottoms of wooden boats or ships (although there are many tales of this happening) but to be flailed around among banks of smaller fish, which are thus killed or stunned.

IN: ikan pedang
 todak
PH: malasugi
CH: jian yu
JA: dakuda, medara

This is a cosmopolitan species, found in the Atlantic and Mediterranean as well as in Indo-Pacific waters. It is not commonly met in S. E. Asian markets, but earns a place in the catalogue, since it is extremely good to eat.

CUISINE Grilled swordfish steaks are a delicacy familiar in the USA and else-where. They should be dressed with a thread of wine vinegar, nothing more. Steaks may also be pan-fried or baked. Sicilians, whose waters attract swordfish in relatively large numbers, have devised many interesting ways of cooking them, including a kind of swordfish pie (see any good book on Italian regional cookery, or my *Mediterranean Seafood*).

SAILFISH   Family *Istiophoridae*
Istiophorus platypterus* (Shaw)

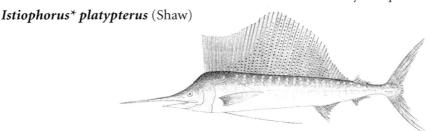

REMARKS These are very large fish, renowned for the
sport which they provide to big game fishermen, and
easily recognised by their enormous dorsal fins, which
look almost like sails.

Total length may be 3·40 m, including the long spear. It
is called myl meennd (Peacock fish) in Tamil because its
dorsal fin is bright blue (with darker spots).

Distribution: a wide range in the tropical and temperate
waters of the Indian and Pacific Oceans. The species has
managed to enter the Mediterranean via the Suez Canal.
(The Atlantic sailfish is usually treated as a separate
species, *I. albicans*. And it has penetrated the south-
western parts of the Mediterranean from the other end.)

TA: myl meennd
BU: nga-ga-lone
TH: pla kathong
thaeng kluay, pla
in see chang
MA: layeran**
IN: ikan layar
PH: pahabela
CA: trey kdaong
VI: cá cò
HK: kai yue
TAI: zheng qi yu liao
JA: bashôkajiki

CUISINE The sailfish rank among the best edible marine fish of the world, but are
not generally known as such, perhaps because they are more often taken by game
fishermen than by professionals who bring their catch to market. Treat the sailfish
as you would the swordfish (page 115).

*This should have been written Histiophorus when the genus was established, but the
mistake persists.
** Layer, a sail.

Flatfish

I confess that S. E. Asian flatfish disappoint me slightly. I draw attention to the best of them in the pages which follow, and these are good, but not in my opinion as good as the sole and plaice and halibut of the North Sea and the Atlantic.

Flatfish start life upright, but when they are still tiny they turn over on to one side, which then becomes the belly and usually stays white or at least pale in colour. The eye and the nostril on the belly side move up over the head and join the other eye and nostril on what has now become the back of the fish. The mouth changes shape, and the back takes on a colour, and often a pattern also, which matches the sea bottom and camouflages the fish.

Some flatfish have their eyes on the left side and some on the right. They are called sinistral or dextral accordingly. This helps identification. Note, however, that the first species listed may be either sinistral or dextral; and that even in those species which are supposed to be one or the other the occasional fish comes out the wrong way.

As a general rule, all the fish in this catalogue are shown swimming from right to left. However, the dextral flatfish must be shown swimming the other way: since otherwise one would be portraying the impossible. Hence the arrangement on pages 120 and 121.

INDIAN HALIBUT, INDIAN SPINY TURBOT

Family *Psettodidae*

Psettodes erumei (Bloch and Schneider)

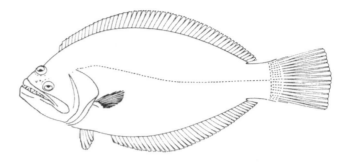

REMARKS Maximum length 64 cm, common length 20 to 40 cm.

This fish, a relation of the North Atlantic halibut, is easily the biggest flatfish in S. E. Asian waters.

The colour of the back is brown. So is that of the underside. Indeed this species is unusual among flatfish in that it will lie down on either side and may be either right-sided or left-sided. The upper eye does not come all the way round to join the lower eye but keeps to what one might call a bridge-of-the-nose position.

Note the mouthful of long sharp teeth and the fact that the dorsal fin does not extend on to the head. These are both distinguishing characteristics.

This species has a very wide distribution. It occurs on the West African coast (as the adalah of Ghana and the boung of Senegal) and ranges also from East Africa into the Pacific (Japan and Australia).

TA: erumei-nakku
BU: nga-khwe, nga-let-kai
TH: pla seek-deo
MA: sebelah*, togok
IN: grobiat, lewe (both Javanese)
PH: kalankao
CA: trey andat kleng
VI: cá ngô
HK: tai wu
CH: da kou jian
TAI: da kou die
JA: bozu garei

CUISINE An excellent fish, which may be grilled, fried or baked with full confidence in the results.

*This name is a general Malay name for flatfish. It means tongue.

LARGETOOTH FLOUNDER

Family *Paralichthyidae*

Pseudorhombus arsius (Hamilton)

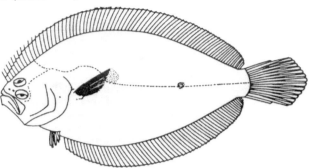

REMARKS Maximum length about 45 cm, common length 20 to 30 cm.

The back is brown, with darker spots and rings, including always the two blotches on the lateral line shown in the drawing. The scales on the back are ctenoid, that is to say toothed and rough, whereas those on the blind side or belly are cycloid and smooth.

P. malayanus (Bleeker), the Malayan flounder, has ctenoid scales on both sides. It is sebelah in Malaysia, pla bai-kanoon in Thailand and may be referred to as the Rough-scaled flounder or Brill. There are several other similar species which may be distinguished by small differences in their vital statistics and markings. Generally, these species have a wide distribution from Africa or India through to the Pacific. However, one of the other large species, *P. dupliciocellatus* Regan (the Ocellated flounder, maximum length 40 cm), is not found west of the Nicobar Islands. The additional drawing below shows the three pairs of spots, each pair surrounded by a ring of small white spots, which distinguish this species.

BE: serbati
TA: nakku
BU: nga-khwe-shar
TH: pla lin ma
MA: sebelah
IN: ikan sebelah
PH: dapang bilog
CA: trey andat
  khsach, trey andat
  phoumea
VI: cá dành
HK: dae boe
TAI: da chi bian yu
JA: tenjikugarei

CUISINE A flatfish of good quality.

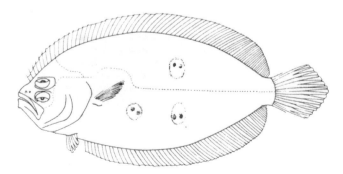

SOLE, ORIENTAL SOLE   Family *Soleidae*
Euryglossa orientalis (Bloch and Schneider)

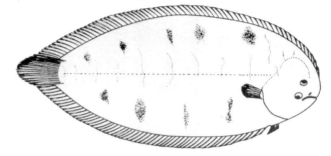

REMARKS   Maximum length about 30 cm.
The back is grey or brown, blotched or spotted, and
may have short bars crossing the lateral line at right
angles.

   This species has a wide distribution from the Persian
Gulf to China and northern Australia. It is also found
in brackish and fresh water, even in inland lakes in
Cambodia.

   There are other soles in the region. **Synaptura com-
mersoniana** (Lacepède) may reach a length of over 25
cm, is greyish-brown and may often be found in Thai
and Malay markets. **Euryglossa panoides** (Bleeker) is
almost as large and has a brown-red back with dark
blotches and spots. **Zebrias quagga** (Kaup) is smaller
and readily distinguished by its zebra-like markings – ten or so dark crossbands
adorn its yellowish brown back – hence its name Fringefin zebra sole. It is pla lin-
ma lai in Thailand and cá lòn bon in Vietnam.

BE: danchoukka serboti
BU: nga-pha-yone
TH: pla lin-kwai kone
    dam, pla pluk
MA: lidah
IN: ikan lidah
PH: tambiki*
CA: trey andat chhkê
    nis
VI: cá lòn, cá bon
HK: chat yat shin
JA: minamishima-
    ushinoshita

CUISINE   All these soles are good. Perhaps the Cambodians are right in thinking
that they are best fried. **E. orientalis** is a great favourite of Hong Kong restaura-
teurs.

* a general name, as is the Visayan name dali-dali.

TONGUE SOLE, LONG TONGUE-SOLE   Family *Cynoglossidae*
Cynoglossus lingua Hamilton

REMARKS Maximum length 45 cm, common length 20 to 30 cm.

The back is brown or grey. Note the two lateral lines. (There is no lateral line on the underside. This state of affairs is typical of the genus, although **C. bilineatus** (Lacepède) has a pair of lateral lines on each side.)

Two other tongue soles of respectable size are **C. arel** (Bloch and Schneider), the Largescale tongue sole), and **C. borneensis** (Bleeker), which, as the name suggests, is particularly abundant in Borneo. Both these may be called Macao sole at Hong Kong. **C. puncticeps** (Richardson), the Speckled tongue-sole, well known as dapang sinilas in the Philippines, is speckled with irregular dark markings.

Distribution: from the Red Sea in the West to the Philippines and Indonesia in the East.

BE: kukurjeeb
TA: kotaralu, vari-allu
BU: nga-khwe-shar
TH: pla lin ma lai, pla bai mail, pla yot muang
MA: lidah-lidah
IN: lidah-pasir
PH: dapang sinilas (general name)
CA: trey andat chhke
VI: cá luỡi trâu
HK: tat sa (or sha)

CUISINE The tongue soles are good to eat, although their long tongue-like shape makes them relatively short of flesh. Steaming is recommended.

Leatherjackets, Triggerfish and Blowfish

These fish are among the more uncouth kinds of seafood which may be found in the markets. One purpose of this short section of the catalogue is to indicate that leatherjackets and triggerfish make better eating than their appearance would suggest.

However, it is sensible to be put off by the ugly appearance of blowfish, since it can be dangerous to eat them without precautions which are best taken professionally rather than in your own kitchen. *Fugu*, the Japanese name for some species of them, is a name associated with sudden death. Yet certain species are considered by the Japanese to be among the greatest of marine delicacies. These are **Fugu rubripes** (torafugu), and **F. porphyreus** (mafugu or namerafugu).

These fish have to be prepared with great skill to avoid any possibility of the fatally toxic parts being eaten or contaminating the flesh. There are whole books in Japanese – I have one – devoted to the necessary technique, and only cooks who have qualified in this are allowed to deal with the fish. Even so, instances occur of Japanese dying from *fugu* poisoning, usually because someone without the necessary skill has attempted to prepare the fish. It is certainly no matter for amateurs, since the location of the toxin varies and years of training and experience are needed if all the signs are to be read correctly. *Fugu* are most often eaten in Japan in the form of *sashimi* and *nabemono*.

Puffer fish in other parts of the world are less dangerous, although it is well to treat all with caution.

LEATHERJACKET, TRIGGERFISH   Family *Monacanthidae*

Aluterus monoceros (Linnaeus)

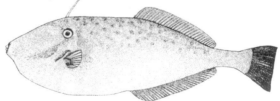

REMARKS Maximum length 76 cm, but 50 cm is a good size.

A greyish-brown fish with yellow fins. Note the isolated dorsal spine which can be locked in this upright position by a little 'trigger' alongside it (which is in fact a rudimentary second dorsal spine). This unusual feature is what has prompted some authorities to distinguish it as 'unicorn leatherjacket'.

The skin of this species is smooth.

This fish, besides being present on both sides of the Atlantic, has a range extending right across the Indo-Pacific.

Among the fairly numerous close relations, some may be called Filefish.

BU: nga-tan
TH: pla raet
MA: barat-barat
PH: papakol
VI: cá bó gau
HK: saa maan
JA: usubahagi

CUISINE This fish usually has its 'leather jacket', i.e. thick and tough skin, removed before it is sold. It is quite good to eat. A recipe is given on page 237.

STARRY TRIGGERFISH
Abalistes stellaris (Bloch and Schneider)

Family *Balistidae*

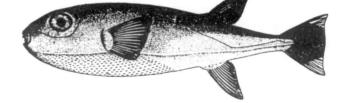

REMARKS Maximum length about 60 cm, common length 25 to 30 cm. Blue-grey to olive above, with numerous blue spots, three large white blotches on the back and a white longitudinal band on each side.

Distribution: Red Sea and East Africa to Japan and northern Australia. Also in the east Atlantic.

BU: nga-tan
TH: pla wua
MA: ayam laut, jebong
PH: papakol
CA: trey kambet kay
VI: cá bò da
HK: saa maan
JA: okihagi

CUISINE As for the preceding species, but this fish '... is preferred to all other fish by many Malays including fishermen ... I think that the main reason for this preference is that the flesh of this fish more nearly resembles that of a chicken than that of any other fish ... The cook should not be allowed to remove the head, which is the best part ...' (Maxwell). A recipe is given on page 237.

PUFFER, BLOWFISH
Lagocephalus lunaris (Bloch and Schneider)

Family *Tetraodontidae*

REMARKS Maximum length 45 cm. Greenish olive above, satin white on the sides and belly. The fins are yellowish. The belly and back are covered with spines (hence the common name 'green rough-backed puffer'). These fish can puff themselves up at will. The teeth are fused into a powerful beak capable of biting through a fishing line.

Distribution: Indo-West Pacific and south-east Atlantic.

BU: nga-pu-tin
TH: pla pao khieo
MA/IN: buntal pisang
PH: butete (general name)
VI: cá nóc
HK: wong po (yellow), ching po (green)
TAI: su se he tun
JA: doku-sabafugu

CUISINE Beware! See page 122.

Sharks and Rays

So far we have been dealing with what scientists call the Bony Fishes, not bony in the sense that they have lots of little bones which stick in our teeth but bony in the sense that they have real bones. There are, however, other fish which do not have real bones but cartilaginous skeletons. These are the sharks and rays, which belong respectively to the Orders *Lamniformes* and *Rajiforms* in the Class *Elasmobranchii*.

Since the Non-bony Fish are more primitive than the others it is customary to place them at the beginning of any catalogue. For gastronomic purposes this makes a discouraging start, which is why I have put them at the end. Let me, however, make clear that many sharks and rays are well worth eating. We may smile at the ruse whereby dogfish (which is a small shark) is presented to British customers as Rock salmon. It is not nearly as good as salmon. Yet the wily fishmonger is making a valid point if his intention is simply to tell us that it is better than we might think. There is certainly one point in favour of sharks and rays; they are non-bony in both senses of the term, and all the easier to eat for this reason.

Being uncouth in appearance, and often inconveniently large, sharks and rays are frequently cut up and dressed before being sold. The amateur will therefore find it difficult to know, from an inspection of what is in the market, exactly what species is being offered to him. However, the drawings which I have provided will be of use to those who do their own fishing and also for the identification of smaller specimens in the market.

In the Orient, especially in China and where Chinese influence is strong, the culinary reputation of sharks rests more on their fins than their flesh. Of the numerous species in the Indo-Pacific only a few are especially sought because they yield fins with the qualities required; and distinctions are also made between e.g. the dorsal fin and the ventral fins and others. Kreuzer (1974) listed what he thought were the most valuable fins, explaining that those of sharks shorter than 1.5 m are preferred, and mentioning the pectoral fins of the sawfish shark now classified as **Anoxypristis cuspidata** (formerly **Pristis cuspidatus**) and, more generally, the upper lobe of the tail of all sharks. He additionally listed fins of one of the nurse sharks; and the more recent publication by Compano (1984) draws attention to the use of one such shark, **Nebrius ferrugineus**. In Hawaii the species **Galeorhinus zyopterus** is known as the 'soup fin shark', for the obvious reason. See page 268 for some account of the preparation of sharks' fins in the kitchen, as a preliminary to making the famous shark's fin soup.

SPADENOSE SHARK
Scoliodon laticaudus Müller and Henle

Family *Carcharinidae*

REMARKS Maximum length 1 metre, market length 50 or 60 cm. This shark is grey-brown to buff, with a Naples yellow tint above and whiteish or creamy below. It is abundant in waters of the Indian sub-continent where the Bombay duck (see page 35) forms part of its diet.

BU: nga-man (general name for sharks)
MA: yu pasir, yu jereh
TAI: sha zi qu chi jiao
JA: togari-ankôzame

Rhizoprionodon acutus (Rüppell) is grey-brown to buff, again with a Naples yellow tint above and whiteish or creamy below. The fins are grey/brown, some with dark upper edges.

Rhizoprionodon oligolinx Springer, the Grey sharpnose shark, which was formerly classified as *Scoliodon palasorrah*, is another smallish shark present throughout the region and of some importance as food.

These small or medium-sized sharks, often known as dog sharks, are quite common in shallow waters, and often seen in the markets, fresh or dried. Of course, there are also much bigger sharks, some edible. *Carcharhinus melanopterus* Quoy and Gaimard, the Blacktip reef shark, may reach a length of 3 metres but is commonly between 50 cm and 1 metre in length. It is considered in Malaysia to be the best. It is pating inglesa in the Philippines (although it has no apparent connection with England), yu nipah or yu sirip hitam in Malaysia and nga-man-taungme in Burma. Its fins have black tips. An even larger shark (up to 3.5 m) is *Carcharhinus falciformis* (Müller and Henle), the Silky shark, seems to be well known in the Gulf of Tonkin (Vietnamese name cá mập mã lai).

Chiloscyllium indicum (Gmelin), the Slender bamboo shark, which is shown on the previous page, is trey chlam kla in Cambodia and chèo beo in Vietnam. It is a cat shark (family *Hemiscylliidae*) and usually less than 50 cm long. Gruvel remarked on its high reputation in Vietnam where he knew it as cá chà bé.

Distribution: the sharks generally have a wide distribution, and some occur in other oceans too. For example, the Silky shark is known in the Atlantic and bears the pretty name Jaqueta in the Canary Islands.

CUISINE The flesh of this and many other sharks is well worth eating. Fry, grill or serve curried.

Dried and slated strips or slices of this fish are sold in Cambodia; and the fins are in keen demand for shark-fin soup.

A Burmese recipe for shark is given on page 227.

HAMMERHEAD SHARK, WINGHEAD SHARK

Family *Sphyrnidae*

Eusphyra blochii (Cuvier)

REMARKS Maximum length about 1.5 m, market length 50 to 70 cm.

Hammerhead sharks are easily recognized by their extraordinary heads. A glance at the illustration will show how they got their name.

There are two other species in the area. ***Sphyrna zygaena*** (Linnaeus), the Smooth hammerhead, is one. It has shorter, more rounded projections on its head but grows to a greater size (4 or 5 metres). The names cited for Hong Kong, the Philippines and Indonesia apply to this species.

Distribution: Persian Gulf to the Philippines, north to China and south to Australia.

TA: koman sorrah
BU: ngaman-te-
  gyoto
TH: pla chalam kua
  khon
MA: yu sanggul*
IN: cucutronggeng
PH: binkungan
CA: (trey) chlam ek
VI: cá cào, cá nhám
  cào
HK: tai tst cha

CUISINE Small hammerheads are often captured and, if small enough, may be cleaned and cooked whole in a court-bouillon. Larger specimens will of course be sold by the piece and may be fried or used in fish soup.

*This name means Chinese ladies' hair style, in reference to the hammerhead shape of a certain Chinese type of coiffure.

SAWFISH, KNIFETOOTH SAWFISH   Family *Pristidae*
Anoxypristis cuspidata (Lathum)

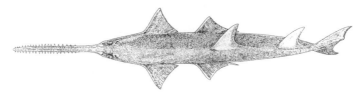

REMARKS Maximum length 6 metres or more.

The colour of the back is drab or grey.

The saw is used for attacking shoals of smaller fish, among which it is flailed about. The 24 pairs of teeth are sharp and make it a dangerous weapon.

This is a viviparous fish. Out of consideration for the insides of the mother the babies wear protective sheaths on their tiny swords until after birth.

Pristis microdon Latham, the Largetooth sawfish, has fewer pairs of teeth on its saw (17 to 20). The Filipino name given above applies to it, but it may also be called barasan. It is htok-nga-man in Burma.

Distribution: the Knifetooth sawfish has a range from the Red Sea and Persian Gulf to New Guinea, north to Korea and south to Australia.

TA: vela schura
BU: khot-nga-man
   (cutting shark)
TH: pla chanak
MA: yu parang, yu
   gergaji
IN: parangpang,
   pamprang
PH: tagan
CA: trey thkar
   damrey
VI: cá dao
HK: kui yue

CUISINE Malays, Chinese and Tamils are all enthusiastic about this fish.

HONEYCOMB STINGRAY   Family *Dasyatidae*
Himantura uarnak (Forskål)

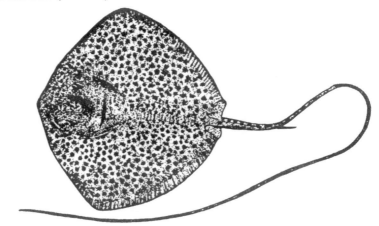

REMARKS The normal maximum width across the disc is about 2 metres.

The back may be anything from sandy to a dark brown, and may or may not be marked by numerous closely set dark spots. A better recognition point is the tail, which is white and bears 30 or more blackish-blue bands.

This species has a wide distribution, from Australia to China and all over the tropical Indian Ocean. So has the related **H. imbricata** (Bloch and Schneider), known as the Scaly whipray because of its scaly back. It is reddish brown and spotted with yellow. It is well-known on the Cambodian coast as babel kreum. **Dasyatis zuegei** (Müller and Henle), is another common species, which is often marketed in Malaysia, as pari nyiru or as pari ketuka. **D. kuhlii** (Müller and Henle), the Blue-spotted stingray, is well-known under the name dahunan in the Philippines.

Another monster in the family is **Pastinachus sephen** (Forskål), the Cowtail stingray, which may weigh as much as 250 kilos and measure 1 metre 80 across. The skin of this species, according to Gruvel, has always been prized in Vietnam, where it furnishes what he describes mysteriously as an article of leatherware known as galuchat and 'used both in ancestral times and nowadays'.

TA: manal-thirukkai
BU: leik-kyaut-hua-
    maungdo
TH: pla kaben lai
    seua
MA: pari beting
IN: pari pasir
PH: paging bulik,
    paging sulatan
CA: babel sluk, chlam
    koup
VI: cá duôi bông
HK: wong po
JA: hyômon-otome-ei

CUISINE Not generally esteemed as a food fish, but has enjoyed some popularity in parts of Thailand and Cambodia, as well as in Malaysia. Cecilia Tan, in her interesting book about Nyonya cooking in Pinang, provides a couple of recipes which are specifically for stingray. See the preceding entry.

GIANT GUITARFISH, SHOVELNOSED RAY

Family *Rhinobatidae*

Rhynchobatus djiddensis (Forskål)

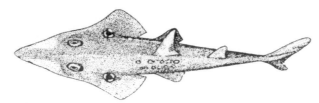

REMARKS Maximum length 3 metres, market length about 50 cm.

Sandy-brown above. The sides and pectoral fins are marked with scattered white rings or 'ocelli', and for this reason the fish is sometimes called 'white-spotted shovel-nose ray'.

A sedentary bottom-feeding fish, which is widely distributed in the Indo-Pacific area. However, some authorities believe that this species belongs essentially to the western Indian Ocean, and that what have been thought to be fish of this species throughout S. E. Asian waters are very, very close relations which should be classified separately.

TA: pal uluvai
BU: nga-man-bu-
     pyauk
MA: yu kemejan
PH: pating sudsod
CA: (trey) babel suy
VI: cá duôi nhám
HK: pay par saa
CH: ji da jian li tou
     yao
TAI: ji da long wen
     fen
JA: tongari-
     sakatazame

CUISINE Quite good. The 'wings' may be grilled or fried.
The rays of S. E. Asia are generally just as suitable as those of the Mediterranean and the Atlantic for preparing Raie au beurre noir in the French manner.

EAGLE RAY, SPOTTED EAGLE RAY
Aetobatus narinari (Euphrasen)

Family *Myliobatidae*

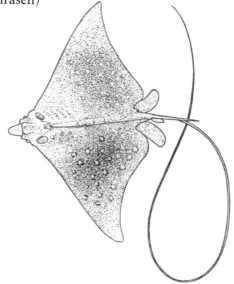

REMARKS Maximum width over 2 or even 3 metres, market size much smaller (e.g. 30 cm).

The back is purple-brown and spotted.

These fish leap out of the sea to a height of 2 metres or more and descend again with a terrific splash. The procedure is reputedly intended to shake off shark suckers which cling to them.

There are other large rays which may be met in the markets, for example the Cow-nosed rays or Whiparees, which may be distinguished from the eagle rays by the cow-like four-lobed snout. *Rhinoptera javanica* Müller and Henle, the Javanese cownose ray, is palimok in the Philippines. Filipinos are also willing to eat the Devil rays, which they know as salanga and which have horn-like projections at the front of the head.

The cow-nosed and the devil rays belong respectively to the families *Rhinopteridae* and *Mobulidae*.

Distribution: the Eagle ray is widespread globally.

CUISINE As for the rays. This one is popular in Cambodia.

A Thai recipe is given on page 240.

TA: kurivi-tiriki
BU: nawsaya, leik-
    kyauk-sun
TH: pla kaben nok
MA: pari lang
IN: pari burung
PH: paol
CA: babel khleng,
    trey babel meam
VI: cá duôi ó
HK: ying po
TAI: xue hua ya zui
    yan hong
JA: madara-tobi-ei

Catalogue of Crustaceans

Shrimp, Prawns, Spiny Lobsters and the Mantis Shrimp

As for shrimp and prawns, one must begin by drawing attention to the different ways in which these names are used by the British and the North Americans. The former preserve what seems to me to be a useful distinction between shrimp, which are small, and prawns, which are generally larger. The latter call them all shrimp (and on the rare occasions when they use 'prawn' it is applied to the small rather than the larger species). I follow British practice myself, noting that it has been retained in South Africa and Australia and New Zealand, while acknowledging that in S. E. Asia one is more likely to find American terminology being used.

Professor Holthuis, by the way, in his excellent survey of *Shrimps and Prawns of the World* (1980) for the FAO, points out that despite the widespread confusion there is a case for deeming species in the family *Palaemonidae* to have the strongest claim to the name 'prawn', **Palaemon serratus** being the 'common prawn'.

The shrimp of S. E. Asia are important because of their use in shrimp paste, a popular foodstuff. The prawns are of excellent quality.

Both shrimp and prawns occur in freshwater as well as in the sea. Although this book deals only with seafood, I must mention here one of the best-known prawns of S. E. Asia, the freshwater species **Macrobrachium rosenbergii** (de Man). It and its close relations are often referred to as 'river shrimp', but besides rivers it may be found in brackish, or even sometimes in marine, waters, so almost qualifies as seafood. Its cultivation has become very important in several S. E. Asian countries. The male reaches a length of over 30 cm. Its name in Malaysia is udang galah, and it is well-known in Thailand and Burma.

The true (Atlantic) lobster is not found in S. E. Asian waters, which are home to the various spiny lobsters which are, some maintain, just as good.

Many people, including myself, are exercised about the question how to kill lobsters (and crabs) in the most humane way. I dealt with the question as well as I could in *Mediterranean Seafood* in 1972. But further research has been done since then – see footnote on page 139.

The Mantis shrimp is an oddity which should not, according to what I have said above, be called a shrimp at all. Indeed the name Sea locust is perhaps better. But Mantis shrimp is the most common English name. The S. E. Asian species are quite as good as the Mediterranean one, and readers who have spent time in the Romagna will know how highly the panochie (or cannocchie) are esteemed there, and how delicious the soup made from them can be.

* The Burmese prepare an interesting dish called pazun-zi by breaking these prawns in half and decanting from the head part the reddish liquid therefrom. When this has boiled for a few minutes it becomes blood-red. It is then mixed with cooked rice and eaten with a certain kind of sweet banana. This is a speciality of Tenesaram, but found elsewhere in the Delta area of Burma. Late September is the best time of the year, since this is when the large prawns are collected in the greatest quantity, at the end of the rainy season.

JAWLA PASTE SHRIMP   Family *Sergestidae*

Acetes indicus
Milne Edwards

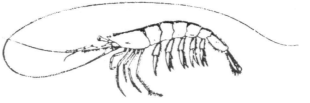

REMARKS These small shrimp do not attain a length
greater than 15 to 40 mm, depending whether male or
female. The species illustrated is one of the best-known in
S. E. Asia. 'Jawla' in its official name is a Marathi word and
'paste' indicates the usual fate of these little creatures.
A. japonicus Kishinouye, the Akiami paste shrimp (aki
ami, or hon ami in Japan) is bigger, with a length from 11
to 30 cm. But there are others and the task of distinguishing between them is not easy.

BU: hmyin, pazun-
    zeik
TH: kwei kung
MA: udang gragok
IN: rebon
PH: alamang
VI: con ruóc
HK: mui ha
KO: baek ha

   Distribution: *A. indicus* has a range from the west coast
of India to Thailand and Indonesia.

CUISINE Mainly utilized for the manufacture of shrimp pastes, as mentioned
above, or shrimp powder.

ROSHNA PRAWN   Family *Palaemonidae*

Exopalaemon styliferus
(Milne Edwards)

REMARKS This species can serve to represent the smaller species in the family
Palaemonidae. The smaller species are mostly shrimp-sized, but are nevertheless
called prawns by the FAO, no doubt because the family as a whole is the one in
which there are numerous larger species which are regarded as the 'true prawns'.
Generally these small species are more likely to be used as bait than as food for
humans; but *E. styliferus* is important and abundant around the whole of the
Indian sub-continent, and eaten there extensively, besides being present in S. E.
Asian waters. Roshna is the name for this species in West Bengal, where it may also
be known as ghora chingri. In Bangladesh it is gara icha.
   Another species present in S. E. Asian waters is *Palaemon concinnus* Dana.
Rather similar small shrimp, *Alpheus* spp., belong to the family *Alpheidae*.

CUISINE These shrimp may be used in the manufacture of shrimp/fish pastes,
but it is also possible to 'pot' them in the English style or to incorporate them
(peeled) in sauces etc. Such shrimp are also available in dried form.

GIANT TIGER PRAWN
Penaeus monodon Fabricius

Family *Penaeidae*

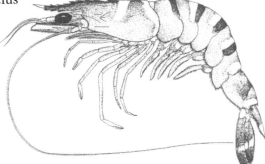

REMARKS This is the largest of the marine prawns of S. E. Asia. It may reach a length of 33 cm. The colours are striking, but variable – light brown to blue with grey, purple or black bands on the abdomen.

The genus *Penaeus* is most easily distinguished from other genera of prawns by the rostrum (or beak), which is toothed both above and below. It is a large genus. Four more members of it are shown on the next two pages, but these are by no means all. I might well have listed in addition: *P. penicillatus* Alcock, a species intermediate between *P. indicus* and *P. merguiensis* (see page 134); and *P. latisulcatus* Kishinouye (called udang susu in Malaysia). The latter is the Western King prawn (Blue-legged King prawn in Australia because its legs and the tips of the tailfan are prominently blue).

UAE: rubeyan (general name)
BE: bagda chingri
BU: jar-pazun, pazun-kya
TH: kung kula-dum
MA: udang rimau
IN: udang windu
PH: sugpo
CA: bangkear
VI: tôm sú
HK: gwai ha (ghost shrimp)
CH: ban jie dui xia, cao xia (grass shrimp)
JA: ushi ebi

Distribution: generally speaking, *Penaeus* spp. have a wide range from East Africa or the Red Sea through S. E. Asian waters to Australia.

CUISINE This particular prawn is so big that it can really be treated like a spiny lobster. However, the great majority of prawns brought to market are of course much smaller. The numerous prawn recipes in this book mostly assume the purchase of prawns of medium size.

The master fisherman who wrote under the pseudonym 'le Nestour' in Cambodia fifty years ago made an interesting comparison between Mediterranean/Atlantic prawns and those of S. E. Asia. He believed that the latter were inferior, having less flavour, but that the Vietnamese never noticed this because of their habit of using a lot of sauce and seasoning. Le Nestour goes on to say that Vietnamese prawns could be given a full measure of 'sapidité' by the following procedure. Cook the prawns in salt water with a bouquet of thyme, bay leaf and parsley. Then hang them up for several hours in a basket in the open air, so that they start to dry out ever so slightly. The meat will become firmer and the process of peeling the prawns later will be easier.

GREEN TIGER PRAWN

Penaeus semisulcatus de Haan – maximum length 23 cm; so 9 or so adults to the kilo. This prawn is green, or brownish green, with darker bands on the abdomen. It may be called feng xia (phoenix shrimp) in China, also 'Flower prawn' in Hong Kong.

TH: kung kula-lai	VI: tôm có
MA: udang harus, udang harimau	HK: fa ha
IN: udang windu	CH: duan gou dui xia
CA: bangkear	JA: kuma ebi

KURUMA PRAWN, JAPANESE (KING) PRAWN,

Penaeus japonicus Bate has a maximum length of 22 cm. Expect 9 to 11 adults to the kilo. The name 'japonicus' reflects the fact that this is the most important member of the family in Japan. This is also an important prawn in Burma. The colour is variable. The abdomen bears ten dark bands, which may account for an alternative Chinese name, zhu jie zia (bamboo section shrimp).

BU: japan pazun, thae pazun	HK: fa ha
PH: hipon bulik	CH: ri ben dui xia (Japanese prawn)
VI: tôm sen	JA: kuruma ebi (tiger prawn)

INDIAN PRAWN, WHITE PRAWN

Penaeus indicus Milne Edwards has a maximum length of 20 cm or perhaps a little more. Expect 10 or 12 adults to the kilo. The dominant body colour is whiteish with blue or brown markings; the tailfan and legs are reddish purple or pinkish blue. The species is of considerable importance in many countries from Bangladesh to the Philippines, both for offshore fishing and in pond culture.

BE: chapra chingri	PH: hipon buti
BU: ye-light-pazun	VI: tôm bac can
TH: kung lai nam ngern	HK: chuk chik ha
MA: udang putih, udang kaki merah	JA: shonan ebi
IN: udang putih	

BANANA PRAWN, WHITE PRAWN

Penaeus merguiensis de Man may reach a length of 24 cm. 7 or 8 large adults make a kilo. Its colour is cream to yellow, sparsely speckled with tiny red spots. The tailfan and legs are red. This is a prawn of very good quality; it is the main species in the prawn farms of Thailand. It is also the most important commercial species of Queensland.

BU: pazun-byu	CA: bangkear
TH: kung chaebauy	VI: tôm bac gân
MA: udang kaki merah	HK: pak ha
IN: udang putih	CH: mo ji dui xia
PH: hipon buti	JA: tenjika kuruma ebi

Prawns of the genus *Metapenaeus* are generally smaller. Two larger members of the genus are catalogued here, together with one species from the genus *Parapeneopsis*.

YELLOW SHRIMP/PRAWN

Metapenaeus brevicornis (H. Milne Edwards) is usually no more than 13 cm in length and 45 to 50 per kilo. The abdomen and the tailfan bear brown dots. It has a distribution from the Arabian Sea east to Malaysia, Thailand and Indonesia.

BE: dhanbone/koraney chingri	IN: udang baratan
BU: sandar-pazun	CA: bangkear kreum
TH: kung lee	HK: sha ha
MA: udang kuning	

GREASYBACK SHRIMP/PRAWN

Metapenaeus ensis (de Haan), like the preceding species, was earlier given (and may still be given by some authorities) the names *Penaeus* or *Metapenaeus monoceros*. Very confusing. However, it is an important prawn, measuring up to 16 cm (13 to 15 adults per kilo). Body colour is variable, 'pinkish white to pinkish red' as one authority puts it.

BU: pazun-baw-gyait	CA: bangkear kreum
TH: kung takard	VI: tôm dât
MA: udang kaki merah, udang merah ros	HK: chung ha
IN: udang apiapi	TAI: sha xia
PH: hipon suahe	JA: yosi (yoshi) ebi

SPEAR SHRIMP/PRAWN

Parapenaeopsis hardwickii (Miers) is best considered in conjunction with the slightly larger *P. sculptilis*, the Rainbow shrimp, with which it seems to have been confused in the past. (The taxonomists have woven a real tangle round some of these prawns.) The Spear shrimp's body colour varies from reddish green to pink and has maximum length of 14 cm. It has a range from Pakistan east to China and Indonesia. The Rainbow shrimp is so-called because of four whitish transverse bands evenly spaced along the body with pink and brown bands in between and has a distribution from the west coast of India east to northern Australia.

BU: pazun-kyaung	CA: bangkear
MA: udang minyak	HK: chung ha
PH: hipon buhangin	JA: ebi (shu)

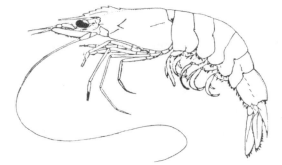

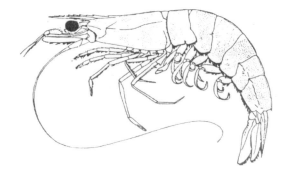

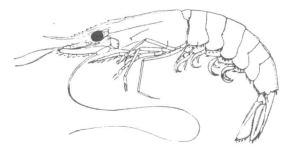

SPINY LOBSTER, MUD SPINY LOBSTER   Family *Palinuridae*
Panulirus polyphagus (Herbst)

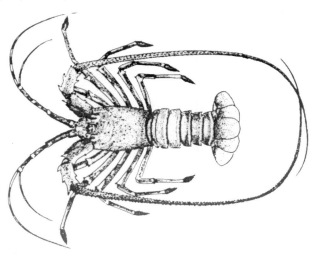

REMARKS Maximum length 40 cm, common length 30 cm. The biggest ones weigh about 20 kilos.

Distribution: from the coasts of Pakistan and India to S. E. Asian waters and north-west Australia.

CUISINE The spiny lobsters are of excellent quality. They are prepared as lobsters are, and just as good. I add

BU: kyauk-pazun
TH: kung mangkon
MA: udang karang
IN: udang barong
PH: banangan, banag
VI: tôm hum

here a recipe which is my own invention. Not everyone enjoys it; but to those like myself whom even the whiff of a distant durian renders ecstatic, it is sensationally good.

Cook a spiny lobster in the usual way. Let it cool and cut the meat into bite-size pieces.

Make a mayonnaise, using whatever is the best salad oil available, and introduce into it no more than a teaspoonful of the flesh of a durian, which you have previously worked into a purée. Mix this thoroughly into the mayonnaise, then add the pieces of spiny lobster.

Take two small pineapples and halve them lengthways. Cut out the flesh, reserving most of it for another occasion but incorporating a dozen or so cubes in the mayonnaise. Then fill the scooped out pineapples with the mayonnaise, dust the top with a very little black pepper, chill and serve.

PRONGHORN SPINY LOBSTER
Panulirus penicillatus
(Olivier)

Family *Palinuridae*

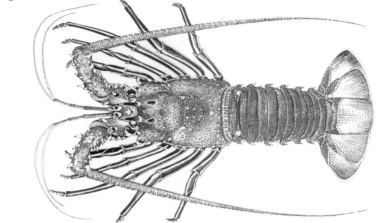

REMARKS This is the biggest and strongest of the spiny lobsters in the region, and maximum length is about 40 cm. It is dark in colour, brown or brown/green.

MA: udang karang
IN: udang barong
PH: banagan,
    kising-kising
    (general name)
VI: tôm hùm
JA: shima ise-ebi

Distribution: from the Red Sea and East Africa eastwards all the way to Japan, Hawaii, Samoa and further east to the west coast of America.

Another dark spiny lobster (usually purple/brown) is *P. longipes* (A. Milne Edwards), the Longlegged spiny lobster, which has striped legs in the West Pacific area and spotted legs in the Indian Ocean.

CUISINE See the preceding entry.

FOOTNOTE: I referred on page 131 to the question of killing lobsters and crabs humanely. I reproduce here the text of a short article in the *Times* of 24 October 1975 – as a matter of general interest rather than a recommendation that readers instal in their kitchens the apparatus recommended!

'Dr John R Baker, FRS, Reader in Cytology at Oxford University, announced yesterday that after two years of investigation in his spare time he has discovered the kindly way of killing crabs and lobsters.

'The apparatus of Dr. Baker's researches was on display in London, arranged by the Humane Education Centre, which provided about £2,000 towards his costs. It was a small metal and glass tank, with a flat metal plate at each end as electrodes, and connected to a 240-volt mains switch.

'The tank should be filled with a weak saline solution in which the animal is immersed and submitted to an electric shock which stunned and immobilized it, Dr Baker said. It was then ready to be boiled, painlessly, without regaining consciousness. It was right that we should try to ensure that crustacea were killed as humanely as possible, he said. Lobsters and crabs had quite highly developed nervous systems and in boiling water made vigorous movements for up to two minutes or longer, which could be interpreted as indicating that they were experiencing pain.'

PAINTED SPINY LOBSTER
Panulirus versicolor (Latreille)

Family *Palinuridae*

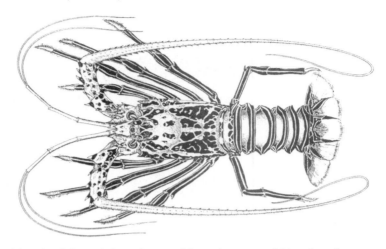

REMARKS This spiny lobster is just about as big as the preceding species. It has a distinctive colour scheme. The abdomen is green and has a series of dark bands running across it, each with a bright white line along its centre. The legs are also green or blue-green and are marked by white lines which run along their length.

MA: udang karang
IN: udang barong
PH: banagan, banag
VI: tôm hùm
HK: huk paak mun
    lung ha
JA: goshiki ebi

P. homarus (Linnaeus), the Scalloped spiny lobster is another greenish lobster, but less striking in appearance.

P. ornatus (Fabricius), the Ornate spiny lobster, on the other hand, is perhaps even more striking. The legs are banded in cream and maroon, the spines on the back of the body carapace are orange at the base and green at the tip, and the general effect is rather like that of a delicately coloured butterfly. This beautiful appearance is reflected in the Chinese name jin xiu long xia (brocade-beautiful lobster). This is a common species in Vietnam, but not one of the best to eat.

Distribution of *P. versicolor* is from the Red Sea and East Africa east to southern Japan, northern Australia and the Pacific Islands.

CUISINE See the entry on page 138.

FLATHEAD LOBSTER, SLIPPER LOBSTER Family *Scyllaridae*
Thenus orientalis (Lund)

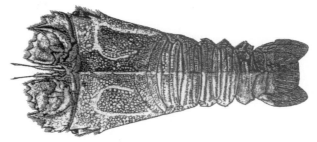

REMARKS Maximum length 25 cm.

The back is greenish-blue, the underside beige or yellowish. The legs do not appear in the drawings, as they are hidden under the body.

This is a gregarious creature, found in much the same sort of habitat as sea crabs and widely distributed in the region from the Red Sea and east coast of Africa eastwards to India, China, southern Japan, the Philippines and tropical Australia. In Australia it is officially known as 'Bay lobster' but has greater fame under the vernacular name 'Moreton Bay bug'.

Ibacus ciliatus (von Siebold) is a similar species, rather broader in the beam and shorter (maximum length 23 cm) than the other, and easily recognised by its bright red back, which gives it the name kung kradan deng in Thailand.

CUISINE The meat of the slipper lobster is not quite up to the standard of good prawns or spiny lobsters, but is nonetheless well worth eating. It may be prepared generally according to recipes for crabs or prawns.

BU: kyauk-pa-zun
TH: kung kradan, kung hin
MA: udang lobok
IN: udang pasir
PH: pitik-pitik
CA: bangkang pak
HK: pei pa ha
JA: uchiwa-ebi-modoki

MANTIS SHRIMP, SEA LOCUST
Harpiosquilla raphidea (Fabricius)

Family *Squillidae*

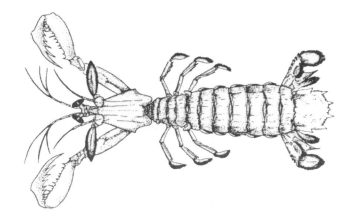

REMARKS Maximum length 35 cm. This is the largest mantis shrimp in the region.

The back is greenish yellow, with purplish tints round the edges, especially near the tail.

The name mantis shrimp is given because of the resemblance between the powerful second pair of thoracic legs, with their jack-knife mechanism for seizing and slicing up prey, and the first thoracic legs of the insect known as the praying mantis.

BU: ye kin
TH: kang takaten
MA: kamun,
    udang lobok
PH: tatampal,
    palpatok
HK: taan ha, lei
    lui ha

These creatures like a muddy bottom, in which they dig themselves holes (from which, however, they emerge in stormy weather lest the mouths of the holes be blocked as a result of the turbulence). They prowl up on to beaches at night in search of food.

Although *H. raphidea* is the largest species of mantis shrimp, it is not the dominant species in the markets. *H. harpax* (De Haan) (maximum length about 20 cm) enjoys that distinction; and the still smaller *Oratosquilla nepa* is second to it in Thailand.

CUISINE Good fare. In Thailand it is customary to boil them, remove the shell and extract the meat which is then dipped in nam pla before being eaten. Or boil them in water to which nam pla has been added, then keep them for a day before eating them.

H. raphidea is a favourite in Japan, where it is known as sako.

The meat may also be pickled in nam pla and then eaten with rice or rice soup. The Chinese like this last dish very much and Chinese rice soup stalls often have these mantis shrimps on hand.

Crabs

I regard crabs as an under-rated food. People will pay much more for anything described as a lobster or prawn; but crabs, for all their low price and plebeian reputation, are often just as good. Fortunately, S. E. Asia is one region where, except for the international hotels and other such haunts, attitudes to foods are unsnobbish and straightforward (except for the weird tendency of the Chinese and others wrongly to ascribe aphrodisiac properties to many foodstuffs, the price of which is thus unwarrantably forced upwards); and the crab therefore holds the place of honour which is its due.

Crabs are often bought cooked. Otherwise they should always be bought alive (preference being given to those which feel heavy for their size) and cooked in boiling salted water for 5 to 20 minutes according to their size. Before cooking the crabs be sure to plug any holes in their carapaces (body or legs) with a compressed piece of bread or a wad of sticky rice. Once the cooking is done let them cool in the cooking water, then remove them and begin the tedious but rewarding business of extracting all the edible meat. First twist off the legs and claws. They are to be cracked and the meat taken out. Then, with the crab on its back, prise the body out. Discard gut and gills, but nothing else. Clean up the shell and return the meat to it in any number of ways either as a cold dish or for heating in the oven or under the grill. Of course small crabs will not be given this treatment but will go into a soup.

The Burmese have an interesting technique for catching crabs. They take the head of a chicken, shave it and attach it to a strong string. When the tide comes in, this is lowered into the water. A crab will try to bite the chicken head, but will have difficulty in doing so. It will grip the head tightly while continuing its efforts. While it is in this posture and oblivious to all else it may be lifted out of the water.

There are many more crabs in S. E. Asia than are catalogued here. One species which is prized by the cognoscenti in Thailand belongs to the genus **Pilumnus** and may be bought from oyster farmers since it likes to live around the poles used for the cultivation of oysters. This crab, which has a purplish black or purplish yellow back, has no swimming legs and four pairs of walking legs. The claws are short but powerful. Some Thai people believe that once they have sunk into a man's flesh the crab will not relax its grip until he hears a peal of thunder. The Thai name is pu bai (dumb crab).

Another crab which deserves a mention here is **Carpilius maculatus** (Linnaeus), the Spotted reef crab; its salient characteristic is more precisely indicated by another English name, Red-spotted crab.

However, although the species are so numerous, and offer good opportunities to the gastronomic explorer, the varieties brought regularly to market are few in number and are all presented in the following pages.

On the difficult question of how to kill crabs humanely please see pages 131 and 139.

Recipes for crab are given on pages 232, 244, 253, 262, 292, 312 and 332.

BEETLE CRAB, HORSESHOE CRAB
Tachypleus gigas (Müller)

Family *Xiphosuridae*

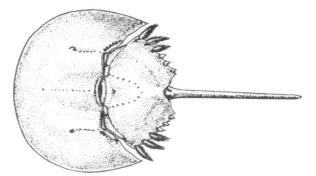

REMARKS The members of the family *Xiphosuridae* are creatures of great antiquity, crabs which bear a large and rounded outer shell as a form of protection. They have small black eyes, but the males are reputedly blind and depend on the females, to whose waists they cling when moving around. One female may have a string of dozens of males in tow.

BU: be-la
TH: maeng da
MA: keroncho,
    belangkas
IN: mimi, ikan mimi

T. gigas, known as the Giant beetle crab, has an outer shell which may measure 30 to 40 cm across and a relatively longer spike at the rear. The male can be distinguished from the female by his noticeably abbreviated front claws. In this species the male is reputed never to leave go of the female at all. The Thai name for a pimp is maeng da and is probably derived from the habits of this crab, always riding around on the back of a female.

Carcinoscorpius rotundicauda is a smaller species (20 to 25 cm across).

The beetle crabs, which are caught in special nets or bamboo traps, are found in shallow water near beaches. They lay eggs in the sand, making a hollow and depositing the eggs therein and covering them up. They hatch after thirty days or so.

CUISINE The eggs are a delicacy. Open the abdomen in order to find them. Take care to discard completely intestine, stomach and excrement, since they can cause dizziness if consumed. (Take care also to avoid completely a related species – distinguished by its small hairy red head – which is not to be eaten at all, as it is highly dangerous.) The eggs can be fried. The meat and gill-leaves are also good, and may be prepared by the addition of sugar and coconut or incorporated in a pineapple soup. This is a favourite dish in Thailand. The crabs are also sold ready boiled or pickled with rice.

The eggs of *T. gigas* are twice as big as those of the smaller species, and are very good fried. A fresh specimen will yield a lot of light blue blood, which should be mixed with the eggs before they are fried.

MASK CRAB, CRUCIFIX CRAB

Charybdis feriatus (Linnaeus)

Family *Portunidae*

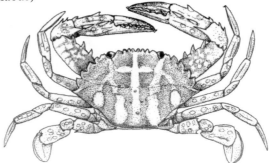

REMARKS Maximum width 15 (or even 20) cm.

This species has distinctive markings on its carapace which account for the Thai name which echoes the Thai name for a zebra. These markings are also thought to resemble a mask, or to suggest a Franciscan friar (the light brown colour and the cross). The second Chinese name means 'animal-faced' – yet another simile.

BU: ga-nan
TH: pu laai
MA: ketam salib
IN: rajungan karang
PH: san francisco
HK: hung haai (red crab)
CH: ban wen xun, shou mian xun

There are several other species in the genus, mostly about the same size as this. But the most interesting one gastronomically is a small species (pu takoy in Thai) which measures no more than 6 or 7 cm across, has a light green carapace and red spots around its pincers, and frequents river mouths. These little crabs are sold in Thailand in bunches of 30 or so.

In Malaysia there is apparently a superstition connected with this crab which discourages people from eating it.

CUISINE The little ones referred to immediately above may be treated in several ways. They are suitable for being pickled in fish sauce. They can be cooked and eaten with rice or rice soup. And, for those in search of an unusual snack, they can be coated with sugar and eaten thus.

MANGROVE CRAB, SERRATED CRAB   Family *Portunidae*
Scylla serrata (Forskål)

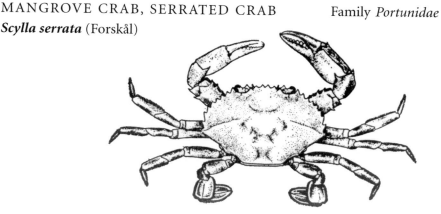

REMARKS The carapace may be up to 20 cm across. The weight may be over 1 kilo. Because of its size it is sometimes called Giant mud crab.

There are two views about crabs of the genus **Scylla** in the Indo-Pacific region. One is that they are all of this species, but vary in colour and in some minor characteristics. The other (for which see the next page) is that there are several species. Those who take the latter view reserve the specific name **serrata** for those crabs which are reddish-brown or near-black in colour, unmarked by spots and most commonly found in mangrove swamps. The pincers are bright red.

Crabs of the genus **Scylla** are swimming crabs. Whether one counts them as one or several, they are the most important edible crabs of S. E. Asia.

BU: lamu-ga-nan
TH: pu thaleh*, pu thong daeng nam teuy**
MA: ketam batu
IN: kepiting
PH: alimangong palaisdaan
VI: con cua lua
HK: chang haai
CH: xun, qing xie

CUISINE An excellent crab. The claws of the male, bigger and meatier than those of the female, are particularly good. The meat may be used in any of the standard ways for preparing crab.

In Taiwan females are kept in special ponds while their eggs develop, so that they can be sold at a high price when fully 'ripe'.

---

* sea crab, a general name.
** nam means thorn and teuy denotes a certain plant.

Other 'serrated' crabs

Family *Portunidae*

REMARKS As I mentioned on the previous page, some experts believe that there are several species in the genus **Scylla**. This is certainly in accordance with the views of fishermen, for example in the Philippines and Vietnam and Thailand. In all these countries there are different vernacular names for crabs which display different colourations.

Of course, such differences and others less obvious to the lay eye are not necessarily sufficient to warrant classifying these crabs into separate species. This is the view taken by Mlle Guinot after her skilful collation of material from the Philippines and Vietnam. However, it does seem clear that there is a broad distinction to be made between crabs answering to the description of **Scylla serrata** on the previous page and certain other crabs which have spots, which are greenish in hue and which live in the sea or estuaries rather than in mangrove swamps. **S. paramamosain** Estampador, the Green mud crab, is the name ascribed to one such, which has a pale green carapace and pale yellow-brown tips to its pincers. It is bulik or banhanwin in the Philippines and con cua chuoi (banana crab) or con cua trăng (white crab) in Vietnam. It seems likely that this is the species or variety known as pu khao si nam tan in Thailand (of which a drawing appears below); and that the Thai also apply the name pu thong lang to it and to the related **S. tranquebarica**, which is of a grey-green or dark green colour with purple tints (whence its English name, Purple mud crab). This last crab is parabanhanwin in the Philippines and con cua sen (green crab) in Vietnam. Finally, there is the species **S. olivacea** (Herbst), the Orange mud crab, which is slightly smaller than the other three.

CUISINE These are all good crabs for eating. Boil and serve with nam pla (fish sauce), as in Thailand. Use the meat in rice soup. Cook in the Chinese fashion with shallots or bamboo shoots. Or, perhaps best of all, deep fry the claws (whole) and then pick out the meat.

BLUE SWIMMING CRAB, FLOWER CRAB   Family *Portunidae*
Portunus pelagicus (Linnaeus)

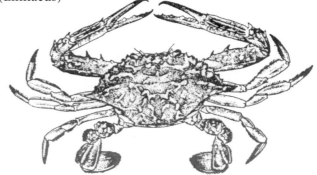

REMARKS The carapace measures 15 to 20 cm across (rather less for the female).

The carapace of the male is light blue in colour with white spots, that of the female brown with white spots.

This crab moults, and in its soft state (i.e. just after it has shed the outworn carapace) it can be eaten whole without the usual cracking of claws and so on, there being nothing hard to crack.

P. sanguinolentus (Herbst), the Three-spot swimming crab, is a related species which bears three distinctive purple spots on its greenish-yellow carapace. In Chinese it may be called san xing suo zi xie (Three-star shuttle crab). It is pu dao (star crab) in Thailand; and saam dim haai at Hong Kong. It is shown below.

UAE: gabgoob
   (general name)
BU: ga-nan
TH: pu ma (horse
   crab)
MA: ketam renjong
IN: rajungan
PH: alimasag
VI: con cua nghê
HK: far haai
CH: yuan hai suo
   zi xie

CUISINE A good species. The meat may be fried or used in rice soup, following the practice of the inhabitants of Chonburi in Thailand. (Brown garlic in hot oil, put it in a cooking pot with rice, pour hot water in, add the crab meat and cook it gently for 20 minutes or more.) The crab meat may also be 'candied' in palm sugar syrup and eaten as a snack (another Thai practice).

MANGROVE CRAB

Family *Grapsidae*

Episesarma spp.

BU: ga-nan
TH: pu samae
PH: damuko
HK: haa la
CH: hong xian li
    ming xie

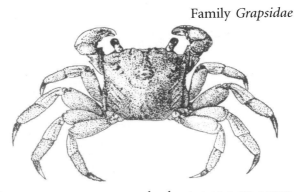

REMARKS Small crabs, whose carapaces measure only about 4 or 5 cm across, belonging to the sub-family *Sesarminae*, members of which are often called Vinegar crabs because they are sold pickled in vinegar. The species illustrated is probably **E. palawanense** or **E. versicolor** but exact identification is not easy.

    The colour may be blackish purple (e.g. for **E. versicolor**, known as the Violet vinegar crab) and the legs can be hairy. These crabs live in mangrove swamps and have the ability to climb the trees at high tide. Fishermen catch the mangrove crabs by picking them off the trees, often at night, with their gloved hands. They then cover them with salt and eat them the next day.

CUISINE Besides being sold in pickled form these crabs may be prepared in various other ways, e.g. cooked and served with nam prik and tamarind, or with a simple dressing of lime juice. Alternatively, pound the meat with tamarind and add a little coconut oil to the mixture thus formed.

MONKEY-GOD CRAB, FLOWER MOON CRAB

Family *Calappidae*

Matuta planipes (Fabricius)

BU: ga-nan
TH: pu haniman
HK: fa long haai

REMARKS Another small crab with a carapace measuring about 7 cm across. Its colour is yellow or banana-leaf green, with a black or purple pattern imprinted all over. A long spine projects from each side of the carapace. This crab is known from certain islands around Vietnam and in the Gulf of Siam. Haniman in the Thai name means monkey-god.

CUISINE Remove the carapace, flour the body and fry it. May also be pickled.

SEA CICADA

Family *Hippidae*

Hippa asiatica (Milne Edwards)

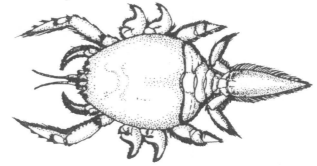

REMARKS The length of this strange and engaging little creature is from 3 to 6 cm.

TH: chak chan thaley

IN: undur-undur

It is more like a crab than a prawn, but the layman may be excused for wondering or thinking that it is some sort of marine beetle.

The colour is whiteish yellow all over. Note the two antennae, and that only one pair of legs sticks out from under the carapace.

The sea cicadas are best sought after high tide when the waters have swept them up on to the beach. But they must be sought quickly, for their habit is to dig themselves holes in the wet sand at high speed, and they are difficult to extract when they have once interred themselves. Phuket in Thailand is famous for them. I was told there that the Royal Family of Thailand order them in large quantities for state occasions, even 20,000 at a time.

CUISINE A delicacy, and quite an expensive one. Cut off the head, remove the carapace, dip the body in flour or beaten egg and then deep-fry it. The advice which I had before visiting Phuket was that they must be served with Sriracha sauce – nothing else would go with them quite so well. I later discovered that 'sriracha' refers to *Molluga pentaphylla*, a slender herb found from India to New Caledonia. However, when I ate the sea cicadas in Phuket I was offered some 'jungle honey' as an accompaniment and found that it suited the crunchy little morsels to perfection.

Catalogue of Molluscs and Other Edible Sea Creatures

Molluscs

Molluscs are soft-bodied, unsegmented animals of remarkably varied appearance. Various classifications into orders have been recommended for them. So far as the edible marine molluscs are concerned, I like the basic division into **Gastropoda** (creatures living in single shells) **Lamellibranchiata** (bivalves, creatures living in double, hinged shells) and **Cephalopoda** (animals like the squid and octopus), and will examine on this basis and in this order the more important species of Asian waters.

Let me begin, however, by saying that, when I first wrote this book, relatively little work had been done on the edible molluscs of Asia. No-one had established what are all the species of octopus and squid which appear in the markets; nor was there any proper list of the bivalves or single shells which are regularly consumed in the area. Fortunately, we now have the benefit of yet another important publication of the FAO, namely the admirable survey of *The Living Marine Resources of the Western Central Pacific* by Carpenter and Niem (see Bibliography – the relevant volumes are I and II). This section of my catalogue is now therefore less tentative. In any case, I can draw comfort from the line of Horace which Risso, the ichthyologist of Nice, once quoted in respect of his own work: 'Est quadam prodire tenus, si non datur ultra'.

Single Shells (Gasteropods)

These are creatures which live in single shells (i.e. not double, hinged ones such as the bivalves possess). They do not constitute a very distinguished collection, from the gastronomic point of view, but the abalone is good and the others catalogued are all worth eating.

HORN SHELL
Cerithidea obtusa (Lamarck)

Family *Potamididae*

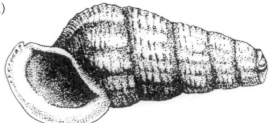

REMARKS Maximum length 6 cm.

The shape of the shell may be regarded, according to the nature of the viewer, as that of an ice-cream cone or that of a temple spire. The colour is red with white or orange, when the shell is clean; but when they are caught they are usually muddy and look almost black.

Telescopium telescopium (Linnaeus) is another horn shell large enough (11 cm) to be worth eating. It may be called the Telescope snail.

BU: kha-yu-zedi
  tjaeng
TH: hoy chup cheng
MA: siput balitong
PH: suso, bayungon
HK: tsim mei law

CUISINE Clean the outside of the shell thoroughly and cut off the pointed tip. Boil for a few minutes. When the shell has cooked sufficiently, place the wide end between your lips and suck. The tender meat will then plop into your mouth.

SAND SNAIL
Natica tigrina (Röding)

Family *Naticidae*

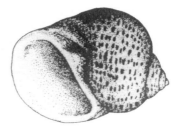

REMARKS The length of the shell is only 4 to 5 cm. The colour is white and yellow, which probably accounts for the alternative name Tiger Moon snail.

A similar species, with less of a whorl to the shell and white all over, is known as hoy ta kai khao in Thailand. The shells are used in gambling games, both as counters and in a game which involves looking at a pile of them and betting on the number being odd or even.

BU: khway
TH: hoy ta kai
MA: tekuyong
  timba
PH: kuhol

CUISINE As for the preceding species. It is not, however, necessary to cut off the tip of the shell, if the sucking routine does not appeal to you. Once these ones have been boiled a tap of the shell will dislodge the meat.

LIMPET
Family *Patellidae*

Cellana nigrolineata (Reeve)

REMARKS This limpet may measure as much as 8 cm. The shell is black and yellow, the creature inside it white.

CUISINE These limpets are just as delicious as the abalone. Once they are cooked (by roasting, some recommend) the meat will drop out of the shell quite easily. However, they are not often marketed.

BU: ami-noe,
si-mee-khwat
TH: lin thaleh
IN: (tiiam batu)
VI: oc cuu khong
HK: cheung
kwan mo

ABALONE, ORMER, EAR SHELL
Family *Haliotidae*

Haliotis asinina Linnaeus

REMARKS Maximum length about 12 cm. The species, which is sometimes referred to as the Donkey's Ear abalone (matching its specific name, *asinina*) is brownish black, with white spots all over.

  H. ovina (Gmelin) is similar but larger.

CUISINE The large muscular foot of the abalone is a well-known delicacy of the Pacific coast of America, and is also esteemed in Europe. It is not very widely available in S. E.

BU: baun
TH: hoy khong
thaleh
MA: siput
IN: lapar kenyang
PH: lapas
HK: pau yue
CH: er bao

Asia (except in canned form), but is likely to become more so as time passes. It is very good in the Chinese dish called pao hu, or bau hu (a name which seems sometimes to be applied to the abalone itself in Thailand). Thai cooks usually make soup from the abalone or fry it with bamboo shoots. See also page 277.

TOP SHELL

Trochus niloticus Linnaeus

BU: kha-yu-zedi
TH: hoy ud (camel)
MA: siput lolak
PH: susong dalaga
HK: sek tao law
CH: gong luo

Family *Trochidae*

REMARKS Maximum length 15 cm. This is the most economically important gasteropod in the tropical west Pacific, serving both as a food and as a source of mother-of-pearl material.

The colour of the shell is black and white. When it is polished a reddish hue appears, but if it is polished further this gives way to the underlying 'pearl'. The shells have some value, not only for ornamental purposes, but also because grinding them up produces a bronze pigment.

Zedi in the Burmese name means shrine, in allusion to the resemblance in shape between this shell and certain pagoda domes. The English name has of course been given because the shape of the shell resembles a child's top.

CUISINE These creatures are to be boiled. The meat may then be extracted and fried or used to make a kind of salad or soup. It may also be dried.

SPIDER CONCH

Lambis lambis (Linnaeus)

Family *Strombidae*

This shell makes a splendid paper weight. It, or rather its inhabitant, is also eaten, mostly by fishermen and other coastal people. The shell may measure 15 cm across and can usually be found in beds of brown algae. The Malay name is rangak betul and the Indonesian names are tedong-tedong and jari-jari.

ROCK SHELL

Family *Muricidae*

Chicoreus ramosus (Linnaeus)

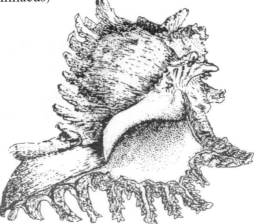

REMARKS A large shell, measuring 25 cm or more.

The outside of the shell is whiteish grey, the inside pinkish. The whole thing is rather beautiful, although the Thai vernacular name ngo is that of the ugly prince in a fable. Perhaps I have been influenced by my childhood admiration for a specimen which my great uncle Willie brought home to Glasgow from the Orient, and which I still have. I do not know whether Willie ate the contents; but the instructions below suggest that the uninitiated would not find it easy to do so.

BU: kha-yu
TH: hoy ngo
HK: gai kwan law

CUISINE The meat is good, but you are unlikely to find it in the markets and have to know how to extract it from the shell. Thai practice is to put the whole thing in the fire until the creature expires, then to remove it and shake or otherwise dislodge the cooked contents. (I have not had the opportunity to try this and am not entirely convinced by the advice.)

BAILER SHELL
Melo melo (Lightfoot)

Family *Volutidae*

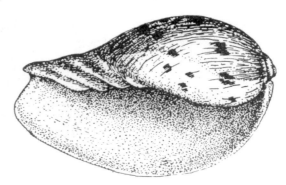

REMARKS Another large gasteropod, with a shell which
may measure 27 cm.

BU: kha-yu-ohn
TH: hoy tan
MA: siput
HK: chaan law
CH: gua luo

   The colour is yellow and red with purplish black spots.
The inhabitant of this striking shell is itself black with
yellow lines, rather like an exotic snail.

   'The flaring apertures of bailer shells make them espe-
cially useful, as their name suggests, for the quick bailing of small boats and
canoes caught in tropical squalls. They are also used in native markets as scoops
for sugar, flour and salt.' (Mary Saul)

CUISINE Again, you are unlikely to find this species in the market. But the fishermen know its merits and keep any they catch. They may be boiled, fried with
vegetables, or roasted and then dipped in nam pla before being eaten.

CONCH, WING SHELL
Strombus canarium Linnaeus

Family *Strombidae*

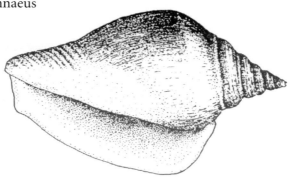

REMARKS Maximum length about 10 cm.

The thick and heavy shell is roughly heart-shaped. It is pale brown or yellowish white in colour, marked lengthways by alternating brown and white lines.

BU: kha-yu-thin
MA: gonggong
IN: kede-kede
PH: balakwit, palagsi
HK: cheung man law

CUISINE 'They are steamed or boiled in the shell or simple baked over a fire, and the meat is generally removed by pulling it out by the hard cuticle or prying it out with a sharp tool. The flesh has a characteristic taste and when eaten plain gives an after-effect that increases one's craving for drinking water.' (Seale)

WHEEL SHELL, BUTTON TOP
Umbonium vestiarium Linnaeus

Family *Trochidae*

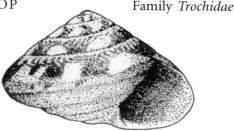

PH: kaligay
HK: tao law

REMARKS Maximum diameter 1.5 cm. The colours are variable and striking.

Another interesting species in this family is the Pagoda prickly-winkle, ***Tectarius pagodus***, which has a wide distribution in S.E. Asian waters and is locally collected for food. It is also collected for its shell which, as the drawing below shows, has a remarkable resemblance to a pagoda. Maximum length 6.5 cm.

CUISINE These little molluscs are worth eating. They may be boiled or steamed. Because the flesh is small and difficult to extract, the tradition in the Philippines is that the vendor gives the buyer thorns of *Acacia pennata* with which to pry the meat out of the shell.

WHELK, CONCH
Pugilina cochlidium (Linnaeus)

Family *Melongenidae*

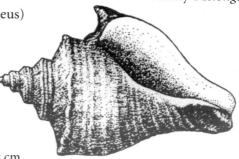

MA: nonam,
    unam
PH: kalaunghuga

REMARKS Maximum length 15 cm.

This big aggressive mollusc lives alone. It likes to take up station by an oyster and waits until the latter opens its shell, whereupon the whelk thrusts in its long tough snout and that is the end of the oyster.

The shell is yellowish or dark brown in colour and is covered with a hairy epidermis which gives a velvety effect. The colour of the aperture is orange or yellow.

Conch, by the way, is a general name applied to most large single shells.

CUISINE Steam or boil or just put on a fire for a while. When the meat is cooked, pry it out; or remove it by breaking the shell.

Bivalves

Edible bivalves are numerous and classified in many orders and families. Some of them, for example the oyster, are excellent and well known. Others have a less wide appeal. Many are eaten raw. The species listed in the following pages are intended to include at least the majority of those likely to be found on sale in Asian markets; but the subject has not been studied much and I shall not be surprised to learn that I have left out some important species!

One thing can be said; that most of the bivalves which are known and prized in Europe or North America have close relations in S. E. Asia. If this little section of the catalogue helps to illuminate such equivalences or relationships it will have served its purpose.

I should mention here that the famous 'clovisse' of the Mediterranean belongs to the genus ***Tapes*** which is also represented in S. E. Asia, for example by a little clam called kha-yu-pan-khat in Burma, where it is used (as in the Mediterranean) to make a good soup, or baked or fried.

Of course some bivalves are exploited for reasons other than eating them. The translucent shells of the windowpane oyster, ***Placuna placenta***, are the subject of a profitable and charming industry in the Philippines, where the material is fashioned into every imaginable kind of pretty object. And the pearl oyster (catalogued on page 170, since it is edible) is used for the culture of pearls, which are produced by the insertion, with surgical skill, of a nucleus (of a special stone, or plastic) into the creature, on which in the course of time it deposits a layer of the pearly material. But here we are concerned only with edibility. In this context I should add that in the Mergui area of Burma ***P. placenta*** is baked whole until the shell cracks, then eaten with lime juice, or you can extract the meat first and then fry it. The Chinese (who call it hai yue, sea moon) recommend eating the white central muscle, but not to boil it, just to immerse it in hot chicken broth.

BLOOD CLAM / COCKLE, ARKSHELL
Anadara granosa

Family *Arcidae*

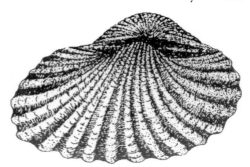

REMARKS Maximum length 9 cm.

The general colour of the shell is brownish black, but it is whiteish near the hinge and there are little white projections along the ridge lines.

Scapharca inaequivalvis (Bruguière) is less common, but often taken with the preceding species. As the scientific name implies, its shells are noticeably asymmetrical.

Both species, and a number of others belonging to the same genus, are known as Blood or Bloody clams, since when they open after being boiled briefly they exude a red-brown juice which looks like blood. The red colour of the meat is apparently an impediment to sales, but even so this bivalve is of great importance commercially in Malaysia and Indonesia.

BU: jin
TH: hoy khreng/ krang
MA/IN: kerang
PH: batotoy
VI: sò huyêt
HK: hum
CH: xue han

CUISINE These cockles are said to be especially rich in iron and thus beneficial as well as delicious.

They may be prepared initially by putting them briefly in boiling water. When the creatures have been taken from their shells they may be fried or used in curries or eaten right away with a sweet and sour sauce (vinegar, a little garlic and chilli, soy sauce). Alternatively they can be left to ferment in soy sauce, or salted.

Chinese authors have recommended the consumption of arkshells as an appetiser and an aphrodisiac. It is perhaps with the latter aspect in mind that one of them insists that after eating a number of arkshells one must go on at once to have a proper meal before doing anything else. The penalty for failing to observe this rule is an unpleasant dryness of the mouth.

GIANT CLAM
Tridacna gigas (Linnaeus)

Family *Tridacnidae*

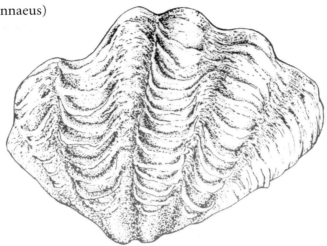

REMARKS This giant among clams can measure as much as 1 metre across and weigh several hundred kilos! But a measurement of 40 to 50 cm is more common.

BU: kya-let-wah
TH: hoy mu sua
MA: kimah, gebang
IN: kimah
PH: taklobo
HK: wan man ho
CH: da che qu

The colour of the shell is black and white. The body within the shell displays many colours – white, yellow, purple and blackish red – and looks like an exotic flower when the clam opens its shell in order to feed.

A smaller giant is **T. maxima** (Röding) which has a dark brown shell. Its Thai name is hoy mu meo, meaning cat's claw clam (the name for **T. gigas** means tiger's claw clam).

These great bivalves live in water from 1 to 20 metres deep, preferably very salty and often in the vicinity of islands or other rocky areas. The Salon tribe in the Mergui area of Burma are among those who are expert in diving for and collecting them. They have been a regular food for people in S. E. Asia and the Pacific Islands for millennia.

CUISINE Surprisingly, the whole of these huge creatures is edible except the kidney. The mantle (meat on the border of the shells) is good to eat. It may be boiled; or fried with curry paste and chilli peppers in the Thai style. It is a good idea to use strong added flavours which will mask or at least compete with its rather strong fish smell.

The adductor muscle, which is of course huge, is the part most prized. It may be sliced, boiled and dried and then used in soups.

OTTER SHELL

Family *Mactridae*

Lutraria sp.

REMARKS Maximum length 10 cm. The shell is purple, as   BU: gone
indicated by the Thai name, but turns white when dry.   TH: hoy muong

This clam lives in muddy or sandy areas where the water is   PH: bantalan
not too salty. The shells can be used for making lime.   HK: hin

This information and the photograph on which the drawing is based are contained in an admirable manual on Thai seafood published in 1969 (see under
Department of Fisheries in the Bibliography), Since then, the species has probably
been reclassified in the genus **Mactra**.

CUISINE The meat is tender and good to eat. The clams can be dried after being
boiled and extracted from their shells. (The liquid should be saved, as it makes a
good soup base.) Or fry with shallots.

TROUGH SHELL, HEN CLAM

Family *Mactridae*

Mactra mera Reeve

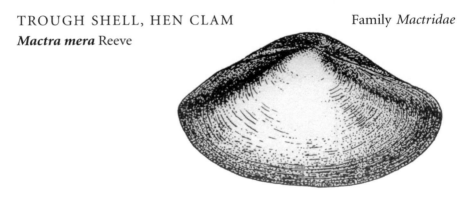

REMARKS These large clams may measure over 8 cm.   BU: shut

The shells, which have been described as triangularly   MA: kepah merah
egg-shaped, are smooth and shining, a rich purplish-   PH: katakao
brown in colour, deep violet at the umbos and marked by   VI: ngheu
fine white rays. The inside is smooth and violet.   HK: hin

CUISINE Some Filipinos think that these clams are a match for oysters in quality.
They are to be steamed or parboiled in their shells, after which the broth can be
served as a soup and the meat either plain or with a sauce. There is a Chinese
tradition that intoxicated persons can be revived by feeding them trough shells.

SUNSET SHELL, MACOMA SHELL
Soletellina diphos (Linnaeus)

Family *Psammobiidae*

REMARKS A large species which may be as long as 12 cm. The shells are often purplish-white or white tinged with pink (hence the name 'sunset').

These clams inhabit sandy shores on the open coast, or sheltered bays, and are largely stationary in habit, burrowing just below the surface.

BU: shut
MA: bagit
PH: paros,
   parosparosan,
   batitis
CH: xi dao she

CUISINE In the Philippines these are among the most highly valued bivalves. They are steamed or parboiled in the shell to produce an excellent broth. The meat is eaten in soup or chowder. A favourite preparation is Sinobukan, made thus. 'Fresh parosparosan are washed and "floated" in a basin of water in order that they may free themselves of sand or dirt contained in their intestinal tract. As soon as they open their shells, boiling water is poured into the basin to kill and partially cook the animal. All the water is now drained off, care being taken not to separate the valves so as to provide a handle to each cooked clam. The diner now picks up a paros by its empty valve and before consuming it soaks the meat in vinegar sauce seasoned with salt, sometimes with finely chopped onions, a dash of white pepper and a little salt.' (Talavera and Faustino, *Edible Mollusks of Manila*)

SURF CLAM   Family *Veneridae*
Paphia undulata (Born)

REMARKS Maximum length 6.5 cm, common length 5 cm.
   The colour of the shell is yellowish-brown with dark brown markings. The shell is concentrically ridged.
   This clam is found in waters up to 8 metres deep. It lives in holes which it makes for itself.

CUISINE A very good clam, which can be used for soup, or fried or in a salad. Be sure to keep and use the liquid obtained when you steam them open.
   This clam is common in the Thai markets, and may be had dried for use in soups.

BU: yout-thwa
TH: hoy lai,
   hoy huaan
MA: remis
PH: halaan
   chichirica
HK: hin

RIDGED SAND CLAM   Family *Veneridae*
Circe scripta (Linnaeus)

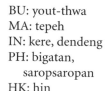

REMARKS The maximum length of the ridged sand clam is just under 5 cm. This one has a reddish yellow and whiteish shell, which (like the shells of clams in this genus) is radiately ridged.
   These clams like to inhabit beaches exposed to surf or strong tidal currents. Each has a large muscular foot with which it can anchor itself to the chosen spot.

BU: yout-thwa
MA: tepeh
IN: kere, dendeng
PH: bigatan,
   saropsaropan
HK: hin

CUISINE Excellent clams, which may be steamed open in the usual way. The broth is very good.

WAVED SAND CLAM
Anomalacardia squamosa (Linnaeus)

Family *Veneridae*

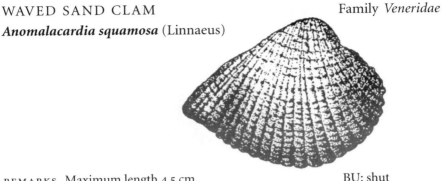

REMARKS Maximum length 4.5 cm.

This clam has a shell which is radiately ridged with concentric undulations on the ridges, giving the effect of latticed sculpture. The colour is whiteish.

Placamen tiara (Dillwyn) also has a whiteish shell, rayed with purple.

The waved sand clams are similar in habits and other respects to the ridged sand clams.

BU: shut
PH: butil, kanturi, moran
HK: hin

CUISINE As for the preceding species. Burmese of the Mergui area make a good clam soup with these clams, but may also bake them, fry them or preserve them by salting. (Powdered shells, by the way, make good duck- or chicken-food.)

VENUS SHELL, ASIATIC HARD CLAM
Meretrix meretrix (Linnaeus)

Family *Veneridae*

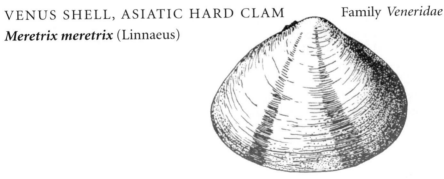

REMARKS Maximum length 7 cm. The colour of the shell is a lovely yellowish-brown and it is smooth.

A species known as **M. lusoria** (Röding) was formerly recognized, but has now been synonymized with **M. meretrix**. It is hard to be sure that one has sorted these clams out correctly. There are others too. One, a Venus shell, is white in colour and is appreciated in Thailand under the name hoy eipuk, but I have not been able to establish its scientific identity.

BU: shut
TH: hoy talap lai
MA: kepah, kepah gading
IN: (bubuel)
HK: hin
CH: wen kuo

CUISINE Purge them in salt water for several hours, then steam them open, taking care to reserve and use the liquor. The Chinese use these clams in soups.

WEDGE SHELL, BEAN CLAM

Donax faba Gmelin

Family *Donacidae*

REMARKS These are small bivalves, no more than 2.5 cm across.

The shells are relatively thick, almost triangular or wedge-shaped, and quite hard to open. The front shell is striated in white, buff, yellow and black. In the Philippines, specimens are likely to be greyish or whiteish pink.

BU: shut
TH: hoy siap
MA: remis
PH: alamis
HK: hin

These creatures like to inhabit sandy areas washed by the tides. They are closely related to a Mediterranean species which the French call olive and the Italians tellina; and this Mediterranean species is held by many to make the finest of all bivalve soups.

CUISINE The practice in Thailand is to boil these little clams briefly and then to pickle them in soy sauce or fish sauce; and they are very good thus.

I propose, however, using them to make Zuppa di Telline, as follows. Heat ½ wineglassful of olive oil in a large, deep pan, let a clove of garlic take colour in it, then discard the garlic. Add 2 tablespoons of tomato purée, diluted with water, or some tinned cooking tomatoes. If you wish, add also a teaspoonful of finely chopped red chilli pepper or a sprinkling of cayenne pepper. Cook for about 5 minutes, then add chopped parsley and 2 kilos of wedge shells, which you have carefully washed beforehand. Wait for the shells to open, moving them around as necessary so that the ones on top do not take too long. Make toast. Soon after all the shells are open pour them and the soup over the pieces of toast.

SCALLOP, ASIAN MOON SCALLOP
Amusium pleuronectes (Linnaeus)

Family *Pectinidae*

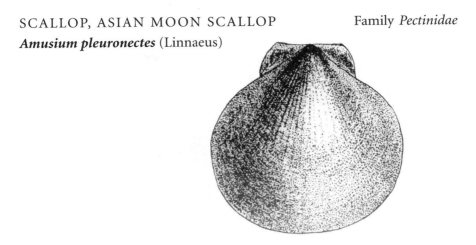

REMARKS This scallop attains a length of 10 cm.

The upper shell is reddish black in colour, marked with red lines (from which the age of the scallop may be calculated). The lower shell is white, sometimes with black spots.

These scallops like fairly deep water, through which they propel themselves by opening and closing their shells.

Of the Thai names cited, the first is the correct one, the second a popular sobriquet which shows what strange things can happen in linguistic practice. The Shell Company, which is prominent in Thailand as in so many other countries, has for its emblem a representation of a scallop shell. Noticing the likeness, Thai people have taken to naming the scallop after the company!

BU: yout-thwa
TH: hoy phat, hoy shell
IN: kipas-kipas
PH: abaniko, kapis
HK: hung mao gan
CH: ri yue shen*

CUISINE The excellence of the scallop has not always been appreciated in the region. However, a brisk demand for scallops from hotels and restaurants catering for Americans and Europeans has put that right.

Having found no special S. E. Asian way of preparing scallops I suggest instead making Coquilles Saint-Jacques à la Provençale. Slice each of the cleaned white muscles into two and season them with salt, pepper and lemon juice. Then sprinkle them lightly with flour and fry them pale golden on both sides in a mixture of olive oil and butter. Next, add the corals and plenty of chopped garlic and parsley. Shake the pan well to mix everything up; and continue cooking for another two or three minutes only.

* 'ri yue' means 'sun and moon'.

OYSTER   Family *Ostreidae*
Crassostrea gigas (Thunberg)

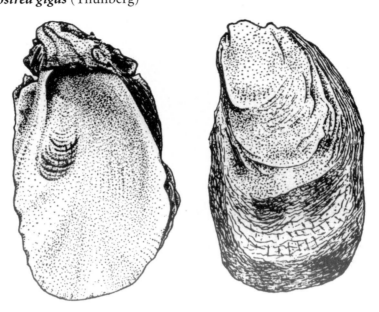

REMARKS This is the largest oyster in the region; it usually
measures about 15 cm but may, exceptionally, attain 45 cm.
C. gigas is markedly elongated in form. However, it is not
easy to identify oysters by their shape, since this is often
dictated by their habitat – the shells growing as they can in
clusters and no two being exactly alike.

BU: kha-mar
TH: hoy nangrom
MA/IN: tiram
PH: talaba
VI: hàu
HK: mau lai
CH: mu li

CUISINE The very large oysters are not eaten raw, but
cooked first, or sun-dried (or sometimes reduced to oyster 'juice'). *C. gigas* is
cultivated at Hong Kong for these purposes. Smaller oysters are dealt with in the
next entry.

OYSTER, HOODED OYSTER
*Saccostrea cucullata** (Born)

Family *Ostreidae*

REMARKS This is an oyster of moderate size (up to 10 cm), which usually has a black exterior with pinkish or purple rings around the margin of the shell. It is well-known in Thailand, Malaysia and Indonesia.

BU: kha-mar
TH: hoy nangrom
 pak jaeb
MA: tiram batu
IN: tiram
PH: talaba
HK: mau lai

Oysters of the genus **Saccostrea** may be distinguished from those of the genus **Crassostrea** by looking at the rims of the shells, where they meet. Those of **Saccostrea** are bumped and dimpled; i.e. the right-hand valve has little tubercles along its edge, which fit into corresponding small pits on the left-hand valve. This arrangement is brought out clearly in the drawing, which shows the right-hand valve, viewed from the inside.

CUISINE The smaller oysters are consumed as they are elsewhere in the world. My own recommendation is to eat them raw from the shell with nothing added but a squeeze of lemon or lime juice. However, it must be admitted that they can be cooked with satisfactory results; and that the smallest ones make an excellent addition to many sauces. They are sufficiently plentiful and cheap in many parts of S. E. Asia to permit so treating them without guilty feelings of extravagance. Whatever you do with your oysters, be sure not to waste their juices!

A recipe for spiced oysters is given on page 253.

* I am told that when the name was first bestowed it was mis-spelled 'cuccullata' and that taxonomic orthodoxy requires that this mistake be perpetuated; a course which I decline to follow.

PEARL OYSTER

Pinctada maxima (Jameson)

Family *Pteriidae*

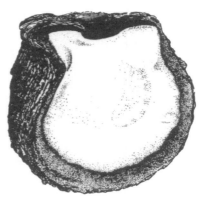

REMARKS Maximum length about 30 cm.

The shells of young pearl oysters are yellow, but they turn purplish black with age. The inside is of a pearl-like brilliance (and there should of course be an actual pearl inside too). The drawing above shows the inside, while that below (using a different specimen) is of the exterior.

The pearl oysters live fairly deep down and divers are needed to harvest them. There are at least two other species, including **P. margaritifera** (Linnaeus), which is dark inside and is called hoy muk chan lai in Thailand.

BU: moke-kaun
TH: hoy muk chan,
    hoy muk kob
    tong
MA: sapanda, togok
IN: (tapis-tapis)
PH: tipay
HK: chun chu law

CUISINE The meat of the pearl oyster is delicious, rare and costly. Neglect no opportunity to enjoy one. Open the shell, extract the meat and fry it (or use it to make a delicious soup).

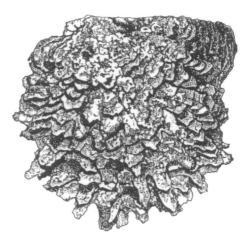

FAN SHELL, PEN SHELL
Atrina pectinata (Linnaeus)

Family *Pinnidae*

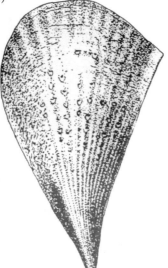

REMARKS Maximum length 37 cm.

The exterior colour is light green, the creature inside whiteish orange.

The fan shell anchors itself in the sand, sharp end down, by a tuft of hairs (the byssus). The upper end of the shell just shows above the surface of the sand.

The first of the Burmese names given and the Thai name mean spade or mattock shell, another interpretation of the shape of the shell.

BU: tha-ywin-pya,
  kha-laun-tu-kun
TH: hoy jawp
MA: billong
IN: (kapak-kapak)
PH: barong
HK: sha chuk
CH: zhi jiang yao

CUISINE This is a fairly large creature, and it is certainly necessary to remove the stomach and intestine (which one does not bother to do from small clams). There is plenty of edible meat left, which may be used in soup or fried (as in Burma and Thailand) and served with coriander. It is rarely eaten in Malaysia.

HORSE MUSSEL

Musculista senhousia (Benson)

Family *Mytilidae*

REMARKS Maximum length 3.5 cm. The shell bears zigzag stripes of brown on its green surface.

Some other species of horse mussel are known in the region, for example **Modiolus philippinarum** in the Philippines, which can measure as much as 13 cm and is shown below. At Phuket in Thailand I met some less large horse mussels (to about 7 cm only) with reddish meat, which a marine biologist told me were classified as **Modiolus penelegans** – an obsolete term, probably corresponding to **M. metcalfei**.

BU: yout-thwa
TH: hoy ka phong
MA: kupang
PH: tahong
HK: chang hau
CH: tu ni gua

CUISINE Horse mussels may be eaten directly or indirectly, as the author of *Seafood for Thai People* points out. For direct consumption, follow the advice given in the next entry, for the common mussel. For indirect consumption, feed the horse mussels to ducks and then eat the ducks' eggs, which will be more numerous and have larger yolks as a result of this diet.

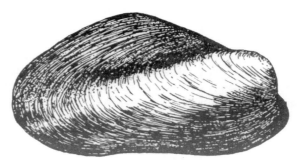

MUSSEL

Family *Mytilidae*

Perna viridis (Linnaeus)

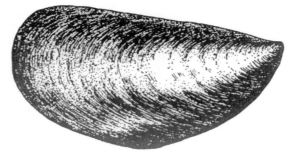

REMARKS Maximum length 16.5 cm, common length (of younger specimens) 8 to 10 cm.

The colour of the shell, or rather of the epidermis which covers it, is greenish-black (bright green towards the margin); but after exposure to the sun it will turn yellow.

Mussels are often found in clusters of 100 or more, which makes it easy to gather them.

BU: kha-yu-nyo
TH: hoy meng phu*
MA: kupang
PH: tahong,
    amahong
HK: chang hau

CUISINE Make mussel soup, or steam the mussels or fry them. They can also be dried (after a boiling) and the practice in Thailand is then to coat them with sugar and fry them. Mussels are sometimes cut in half and dried thus, ready for frying or pickling.

One Chinese author recommends boiling them with turnip or squash. The Chinese think well of them, especially in the south, but warn against eating too many. (Dizziness, blurred vision and constipation are the consequences. Even more dreadful is the result of eating them 'continuously'; the hair falls out.)

Interesting Filipino recipes for mussels are given on pages 294 to 296.

*meng phu is the carpenter beetle which has a yellow head and a dark blue body and frequents sunflowers.

PIDDOCK, ANGEL'S WING   Family *Pholadidae*
Pholas orientalis Gmelin

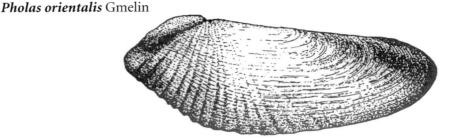

REMARKS Maximum length 12 cm. The exterior colours
are black and white, and the two shells are noticeably
assymetrical, one being longer than the other. These
piddocks inhabit muddy and sandy tidal areas near river
mouths, often choosing fairly hard mud in which to
establish their holes.

TH: hoy phim, hoy
  phim pakarang
MA: siput selat batu
PH: diwal (Visayan)
HK: haw chung
CH: dong fang hai sun

CUISINE Piddocks may be prepared in various ways: for example, boiled and
served with sauce and rice; or sautéed with shallots and bamboo shoots; or used to
make a Thai curry of the kind called phat phet.

RAZORSHELL CLAM, RAZOR CLAM   Family *Solenidae*
Solen grandis Dunker

REMARKS Maximum length 15 cm. The shells which are
generally yellow, sometimes fairly dark and sometimes
whiteish, are very sharp and brittle and need to be
handled with great caution. These razor clams dig holes in
the sand and can be hunted at low tide, either with a
spade or by sprinkling lime on the holes, which causes
them to pop up.

BU: thin-done-dar-
  yout-thwa
TH: hoy tha, hoy
  lawt
MA: sumbun
PH: tikan
HK: chi kap law
CH: zhu cheng

CUISINE The meat is white and may be used either fresh
or dried. See above, and the recipe on page 247.

RAZOR CLAM
Pharella javanica (Lamarck)

Family *Solenidae*

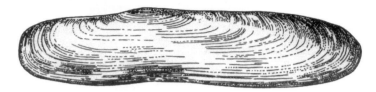

REMARKS The typical shape of a razor clam, exemplified by **Solen grandis** on the preceding page, is long and narrow. However, there are at least two, in the genus **Pharella**, which are noticeably less narrow and have a sort of 'hump' in the middle. Generally, these species share the same common names as their narrower relations.

The shell of **P. javanica**, the subject of this entry attains a length of 8 cm; the outside is off-white, the inside pale cream to bluish white. **P. acutidens** Broderip and Sowerby is rather similar in length and colouration, but has a more restricted distribution in the region. **Glauconome** spp., are of somewhat similar appearance and may be marketed together with **Pharella** spp.

Razor clams live in burrows in the sand, down which they can 'jack' themselves very quickly if disturbed; hence the name 'jack-knife clam', sometimes used. They are all able to survive with reasonable efficiency by opening and closing their valves in a snapping motion.

CUISINE The meat is white and attractive in appearance, and of good quality. In Thailand it may be used in soup, or fried with shallots, or used in the recipe for hoy lawt on page 247. Filipino cooks think highly of the species. They steam or parboil the creatures in their shells to produce an excellent broth. The meat is tender and has a good flavour.

SHIPWORM, SIAMESE SHIPWORM
Lyrodus pedicellatus (Quatrefages)

Family *Teredinidae*

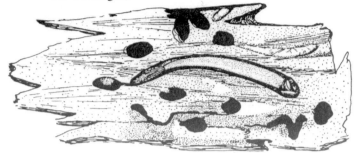

REMARKS The maximum length of this strange creature is 30 cm.

BU: thit-pauk-poe
TH: phriang
MA: kapang
PH: tamilok
HK: haw chung

It is really a kind of marine snail, which starts life in a double shell. It then seeks a suitable piece of wood, often a floating log or the trunk of a 'sam' tree such as grows in mangrove swamps, digs into the bark and establishes itself within. It is at this point that it becomes long and wormlike, with the original two shells transformed into mere appendages, one at each end. All that one normally sees of the shipworm is the snail-like head peeping out of the bark.

The shipworm may bore into the timbers of boats and do considerable damage.

Coastal people in Thailand, and possibly elsewhere, have for long cultivated the shipworm in logs anchored in the sea. Dr Vagn Hansen, while directing the Marine Biological Centre at Phuket in Thailand, formed the opinion that this operation may have been among the very first examples of 'sea farming' in the world.

CUISINE The shipworm is not often marketed, but is eaten with some enthusiasm in certain places. The raw flesh has a good flavour. But it is important to choose shipworms which have been living in 'sam' trees rather than in, e.g., floating logs.

The meat may be fried with eggs, and the dish will be doubly exotic if you choose for this purpose the large (almost pea-sized) eggs of the red ant which is found on pommelo and longan trees.

Shipworms may also be pickled in vinegar or in nam pla.

The Cephalopods

This group of creatures, except for the nautilus, presents an unattractive appearance. They look like rubbery bags with eight or ten tentacles sprouting therefrom. But they are good to eat, and potentially of great importance since they constitute one of the few reserves of seafood which have not yet been over-exploited in S. E. Asia.

They are also of interest as the only molluscs with centralized nervous systems. There are brains within those heads; and the octopus, for example, may be taught to perform quite complicated manoeuvres. Indeed it performs some without being taught. Like almost all the cephalopods, it has ink sacs and the ability to expel clouds of ink from these when it wishes to take evasive action. The cloud is not large enough to mask its retreat; but research has shown that the cloud itself simulates an octopus in shape, thus diverting the attention of the attacker while the octopus, which will in the meantime have made itself transparent, escapes; and that the ink may also numb some of the sensory powers of the attacker to such an extent that the escaping octopus might even brush against it without attracting attention.

The first cephalopod listed, the nautilus, is the most primitive. These unusual creatures are the only survivors of the ancient order of nautiloids, which comprised several thousand species millions and millions of years ago. Indeed, the nautilus, which is only found in the South-West Pacific, may well be called a 'living fossil'. (It has been included in the catalogue partly for this reason. Although it is edible, it is not often available to the cook.) It has the distinction of still living in a shell (and a very beautiful one), whereas the other cephalopods have in the course of evolution found it convenient to allow their shells to degenerate into internal 'bones', of which the cuttlefish 'bone' given to birds as a pecking object is the most familiar.

Cuttlefish and squid are both equipped with eight short and two long tentacles. The long ones can be shot out to catch prey. The cuttlefish are more compact than the squids, many of which have elongated bodies and may grow to an alarming size in some parts of the world (the record overall length of a squid being over 20 metres). Both cuttlefish and squid have fins. The octopus, in contrast, has none; and it has only eight tentacles.

In all parts of the world one finds ingenious and interesting methods of catching the octopus. I enjoyed the following passage in the monograph* written by Bartsch after he had made a research expedition to the Philippines.

Well do I recall my first octopus hunt with them in the southern islands. It was a dark night. The good ship Albatross lay peacefully at anchor some half mile off a Moro village, whose dim outline was faintly silhouetted against the sky. We had just finished our dinner, returned to the deck to take up submarine light fishing, when we noticed a torchlight procession proceeding from the village down the sand spit that fringed a reef. The orderliness

*Bartsch, Paul: *Pirates of the deep — stories of the squid and octopus*, in the Annual Report of the Smithsonian Institution for 1916 (pp. 547–775): Washington, D.C., 1917.

of the procedure soon changed to what at our distance might have (been) considered some wild ceremonial dance.

Our curiosity being thoroughly aroused, we lowered a boat and soon joined the party of men and boys, who were clad in the conventional G-string costume, each provided with a torch varying from about 4 to 6 inches in diameter and probably 10 to 12 feet in length, made of slender segments of dried, split bamboo, carried on the left shoulder, held by the left hand, and lighted in front. The right hand was reserved for the ever-present bolo or a spear. The light of these torches would show through the shallow water and thus reveal the luckless devil fish, which seemed to have forsaken the secure caverns of the reef and to have gone a-hunting on the shallow flats within. They are curious creatures, and their humped up attitude and large eyes render them rather mirth provoking at such times. But there is little time given to contemplating, for a native bolo or spear brings him in and he is promptly strung on a rattan string, where he may continue to squirm with his fellow captives until dead.

This method is still in use. Voss records that some Filipinos also use another method of capturing octopus, which involves using the juice of the plant called *tubli* in the Visayan dialect. 'The plant is macerated and the juice squeezed into an octopus hole. The octopus immediately deserts its home and is grasped by the fisherman.'

EMPEROR NAUTILUS, PEARLY NAUTILUS   Family *Nautilidae*
Nautilus pompilius Linnaeus

REMARKS Maximum diameter of the shell is about 20 cm.

BU: kha-yu-sin-na-maung

TH: muk hoy, hoy nguang saang*

PH: toksi

Let it be said at once that this creature is not a gastero-pod. True, it has a single shell; but it is really a sort of squid. It is sometimes called the chambered nautilus, since its spiral shell is built up, as it grows, by the addition of one chamber after another, until there may be as many as three dozen. The animal's body always lies in the last, outer and largest chamber, and is equipped with several score of small arms, so that it sometimes looks like a sea anenome lodged in a shell. The shell contains gas, which makes it semi-buoyant, permitting the nautilus to change depth and to swim.

It is not easily caught, but Burma is one place in which it is taken (in large quantities, perhaps because the shell, polished down to the 'pearl', can be conveniently carved into the shape of a peacock, the national emblem, and will then fetch a good price). In the Mergui area (and, no doubt, elsewhere) they may be found stranded on beaches, but fishermen also take them in trawls and dive for them.

Distribution: from the Andaman Islands to the Philippines, Australia and Fiji.

CUISINE May be prepared like any small squid (see following entries). Indeed all you really need do is remove the eyes.

* literally, long-nosed elephant shell.

CUTTLEFISH, PHARAOH CUTTLEFISH
Sepia pharaonis Ehrenberg

Family *Sepiidae*

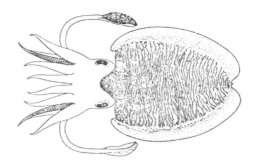

REMARKS Maximum mantle length of the male just over 40 cm, market length 25 to 30 cm.

Male adults have bold brown stripes across the back of the mantle and the head. The females are less boldly marked.

This species has a wide distribution from the Red Sea to Japan and Australia. It is the most abundant cuttlefish in the Hong Kong markets, and probably in others through the region of S. E. Asia. It is also one of the largest; but there are many others.

BU: kha-wel, kim-
mun-leit
TH: muk kla dong
MA: sotong katak
IN: biekutak
PH: bagolan
CA: muk snauk
VI: cá muc
HK: mak mo*
JA: torafukouika

The ink of the cuttlefish was used in the past to make the colour sepia. The interior 'shell' of the cuttlefish is used by goldsmiths in Burma, but exactly how I have not discovered. The Chinese, remarking that 'the cuttle has ink in its bosom', have called it the 'sea-god's clerk' (Read). They have also used powdered cuttlefish bone extensively in medical practice.

CUISINE As for the octopus (page 184), but the cuttlefish are more tender and do not need to be beaten before cooking. The Burmese of the Mergui area like to cook cuttlefish with sticky rice and coconut cream. Very small cuttlefish, after being cleaned, washed and dried, may be deep-fried whole. The result (which is what the French call Supions frits) is delicious. Canned cuttlefish is available from China, put up in either soy sauce or tomato sauce.

Recipes for cuttlefish will be found on pages 235, 254 and 332.

---

* This means 'nanny inkfish'. Another Chinese name in use at Hong Kong is foo ban woo chak, meaning tiger-blotched black thief (the reference to a tiger being based on the colour pattern of the male).

SQUID, SWORDTIP SQUID

Family *Loliginidae*

Photololigo edulis Hoyle*

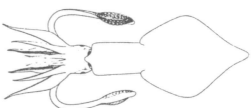

REMARKS Maximum length 30 cm or more, even 40 cm in some areas.

All one can say about the colour is that it may vary from translucent to bright red, depending on the situation in which the individual finds itself. Squid have a remarkable facility for changing colour by expanding or contracting their chromatophores (contractile sacs, containing pigments, which are situated in their outer skins).

Photololigo chinensis Gray, the Mitre squid, is a closely related species. The two of them together account for half the cephalopod landings at Hong Kong. *P. duvaucelii* Orbigny, the Indian squid, is a smaller squid, the habits of which are indicated by the Chinese name chin sui yau yue, meaning shallow water soft-fish.

Distribution: *P. edulis* has a range in the Western Pacific from northern Australia to the Philippines and Japan.

BU: ba-wel, kin-
      mun-yet-phout
TH: muk kluay
MA: sotong blasa
IN: cumi-cumi,
      sotong
PH: pusit, calmar
CA: muk bampoung
HK: tor yau yue
      (trawl softfish)
JA: gotouika

CUISINE Squid are ideal for stuffing. Clean them, cut off and chop up the tentacles, then devise whatever stuffing you please and include the chopped tentacles in it. Be careful, however, to leave room in the body for the stuffing to expand during cooking.

RECIPES
Squid sauté with pineapple, page 263
Ca muc noi thit (stuffed squid),
   page 266
Stir-fried squid, page 277

Adobong pusit, page 293
Calamares rellenados (stuffed squid),
   page 294
Ikan cumi-cumi Kalimantan,
   page 313

* Carpenter and Niem (1998) remark that knowledge of the taxonomy of the genus *Photololigo*, which includes the majority of the large commercially important species, remains poor. They observe that assessments of these squid as a food resource and decisions about the management of the stocks depend on accurate identification of species. 'Therefore, there is an urgent need for a substantial cooperative regionwide taxonomic study of the genus *Photololigo* using classical morphology supported by modern techniques including allozyme, electrophoresis and DNA analysis.' One supposes that this will take quite some time!

Photololigo singhalensis Ortmann,
the Long barrel squid, has a maximum mantle
length of about 50 cm and a weight of 1 kilo.
It is one of several Indo-Pacific species in this
genus which have a distinctive shape,
shown in the drawing and reflected in the
Chinese names cheung yau tung
(long-barrelled soft-fish) and cheung woo
chak (long black thief). Distribution is from the
Eastern Arabian Sea, the Bay of Bengal to
the South China Sea and the Philippines.

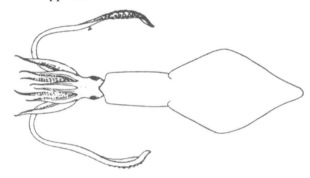

Sepioteuthis lessoniana Lesson, the Big fin reef
squid, is conspicuously different in shape.
Although the maximum length of the mantle is
only 36 cm, the maximum weight is well over
1½ kilos. The Chinese name is daai mei yau yue
(big-tail soft-fish). The back is rich brown or
spotted or pale and translucent, but always
marked by transverse bars. Its distribution
is wide; from Africa to Hawaii and from Japan
to Australia.

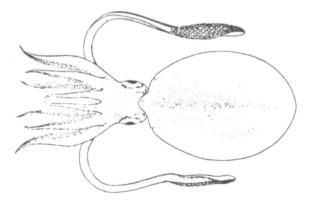

FLYING SQUID, PURPLEBACK FLYING SQUID

Family *Ommastrephidae*

Sthenoteuthis oualaniensis (Lesson)

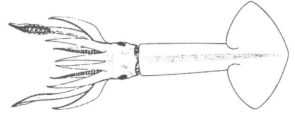

REMARKS Maximum mantle length of the male is around 30 cm, maximum weight over ½ kilo.

This species is shown as a representative of the ommastrephid squids, which are called flying squids and of which there are several species in the region. They do not really fly, but they can propel themselves out of the water and glide. These are oceanic creatures.

BU: kin-mun-pyan
TH: muk lawt
PH: pusit
VI: cá múc
HK: (yat boon yau yue)
JA: tobiika

Gruvel gives an interesting description of a method of fishing for the calmar (as the French call flying squid) in the region of Qui Nhon (Binh Dinh) in Vietnam, by night. The fisherman first tows a line with little blobs of white material on it. These attract the flying squid, one of which will eventually come near enough to be scooped up in a dip-net. The fisherman then takes a bamboo scalpel and excises from this first victim the little phosphorescent organ on the back of the mantle. After triturating this lightly to increase its luminosity, he wraps it in a thin covering of very fresh and translucent fish flesh. The 'light' thus fashioned will shine for six hours. It is used to illuminate the bait on a fishing line, being hung just above it. Other calmars, seeing a snack thus lit up in front of them, swim forward to their doom. The line is rebaited after each capture.

Distribution: widespread in both the Indian Ocean and Pacific Ocean.

CUISINE Calmars are highly esteemed in France and other Mediterranean countries. However, they seem to be little known in S. E. Asia, although available. They may be prepared like the other squid, except that their very long thin bodies are less suitable for being stuffed.

SANDBIRD OCTOPUS, MARBLED OCTOPUS

Family *Octopodidae*

Octopus aegina Gray

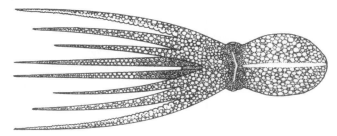

REMARKS Maximum length of mantle 10 cm (total length 30 cm), corresponding to a weight of 400 grams. The first English name above echoes the name used in Hong Kong.

BU: ba-wel*
TH: pla muk yak, pla muk sai
MA: kereta, sotong kereta
IN: gurita
PH: puguita
CA: muk ping peang
HK: saa lui (sand bird)

The dorsal surfaces of body and arms are brown, with a reticulated pattern. Note the small size of the head and the 'cirrus' beside each eye. The arms are long and sturdy; the two dorsal arms being noticeably shorter than the others. Each arm bears a double row of suckers.

This species has a wide distribution from the Red Sea and East Africa to the Western Pacific. A less good species, *O. macropus* Risso, the White-spotted octopus, has an even wider distribution including the Mediterranean and the Caribbean. It has longer and thinner arms, each bearing one row of suckers, not two. The Chinese call it sui gwai, or water ghost, like the Burmese name for *O. aegina* (on which see the footnote).

CUISINE An octopus must be cleaned by removing the beam, eyes and interior organs. Large ones must be beaten, e.g. against a stone, to make them tender, or alternatively (as a cook in Nice advised me) hung up overnight, tentacles down. They should then be cooked by some slow method, such as stewing. But the best octopus which I have ever had were baby ones prepared according to the Neapolitan recipe Polpetielli alla Luciana (to be found on page 339 of my *Mediterranean Seafood*, which is worth buying for this recipe alone, although full of other good ones which may be used in S. E. Asia).

* The name in the Rangoon markets is yay-tha-yeh, meaning water ghost, but it seems to be applied also to cuttlefish and squid.

OCTOPUS, OLD WOMAN OCTOPUS   Family *Octopodidae*
Cistopus indicus Orbigny

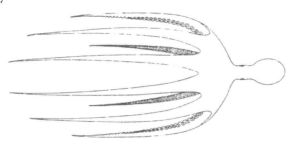

REMARKS The mantle can measure as much as 18 cm in length, corresponding to a weight of 2 kilos. The colour is brownish or greyish, with a green iridescent sheen on the underside of the mantle.

BU: yay-tha-yeh
TH: pla muk yak, pla muk sai
MA: keretah, sotong kereta
IN: gurita
PH: pugita
HK: laai por (muddy old woman)

This octopus has a distribution from India to China and east to the Philippines. It has been recorded off Mozambique. It is the major commercial octopus in the Asian markets. Again, the Chinese name used in Hong Kong has provided the basis for the English name approved by the FAO.

The traditional enemies of the octopus are the predatory eels such as the Moray eel. Both live in rock crevices (although the octopus will sometimes build a 'home' for itself with stones or debris, or take over an abandoned pot on the sea floor). The moray usually wins a battle between them, often by the use of unscrupulous tactics (for example, it will sink its teeth into one tentacle of the octopus, then straighten its own body out and spin it round and round until the tentacle breaks off; after which the process can be repeated until no tentacles are left).

CUISINE As for the preceding species.

Sea Turtles

The seven living species of sea turtle are survivors from the period of the dinosaurs, 90 million years ago. Most of them have, or had, a world-wide distribution; but nowadays there are fewer beaches where they can safely excavate holes and lay their eggs. The populations have therefore decreased, in some instances to the point where the species is endangered.

The sea turtles are shy, harmless creatures and I would rather recommend means of conserving them than methods of eating them. However, their eggs are prized as food and the calipee (that part of the flesh which is next to the lower shell) of the Green turtle is in demand for turtle soup, so they must have a place in this book. Besides, there are developments in turtle 'farming' which may lead to a situation in which we could eat at least some turtles and their eggs with a clear conscience. (I recall hearing of a 'farm' for rearing the hawksbill turtle at Ha-Tien in Vietnam, near the border with Cambodia.)

I have catalogued the three turtles which are of most interest to the consumer in S. E. Asia. However, I mention here **Caretta caretta**, the Loggerhead turtle, which is known from the United States and Australia and Africa and is also sometimes found in S. E. Asia. It is not often eaten, but its eggs are relished. It may be recognized by its large head and parrot-like beak.

Readers who would like to know more about the habits and prospects of these engaging creatures will find much fascinating information in the admirable book by Bustard cited in the Bibliography. The FAO catalogue of 'Sea Turtles of the World' (see under Márquez in the Bibliography) is a very useful reference.

GREEN SEA TURTLE
Chelonia mydas (Linnaeus)

Family *Cheloniidae*

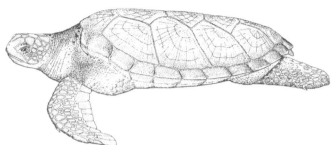

REMARKS This turtle has a very wide distribution in tropical and sub-tropical waters. It may be that there are two distinct sub-species, one in the Atlantic and the other in the Indo-Pacific. Colour of back and underside varies not only between these regions but also within them. The back may be green-brown or brown with darker markings, sometimes so many that the general effect is almost black; or it may be pale olive-green without noticeable markings.

TA: gal kasbava, pal amai
BU: pyin-tha-leik
TH: tao tanu
MA: penyu agar
IN: penyu daging
PH: pawikan
VI: con vích
HK: hoy kwai
JA: ao umi-game

The maximum size of individuals in the Indo-Pacific region is not certain. One might say that they can attain a weight of over 200 kilos and that the shell, measured over the curve from front to back, may be 1½ metres long. But most specimens are much smaller than this.

CUISINE The flesh of the green turtle is the best for making turtle soup and for eating generally. In the days of the early navigators, when it was difficult to provide fresh meat on long voyages, the green turtle was much in demand since it could be kept alive on board ship until required.

The eggs 'are round, rather like a ping-pong ball, and have a parchment-like skin. They are best boiled for eating but do not set hard like a fowl's eggs, the albumen or white remaining quite liquid'. (Tweedie and Harrison)

HAWKSBILL SEA TURTLE
Eretmochelys imbricata (Linnaeus)

Family *Cheloniidae*

REMARKS This is a smaller turtle. The length of the carapace is unlikely to exceed 75 cm.

    The hawksbill takes its name from the hooked jaws which are adapted to deal with its diet of crabs and prawns. It is best known as the turtle which provides tortoiseshell. 'The thin translucent horny plates which cover the dorsal surface of the shell ... are removed, after the animal is killed, by immersion in hot water. Heating of the plates renders them plastic and they can be welded together, so that the form of the articles manufactured is not limited by the thickness of a single plate.' (Tweedie and Harrison)

BE: samudrik kasim
TA: alung amai
BU: leik-kyet-tu-ywe
TH: tao kra
MA/IN: penyu sisek
PH: pawikan
VI: dôì môì
HK: hoy kwai koupi
JA: tai-mai

    The diet of hawksbill turtles includes algae, single shells, certain crabs, mangrove leaves and fruit, and even sponges (eaten by no other sea turtles).

    Distribution: this is the most tropical of all sea turtles, distributed throughout the central Atlantic and the Indo-Pacific.

CUISINE Although hunted mainly for its shell, the hawksbill is eaten and the calipee may be used in the preparation of 'green turtle soup'. Its eggs are prized.

LEATHERBACK TURTLE
Dermochelys coriacea (Linnaeus)

Family *Dermochelyidae*

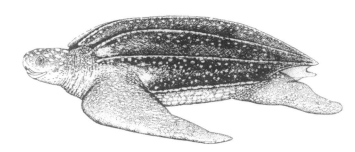

REMARKS This is a large turtle which may weigh over 500 kilos; the largest specimen ever recorded, a male found dead on Harlech beach in Wales in 1988 weighed 916 kilos. The carapace length may measure as much as 2 metres (over 2.5 metres in the case of the Welsh specimen) and is distinguished by seven longitudinal ridges and by its smooth, leathery surface. The back is black in colour, but spotted with white.

BU: leik-khwe
TH: tao ma pheuang*
MA/IN: penyu
    belimbing*
PH: pawikan dagat
VI: con ba-tam
HK: hoy kwai
CH: leng-pi-gui
JA: osa game

Although the leatherback turtle is the most widely distributed of all sea turtles (since it is better adapted than the others to colder waters, e.g. of New Zealand and Chile), it has seemed to be in serious danger of extinction. The species has had a very large number of breeding grounds where eggs are laid in clutches of up to 150 at a time in 'nests' on beaches. These breeding grounds have been especially important in the eastern Pacific and western Atlantic. However, the range of predators which are eager to attack the eggs, or the little turtles when they first emerge from the eggs and before they have time to dash down to the sea, is formidable. The hatchlings are too large for many of the smaller predators which attack other species, but even so they are exposed to the hostile attention of vultures, dogs, jackals, pigs, wild boars and monitor lizards. While they are running frantically to the surf zone they may be attacked by other birds and by mammals such as mongooses, skunks, raccoons, and even jaguars. And, once through the surf zone and into the ocean, they may still be eaten by various sea birds, carnivorous fish and squids. Those who survive to grow up into full size turtles can count themselves very fortunate.

S. E. Asia is not particularly rich in breeding grounds but one which has attracted attention is a 13-mile stretch of beach in central Trengganu in eastern Malaya. About 1500 female leathery turtles would use this beach during the egg-laying season, from June to September. Each female might lay a number of clutches of about 80 or 90 eggs, or even more in deep pits in the sand. These eggs were systematically gathered for sale as food. Although efforts have been made to reserve some for incubation in hatcheries, so that little leathery turtles can later be released into the sea, the operation was hampered, at least in its early stages, by a tendency towards over-exploitation, and by the early 1990s the number of nesting females on this beach had already decreased dramatically.

CUISINE This turtle is not itself eaten, so far as I can discover, but its eggs are in great demand. They are almost as big as tennis balls and are believed to have aphrodisiac properties.

---

* with reference to the ribbed fruit called ma pheuang in Thai and belimbing in Malay.

Miscellaneous Marine Creatures and Edible Seaweeds

What remains to be described is a real miscellany of items, belonging to widely
different categories of the animal and vegetable kingdoms. These notes are rather
sketchy, especially that on the edible jellyfish; but it seems to be to me worth drawing attention to everything edible which comes from the sea, since it is likely that
some resources which have so far been neglected except by such people as the sea
nomads will be exploited more fully in the future.

I take the opportunity to explain briefly about the sea nomads (often called sea
gypsies, but this is a misleading term since it could imply some ethnic connection
with the gypsies of Europe and Asia).

Sea nomads are people who live at sea, exploiting marine resources in a relatively unsophisticated way, during the dry season and take refuge in temporary
shore settlements during the monsoon. They occur in various parts of S. E. Asia,
especially around inhospitable areas such as mangrove swamps, where physical
difficulties of movement and other unfavourable conditions preclude the estab-
lishment of conventional communities. They seem all to be primitive, timid and
amiable, but do not represent a single ethnic group. They are found, under the
name Mawken, in regions such as Tenasserim and the Mergui peninsula on the
west coast of Malaya and Thailand. Mawken apparently means 'sea-drowned'; but
these people have been described as being among the most expert boatmen in the
world. Many groups of sea nomads also survive in Indonesia and in parts of the
Philippines.

The paper cited in the Bibliography under Sopher contains much fascinating
information about these communities.

TONGUE CLAM
Lingula unguis Linnaeus

Family *Lingulidae*

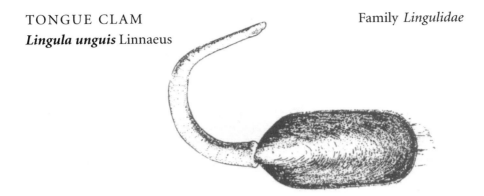

REMARKS The maximum length of the shell is about 45 cm, but with the peduncle protruding one can have a total length of 80 cm.

The colour of the shell is green, of various shades.

These creatures are of great antiquity. **Lingula** is indeed the oldest living genus of animals, having survived almost unchanged through 500,000,000 years.

The tongue clam lives in a vertical burrow which may be 35 cm deep. The opening of the burrow on the surface of the mud or muddy sand is usually marked by three little circular holes (or a single slit).

Surakanee in Thailand is one place where tongue clams abound. The name name means the duckbilled shell fish.

BU: pakali
TH: hoy paak pet
MA: balai
IN: lurjuk
PH: balay
HK: sek kip

CUISINE The peduncle or 'stalk' is extensively eaten in the fresh stage, after being boiled or steamed. The morsels are also available pickled in vinegar.

SEA URCHIN
Diadema setosum (Leske)

Family *Diadematidae*

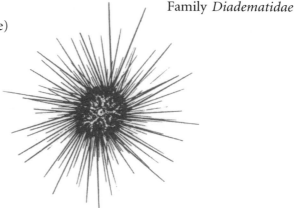

REMARKS There are many varieties of sea urchin, mostly about the size of an apple. Their spines are a notorious hazard to bathers. However, this particular species is edible, which is some compensation.

BU: ye-khu, sin gaun
PH: tinikangitim
VI: con chom chom
HK: hoy daam
CH: ci guan hai dan

CUISINE Cut off the upper half of the shell and you will expose the small ovaries, which are what you eat. Tiny mouthfuls, but delicious. Take them with a little lime juice or fish sauce or chilli sauce, according to your preference. (Mine is for lime juice, but very little.) For anyone who knows how much the sea urchin is prized in the Mediterranean it is strange to find that it is only eaten in some places in S. E. Asia. Thus in Thailand people eat them at the island of Kor Samuy in Suratanee; but not at Phuket.

EDIBLE JELLYFISH
Rhopilema esculenta (Kishinouye)

Family *Rhizostromidae*

REMARKS Dr Vagn Hansen has told me, from his experience at Phuket in Thailand, how the sea nomads exploit this marine resource, bringing down from Burmese waters the gonads (in dried form) of this jellyfish.

CUISINE Jellyfish is among the foods which the Chinese value for its texture. It is sold in dried discs of 15 inches or so in diameter, formed from the umbrella part. These are softened by being soaked in water, then cut into strips and scalded. This procedure causes the strips to form curls, the texture of which has been described as 'tender, crunchy and elastic', an unusual combination. The jelly-fish curls are served in a dressing composed of three parts of sesame oil to two of soy sauce, with a little vinegar and sugar.

MA: ubor-ubor
PH: dikya
VI: sua
HK: hoy cheek

SEA CUCUMBER, SEA SLUG
Holothuria scabra Jaeger

Family *Holothuridae*

REMARKS This species, probably the most important in the Indo-Pacific from the commercial point of view, has a maximum length of about 35 cm. The back is whitish, sometimes with black and yellow rings and marks showing through. The underside is plain white. It is harvested throughout the area in artisanal fisheries.

BU: pan-le-pet-kye
TH: pling khao
MA\IN: trepang
HK: hoy sum
CH: hai shen

Sea cucumbers have a great appeal to the Chinese because of the interesting slippery texture which they acquire after being suitably prepared, and also for their flavour. It may also be connected with their reputation as a tonic (the Chinese name means 'sea ginseng') and an aphrodisiac (the shape is phallic and if one squeezes a live specimen it will eject sticky threads).

The method followed in preparing them, often done in the Pacific islands where they are collected and processed as a cottage industry, is first to boil them in water until they swell; then to slit them open along the underside, wash them, and boil them again, to the point at which they are rubbery but not too hard; next, to remove the guts and then smoke and dry the creatures over a fire of mangrove wood or coconut husks; and finally to cure them in the sun for a few days. When the time comes to use them, they are soaked to soften them and make them swell in readiness for being cooked.

One species highly prized by the Chinese is *Holothuria (Microthele) nobilis*, which comes in two forms, white and black, depending on habitat. It is often called teatfish or mammy fish, the latter name being apparently derived from the native name *mama* in the Gilbert Islands.

Next in order of estimation come some somewhat smaller species, both of the genus *Actinopyga*: the Blackfish (several species, not distinguished in commerce) and the Deep-water redfish, *Actinopyga echinites*. The Prickly redfish, *Thelenota ananas*, is of generous size (maximum length nearly 80 cm, average live weight about 2.5 kg). Its 'prickles' are large teats which occur in groups of two or three all over the body.

A sea slug can regenerate its own viscera. The viscera, salted and fermented, are eaten by beer drinkers as a savoury in Japan and known as konowata.

CUISINE After the preparation described above, the sea cucumbers may be made into a soup or cooked in other ways which will show off their special texture and 'mouth-feel'. See also the recipe on page 278.

DOLPHIN, BOTTLE-NOSED DOLPHIN   Family *Delphinidae*
Delphinus spp. and *Stenella* spp.

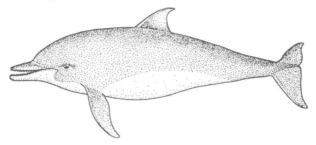

REMARKS The dolphins are called la-byne in Burma and lomba-lomba in Malaysia, but these are the only current names I have found. As in the Mediterranean and other parts of the world too, so in S. E. Asia the dolphin is regarded by most people as a friend of man rather than a source of food.

Gruvel explains that the people living on the coast of Annam (the south of Vietnam) had strange legends which applied to both the dolphins and the whales (the two major sorts of marine mammal known to them). The Annamites called them cá ong (poisson seigneur), and believed that these creatures had been sent by the god of the waters to protect sailors and to convey shipwrecked persons on their backs to the nearest safe landing-place.

The Annamites further believed that dolphins and whales were always preceded, as they swam along, by helpful cuttlefish which obscured the water in front of them by emitting their ink and which pushed out of the way fish which might have harmed them, such as the shark-sucker (which the Annamites called cá hep or cá gio-ep and which they believed to be in the habit of fixing themselves to the pectoral fins of marine mammals and pricking them deeply).

If a fishing boat came upon the corpse of a dolphin or whale, the men would bring it to land and the whole village would attend the funeral, which would be royal in style. The captain of the boat or the man who first saw the corpse would take the role of Eldest Son of the Deceased Cetacean and would wear a mourning turban for 3 months and 6 days. Afterwards he would burn the turban, exhume the bones of the cetacean and deposit them in a sanctuary of quasi-royal status.

Whenever a dolphin or whale died, the rain and wind would rage for three days. Thus, if one noticed continuous rain and wind for such a period, one would know that a death had occurred and would go to look for the corpse. Finding it would stop the rain.

When a cetacean died on the shore, everyone would hasten to the spot with little cups in which to collect a liquid flowing from the outlet of the nasal aperture which apparently had the property of curing numerous maladies.

CUISINE In regions where beliefs such as those described above were or still are held it would seem sacrilegious to discuss eating a dolphin. Moreover, the flesh of dolphins is generally rather tough. But some are eaten with enthusiasm, for example ***Delphinus delphis*** and ***Stenella fraenatus*** (the species illustrated) in Taiwan.

DUGONG, SEA COW

Halicore dugong

Order *Sirenia*

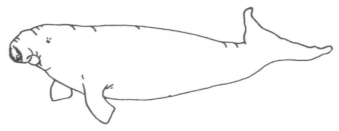

REMARKS In various parts of S. E. Asia one hears stories of a creature like a mermaid, with breasts and a forked tail. This is the dugong, which is not a fish but a mammal. It belongs to a family which is represented in other parts of the world, notably by the manatee in the West Indies.

The name dugong appears to be a corruption of the Malay name duyong. The creature was at one time quite common in Malayan waters, but has become rare. It is a marine animal, but it is usually found in estuaries or other such areas, and may also travel quite a long way up rivers. Thus it is known at the Falls of Khong in Laos, far up the Mekong. I was told there that the tears of the dugong, if they can be gathered, are thought to make a fine love potion; and the oil from its body is used to light lamps.

I have not heard of the dugong being eaten in Laos. However, it is, or used to be, eaten in Malaya; and the manatee, according to data collected by Simmonds (*Curiosities of Food*, London, 1859, and Berkeley CA, 2001), is delicious. 'It appears horrible to chew and swallow the flesh of an animal which holds its young (it has never more than one at a litter) to its breast, which is formed exactly like that of a woman, with paws resembling human hands'.

This sort of consideration is reinforced in Laos by the reputation which the dugong enjoys for protecting fishermen. I have had a vivid description of how, when a pirogue sinks, a score or more of dugongs will appear and form a circle round the crew as they flounder in the water. The dugongs utter wheezing sighs of concern and are evidently bent on protecting the men from possible attacks by large and predatory fish. This belief is an interesting counterpart to the Annamite ideas about dolphins and whales, explained on the preceding page.

However, whether or not the dugong is animated by such philanthropic sentiments, there is no doubt about what the attitude of human beings should be. Leave it alone. The quaint and inoffensive creature is in danger of extinction.

Edible Seaweeds

These could be the subject of a small book. Many seaweeds are edible and many are eaten in S. E. Asia. They are, however, a different kind of food from fish, crustaceans and molluscs; and it is the latter which people expect to find in a book about 'seafood'. I therefore make no apology for treating the edible seaweeds in summary fashion, while hoping that what little I have to say about them will stimulate interest in a valuable food resource. Incidentally, the little I have to say is drawn mainly from the admirable paper by G. N. Subba Rao, listed in the Bibliography; note, however, that some of the scientific names he gives are not to be found in more recent reference works.

Seaweeds belong to a group of plants known as Algae which differ from the true plants in that they do not possess true roots, leaves and stems, although some of them have parts which look like roots, leaves and stems. In what follows I have not treated the, usually microscopic, blue-green algae, although these are used as food, e.g. **Mostoc** spp. The important marine algae are classified into three phyla, as follows:-

CHLOROPHYTA, green algae, widely used as food;

PHAEOPHYTA, brown algae, used both for food and for industrial purposes;

RHODOPHYTA, red algae, the most valuable, also used both for food and for industrial purposes.

Some seaweeds are very useful to us as an addition to food rather than a food in themselves. The jelly which can be extracted from seaweed has almost magical properties in stablizing things like icecream. This product is known as agar, from the Malayan name agar-agar which was originally applied to one red seaweed but has now come to be used for the gelatinous extract of a number of seaweeds. Though the agar seaweeds were mentioned in Chinese literature as early as A.D. 300, 'the method of extraction is believed to have been discovered in the seventeenth century, when a Japanese emperor and his party were stranded one night in the mountains by snow, and a peasant who entertained them prepared a dish of seaweed jelly. What remained was thrown out and froze on the bush where it had been cast. Next day, when the sun came out, the peasant found that all the watery part of the jelly had run away leaving only a papery substance which could be remade into a jelly by boiling it up with more water. Later on, this process was found to purify the seaweed extract, and the method of carrying out the purification by freezing and subsequent thawing still persists in some commercial practice today.' (Lily Newton)

It is in Japan that the consumption of seaweeds is most extensive and attended by the greatest artistry and sophistication. However, various countries of S. E. Asia consume appreciable quantities, either in the natural state or in the form of extractives. Notes follow on what is known about consumption in a number of these countries.

BURMA

Various seaweeds are collected along the Tenasserim coast and sold for human consumption, usually as salads, raw or boiled. These include the red algae **Bostrychia radicans**, **Caloglossa** sp., **Catenella impudica** (the Burmese pour boiling water over this and then add it to salads) and **Catenella nipae** (which may be eaten raw, but can also be boiled for an hour and then mixed with sesame oil, salt, chilli powder, fried ginger, onion and garlic). The general Burmese name for edible seaweeds is pin-le-ye-hmaw.

THAILAND

The seaweeds eaten in Thailand include a red alga of the genus **Gracilaria** which is sometimes eaten fresh, sometimes dried and then cooked as a sweet. Other red algae, of the genus **Porphyra**, are an ingredient of soups. They too may be used fresh or in the dried form.

VIETNAM

On the southern coast the red alga **Griffithsia corollina** is bleached, compressed, cut up and eaten with sugar. Other seaweeds are also eaten. A general Vietnamese name for them is rau câu.

PHILIPPINES

About twenty species of seaweed are eaten, fresh or dried. The most common are:
- Gulaman-dagat, **Gracilaria** spp., red algae;
- Gamat, **Porphyra** sp., red algae sometimes called laver and rich in protein;
- Pokpoklo, green algae of the genus **Codium**;
- Bitukong manok, green algae of the genus **Enteromorpha**;
- Gulaman, **Agardhiella** spp., red algae which are brought into the Manila markets during the rainy season (and are boiled with sugar and spices to make a popular gelatine-like sweetmeat);
- **Sargassum** spp., brown algae which are eaten either raw or cooked;
- **Caulerpa lentillifera**, a green alga which is cultivated in large containers and eaten raw as a salad; often seen in the markets of Manila (Tagalog name ararucip). See the drawing below.

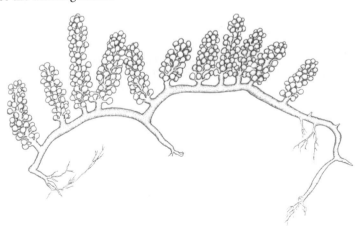

INDONESIA AND MALAYSIA

Consumption of seaweeds is widely prevalent, especially after a poor rice harvest or when food prices are high. They may be eaten raw, or after being blanched, or as a condiment after being cooked in palm sugar or with soy beans.

Chaetomorpha javanica, a green alga, is eaten in Ambon, where the practice is to soak it in fresh water overnight, dry it in the sun, boil it and serve it with bacon.

Ulva lactuca, another green alga known as sea lettuce, is commonly used in soups, salads and for garnishing.

Various brown algae such as *Sargassum* sp., (of which 58 species are known in Indonesia) are eaten raw or cooked with coconut cream and vinegar.

Many red algae are used to make agar-agar, especially *Eucheuma* spp. (of which the vernacular name is agar-agar), and *Gelidium* spp.

An illustrated catalogue of the seaweeds eaten in Indonesia is included in the publication listed under *Lembaga Oceanologi Nasional* in the Bibliography.

Seaweed as the basis of Bird's Nest Soup

People who baulk at eating seaweed in its natural state may nonetheless rave about a certain seaweed product, namely the edible bird's nest which, as Patrica Arroyo explained in the following passage (*The Science of Philippine Foods*, 1974), is produced by the regurgitation of seaweed.

'The so-called Nido soup popular among Chinese gourmands and well accepted among Filipinos, is unique in that its main ingredient is the edible bird's nest of a breed of swallow (*Collocalia white-headi* Tsumbame) the cave swiftlets, locally called balinsayaw. The gathering of these nests is a formidable task of the intrepid souls who scale cliffs and mountains. Contrary to popular belief, the bird's nests are not found in the faces of cliffs but in caves. Hence the gathering involves work in the nooks and crannies of caves which are dark and slippery. This makes it a rare and high priced delicacy which is most precious to a Chinese food gourmet and which has become popular among Filipinos. One kilo costs P 1300 (Macatuno, 1972). However, due to its ability to swell in boiling water, very small amounts are needed to make soup. But still, to lower its costs, it is common to adulterate the soup with chicken eggwhite and cornstarch. One can easily detect the presence of real bird's nest in a soup by the presence of tiny twigs which are coloured brown. These are absent if the soup is made purely of eggwhite and cornstarch.

'The nest is believed to be of biological origin – the saliva of the bird. This particular breed of swallow is found only in the Indo-Malaysian region such as in the island of Mantanini, North of Borneo, sometimes called Soup Island and in the Philippines. People of El Nido, Palawan (El Nido is "the nest" in Spanish and hence the name El Nido soup) where these nests are most found in the Philippines, believe that the birds pick up bits of seaweed and regurgitate them in their crops which they ultimately use as the building blocks for their nest. Others believe that the nest is made of twigs and the swallow's saliva is secreted to serve as adhesive. Collectors like to claim that the nest is cemented with sea foam and not with saliva. However the absence of sodium salts in its chemical composition disproves this romantic theory.

COOKERY SECTION

Introduction to Cookery Section

The recipes given in this book are as I found them in S. E. Asia. They have not been adapted for use elsewhere, although they can be. Not all the exotic ingredients are essential, and those which are can be tracked down in most parts of the world by persons sufficiently enterprising to ask S. E. Asians living in their vicinity to divulge their own sources of supply, and who know what they are looking for. This last point is important. Hence the long note on ingredients, which begins on the next page but one.

The recipes themselves are intended to comprise a representative selection from each country (or group of countries – Singapore and Brunei have been accommodated together with the two parts of Malaysia). Some seafood dishes occur in almost identical form in two or several countries. I have avoided needless repetition of such recipes, but have been ready to include different versions of the same dish if the differences are interesting.

Each recipe section has its own little introduction. These furnish some comments on what might be called the trans-national culinary influences in the region. In this general introduction I point out that these influences are so important that they blur what might otherwise be a neat picture of 'Malaysian cookery' in one compartment, 'Indonesian cookery' in another, and so on. The Chinese influence suffuses the entire picture. The legacies of European colonial rule are still visible in at least the big cities. Dishes imported from the Indian sub-continent extend in an arc through Burma, Thailand, Malaysia and parts of Indonesia. This is one good reason for looking at the cookery of the region as a whole rather than piecemeal.

This thought leads me to make other general remarks which may help readers who are not acquainted with S. E. Asia to see the recipes in the right setting.

- The preparation of food in S. E. Asia is usually done on a relatively large scale, for the 'extended family' which is the normal social unit. Even when the group is small it is usual to offer many different dishes at one meal.

- The concept of one 'course' followed by another is hardly known in S. E. Asia. The usual practice is to put all the food on the table (or on a mat on the floor) together – a soup; rice; whatever the family can afford in the way of meat, fish or poultry; side dishes such as sambals; vegetables; and fruit or dessert-type confections.

- The food is lukewarm or at room temperature. It is usually eaten from a bowl, with a Chinese soupspoon (for liquids) and chopsticks or the fingers.

Everything is cut into pieces of a size suited to the chopsticks or prepared so that bits (of a fish, for example) can easily be lifted off with them. Tea is commonly drunk with meals.

- Strangers often suppose that these lukewarm S. E. Asian dishes are all 'hot' in the other sense. It is certainly true that S. E. Asians can tolerate more chilli pepper than the average European, and it is silly to try to match this high degree of tolerance at the risk of burning one's own unhabituated tongue. (One may, after all, reflect that before the chilli pepper arrived in S. E. Asia from the New World the S. E. Asians themselves had to do without.)

- Fish play a more important role as food in S. E. Asia than in most other parts of the world. Freshwater fish are abundant and more commonly eaten, except in the coastal areas, than marine fish. Indeed, many S. E. Asian fish recipes are used primarily or even exclusively for freshwater fish. Some such figure in this book, but only those which I have found to be used at least occasionally for seafood.

There remains one general point to be made about the recipes.

WEIGHTS AND MEASURES

Cooks in S. E. Asia do not do much weighing and measuring, except in the market place. In the kitchen they work by eye and by tasting. It is often difficult to persuade them to give any indication of quantity beyond such phrases as 'not too much' or 'enough to make the taste right' or 'the amount that is needed'. I have however found that if one depicts to them the problem facing an ignorant foreigner who does not know whether to add one drop or one litre of fish sauce they quickly respond with more precise information such as 'between one and two soupspoonfuls'.

In practice one does not need to be precise in the confection of most fish dishes. Marcel Boulestin once wrote, in his forthright way, that 'the dangerous person in the kitchen' is the one who goes rigidly by weights, measurements, etc, since exact weights are only important in the making of pastry and jams. But even in fish cookery one does need to know roughly in what proportion the ingredients are to be used. It is therefore useful to have recipes which give quantities, so long as one does not suppose that the quantities are immutable, that measuring out level tablespoonfuls is a rite more important than tasting as you go, or that it really matters how many millimetres thick your slices of ginger are.

My custom is to use the metric system. But in S. E. Asia there are many local systems of weights and measures, and many places where the pounds and ounces and pints and inches which the British used to teach people are still employed. Hence the need for the tables which are printed at the end of the book; tables which I have made fuller than is strictly necessary, since I have always found it a bore to have to skip from one volume to another in search of some equivalence which I need to recall but which the author of the cookery book in front of me could not have foreseen my needing.

Notes on Ingredients

It is not my purpose here to describe and illustrate every ingredient used in seafood cookery in S. E. Asia. Many of the ingredients are familiar to all, or require no explanation. However, some are exotic from the point of view of Europeans or North Americans; and there are some whose use needs to be explained. The following pages provide explanations.

The traditional method of cooking in S. E. Asia is on a charcoal brazier. The pan most used thereon is the wok in its various forms. It is shown in the drawing on the right, accompanied by the special sort of spatula which is used with it. The wok is a versatile pan, found all over S. E. Asia as well as in China, where I believe it was first evolved. Its shape permits frying with the minimum quantity of oil, while requiring the cook to move things around inside it to ensure even cooking.

Another feature of cookery which is common to all the S. E. Asian countries is the practice of pounding ingredients together and then frying the result. Such a pounded mixture is called rempah in Malaysia. It is prepared with great care and patience. It is the S. E. Asian equivalent of the Italian soffrito (a mixture of chopped-up onion, garlic, parsley, tomato etc lightly fried in olive oil, which has its counterparts in Provence and in Spain), but is usually more complex. As with the soffrito, it is important not to cook the rempah too long and risk, for example, burning the garlic (an ingredient common to both).

Among the ingredients which recur again and again in S. E. Asian recipes are fish sauces and fish pastes. Although the fish sauce would have been familiar to the Romans, there is little in Europe nowadays to match them. Anchovy essence might be regarded in this light, and the Provencal peï salat (or pissalat); but generally speaking fish sauces of S. E. Asia inflict quite a gastronomic shock to visitors. So we start with them, overleaf.

FISH SAUCES AND FISH PASTES OF THE REGION

Why, the visitor may wonder, should fish sauce be so important in S. E. Asia? The question deserves an answer, and the nature of these sauces and pastes merits some explanation. Hence this note.

From prehistoric times man has used preservative processes in order to store surplus food against seasonal or other scarcities. Most of these processes have involved dehydration, that is to say extracting the water from the food. Sun and wind have been used to achieve this, also smoking processes and extraction of the tissue fluid by osmosis (which is what happens when foods are salted). But fish have always posed a special problem. They decompose faster than other animal protein foodstuffs, and faster still in hot climates. Fortunately, men found that the degradative processes which affected fish, and which they could not arrest to their satisfaction, could nonetheless be controlled in such a way as to confer an acceptable or even desirable flavour on the decomposing food. The process that induces these changes is fermentation.

The first real enthusiasts for this discovery were the Romans, who consumed large quantities of a fermented fish sauce known as 'garum' which was remarkably similar to the fish sauces made in S. E. Asia nowadays[*]. But the popularity of preparations like 'garum' did not outlive the Roman Empire; the Middle Ages saw the introduction of new techniques for preserving fish which, at least in European conditions, wore better.

However, a number of reasons have made it natural for people in S. E. Asia to continue to use the fermentative processes. This method of preservation is cheap. The whole fish is often used, which is economical. And the demands on technology are slight. Nor is there any need to chill the fish or to have complex storage, transport and distribution facilities. The fact that it is hot and humid in S. E. Asia does not matter, in this context, whereas it would and does create considerable difficulties for any straightforward fish-drying operation.

Further, S. E. Asia is a region where the demand for protein is hard to satisfy in the form of fresh meat and fish at prices which people can afford. There is a great need for a cheap source of protein, such as can conveniently be combined with rice. It is this need which is met by fish sauce.

The table which appears on the next page is intended to sort out for the reader the various preparations of the various countries. There are very many of them, and my scheme is perhaps misleadingly simple. But it does show the three main categories of preparation, with the most commonly used national names.

---

[*]Mr Dolf Riks has pointed out that the Malay name for salt is garam. He wonders, as do I, whether there is a connection. Fish sauce is not salt, but in many parts of S. E. Asia it usurps the condimental function of salt (except for desserts, on which salt is used with surprising and pleasing results – try sprinkling a little on fresh pineapple, for example).

First, fish sauce. This is a clear liquid, which may be anything from amber to dark brown in colour. It is rich in salt and soluble nitrogen compounds; and its composition bears a striking resemblance to that of soy sauce (which the Chinese consume in much the same way and for the same reasons that the S. E. Asians consume fish sauce). It may be prepared from marine or freshwater fish, or from a mixture. In commercial manufacture, large vats are used, with taps near the bottom. The vats are filled with layers of fish and salt. A preliminary draining is done, the fish and salt are then trampled down, some of the liquid restored so that they are fully immersed, and the whole lot covered with weighted bamboo trays and left for a few months. Afterwards the vats are tapped and the fermented liquor drawn off. Fresh brine may then be added to the residue and fish sauce of less good quality obtained therefrom. The fish sauce is often left to mature, in earthenware or glass containers, in the sun before being marketed.

The writer 'le Nestour', in describing the manufacture of fish sauce (nuoc mam) in Vietnam, comments: 'Par les manipulations qu'elle nécessite, ses transvasements délicats et le temps nécessaire à sa bonification, elle rappelle assez la préparation de nos eaux-de-vie de choix'. That a Frenchman should see an analogy between making fish sauce and making fine brandy is remarkable; it brings home to us the complexities of the manufacture of fish sauce and the importance which it has in S. E. Asia.

Secondly, fish pastes. They vary in quality and composition. Some of them are really liquids with some chunks of fish floating about in them. Others are real pastes. It is usual to add carbohydrates in the form of roasted rice, bran or flour. The famous fish paste of the Philippines, bagoong, may be coloured red by the addition of a red yeast-like organism, *Monascus purpureus*. The Cambodian fish paste, prahok, is prepared from cleaned fish by a process which yields both fish sauce and fish paste.

Shrimp pastes are no different in principle from fish pastes, but I have shown them in a separate column since the taste does differ.

	FISH SAUCE	FISH PASTE	SHRIMP PASTE
BURMA	Ngan-pya-ye	Nga-pi	Pazon-nga-pi
THAILAND	Nam pla	(Kapi?)	Kapi
CAMBODIA	Tuk trey	Prahok	Măm tôm
VIETNAM	Nuoc mam		
PHILIPPINES	Patis*	Bagoong* (fish)	Bagoong* (shrimp)
INDONESIA	Ketjap ikan/Petis		Terasi/Trassi
MALAYSIA			Blachan/Belacan

*An excellent account of these products is given in Miss Arroyo's book cited in the Bibliography.

INGREDIENTS WITH LEMONY OR SOUR TASTES

Lemons and the like are the traditional and ideal accompaniment for fish. The lemon itself, although it grows well in some parts of Indonesia, is not generally available in S. E. Asia. As usual in tropical areas, the **LIME**, which is too well-known to require illustration, takes its place. (In the Philippines a variety known as Calamansi, small and with orange flesh, is used.) But another member of the citrus family does require identification. This is *Citrus hystrix*, the **MAKRUT LIME** (a name which in English has replaced the derogatory term 'Kaffir lime' which was formerly used by some authors). Its leaves, broken into small pieces, are used in many fish dishes. Saunt (1990) describes the fruit thus: '. . . is small, with an unusual and distinct shape and rind texture. The stem-end is pronounced and the rind of irregular and extremely bumpy texture; Malaysians liken its appearance to that of a crocodile's eyebrows!'

BU: shauk-nu, shauk-waing
TH: makrut
CA: krauch soeuch
PH: swangi
IN: jeruk purut, jeruk sambal
MA: limau purut

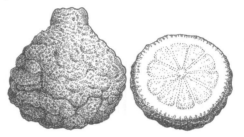

Another important ingredient which gives an acid taste is the **TAMARIND**, *Tamarindus indica*, of which both the pulp and the tiny leaves may be used. The pulp is often sold ready prepared, in a near-black sticky mass. It is diluted with water to produce what is called tamarind water in the recipes.

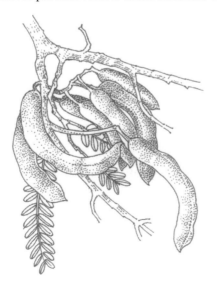

BU: ma-gyi-thi
TH: makaam
CA: ampil tum (ripe),
    ampil kheei (green)
VI: me
HK: asam koh
PH: sampaloc
IN: asam jawa
MA: asam jawa (pulp)
    asam keping (pieces)

Cymbopogon citratus is the scientific name of **LEMON GRASS** or **CITRONELLA**, a plant which has the taste of lemon and is therefore often used in fish cookery. The usual procedure is to crush the stalks and then chop them, thus releasing fully the lemon flavour.

BU: sabalin
TH: takrai
CA: slek krey
VI: xa
HK: heung mao tso
PH: salay
IN: serai
MA: serai

GINGER, GALINGALE AND TURMERIC

The ginger plant, *Zingiber officinale*, is a native of Asia. The parts which are eaten are the irregular rhizomes (shown on the right) which form just below the surface of the soil. Fresh ginger is normally used in S. E. Asia cut in slices about as thick as a coin.

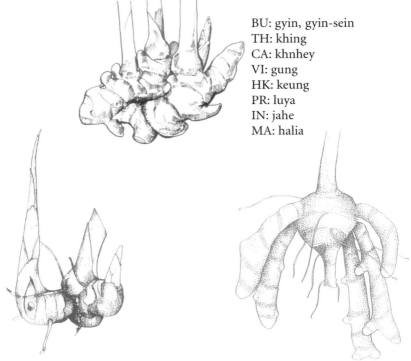

BU: gyin, gyin-sein
TH: khing
CA: khnhey
VI: gung
HK: keung
PR: luya
IN: jahe
MA: halia

GALINGALE (or GALANGA)

Again, the rhizomes are the edible part of this plant. Those of the galingale are harder than ginger and have a slightly different flavour, but are used in the same way. The scientific name is *Alipinia galanga*.

BU: pa-de-gaw-gyi
TH: kha
CA: romdeng
VI: rieng
HK: lam keong
PH: luyang, ligaw
IN: laos, lengkuas
MA: lengkuas

TURMERIC, *Curcuma domestica*, is similar but the rhizomes are yellow/orange inside. Powdered turmeric is available, but you can pound or grind your own. Turmeric is sometimes referred to as saffron, which is something quite different.

BU: sa-nwin
TH: kamin
CA: romiet
VI: bot nghe
HK: wong keung
PH: dilaw, dilao
IN: kunyit
MA: kunyit

THE COCONUT AND OTHER NUTS

The **COCONUT**, fruit of the coconut palm, *Cocos nucifera*, is of fundamental importance in S. E. Asian cookery.

Coconut oil is good for cooking (especially when fresh and home-made).

The liquid which you can hear slopping about inside a coconut before it is opened is known as coconut water or coconut juice. It is normally used in the preparation of soft drinks rather than for cooking.

Coconut cream and coconut milk (terms which are sometimes used as though they were interchangeable, but which I distinguish as explained below) are produced by taking out the white flesh of the coconut, grating it, adding water and then squeezing the mixture through a muslin or other suitable cloth. The process can be carried out twice with the same grated coconut. The first extraction will be thicker than the second; which is why recipes must specify one or the other.

In this book I have frequently followed the useful and logical convention that:

> COCONUT CREAM means the first extraction;
> COCONUT MILK means the second extraction.

Coconut cream may also be prepared from desiccated coconut, following the directions on the package This is fortunate, because many S. E. Asian dishes depend for their distinctive flavour on coconut cream and could not otherwise be recreated in places where fresh coconuts are unobtainable.

When cooking with coconut cream, never cover the pot. Before boiling point is reached, reduce the heat and start stirring with a down-up-over motion. Go on stirring thus after the mixture has come to a gentle boil. Otherwise the coconut cream will curdle. Here is some useful advice from my friend Dolf Riks. 'The milk should be boiled soon if it is not immediately used as it spoils rapidly. While doing so stir from time to time to prevent it from curdling. It may be frozen in plastic bags but then it will separate into a transparent liquid, which is mainly water, and a thick milk. This I find very handy, when you want a thick milk just chop the white pieces of the frozen block of coconut milk.'

CANDLENUTS, *Aleurites moluccana*, are important in Indonesia as kemiri and Malaysia as buah keras, where they are a staple feature of the 'pounded ingredients' which are called for in many fish recipes.

KELUWAK NUTS, from *Pangium edule*, are also known as pangi, pakem, kepayang. Before use for food, they have to be purged of the toxic hydrocyanic acid which they contain. They are used in Indonesia, Malaysia and the Philippines. The name keluwak refers particularly to ripe nuts which have been fermented. The nuts are flattened, and measure about 5 cm by 3 cm.

PEANUTS or **GROUNDNUTS**, *Arachis hypogaea*, are particularly important for the excellent cooking oil which is made from them; but peanuts themselves appear in or with some fish dishes.

THE ONION FAMILY

Allium cepa is the scientific name of various onion plants. The whole subject of onions is confusing, since from the scientific point of view there are, it seems, no clear dividing lines between varieties which seem perfectly distinct to the ordinary person. The situation in S. E. Asia is that the regular large onion, often called Spanish onion, is available in many markets. But the onions which are normally used are the small reddish onions which are shown top right. These correspond in size and function to shallots, which are also used, but less common.

BU: kyet-thun-ni
TH: hom phua lek
CA: khtim kraham
VI: hanh kho
HK: ts'ung
PH: sibuyas Bombay
IN: bawang merah
MA: bawang merah

The regular large onion is shown below.

CA: khtim baraing
VI: hanh tay
PH: sibuyas
IN: bawang Bombay
MA: bawang besar

Allium sativum is the familiar garlic. The heads of garlic grown in S. E. Asia are smaller than those of, say, France. The cloves are smaller too, and this is why the recipes often call for what seem like surprisingly large numbers of them. Garlic is of course almost always used in the form of dried heads; but sometimes a recipe calls for fresh garlic and for using the foliage.

BU: kyet-thun-byu
TH: krathiem
CA: khtim
VI: toi
HK: suen t'au, taai suen
PH: bawang
IN: bawang putih
MA: bawang puteh

A different sort of onion, which we know in the West as the **SPRING ONION** or **SCALLION**, is used in one way or another in many S. E. Asian fish dishes. All of the spring onion is edible, raw; but the part most commonly used is the green part, sliced across very thinly into tiny rondelles or cut into sections and used as a garnish.

TH: ton hom
CA: khtim slek
VI: hanh tuoi,
   hanh la
HK: t'sung
PH: sibuyas na mura
IN: bawang daun
MA: daun bawang

This is one of the most important elements in S. E. Asian cookery. In many parts of the region each family will have its own little bed of onions, often on a raised platform to protect the crop, even if they grow no other vegetables.

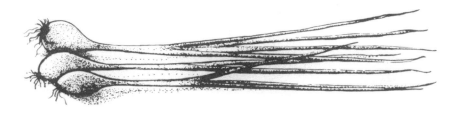

SOME OTHER VEGETABLES, ETC.

The **ORIENTAL** or **CHINESE RADISH**, illustrated below, is *Raphanus sativus* var. *longipinnatus*. Whiteish outside and white inside, it may be eaten raw and is rich in various nutrients. The Chinese usually peel and slice or dice it before adding it to soups, e.g. fish soups. This radish is often called by the Japanese name daikon or the Hindi name mooli.

BU: mhon-la-u
TH: phakkat-hua
CA: moeum spey sar
VI: cu cai tau
HK: loh baak
PH: labanos
IN/MA: lobak

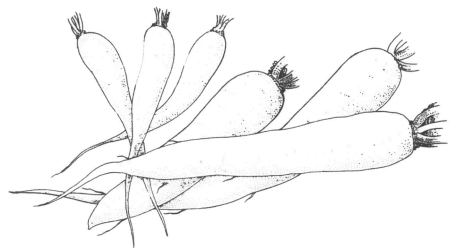

The **BITTER CUCUMBER**, *Momordica charantia*, is also known as the Bitter gourd or Balsam pear It is important in the Philippines, and also in India, where it is known as karela.

BU: kyet-hin-ga
VI: kho kwa
HK: fu kwa
PH: ampalaya
IN/MA: peria

The **BOTTLE GOURD**, *Lagenaria siceraria,* takes its name after its shape. It is especially popular in Burma and the Philippines.

BU: bu-thee, bu-
   thabeik
TH: naam tao
CA: khlok
HK: woo lo gwa
PH: upo
IN/MA: labu air

WATER SPINACH, *Ipomoea aquatica*, is a common vegetable in the Philippines and other S. E. Asian countries. It may also be called Water convolvulus or Swamp cabbage.

TH: pak boong
CA: takuon
VI: rau nuong
HK: oong choy
PH: kang kong
IN: kang kung
MA: kang kong

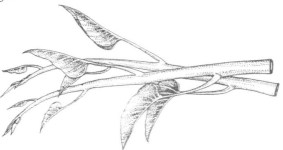

CHINESE CABBAGE, *Brassica rapa* var. *chinensis* etc, occurs in many varieties and is not illustrated, since it is more helpful to grasp the idea that it is polymorphic than to focus attention on one particular form. The name pak choi (or bok choy) is commonly used in Western countries.

TH: phakkat kha oplee
VI: cai xanh
HK: baak choi
PH: petsay, pechay
IN: petsai, sawi
MA: sawi, kobischina

The **EGGPLANTS** or **AUBERGINES**, *Solanum melongena*, occur with the familiar purple fruit, large and glossy. But two other forms of eggplant, shown below, are also found in S. E. Asian markets. There is also an even smaller variety which has a very bitter taste.

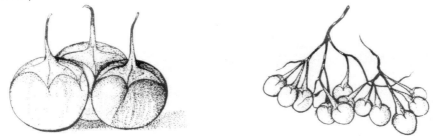

STAR-FRUIT, or **BELIMBING** (as it is known in Malaysia and Indonesia; the Filipino name is Bilimbi and the Cambodian name is Tralung tung) occurs in two species. *Averrhoa carambola* is the larger and its fruits may be sweet enough to be eaten as dessert. *Averrhoa bilimbi*, shown below, is the one of interest here. Its fruit is sour (hence the name belimbing asam) and it is often used in cookery. Dried slices (cut across the fruit and thus preserving the star shape) are available in the markets. (The name Star anise, by the way, refers to something quite different, illustrated on page 218, namely *Illicium verum*, which is a spice.)

BAMBOO SHOOTS are widely used in Chinese and S. E. Asian cookery.

BU: wah-bho-kmyit
TH: naw mai
CA: tumpeang
VI: mang
HK: choke shoon
PH: labong
IN: rebung
MA: rebong

BEANS

The **SOY BEAN** is of great importance in S. E. Asia. It is extremely nutritious. The scientific name of the plant, which is shown on the right with its seed pods, is *Glycine maximum*. The soy bean produces an excellent cooking oil and various other products of which **SOY SAUCE** is the best known. It goes under various local names, including kecap (old spelling, ketjap) in Indonesia. It comes in two main varieties – one light and clear, the other dark and salty. But there is also a sweet and very dark kind which is especially popular in Indonesia.

SOY BEAN CURD, in its fresh, soft, unpressed form, is taho in the Philippines and tahu in Malaysia and Indonesia. As a hard, pressed cake it is tokua (Philippines), taukwa (Malaysia and Indonesia) and dau hu (Vietnam).

FERMENTED SOY BEANS are tahure or tausi in the Philippines (depending on the degree of fermentation), tempe in Indonesia, taucho in Malaysia and tuong in Vietnam.

BEAN SPROUTS may be of the soy bean, but the best (shown here) are of the **MUNG BEAN.** They go under such names as taoge (Indonesia), taugeh (Malaysia) and gia (Vietnam).

I should mention, among the other beans of the region, *Vigna unguiculata* ssp *sesquipedalis*, which is shown below. It is sometimes known as the **YARD-LONG BEAN** (or long-podded cow-bean; or haricot baguette in French) and occurs in a number of seafood recipes.

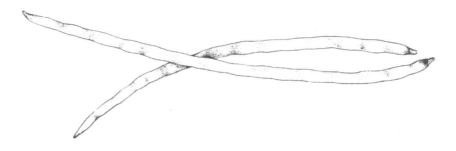

PEPPERS

The word pepper has various different meanings and can often cause confusion, especially when people refer to green and red peppers as though these were two different kinds. (Pepper fruits are green when unripe and orange or red when ripe.) But popular confusion is justified, since each of the species of pepper plant displays variants in fruit characters.

Two cultivated peppers are widespread in S. E. Asia, *Capsicum annuum* and *Capsicum frutescens*. The first has a clear white flower, borne singly; the second has greenish-white flowers, usually borne in pairs. Dr Barbara Pickersgill of the University of Reading, whose advice I follow here, says that fruit characters are not reliable in distinguishing between the species. Both have pungent (hot) and non-pungent forms. However, we can make some useful distinctions. The **BELL PEPPER** shown on the right is typical of a kind of large-fruited pepper which is never very hot. It is often called **SWEET PEPPER** or **PIMENTO**.

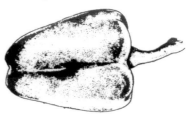

There are also various smaller peppers, more elongate in shape, which are bright red when ripe and usually very pungent. They come in three sizes. These are the **CHILLI PEPPERS**, which come in several sizes of which the largest and smallest are shown below. They are to be used with caution. The larger ones are a lovely pale jade green when marketed fresh and young. At this stage they are much less pungent than later on. They are often dried when red and may then be used, after a soaking in water, to add pungency and red colouring to dishes.

BU: nga-yok
TH: prik yuak
VI: ot lon
PH: sili
IN: cabe hijau (when green),
    cabe merah (when red)
MA: chilli, chabai

BU: no-hmyaw nga-yok
TH: prik keenu
VI: ot hiem
HK: lat chui chai
IN: rawit
MA: chilli, chabai

Piper nigrum (not shown) is something yet again – a kind of vine which bears the small fruit which we know as peppercorns. **BLACK PEPPER** is made from unripe peppercorns, the milder **WHITE PEPPER** from ripe ones which have had the outer pulpy layers removed.

SOME HERBS
AND EDIBLE LEAVES

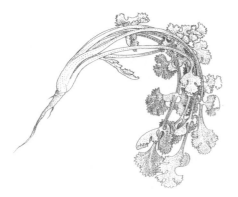

CORIANDER or (U.S.) **CILANTRO,** *Coriandrum sativum.* The leaves of young coriander plants, sometimes known as Chinese parsley, are used as a garnish and have a strong and distinctive taste, often unattractive to Europeans. (The name coriander is derived from the Greek word for a bug; the smell is reminiscent of bed-bugs.) I advocate using fairly small amounts; but many S. E. Asian cooks use a lot.

BU: nan-nan-bin   VI: rau ngo
TH: pak chee   HK: uen sai
CA: van suy   PH: ketumbar
           IN/MA: daun
               ketumbar

DILL, *Anethum graveolens.* The young leaves are sometimes used in S. E. Asian fish cookery, as they are in Scandinavia. But I have not found many local names for dill. Pak chee Lao (Laotian coriander) is what the Thai call it.

Dill and fennel leaves look alike; indeed the French call dill 'fenouil bâtard'. Fennel leaves are also used in S. E. Asia, as is the fennel root. But dill leaves are to be preferred for their flavour.

MINT plays a part in S. E. Asian fish cookery and various species and cultivars are available. The best is the sort with purplish leaves, shown in the drawing.

BU: hpo-ti-nan
TH: bai saraneh
VI: bac ha
HK: por hor yip
PH: menta
IN: kresmen
MA: daun pudina kodak

BASIL also occurs in various forms. What is shown below left is one of 4 or 5 forms of *Ocimum basilicum*, Sweet basil. The genus also includes *Ocimum canum* (maenglak in Thailand); the shrubby and pungent *Ocimum gratissimum* (kaphrao-chang in Thailand); and 'holy basil' *Ocimum sanctum*, shown below right (kaphrao in Thailand), which has a clove-like fragrance.

BU: ziga-aphyu
TH: mangluk,
    horapa, krapow
CA: chi mreas preou
VI: rau que
PH: belanoi, sulasi
IN: kemangi
MA: kemangi

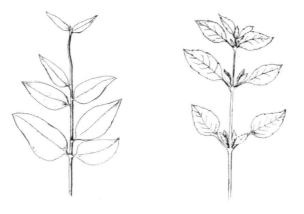

Some leaves which are used for flavouring dishes seem to be much better known in Malaysia than elsewhere. Among these are curry leaves, daun kari in Malay and bai garee in Thai. These leaves, which belong to *Murraya koenigii*, the curry plant, are dark green, elongated in shape and about 2 cm long. See the drawing bottom left. They are an important ingredient in South Indian cooking, the influence of which is particularly visible in Malaysia.

Leaves of *Polygonum odoratum*, best known as rau ram in Vietnam, are shown bottom right.

MISCELLANEOUS SPICES ETC

It is not necessary here to catalogue various spices which are familiar all over the world, such as nutmeg and cinnamon; nor to deal with things like cumin seeds and coriander seeds, of which the use is also widespread. However, two things do deserve some explanation.

The Chinese **'FIVE SPICES'** are met all over S. E. Asia. This is a ready-made mixture compounded from star anise, fennel, cloves, cinnamon and pepper. In Hong Kong it is ng heong fun and in Malaysia serbok rempah cap lima. A drawing of star anise, the first of the five spices, and the least familiar, appears lower down on this page.

MONOSODIUM GLUTAMATE, known as MSG, is supposed to bring out the flavour of other ingredients and has been used liberally by cooks in S. E. Asia as ve-tsin as well as in China and Japan as ajinomoto. However, I have not included it in any recipes here, since there is evidence (including my own testimony) that adding significant quantities of it to dishes can cause head and chest discomfort, more severe in some people than in others. Its 'natural' presence, in small amounts in certain foodstuffs, seems to be non-controversial.

RICE AND RICE PRODUCTS

It is unnecessary to say that rice, whether or not of the glutinous (sticky) kind preferred in some countries and for some purposes, is the staple food of S. E. Asia. But it may be useful to say something about various rice products. **RICE FLOUR** is frequently used. And many seafood dishes incorporate **RICE NOODLES,** just as some of the best seafood dishes of Italy involve the use of pasta in various forms. The names of these noodles are fairly constant throughout the region. Kwayteow means flat rice noodles, laksa thick ones, mee thin ones and meehoon very thin ones. It is worth while to acquaint oneself with the different varieties.

Charmaine Solomon (1996) has a particularly good account of rice and rice products throughout Asia.

Recipes from Burma

In writing about Burmese seafood recipes one must first make clear that the Burmese are much more interested in eating freshwater fish, which account for over 80 per cent of their consumption of fish. Sea fish, some believe, have a soporific effect on people who eat them; a belief which I have not met elsewhere, but which is entitled to sympathetic examination by any research worker who can devise methods of testing the hypothesis. A more wide-spread belief is that eating sea fish upsets people, making them nervous and agitated. For that reason invalids and pregnant women are expected to eat freshwater fish only. The same belief may account for the Burmese tendency, when sea fish are being cooked, to do everything possible to suppress their characteristic smell. The use of turmeric achieves this.

It is likely, however, that the proportion of marine fish eaten in Burma will increase. The resources are great, and by no means fully exploited. The Hilsa (a shad which counts as a marine fish, see page 27) is anyway one of the best-known Burmese fish; and the Burmese coast is exceptionally rich in crabs, of which there are said to be over 200 species.

The recipes which follow demonstrate a certain connection between the Burmese cuisine and those of India and China, a dual relationship which is symbolized by the choice which Burmese cooks frequently exercise between 'Indian curry powder' (garam masala) and 'Chinese curry powder'. There is, however, a distinctive Burmese flavour to many dishes, notably the famous Mohinga which is uniquely apt to induce nostalgia in anyone who knows Burma, but is well worth eating on its own remarkable merits.

A number of the recipes call for coconut cream, which would not be freely used except in areas where the coconut grows. Adding it often improves the taste; but also has the effect of converting an everyday dish into one for special occasions.

Some recipes call for sugar. Ordinary Burmese people would not be able to afford white sugar. However they do use jaggery, a fine natural sugar tapped from the tops of palm trees and sold in cakes. The best jaggery comes from Martaban near Moulmein.

Where a reference is made in the recipes to ground chilli pepper, this means dried red chilli peppers, roasted and then ground immediately before use.

The most common cooking technique in Burma is frying; and the usual medium is peanut oil. (Sesame oil is preferred for other purposes.)

Mohinga

The national dish of Burma   serves 12

It must be admitted that many of the fish dishes of S. E. Asia arouse more interest than appetite on the part of Western visitors. 'Interesting,' we exclaim, declining a second helping. Mohinga does not fall into this category. Its appeal seems to be just as strong to foreigners as to the Burmese.

Mohinga is usually made with freshwater fish (*Heteropneustes fossilis*, a catfish, being preferred). However, it may be made with sea fish and there are indeed Burmese who think it better thus, notably the people of Arakan who believe that Mohinga made with nga-shwe (the pike-conger, page 34) is the best of all. Nga-thalauk (shad, page 27) is another possibility.

The recipe which follows is essentially that of Naw Bway Htoo, whose Mohinga was the first which I ever tasted, and particularly delicious.

800 grams (½ viss) of sea fish (see above)
2 stalks lemon grass, crushed
200 grams fish sauce (ngan-pya-ye)
2 or 3 chilli peppers (preferably fresh, but dried will do)
½ teaspoonful turmeric powder

> 400 grams onions, finely sliced
> cooking oil
> 4 cloves garlic
> 1 small piece fresh ginger   ⎫
> ½ stalk lemon grass   ⎬ pounded together
> 2 more chilli peppers   ⎭

coconut cream (the product of half a coconut)
70 grams (4 ticals) rice flour   ⎫ roasted light brown in a
50 grams (3 ticals) dhal powder   ⎭ hot dry pan before use
a 20 cm section of banana trunk, cut from high up
400 grams onions
3 duck (or 4 hen) eggs, hard-boiled
2 kilos (cooked weight) rice noodles, previously cooked

> lime wedges
> more pounded chilli pepper (perhaps in oil)
> fried cloves of garlic
> fried onion rings
> Burmese bean patties (bajos)

Clean the fish, but leave the head in place. Set it to boil in just enough water to cover, with the remainder of the first batch of ingredients. Do not let it cook for long; 5 minutes should do. Then take the fish out and remove the flesh from it in little bits.

Turning to the second column of ingredients, fry the sliced onions golden brown. Add the pounded mixture of garlic etc. When a good aroma arises, add the flesh of the fish. Remove from the fire and keep aside.

Mix the coconut cream with the reserved fish broth and nearly 2 litres of water. Bring this to the boil. Meanwhile mix the rice flour with a little water; and do the same with the dhal powder. Add both to the main brew, stirring the while. Peel the section of banana trunk and slice it thinly. (The slices form delicate patterns of pink and white, which remind me of Bohemian glass.) Cut the remaining onions in quarters. Add these ingredients. When they are tender, add the fish mixture, a pinch of salt and the eggs.

Now you have your hinga. It remains to place the mo, or rice noodles, in bowls, one for each person. Then ladle the hinga over it. Each guest should add what he wants from the accompaniments listed in the fourth column of ingredients. The Burmese bean patties are especially good.

Nga-Si-Phaung-Hin-Cho

Fish bladder soup

This is an interesting and economical soup. The fish used are sometimes freshwater fish, such as the Swamp eel, but experts recommend the Threadfin (nga-kat-tha, page 45) or – perhaps best of all – the Sea catfish listed on page 33.

150 grams fish bladder, fried so that it puffs out
250 grams of small fish balls (made by boiling the chosen
    fish, on which see above, then finely mincing the flesh
    and pressing it into small balls)
200 grams cabbage, cut into strips
100 grams carrot, cut in thin long strips
salt
sugar (optional)   } to taste
fish sauce (ngan-pya-ye)
pepper

Bring 1½ litres of water to the boil; then add to it successively the fish balls, the fried bladder, the cabbage and the seasoning of salt/sugar/fish sauce. Cook gently for 10 to 15 minutes, and sprinkle a little black pepper over the soup just before it is served.

Hingyo

Prawn and gourd soup

This is an everyday Burmese dish, economical and simple. Put 4 cups of water in a pot, add half a cup of pounded dried prawns or shrimp, 3 teaspoonfuls of salt, 1 tablespoonful of fish sauce and 3 or 4 cloves of garlic, pounded. Bring all this to the boil, meanwhile peeling about a quarter of a gourd and shredding it. Add the shredded gourd to the boiling broth and let it go on boiling for 5 minutes. Just before serving the soup, add half a teaspoonful of ground black pepper.

Day Mya Mya Aye, whose directions these are, adds that pumpkin or eggplant or tomatoes may be used instead of the gourd.

Nga Kutleit

Burmese fish cutlets

On the day when I had resolved to test this dish there was no decent fish to be had in the market except hairtail (page 104). I bought one weighing 800 grams, chopped it into three parts (after cleaning it) and let these simmer for 15 minutes. The outcome was ½ kilo of prepared flesh, free of skin and bone, which did very well in the dish. But one could use instead sea catfish (pages 32 and 33) or pike-conger (page 34) or wolf herring (page 22).

400 to 500 grams fish (see above), cooked, boned and finely pounded
peanut oil
½ teaspoonful powdered turmeric
2 cloves garlic, sliced thinly
2 green chilli peppers, sliced thinly
1 medium or 2 small onions, sliced thinly
1 level dessertspoonful ground black pepper
1 level tablespoonful Indian curry powder
salt to taste
1¾ kilos potatoes, boiled, peeled and pounded with
2½ tablespoonfuls flour to obtain a soft, sticky consistency

Heat about ¼ cup of the oil, put the turmeric in and immediately afterwards the garlic. Let them brown. Then add the pounded fish and stir thoroughly. Next, put in the chilli pepper, onion, black pepper, curry powder and salt. Continue to cook the mixture for about 5 minutes more until all traces of the fishy smell have been banished (by the turmeric) and a really good aroma is arising. During this cooking period you must keep moving the mixture around in the pan and turning it over, using the useful implement illustrated on page 203. When the cooking is completed, remove the pan from the fire.

Now take the potato mixture and separate it into balls about 4 cm in diameter. Work each ball into the shape of a thick bowl, put a generous heaped teaspoonful of the fish mixture into the hollow of the bowl and then pull the sides together over this stuffing. Each stuffed ball is then flattened into the shape of a thick rissole or cutlet, and fresh peanut oil is used for frying these, 4 or 5 at a time, in a large frying pan. Remove the cutlets as soon as they are brown and crisp. You should have about 30 of them when you have finished.

Tauk-Tauk-Kyaw

'A flaming fry' was the translation (not literal) offered to me of this recipe title. The dish seems to be of Chinese derivation. Tauk tauk refers to the noise made by the twin chopping knives of a Chinese chef as he minces fish etc. The choice of fish is not of great importance. The Burmese themselves might use: barracuda (page 40), pike-conger (page 34), grunts (*Pomadasys* spp., page 86) or the king soldier bream (*Argyrops spinifer*, page 81, well known in Burma as nga-ba-yin).

800 grams fish (see above), boned and minced
½ cup cooking oil, no less and perhaps a little more
2 or 3 cloves garlic, chopped
4 or 5 tiny onions, chopped or sliced
salt to taste
fish sauce (ngan-pya-ye) to taste
1 teaspoonful sugar
50 grams carrot, thinly sliced
50 grams Chinese radish, thinly sliced
1 small bunch of leeks, cut into lengths of 1 cm or less
2 eggs, beaten

The method is simple. Fry, fry, fry. First fry the garlic and the tiny onions, then add the fish with salt, fish sauce and sugar. When the fish seems to be cooked sufficiently, add the thin slices of carrot and radish. When they are half cooked, which is to say almost at once, add the leeks and the beaten eggs. Continue stir-frying for a few minutes, then check the taste and serve the dish.

Nga-Khabut-Kyaw *Fried fish, curried*

¾ kilo (cleaned weight) of suitable fish (e.g. threadfin, pages 44 and 45; sea catfish,
    pages 32 and 33; Spanish mackerel, pages 110 and 111)
salt
ginger, a piece 3 cm long, well pounded
oil for frying
5 large onions, cut into rings
1 dessertspoonful of garam masala (Indian curry powder)
8 small green chilli peppers, each halved lengthwise
mint, a small bunch, washed

Free the fish of skin and bone, wash it and cut it into bite-size pieces (e.g. 2 cm cubes). Rub these with the salt, then with the pounded ginger.

Heat the oil in a pan and fry the pieces of fish in it until they begin to stiffen, then remove them. Next, fry the onion rings. When these are half cooked, restore the pieces of fish to the pan and add the garam masala (or curry powder) and the chilli peppers. Continue cooking gently until (after 10 minutes or less) the sauce thickens and an appetizing aroma arises. Then strew mint on the dish, pause briefly, take the dish from the fire, add salt to taste and serve.

Nga-Hmwe-Hin *A basic Burmese fish curry*

¾ kilo fish
1 one-inch piece ginger,
   thinly sliced
salt to taste
a little pounded turmeric
2 tablespoonfuls fish sauce
1 stalk lemon grass
½ cup cooking oil
sprigs of coriander

pounded ingredients:
5 small onions
4 cloves garlic
5 dried red chilli peppers

Boil the cleaned fish in a small quantity of water, adding the ginger, salt, turmeric, fish sauce and a small piece of the lemon grass. When the fish is cooked, remove it and take out the bones.

Bring the oil to the boil and add the pounded ingredients and the rest of the lemon grass. When the pounded ingredients turn golden brown and a good smell arises, add the boned fish (and any broth left over from boiling the fish). Continue cooking until the oil separates on the surface. The dish is then ready. Take the pot from the stove and sprinkle sprigs or leaves of coriander upon it.

Daw May Khine adds that green chilli peppers can be incorporated in the dish if you wish.

Nga-Hmyit-Chin-Hin

Fish and salted bamboo curry

The Burmese like to combine salted bamboo (hmyit-chin) with fish, crustaceans or pork. This simple curry is one of their favourites. They would usually select a freshwater catfish for this dish; but sea fish are used in coastal areas.

1 kilo sea catfish (page 33) or other suitable sea fish
3 tablespoonfuls peanut oil
5 small red onions, chopped and pounded
2 tablespoonfuls of ground fresh ginger ⎤ combined and mixed
1 tablespoonful ground red or green chilli pepper ⎬ with the equivalent
2 teaspoonfuls powdered turmeric ⎦ volume of hot water
1½ kilos salted bamboo (washed, sliced across, then cut into
   strips and boiled until tender)
fish sauce (ngan-pya-ye) to taste
salt to taste

Heat the oil in a pan. When it is good and hot add the pounded onions and the spice mixture. Cook this until the water has evaporated and the oil rises to the top, giving off a good aroma. Then add the minced fish with a little more hot water. Stir well and continue cooking until everything is simmering again. At this point add the boiled salted bamboo strips and hot water to cover. Bring the dish back to simmering point, then add the fish sauce and salt and serve (with rice).

Pinle-Ka-Kadit-Hin

Sea perch curry

Lates calcarifer is a magnificent sea perch whose characteristics are described on page 48. It is well-known in Bengal as the bhekti, and greatly appreciated next door in Burma under the name ka-kadit. The recipe which follows appears to me to be Indian/Burmese, and is a particularly good one.

1 kilo sea perch	*pounded ingredients:*
½ cup cooking oil	2 medium onions
coconut cream (first extraction)	4 cloves garlic
from ½ large coconut	1 one-inch piece ginger
2 teaspoonfuls tamarind water	1 teaspoonful powdered turmeric
(page 206) or lime juice	3 teaspoonfuls coriander seed
1 teaspoonful salt	2 teaspoonfuls cumin seed

The sea perch is a large fish; so the kilo which you have bought is likely to be a section of one. Ask the fishmonger to cut this for you into rounds, about 1 inch or 2½ cm thick. These should then be washed, patted dry and lightly salted.

Heat the cooking oil, then add to it the pounded ingredients. Let this fry until it gives off a good aroma, then lay the pieces of fish side by side in it. When all this is simmering satisfactorily add the tamarind or lime juice and salt, and continue to cook the fish, shaking the pan gently from time to time to prevent it from sticking, until it is just sufficiently cooked. Then add the coconut cream. As soon as this has become hot, serve the dish.

Sha-Nga-Paung-Hin

Sliced fish cakes in coconut cream

½ kilo fish	*pounded ingredients:*
1 small red onion, finely sliced	4 red chilli peppers
1 cup sesame oil	6 cloves garlic
coconut cream from 1 coconut	1 one-inch piece ginger
	1 small piece turmeric (optional)
	1 short stalk lemon grass (white part only)
	1 small red onion

Clean, skin, bone and pound the fish. Remove the seeds from the chilli peppers and soak the peppers in a little water. Drain them and pound them with the other ingredients to be pounded. Mix the result with the pounded fish and form the mixture into small flat rissoles or cutlets.

Heat the oil until it is smoking. Fry the finely sliced onion until brown. Next, fry the fish cutlets until golden brown, then lift them out and slice them thinly. Pour the coconut cream into the pan, bring it to the boil and add the sliced cutlets. Cover, and simmer for 5 to 10 minutes. The dish is then ready to serve.

These directions come from Daw Kyi Aung, who made the dish for me in Rangoon. It is delicious. The recipe is usually applied to freshwater fish, but may be used for sea fish just as well, for example nga-shwe (pike-conger, page 34).

Nga-Tha-Lauk-Paung

Hilsa boiled all day

The small bones of the hilsa make it difficult to eat. The French deal with it by cooking their shad (alose) with sorrel, which softens the bones. The recipe given here is the Burmese solution.

1 hilsa (nga-thalauk, page 27) of about 1 kilo	½ teaspoonful salt
1 cup vinegar	¼ teaspoonful powdered turmeric
	1 piece ginger, powdered
garnish:	4 cloves garlic, pounded
tomatoes	juice of 2 small onions
potato chips	2 tablespoonfuls peanut oil

Gut, scale, wash and dry the hilsa. If it is too big for the casserole in which it is to be cooked, cut it into halves. Rub it with a mixture of all the ingredients in the right-hand column above.

Put the fish in a casserole, pour over it the vinegar and an equal quantity of water. Simmer on a slow charcoal fire for 10 hours, topping up the liquid with more water as necessary. Towards the end of this period you will find that the bones of the hilsa have become quite soft. At this point, stop adding water, but continue cooking until all the remaining water has evaporated and the fish becomes oily. Then stop.

Garnish the fish with cooked whole tomatoes and fried potato chips.

Nga-Sin-Kaw-Kyaw

Minced fish fried with sago flour

Any fish will do for this recipe, so long as it has white flesh which can conveniently be separated from the bones and minced.

¾ kilo fish, boned and minced	1 carrot, shredded
1 teaspoonful 'Chinese curry powder'	50 grams sago flour
1 teaspoonful pepper	1 bunch leeks, cut into 2 cm strips
4 cloves garlic, 2 pounded and 2 chopped	4 small red onions, chopped
salt to taste	cooking oil
Burmese fish sauce (ngan-pya-ye) to taste	3 eggs, beaten (optional)

Pound the minced fish with the curry powder and the pepper, then mix all this thoroughly with the pounded garlic, salt and Burmese fish sauce. This done, add the shredded carrot. Mix the sago flour with a little water, then work it into the main mixture. Add the pieces of leek.

Now fry the chopped garlic and onions in hot oil. When they are turning golden, add the main mixture. When this begins to turn brown, add the beaten eggs and continue cooking for only 2 or 3 minutes before serving.

Ngamantha Khayanchinthi Si Piyan

Shark baked with a tomato and citrus juice sauce

Any of the better sharks, for example those listed on pages 125 and 126, may be used for this dish. However, I think that Burmese friends who particularly recommend using sawfish are right. And it is worth saying that 'wings' of ray may be cooked according to the same recipe.

1 pound (cleaned weight) shark meat (see above)
1 teaspoonful salt
cooking oil (¼ cup may be enough)
2 to 4 cloves garlic, pounded
1 bunch coriander
6 tablespoonfuls fresh tomato purée
2 tablespoonfuls citrus juice (e.g. lime, lemon or bitter oranges)
1 teaspoonful freshly ground chilli pepper

Clean the fish, cut it into six pieces and rub the salt well into them.

Oil a suitable oven dish (large enough to take the pieces of fish side by side, but no larger) and put the fish therein.

Use some more cooking oil to fry the garlic in another pan until it turns golden. Then add the celery, followed a few minutes later by the tomato purée and the citrus juice. Keep stirring the mixture. It will soon give off an irresistible aroma, the sort of smell which creates total confidence in the cook. At this point, pour it over the fish, sprinkle the chilli pepper over all and add about ¾ of a cup of water.

Cook thus in a hot oven (430°F, 220°C, gas 7) for 25 to 30 minutes. The exact cooking time will depend on the thickness of the pieces of shark, but you can tell when the dish is ready by seeing oil collect on top of the meat and by probing the fish with a fork.

Nga-Htoke-Paung (may be written Nga-Baung-Doke)

Steamed fish in banana leaf

One evening in Rangoon we had the agreeable experience of eating two slightly different versions of this dish, prepared respectively by Daw Matilda Ba Thein and Daw Kyi Kyi Aung, and of discussing the niceties of their techniques with both these skilled ladies. The directions which follow are distilled from this colloquy. This is another of the Burmese fish recipes which are normally applied to fresh-water fish, such as the butterfish (nga mhyin), but which are also used for sea fish by some Burmese. Be sure, however, to choose a sea fish of good quality, with white flesh and a delicate flavour. A pomfret (pages 100 and 101) would be a good fish for the purpose.

½ kilo (cleaned weight) fish (see above)
¾ tablespoonful salt
1 teaspoonful fish paste (nga-pi) } mixed together for rubbing
1 teaspoonful fish sauce (ngan-pya-ye) } into the fish
¼ teaspoonful powdered turmeric

6 cloves garlic
2 small red onions
1 one-inch piece ginger } pounded together
1 short stalk lemon grass (white part only)
5 or 6 chilli peppers (or 2 teaspoonfuls
   powdered chilli)
1 tablespoonful roasted rice, pounded to become rice flour
2 tablespoonfuls grated coconut
¼ teaspoonful more turmeric powder
¼ teaspoonful more salt
6 more small red onions
a six-inch piece of bottle gourd, peeled and thinly sliced
banana leaves cut into 6-inch squares
15 to 20 yai-yo leaves (*Morinda citrifolia*, 'Indian mulberry')

Gut and wash the fish. Cut it into pieces about 3 inches long by 1½ inches wide. Rub these slices with the mixture indicated above.

Pound the ingredients to be pounded and combine this mixture with the flour, the grated coconut and the second doses of salt and turmeric. Mix the sliced onions and bottle gourd into the paste thus formed.

On each square of banana leaf place a yai-yo leaf (or two if they are small); on this a spoonful of the paste, followed by a layer of fish; then another spoonful of the paste; and finally another yai-yo leaf. Fold the banana leaf into a neat packet, secure it with a toothpick. Steam the packets for about 15 minutes and serve them entire, leaving it to the guests to unwrap them.

The yai-yo leaves need not be included. The dish is more bland without them, since they have a distinctive, slightly bitter, flavour. My own view is that they should be included if possible.

Balachaung

A relish made from fried prawns with shrimp paste

There are many versions of this well-known Burmese preparation. The one which I have followed most closely was printed in the International Cookbook first published in Rangoon in 1948 by women of the English Methodist Church. The recipe concludes with the comment that the quantities prescribed are sufficient to fill a 1 lb jar of Horlick's; an evocative remark for students of imperial history.

¼ kilo dried prawns (little ones, dried whole)
10 cloves garlic ⎫
1 medium onion ⎬ peeled, and sliced very thin
1 piece fresh ginger ⎭
3 chilli peppers (optional)
1 cup sesame oil
1 level teaspoonful turmeric powder
50 grams or a little more shrimp paste (pazun-nga-pi),
   diluted with an equal or slightly greater quantity of water
salt to taste

Wash the dried prawns and pound them in a mortar, until they are reduced to small strands of flesh (not to a powder). Heat the oil and fry in it, in turn, the garlic, onion and ginger. Remove them and reserve them.

If you wish you may now fry the ground chillis in the oil. Whether you do or not, the next step is to put in the turmeric and the pounded prawns and fry them until crisp. Then strain them out of the oil. Some oil will still be clinging to the sides of the pan. Stir the shrimp paste into this and keep stirring until it is cooked, which will take about 2 minutes. Return the dried prawns to the pan and mix thoroughly with the shrimp paste. Add salt to taste and garnish with the fried garlic, onion and ginger.

This preparation may be eaten with mixed raw vegetables or served with a curried dish and rice.

Pazun-Paung-Ni

Steamed minced prawns

This is a recipe from the comprehensive Burmese cookery book by Daw Khin Than Way. The prawns to be used should be of a fair size, say 3 inches in length.

1½ kilo prawns
½ cup peanut oil
150 grams small onions, finely
   chopped
30 grams (6 cloves) garlic,
   finely chopped

150 grams tomatoes
a little black pepper
4 tablespoonfuls salty peanut
   sauce
2 tablespoonfuls fish sauce
6 duck eggs, stirred together

Clean and devein the prawns and mince the meat. Then mix it with all the other ingredients in a bowl. Steam the mixture over boiling water until it is cooked.

Pazun-Si-Pyan-Hin

Prawn curry

This recipe comes from Daw May Khine's pocket cookery book. It is a very popular dish in Burma.

750 grams prawns
a little salt
a little pounded turmeric   } mixed together
1 tablespoonful fish sauce
5 small onions
5 cloves garlic   } pounded together
4 red chilli peppers, previously roasted
½ cup peanut oil

Peel and devein the prawns and marinate them in the mixture of fish sauce, salt and turmeric. Fry the pounded ingredients until they are golden-brown and give off a good smell, then add the marinated prawns and stir all together. Add a little water. When the oil comes to the top of the mixture it is ready.

Daw May Khine adds that the chilli peppers may be left out.

Pazun-Hmyit-Hin

Prawn and bamboo shoot curry

The Burmese like the combination of prawns and bamboo shoots. This curry is best made in July or August, when the tender shoots of the variety of bamboo known as wahbho are sprouting. The shoots should be picked when they are standing about 6 inches high, and must be used on the same day. The best part to use is that just under the surface of the soil. (Canned bamboo shoots may, of course, be substituted.)

1 kilo prawns (weighed whole), cleaned and peeled
1½ kilos bamboo shoots, boiled and sliced
4 medium onions, sliced
3 tablespoonfuls cooking oil
2 teaspoonfuls powdered turmeric
2 teaspoonfuls ground chilli pepper
2 tablespoonfuls ground onion
2 tablespoonfuls ground fresh ginger
coconut cream (first extraction) from 1 large coconut

Fry the sliced onions in hot oil until they are golden brown. Add the turmeric and the ground chillis with a little hot water. Simmer for a minute or two, then add the other ground ingredients and a little more hot water. Continue cooking until oil rises to the top of the mixture, then add the prawns and cook them until they are good and firm.

Now add the slices of bamboo shoot, stir and pour 1 cup of hot water over all. Simmer for another few minutes, then add the coconut cream and remove the pot from the fire as soon as this has had time to become hot. Serve with rice.

Pazun-Let-Thote

A 'hand-mixed' prawn salad

This unusual salad is deservedly popular in Burma itself and also among all foreigners who have tasted it. It can be made perfectly well with fish (but choose one with firm flesh) or cephalopods (e.g. octopus) or bivalves (e.g. *Anadara* spp., page 160) or for that matter with pork, or even without any fish or meat at all; but the version with prawns is to my mind unbeatable. It was demonstrated to me by a young Burmese chemist, U Aung Myint. Allow an hour and a quarter for preparing the dish in the quantity given.

1/2 kilo (unpeeled weight) medium prawns (or more if you wish)
10 large cloves garlic
6 small red onions (or 1½ medium Spanish onions)
1 cucumber about 20 cm long or part of a larger one
½ white cabbage
a dozen young lettuce leaves
5 to 10 small (red or green) fresh chilli peppers
1 small packet prepared tamarind pulp, diluted with water
½ cup peanut oil
1½ teaspoonfuls powdered turmeric
1 tablespoonful fish sauce
2 teaspoonfuls salt

Peel and finely slice the cloves of garlic and the small onions, leaving about a third of the onion with the garlic and putting the other two thirds aside. Halve the half cabbage, cut out and discard the thick centre stalk and shred the leaves. Wash and chop coarsely the lettuce leaves. Peel the cucumber, slice it into rounds about 4 mm thick, then slice these across into strips about 4 mm wide. Cut each of the little chilli pepppers into about six pieces.

Behead, peel and devein the prawns. If you are using prawns which are absolutely fresh from the sea, do not cook them; simply sprinkle a little lime juice over them. Otherwise put the cleaned prawns into gently boiling water for a couple of minutes or so (not even long enough for the water to come back to the boil). In either event, cut the prepared prawns into bite-size pieces.

Heat the peanut oil in a large frying pan. While it is on a low flame, put in the turmeric and stir it around gently with a spatula. It must not turn black, only a darker shade of golden brown. After two minutes, add the garlic and onion (which should also become golden-brown, no more). Check the aroma, which should be free of any turmeric smell.

Now combine everything in a large bowl – prawns, cabbage, cucumber, remaining (raw) onion, lettuce leaves, contents of the frying pan (including what oil is left in it), tamarind water, fish sauce and salt – and toss it well together so that everything is well mixed. (The little pieces of chilli pepper would go in too if you follow normal Burmese practice; but it is permissible to serve these separately.)

Chin-Baung-Pazun-Kyaw

A traditional Burmese preparation of prawns and leaves

We paused in one of the Rangoon markets to examine some greenery and were told by the vendor that these particular leaves went very well with prawns. Even before we decided to buy a bunch our alert hostess had changed her lunch menu and was negotiating for prawns nearby. Soon we were sitting down to eat the combination, which is extremely good. (We need not have hurried, since I later learned that the dish keeps well and that a Burman setting off for foreign parts is likely to be given a jar of it to take with him.)

¼ viss (just under 1 pound) prawns
2 tablespoonfuls or so of peanut oil
1 large bunch chin-baung-byu (a sort of sorrel – don't buy the red kind,
    which is chin-baung-ni)
2 small red onions, sliced
3 or 4 green chilli peppers, chopped
salt and pepper

Heat the oil, cook the onions and chilli peppers in it briefly, until the onions are golden. Add the prawns and continue cooking for another 5 minutes or so. Then put in the chin-baung leaves (stripped from their stems) with the seasoning. The dish will be ready after 2 or 3 minutes' more cooking. Serve at once or allow to cool and store in a jar.

Ganan-Paung

Baked crab

Most S. E. Asian recipes for baked crab include a number of hot and spicy ingredients. This one, related to me succinctly and enthusiastically by a Burmese elder statesman, does not. It relies on the taste of cinnamon to complement the flavour of the crab.

   Buy live crabs of a good size. When the time comes, kill them by whatever method you favour. Then cut off the tops of their carapaces and scoop out the flesh. Extract the meat from the claws too. Mix it all with some pounded onion and a little cinnamon, then put it back in the carapaces (which have in the meantime been carefully cleaned), dust with flour (rice flour or wheat flour) and bake until done.

Recipes from Thailand

Thailand is unique among the countries of S. E. Asia in having no colonial legacy, political or culinary; and this may help to account for the relative purity of its traditional cuisine. It is true, and evident, that influences from the Asian subcontinent, from China and from the Malayan peninsula and beyond have long been at work; but both in Bangkok and in the countryside and fishing ports one still recognizes Thai food as Thai.

In Bangkok, do I say? This formerly beautiful city is now so overgrown and has received, in politely adapting itself to the exigencies of the tourist trade, such an exposure to current foreign influences that it is no longer the easiest place in which to look for authentic Thai food. Yet in Bangkok is to be found, since 1975, the shrine to which all who seek this should at once proceed, namely the Rung Taw Kitchen*. Here, in an atmosphere of the most delicate attention, such as one would expect in a private house, in a garden scented by orchids and untainted by either motor-car fumes (the nearest busy street being some distance away) or commercial pressures (the desire of the proprietress being patently to maintain Thai traditions and to delight her guests rather than to secure the profits which her venture deserves); here, I say, one may really see, smell and of course taste Thai cooking at its finest. (Be sure to have the homemade ginger drink** with and several desserts after your fish or other main dish.)

However, do not allow this experience, supreme as it must remain, to be your only one. Sample also the popular dishes in popular eating-places; and note that the same artistry, the same patience in carving fruits and vegetables, in blending tastes and imparting a visual harmony to dishes is reflected therein too.

The Thai versions of the ubiquitous Mi (or Mee – see the recipe on page 247) seem to me to be among the best, just as the cockles (*Anadara granosa*, page 160) which sea nomads prepared for us one night under the palms beside a Phuket beach survive in our memory without peer.

* I hope that it still survives, a quarter of a century later.

** This is called Khing sot and is made from young ginger in the rainy season. The menu on one occasion when we enjoyed this drink was (1) Kao Tom Pla Muk (see recipe): (2) Hoy Maeng Pu Mok ('stuffed' mussels in their shells decorated with tiny pieces of red chilli and Makrut lime leaf): (3) Pla Puak (little fish-shaped fish cakes made from Pla kaphong and taro): (4) Pu Ma Chood Pang Tawt (served with Sriracha sauce – see page 150): (5) Miang Pla Thu (see recipe): Gaeng Phet Kung (a green shrimp curry): and Mang Lak Nam Ka-ti (the dessert, which gave the effect of tiny black jelly-baby fish afloat in a caviar-studded sea of milk, what looked like caviar being sweet basil seeds).

Cholburi Fish Soup

This recipe was contributed by MR Sangiem Svasti to a book of recipes commemorating the cremation in 1935 of HH Princess Yaovabha-bhongse-snid at Wat Benjamabophit.

shallots	small young eggplants
lemon grass	fresh sea shrimp
fresh sea fish	chillis
salted sea fish (pla kulao)	nam pla
shrimp paste	palm sugar
salt	makrut lime leaves
very young water melons	lime juice

Slice shallots and lemon grass. Grill fresh and salted fish, removing bones, reserving flesh. Wash and peel water melons cutting them into cubes. Halve eggplants or leave them whole if they are very young. Shred chillis. Peel shrimps, remove heads and black veins. Cut them up small.

Pound together shallots, lemon grass, fresh and salted fish, shrimp paste and salt. Dissolve this paste in water and bring this stock to the boil. Add melons, shrimps, eggplants, and chillis. Taste and season with nam pla and palm sugar as liked. Garnish with makrut leaves and a squeeze of lime juice just before serving.

Tom Som Pla

A sour fish soup

This recipe comes from a faded green book published to mark the 48th birthday, in 1935, of a monk. The 48th birthday is important as the end of the fourth twelve-year period in a man's life. The monk, whose name was Pra Kru Bhinitviharkaan and who belonged to Wat Boromnivas, had collected the recipes and wished to see his collection in print; so friends provided the money and the book was produced.

1 pla kaphong (snapper, pages 74 to 79)	*Pounded ingredients:*
4 one-inch pieces ginger	5 coriander roots
½ cup tamarind water	7 shallots
fish sauce (nam pla) to taste	15 peppercorns
1 tablespoonful sugar	1 dessertspoonful shrimp paste (kapi)
7 spring onions (optional)	

Clean the fish. Cut the flesh, including that in the head, into bite-size pieces. Make a curry paste by pounding the ingredients indicated. Wrap the paste in a piece of banana leaf and grill it until it gives off a good fragrance.

Shred the ginger. Put it and the curry paste into the water in which you are going to boil the fish. Bring it to the boil, then add the fish, bring it back to the boil and add the tamarind water, fish sauce and sugar. When it boils again, taste it to check the seasoning. Then serve it, using chopped spring onion leaves as a garnish if you wish.

Tom Klong Bai Makarm *Fish soup with tamarind leaves*

½ kilo (cleaned weight) pla kaphong (snapper, pages 74 to 79), cut up into
    small pieces
4 to 6 cups coconut milk
1 tablespoonful shrimp paste (kapi)   }   pounded together
3 coriander roots
6 to 8 shallots, crushed
5 slices galingale
1 cup of young, tender pink shoots and leaves of tamarind
3 stalks of lemon grass, cut into 2-inch lengths and bruised
5 young makrut lime leaves
2 dried red chilli peppers, roasted
sprigs of coriander (or spring onion leaves, cut into sections)
seasoning: fish sauce (nam pla), palm sugar and a little lime juice

Bring the coconut milk to the boil and wait for the oil to separate on the surface.
Then add to the separated mixture the pounded coriander root and shrimp paste,
together with the shallots and galingale. Let it boil for about 15 minutes, then add
the tamarind shoots and leaves. Mix these well in. Next add the pieces of fish, the
lemon grass and the makrut leaves. Boil for another 10 minutes.

    Garnish the soup with the roasted chilli peppers, cut into pieces lengthwise, and
the coriander (or spring onion). Season with fish sauce, palm sugar and lime juice.

    This recipe was given to a friend of mine in Bangkok by the man who came to
prune her tamarind trees.

Kaeng Cherd Pla Muk Yud Sy

A clear soup with stuffed baby inkfish

Wash and remove the ink sacs from very small inkfish (cuttlefish), which should
be about 1" to 2" long. Stuff them loosely with a filling made of ground pork and a
pounded mixture of equal quantities of garlic and coriander root, with salt and
pepper. Steam the inkfish until they are cooked. Bring some good soup stock to
the boil and add finely sliced Chinese mushrooms.

    Put two or three inkfish into each individual soup bowl and pour hot soup over
them. Garnish with garlic (fried crisp and golden in plenty of oil), pepper and
coriander leaves. Chinese celery may be substituted for coriander.

    If you prefer a thicker soup, add a few tapioca pellets just before serving.
Alternatively (and especially if you want a substantial snack for breakfast or
supper) make the soup thicker still by adding a quantity of pounded (but not
pulverized) uncooked rice. You will then have **Khao Tom Pla Muk**, which is both
delicious and filling. When we ate it at the Rung Taw Kitchen (the source of this
recipe) we asked about the garnishing – little crisp brown crumbs which we could
not identify. The answer was interesting. When rice is cooked, there is often a thin
layer of hard grains left stuck to the bottom of the pot. This can be removed, fried
or toasted, and then crumbled over the top of the soup, leaving the dish with a
pleasing contrast of texture.

Nam Prik Num

Green chilli sauce made with pla thu

This seafood recipe comes from the north of Thailand, near the Shan border and far from the sea. However, seafood (often in dried or ready-steamed form) is available there. In the old days it was not always easy to obtain shrimp paste in those parts; hence the use of tua nao, which plays a similar role in the recipe but has its own distinctive and agreeable taste. (Tua nao is bought in stacks of thin round crêpes, brownish in colour. They are prepared thus. Soak yellow beans for 36 hours, until the outer skin peels off. Pound the inside part to a paste. Take a small ball of this paste and pat it from hand to hand, each hand being covered by a leaf to prevent sticking, until the ball has turned into a paper-thin crêpe. Repeat until all the paste is used up. Then dry the crêpes in the sun.)

½ cup roasted white meat of pla thu (pages 108 and 109)

to be roasted together:	*and for flavouring:*
5 shallots	2 pieces tua nao (see above)
3 small heads garlic	makrut lime juice
1 stalk lemon grass, cut up	fish sauce (nam pla)
5 slices mature galingale	1 teaspoonful coriander leaves,
7 green chilli peppers (long,	finely cut
thin and young)	1 teaspoonful spring onion
	leaves, finely cut

Pound together the first four roasted ingredients and the tua nao, until you have a paste. Then add the fish and pound again. Finally, add the green chilli peppers and pound very lightly, just enough to squash them and make the juice come out.

Season to taste with makrut juice and fish sauce before adding the finely cut coriander and spring onion leaves and serving.

(Recipe of Mrs Udom Panit from Meuong Pai)

Pla Tod Laad Prik *Fried fish with chilli sauce*

1 pla karang (grouper – pages 54 to 57 – these fish may also be called pla kao in the market) weighing 750 grams to 1 kilo
fish sauce (nam pla)
2 to 4 small heads of garlic, crushed and chopped
3 to 6 large red chilli peppers, thinly sliced
2 to 4 tablespoonfuls of ready-made sweet and sour sauce (buey chiew) or a mixture of 1 tablespoonful each of lime juice, honey or marmalade

Clean the fish, score it on both sides and marinate it in fish sauce for 15 minutes or so. Heat oil in a wok (not too much – the fish should not be completely immersed in it) and then fry the fish in this until it is crisp and brown on both sides. Put half the garlic in about 5 minutes before you expect the fish to be ready. Take the fish out when the garlic is browned (taking care not to let it burn). Keep it on a heated plate.

In the oil which is left in the wok cook the rest of the garlic with the chilli peppers, some fish sauce and the buey chiew. When this second lot of garlic is done, pour the mixture over the fish and serve it.

Pla Wua Tom Kar

An illegitimate curry of triggerfish

This recipe was pronounced illegitimate by Dr Vagn Hansen when he was direct-ing the Marine Biological Centre at Phuket. What happened was that we tasted in his house a superlatively good chicken curry. He called it 'Koh Lanta thicken' and explained that it was made from the recipe of a gifted girl from a remote island who had come to Phuket to cook for two years until she was recalled by her family. I asked whether the recipe could be applied to fish and was told definitely not; a curry for fish would be different. However, the triggerfish is dubbed by some the chicken of the sea and I stubbornly hold that the recipe is exactly right for it.

2 triggerfish (page 123) of nearly 1 kilo each (uncleaned weight)
2 coconuts
salt to taste
2 pieces galingale
9 stalks lemon grass
15 small onions
1 large head garlic
10 chilli peppers
5 leaves of makrut lime (*Citrus hystrix*), torn into pieces

Clean and skin the triggerfish and cut the flesh into fairly large pieces. Use the two coconuts to make 1 cup of thick and 5 of thin coconut cream.

Put the 5 cups of thin coconut cream into a pot, put the pot on the fire and soon afterwards add the fish and salt. Cut the galingale into small pieces. Cut the lemon grass into lengths of 2 or 3 cm and beat them to make them soft. Add both to the pot.

Peel and crush the small onions and the cloves of garlic. Add them and the chillis to the pot. Boil until the triggerfish is tender, then add the cup of thick coconut cream, bring back to the boil, add the makrut leaves, remove from the heat and serve.

Ho Mok Pla *Steamed fish with curry paste in banana leaf cups*

A famous Thai fish dish. Like its counterparts in the neighbouring countries, it is most frequently made with freshwater fish, but may be used for sea fish too. The version which I give below is an old recipe of the Viseschinda family, adapted by Susie Caro from her grandmother's instructions.

2 cups flaked fish, of good quality	*for the curry paste:*
2 cups coconut cream	1 teaspoonful finely chopped garlic
½ tablespoonful fish sauce (nam pla)	1 tablespoonful small purple onions, chopped
1 egg	5 dried chilli peppers
1 cup sweet basil leaves OR cabbage leaves cut into small strips	½ teaspoonful chopped galingale
	1 teaspoonful chopped coriander root
1 tablespoonful finely cut strips of red chilli pepper	½ teaspoonful chopped makrut lime peel
	1 teaspoonful chopped lemon grass
2 tablespoonfuls chopped spring onion	1 teaspoonful shrimp paste
	1 teaspoonful salt
1 tablespoonful chopped coriander leaves	1 teaspoonful peanuts, cooked and shelled
2 makrut lime leaves, finely chopped lengthwise	(all the above to be pounded with pestle and mortar until you have a firm paste)

Put 1 tablespoonful of the coconut cream aside. Divide the rest into two parts. Put one part into the blender with the fish meat and the fish sauce and blend at low speed for 3 minutes. Add the second portion of coconut cream, the curry paste and the egg yolk. Blend at medium speed for 5 minutes or so. Then refrigerate the mixture for a while.

Meanwhile mix the reserved tablespoonful of coconut cream and the white of the egg together and keep this mixture aside.

You will need 10 banana leaf cups. Put the sweet basil leaves or strips of cabbage in the bottom of these, followed by the fish mixture and topped by a teaspoonful or so of the coconut cream and white of egg mixture. Decorate with the remaining ingredients, place the cups in the top of a very hot steamer for 15 minutes and serve at once.

Miang Pla Thu *A salad of Spanish mackerel*

If you wish to make an authentic Thai dish with the minimum of effort and the maximum of flexibility, this is it.

Buy your pla thu (Spanish mackerel, pages 110 and 111) ready-steamed. Fry it briefly in vegetable oil, flake the flesh and add to it either lime juice or chunks of lime with the peel on, cut small as for marmalade. Then mix the fish with as much as you please of any or all of the following ingredients:

shallots, sliced; ginger, shredded; peanuts, whole or crushed; chilli peppers, seeded and cut into thin strips (or whole); green mango, shredded.

Kaeng Tai Pla

Fish liver curry, a speciality from Songkhla

This recipe was kindly contributed, with an introductory paragraph, by Mom Rachawong Pimsai Amranand. It is one of those which appeared in a commemorative book of recipes* distributed to the mourners at the cremation of a Thai lady.

Fish livers, usually from pla thu, are prepared in brine and so there is no need for salt or nam pla in this recipe. The curry is exceedingly hot and usually only a very small bowl is served to each person, with quantities of rice and fresh vegetables. The curry should taste hot, salty and a little sour but Bangkok people add sugar because they like a sweeter taste. In Songkhla there is no sugar. The sourness comes from a citrus that grows in the South, called som khaik or Indian orange, which is akin to the Seville or bitter orange familiar elsewhere; it is sold cut and dried and obtainable at the week-end market in Bangkok. (If you cannot get this, tamarind pulp will do – soak it in a little water and squeeze it and use the resulting juice.)

20 tablespoonfuls of fish livers	20 cloves of garlic
1 kilo of grilled fish (any fish will do)	9 slices of 'Siamese ginger' (galingale)
3 tablespoonfuls of fresh sea-shrimp meat	½ teaspoonful grated makrut lime peel
3 stalks of lemon grass	makrut leaves, very finely cut up
10 peppercorns	a little kapi (shrimp paste)
2 tablespoonfuls bird chillis	10 slices of turmeric
3 dried chilli peppers	sugar
5 shallots	som khaik or tamarind pulp

Put the fish livers and 2 cups of water into a saucepan and allow to boil.

Pound together in a mortar the shrimp, lemon grass, peppercorns, dried chillis, shallots, garlic, galingale, makrut peel, shrimp paste and turmeric root until fine. Dissolve this paste in some water and bring it to the boil. Add the meat of the grilled fish, the fish livers and the water in which they cooked. Allow to boil; then add sugar, som khaik (or tamarind water) and makrut leaves. Taste and adjust seasoning. Boil for a little longer and serve with raw vegetables such as long beans and sa-taw, the seeds of *Parkia speciosa*. The latter have a peculiar smell of their own and are much loved down South. They are known as peteh/petai in Indonesia/Malaysia.

---

* For more information about this pleasant custom, see my collected essays, *A Kipper with My Tea.*

Kaeng Phet Kraben

Curried eagle ray or sting ray

For this recipe you need 3 good pieces of eagle ray (pla kaben nok, page 130), weighing about ½ kilo in all. Cut them into small bits. You will also need 1 kilo grated coconut, to be made into about 4 cups coconut milk (on this occasion it includes the first extraction, so is a cross between cream and milk).

You must also prepare a curry paste by pounding together the following ingredients with some salt:

1 tablespoonful coriander seed	1 stalk lemon grass
¾ tablespoonful cumin seed	9 dried chilli peppers (soaked in
3 slices of mature galingale	salt water and de-seeded)
2 to 3 tablespoonfuls each of	3 slivers makrut lime rind
finely cut shallot and garlic	1 teaspoonful shrimp paste (kapi)

Finally, you will need for flavouring a bunch of sweet basil leaves, a bunch of mak hua duang (the tiny little eggplants which are about the size of large peas) and young, tender leaves of makrut lime.

Bring the coconut milk to the boil and wait until the oil separates on the surface. Then put in the fish. Stir it from time to time as it cooks. This will not take long. Once it is done, turn off the flame, lift out the fish (using a strainer spoon to collect any little remaining bits) and reserve it all in a separate bowl.

Skim off curd and oil from the top of the boiled coconut milk. Now sauté the curry paste in the pan, adding the skimmed curd and oil as you go, bit by bit. Continue until the liquid has been reduced to a thick oil, by which time a splendid aroma will be rising from it. At this point transfer the contents of the pan back into the pot of boiled coconut milk, bring it all to the boil again and add the fish. When the fish has been fully warmed up add the flavouring, leaving the sweet basil leaves until last. Season with fish sauce and serve.

I mention here another popular Thai curry with the striking title Jungle curry (**Kaeng Paa**). This is made on similar lines, but without coconut milk or shallots. The amount of garlic is increased and some other ingredients added, notably a coriander root and dee pree (which is long pepper).

Kaeng Sai Bua with Pla Thu Nung

A 'kaeng' in which lotus stems are featured with steamed pla thu

This recipe was given to me by Ti Garden, whose meticulous approach to cookery, and indeed to everything is exemplified in the precise instructions.

6 pla thu, bought ready-steamed (several species go under this name – see pages
    108 and 109 – choose good-sized specimens of one of the smaller species)
oil for frying
½ kilo grated coconut, to produce 1 cup coconut cream and 4 to 6 cups coconut
    milk
10 or so long lotus stems (which can be bought in coils in the market), with the
    outer skin peeled off and the peeled stems cut into sections about 1½ inches long
8 of the sour little fruit known as madan (*Garcinia schomburgkiana*) finely cut up

ingredients to be pounded:	*for the seasoning:*
3 large red dried chilli peppers	1 teaspoonful salt
(previously soaked in warm,	fish sauce (nam pla) to taste
salted water)	a little tamarind extract (if needed)
5 shallots	a pinch or two of sugar
5 coriander roots (optional)	
15 black peppercorns	
1 rhizome of young galingale	
(or 4 to 5 'fingers' of krachai*)	
½ teaspoonful shrimp paste (kapi)	

Take 3 of the steamed pla thu, extract the flesh (free of bone and skin) and reserve it. Fry the other 3 whole until they are crisp and brown and keep them aside too, having first cut off their heads.

    Pound together the ingredients to be pounded. Bring the coconut milk to the boil; add the pounded mixture to it. Next, add the sections of lotus stem; the flaked flesh of the first 3 pla thu; the 3 whole fried pla thu; and the madan. Bring everything back to a gentle boil and continue cooking for 5 to 10 minutes until the lotus stem is sufficiently cooked. Then season to taste with the salt and fish sauce. If the taste is not sour enough, add a little tamarind extract.

    Finally, put in the pinch or two of sugar and the cup of coconut cream, bring back to simmering point and serve.

*Krachai is *Boesenbergia pandurata*, a plant of the ginger family, whose roots, hanging in clusters, are thought to resemble a bunch of 'Chinese keys', a name by which they are sometimes known. The roots, brown outside and yellow/orange inside, are used as an aromatic ingredient.

Jaew Pla Thu

This recipe was among those distributed, in the form of a little booklet, to the guests at the 60th birthday celebration of a Thai lady who was renowned for her skill at cookery. The result of following the directions is a thick sauce to be eaten with raw vegetables rather in the same way as you eat a dip. You can cut down on the chillis but it is supposed to be very hot.

2 large steamed pla thu (page 108)
20 fresh chilli peppers, red yellow and green
30 bird chilli peppers (the smallest kind)
4 or 5 slices of galingale
2 heads of garlic

8 shallots
lime juice
fish sauce (nam pla)
palm sugar

Grill the fish until crisp, de-bone it and reserve the flesh. Grill the chilli peppers, galingale, garlic and shallots until nicely charred outside and cooked inside. If you are using a charcoal fire, drop the lot into the hot coals and remove them with tongs.

Peel the garlic and shallots, and pound them together with the chilli peppers and the galingale. When all this is finely pounded, add the fish and pound to blend well. Season with lime juice, nam pla and palm sugar. Taste to see that the balance of salty, sour and sweet is just right. Serve this sauce with raw vegetables such as cucumbers, Chinese cabbage and lettuce.

Pla Kuey *How they preserve anchovies at Chanburi*

Archarn Sunthorn Bunnotok, of Chanburi, contributed this recipe. She explains that the anchovies should be fresh from the sea and of the most soft tender variety. Should you prepare the dish with less tender anchovies, add a dash of the tenderizer known as din prasew to the vinegar and salt – this will soften the backbones of the fish satisfactorily.

2 cupfuls anchovies (see above), well cleaned with sea water
3 to 4 cups rock salt
2 tablespoonfuls best quality plain vinegar
3 tablespoonfuls brown sugar
½ cup kao koi (uncooked rice which has been toasted in a skillet and then pounded to a powder while still hot)
2 tablespoonfuls of galingale which has been grated and then dried out in the sun to make it fluffy

Marinate the fish in a mixture of the salt and vinegar for 1 to 2 hours, until they are soft and juicy, then mix well with the brown sugar and add the kao koi and galingale. Let the preparation mature in a sterilized glass container for 3 to 4 months, or until the anchovies turn brown, with a clear liquid formed on top and a good aroma arising from the brew.

When you come to eat these preserved anchovies, season them with finely cut lemon grass, young ginger, spring onion, tamarind juice (made by squeezing fully ripe tamarind fruit with warm water until it turns into a brownish liquid), a little sugar and lime juice to taste.

Tod Mun Kung *Fried shrimp dumplings* (recipe of Khun Suda of Thonburi)

1 kilo of good sized fresh shrimp (prawns), peeled and deveined (but keep the
    yellow part from the body)

2 small heads of garlic

15 black peppercorns

1 dried red chilli pepper (optional)

salt

2 tablespoonfuls flour

fish sauce (nam pla)

1 egg white, unbeaten

Select your largest klok, i.e. stone mortar, and pound in it the garlic, peppercorns
and chilli pepper with a little salt, adding the shrimp a few at a time as you go.
Continue until you have a smooth, sticky mass. Then sprinkle in the flour and
season with fish sauce and pound some more. (The more you pound, the better
and the chewier will be the dumplings.) Finally, 'squish in the egg white'.

Take a handful of the mixture at a time and squeeze it out (between thumb and
forefinger) into balls. Flatten these a little and deep-fry them.

The Tod mun (which some would write Tawt man) is usually taken with chilli
sauce or with a cucumber sauce made as follows. Mix well together ½ cup vinegar,
1 teaspoonful salt and 2 tablespoonfuls palm sugar or honey, adding a little more
sugar if necessary. Put into this mixture 2 tablespoonfuls of roasted peanuts,
crushed; and 2 or 3 chilli peppers, crushed and chopped. Finally, add 1 cup of
chopped cucumber (pieces about 1 cm square – if you use a large cucumber, take
out the seeds; if small ones, do not bother).

Kung Sang Wa *A prawn dish in the aristocratic tradition*

Begin by buying 5 or 6 large prawns. Clean and devein them, but retain the yellow
part from the body section and the liquid which comes out from the body. Steam
the meat just enough to make it lose its transparency. Then shred it and mix it
well with the yellow part and the liquid. Thereafter you will need the following:

some fresh green, yellow and red chilli peppers

2 stalks lemon grass

young ginger, enough to produce 4 tablespoonfuls

7 shallots

3 spring onions

2 sprigs coriander

5 tender leaves of makrut lime

all cut up finely,
i.e. almost to
grated form

5 sprigs mint

3 or 4 sprigs of *Eryngium foetidum* (phak chee farang, 'false coriander', fitweed)

1 teaspoonful rind of som sa (citron, *Citrus medica*)

and for the seasoning:

fish sauce (nam pla); juice of 1 large makrut lime; more juice – of lime, lemon or
som sa; a little sugar

When you have cut up the ingredients marked for this treatment, mix them with
the shredded prawn, add the seasoning and garnish with either coriander leaves or
mint leaves and a few chilli peppers.

Kang Dong   *Pickled mantis shrimp*

Buy 20 mantis shrimp (page 142) with eggs (this is important), clean them thoroughly and spread them out on a grid to dry thoroughly. Meanwhile bring to the boil 2 to 3 cups of good quality fish sauce (nam pla) with 3 tablespoonfuls, or even 4, of brown sugar (palm sugar, if possible). Then let the mixture cool.

Sterilize a glass jar of suitable size, place the mantis shrimp in it and pour the fish sauce mixture over them, so that they are completely covered. The mantis shrimp will be ready for eating in about three days. (The best plan is to keep the jar in the sunlight during the day and then refrigerate it at night during this period. Afterwards, if you do not eat the mantis shrimp right away, keep the jar refrigerated, or at least in a cool place.)

Serve the pickled mantis shrimp with a squeeze of lime juice, a pinch of sugar and slivers of hot chilli pepper.

Kaeng Khoua Saparot Kab Kai Meng Da

Horseshoe beetle crab eggs with pineapple (based on a recipe in *Tamra Arhaan Kao-waan*)

1 cup horseshoe beetle crab (page 144) eggs, scalded	*ingredients to be pounded:*
	salt
grated coconut to produce 1 cup cream and 4 cups milk	7 large red dried chilli peppers (previously soaked in salted water and de-seeded)
½ cup shrimp (prawn) meat, cut up finely	1 teaspoonful finely cut shallots
fish sauce (nam pla)	2 tablespoonfuls crushed garlic
3 cups sour pineapple, cut up finely	5 slices galingale
palm sugar	2 stalks lemon grass, chopped
tender makrut lime leaves	1 tablespoonful coriander root, finely chopped
	1 tablespoonful finely chopped rind of makrut lime
	1 tablespoonful shrimp paste (kapi)

Bring the coconut milk to the boil and wait for the curd and oil to separate on the surface.

Meanwhile make your pounded mixture (see right hand column above) and combine it with the shrimp meat. Transfer the curd and oil from the boiled coconut milk to a pan and sauté the pounded mixture in it, adding a little fish sauce. This done, add the pineapple and the horseshoe crab eggs and put the whole mixture back in the first pot, where the boiled coconut milk (less what you skimmed off the top) still is. Bring to the boil and cook for 20 minutes or more. It is important to ensure that most of the liquid is boiled away before you proceed to the next step, which is to add the cup of coconut cream. Finally, season with more fish sauce and some palm sugar, garnish with makrut leaves and set aside for a while. (It is usual to let this dish stand for some time and then to bring it back to the boil for a moment just before serving it.)

This kaeng should be creamy and thick, with the pale yellow colour of the pineapple.

Kanom-Chin Nam Prik Pu, Kung

Rice noodles with a crab and prawn sauce

This is a long recipe, but the result is a meal in itself and a very good one too. The version which I present is adapted from that in *Tamra Arhaan* by Chitsamaan Komolthiti. You will need some cooked rice noodles, and the following.

Preparation of the sauce (kaeng):
½ cup crab meat, steamed or boiled and then ⎫
   flaked, with the cooking juices   ⎪
½ cup prawn meat, similarly treated   ⎪
a little salt   ⎪
1 tablespoonful chopped roasted shallots   ⎬ pounded together
1 teaspoonful finely cut coriander root   ⎪
1 red dried chilli pepper, previously   ⎪
   soaked in salted water   ⎪
2 to 3 cups coconut milk   ⎭
¾ cup green chick peas, roasted, skinned, crushed and ground
1 tablespoonful peanuts, roasted and crushed
additional seasoning – fish sauce (nam pla), salt, tamarind water, juice of makrut
   lime, 1 teaspoonful ground chilli pepper, palm sugar and (if available) some
   chopped rakam (bunches of spiny little brick-red fruit from the palm tree
   Salacca wallichiana, with brown flesh inside, which is what you chop up)
additional garnishing – 1 tablespoonful each of finely cut coriander leaves and of
   spring onions; and 2 tablespoonfuls of garlic, finely sliced and fried

Bring the coconut milk to the boil until the curd and oil separate on the surface. Mix one cupful of this with the pounded ingredients, then transfer this new mixture back to the pot and blend it well with the rest of the coconut milk. Sprinkle in gradually the chick peas and peanuts and make sure that they are well blended too. Then add the seasoning indicated (to taste, where quantities are not given – this is a matter of personal preference) and the garnishings. Now you have your sauce.

Presentation of the dish:
Pour the sauce over cooked rice noodles. Serve the dish with dried red chilli peppers, crisply fried, and thin slices (or wedges) of hard-boiled egg served on the side together with an array of vegetables. The vegetables recommended are:

- banana blossom (sliced lengthwise, using only the white and tender parts and soaking these first in diluted lime juice)
- shoots of kathin (*Leucaena latisiliqua*)
- lep krut leaves (*Polyscias* sp.), dipped in batter and deep-fried in oil, tempura-style, until crisp

and the following four ingredients, all finely cut up, deep-fried in oil and drained:
- phak bung (water spinach, *Ipomoea aquatica*)
- tua poo, (winged bean, *Psophocarpus tetragonolobus*)
- tua dam (cow pea, *Vigna unguiculata*)
- phak krachet (water mimosa, *Neptunia oleracea*)

Hoy Tod

Thai crêpes with clams or oysters

I was introduced to this dish, which would intrigue a Breton crêpe-maker, in the little village of Ban Sapaam in Phuket Island by Churairat Pupha, who makes it scores of times daily and whose reputation for it extends well outside Phuket.

2 ladlefuls clams, e. g. *Paphia* sp., or small oysters, ready shucked
coconut oil
a little mixed flour (rice flour and tapioca flour should both be used, and Churairat
    Pupha adds wheat flour too if she has some), greatly diluted with water
1 large egg
2 handfuls of bean sprouts
stalks of Chinese cabbage or other edible green leaves

You need a large iron frying pan, rather like a Spanish paella pan, and it must be slightly tilted. Churairat Pupha uses a waist-high structure embodying a charcoal fire and a tilted top on which the pan rests in just the right posture.

Place the pan over the fire and pour in enough coconut oil to coat the bottom. When this is hot, spatter the rice and tapioca flour mixture in small quantities across the pan, from edge to edge. It will splutter and then set in an irregular lace-work pattern, rather like streaks of white egg. Flick a little hot oil (from the lower end of the pan) over it as it sets. Next, add half the clams, sprinkling them all over the pan. They will be cooked in a minute or two, during which time you must beat the egg. Using a fork, 'string' the beaten egg across the pan and again flick some of the hot oil over it.

Make a cut right across the unorthodox, clam-studded crêpe which you have thus prepared. Then use a spatula to loosen both halves and to flip them over. Add the bean sprouts, at one side of the pan, and the green cabbage stalks. They are not to be cooked, merely heated and slightly crisped. Once this is achieved, take them out, put them on a small serving dish and place the crêpes on top of them.

At this stage the remaining clams are put in the pan and cooked for a minute or two, after which they are sprinkled on top of the crêpes.

Serve with a mildly piquant sauce made by adding a little sugar to ordinary bottled mild chilli sauce.

Mi (or Mee)

Fruits de mer with noodles

There are many versions of Mi. The word itself just means rice noodles. The dish seems to be of Chinese origin and is popular fare in most of the S. E. Asian countries. I give it here, in the Thai recipe section, because Thai cooks enjoy a special reputation for preparing it (to such an extent that in Malaysia, for example, one is offered 'Siamese Mee') and because the best version which I have ever had was that prepared by Chien Pupha at Ban Sapaam in Phuket. The recipe below is, I hope, a faithful reflection of the demonstration which she performed for me, not once (for the whole thing is done at great speed) but thrice.

1 ladleful small oysters or clam (surf clams, *Paphia undulata*, were used at Phuket)
1 ladleful tiny squid
1 ladleful small prawns
1 ladleful bits of raw pork
coconut oil for frying
3 cloves garlic, chopped
½ to 1 tablespoonful soy sauce
Chinese cabbage or other edible green leaves
1 Chinese soupspoonful chicken stock
a handful of cooked rice vermicelli
1 large egg

Heat the coconut oil in a wok and toss in the garlic. Let it cook for a minute, then sprinkle the soy sauce over it. Half a minute later add the clams, squid, prawns and pork, followed by the cabbage or other leaves. After another half minute add the chicken stock, put a lid on the wok and leave it thus for 2 minutes.

Now take the lid off and push what has been cooking to one side of the wok so that you can add the vermicelli in the middle. Break the egg over the vermicelli and stir the white into them while deftly leaving the yolk unbroken. All this takes only a couple of minutes. To serve the Mi, put the vermicelli on a platter and add everything else on top of them. As accompaniments, offer mild ground chilli pepper and the liquid only from a little pot of sliced hot green chilli peppers in vinegar.

Hoy Lawt

How to cook salted and dried razorshell clams

Razorshell clams are available in salted and dried form. If they are very salty, soak them in water first and then lay them out to dry in the sun.

Fry the razorshell clams (with a little garlic, if you like) in oil until they are just crisp. Then pour out the oil and add plenty of brown sugar, which should be allowed to melt (without being burned) and in which the clams should be stirred around until they are completely coated and slightly sticky.

These 'glazed' razorshell clams make a very good accompaniment for a hot curry, or may be eaten by themselves as a snack. They are popular and inexpensive in coastal areas, but are also a real delicacy.

Mango Prawns

I was a long way from the sea when I heard about this one; precisely, at Ban Houei Sai, the enchanting village which stands on soil studded with sapphires in the Golden Triangle area of Laos. I was on the trail of *Pangasianodon gigas*, the giant catfish of the Mekong. Peter Law, a narcotics expert from Hong Kong, was following other trails of his own; but he is also a gastronome and was moved by some turn in the conversation to impart this recipe to me. I have accommodated it here in the Thai section on the basis that it comes from a resident of Bangkok and that both mangoes and prawns are exceptionally good in Thailand; but its ultimate provenance is unknown to me.

The recipe may be used for crab instead of prawns. Whichever you use, the amount of crustacean and the amount of mango should be about equal. The quantities given are right for 4 people.

8 medium prawns
4 mangoes

and for the dressing:
½ **pint mayonnaise (or thick cream or TCD, see below)**
2 **tablespoonfuls horseradish* (freshly grated if possible)**
a squeeze of lemon or lime juice
1 **teaspoonful sugar**
a little freshly ground pepper
(only if required) a little cream or creamy milk with which to thin the mixture

What, you may ask, is TCD? It is Thick Cream Dressing, Peter Law's alternative to mayonnaise. Make it by putting in a mixing bowl 1 level teaspoonful English (or French) mustard, ½ teaspoonful salt, 1 teaspoonful sugar, ½ teaspoonful white pepper and ¼ pint evaporated milk. Mix all this and beat in by degrees ¼ pint olive or other salad oil, gradually adding also 2½ tablespoonfuls white wine vinegar.

However, back to the main recipe. You must boil and peel the prawns, and cut up the tails into chunks. You must also prepare the mangoes, with some care. First cut them in half lengthways, removing the stones. Then, keeping the skin of the mango halves intact, remove the flesh in cubes or balls. (One way to do this is to make several cuts down to, but not through, the skin lengthways, then to do the same crossways; after which the cubes may be removed by running a spoon under the flesh and close to the skin.) Keep the skins.

Meanwhile you have made the dressing by mixing together the ingredients. Now mix the pieces of prawn and mango with the dressing. There should be enough dressing to cover them well, but without creating a soupy effect. Fill the mango skins with the mixture, garnish with strips of pimento (mild red or green pepper) and mint leaves. Serve chilled.

---

* I should mention a substitute recommended by 'Wyvern', the learned author of *Culinary Jottings for Madras* and one of the best writers on cookery in the English language. He states that the root of the Moringa or Drum-stick tree in India may be used instead of horseradish with entirely satisfactory results.

Recipes from Cambodia

The traditional cuisine of Cambodia has been described as the most arduous in the world for the cook and the most pleasing to the eye of the diner. The capacity for taking pains and the highly developed techniques which were displayed by the builders of Angkor Wat could still be seen, reflected across the centuries and translated to the smaller scale and different materials of the kitchen, in the work done by the cooks of the Palace and of the aristocracy at Phnom Penh during the first half of this century. But these days are gone, and I prefer anyway to devote my space to describing popular dishes such as are no doubt still eaten throughout the country.

The ordinary Cambodian eats two meals a day, one at about 11 a.m. and one at dusk. The heart of each meal is rice (bay), the invariable accompaniment soup (sâmlà). But whenever possible the Cambodians add further accompaniments, taking one from each of the three broad categories known as:

Chhâ – a sauté of meat or poultry (or certain crustaceans and molluscs) with vegetables (chhâ banle) or vermicelli (chhâ my-suor) or condiments only (chhâ kroeung);

Aing – a dish of grilled meat, poultry or fish;

Chion – a dish of fried meat, poultry or fish.

Fish dominate the last two categories of dish, but not the first. However, there are chhâ made with marine crustaceans or molluscs; and an example is given on page 254.

When I say that fish are dominant in the grilled and fried dishes, I mean fresh-water fish. The geography of Cambodia is such that it is probably the richest country in the world for these. The sea fisheries, based on a relatively short coastline, are less developed and consumption of seafood is largely restricted to the coastal areas. However, many of the best-known Cambodian recipes may be applied to marine fish as well as to freshwater fish and thus qualify for inclusion in the collection which follows.

Two Cambodian Fish Soups

Cambodians, like the Burmese and perhaps even more so, consume much more freshwater fish than sea fish. Their well-known and distinctive fish soups are normally prepared with freshwater fish. It is, however, perfectly proper to make them with sea fish and the results are just as good.

Professor Hellei has pointed out, in his admirable monograph on Cambodian eating habits, that the two essential elements in any meal are rice and a bowl of soup (sâmlâ). He has also furnished a convenient classification of the principal soups, as follows:

A) Sngor, including fish, meat or fowl, but no vegetables;
B) Plain sâmlâ including fish, meat or fowl, with vegetables;
C) Sâmlâ mchou, similar to (B) but acidulated;
D) Khor, a remarkable group of soups, based on a caramelized sauce.

I describe below the fish versions of (C) and (D), which are of particular interest.

Samla Mchou Banlé   *Acidulated fish soup*

This, the most popular soup in Cambodia, is a combination of fish and vegetables with an acid flavour.

Miscellaneous little fish, duly cleaned, and small prawns constitute the first element.

The vegetables may include tralach (gourd or vegetable marrow), trap ropou (round aubergines), peng pas (tomatoes), trakuon (water bindweed), pralit (water lily) and kra ao chhouk (lotus buds); each fitly prepared.

The third element consists of condiments which are chopped and then pounded together in a mortar with a little garlic. These should include tamarind, citronella, galingale and leaves of ma am (*Limnophila aromatica*).

Fourthly comes prahok (a fermented fish product, see page 205) which is pounded to a paste and added to boiling water with salt and some Tuk trey (fish sauce). The fish are then put in, followed by the vegetables and condiments and the whole cooked for 20 minutes, when it is ready to serve.

Khor Trey   *A more exotic fish soup*

The basis of this soup is a sauce made by heating palm sugar until it is caramelised and then adding tuk trey (fish sauce).

The fish may be small (gutted but otherwise whole) or large (dressed and cut into convenient pieces). The fish or pieces of fish are left to stand for an hour or two in a bowl with salt, dark soy sauce, pepper and crushed garlic. Then, the caramelized sauce being ready in a large pan, the fish are added. When the sauce has been boiling for ten minutes, with the fish in it, cold water is added. The fire is kept high and more cold water added whenever necessary, but never very much at a time, until the fish is well cooked. (If small, bony fish have been chosen, the cooking will go on for 10 hours or more, with a little vinegar or rice alcohol added, so that the fish and their bones dissolve completely.)

Trey Aing

Grilled fish in the Cambodian style

This is a common accompaniment for rice. As Professor Hellei remarks: 'Le petit peuple se sert de petits poissons vulgaires simplement grillés à la braise avec de la saumure ou des légumes conservées'. But he goes on to give a summary account of how the dish is prepared in better-off households.

Larger fish are chosen, usually from the wealth of freshwater fish for which Cambodia is famous; but seafish are used in the coastal areas and are even better. The chosen fish is washed, sometimes gutted, but not scaled. It is grilled over charcoal, being turned frequently but with care so that the whole of it is cooked through.

A second platter is prepared, of vegetables, green salad and aromatic leaves. The vegetables may be cucumber (peeled) and bean sprouts (well washed). Citronella and mint would be likely to figure among the aromatic leaves.

A sauce is prepared separately. The basis of it is the staple fish sauce, to which are added garlic, fresh chilli pepper, lime juice, galingale, roast peanuts, sugar and coconut juice. Morsels of grilled fish and of the vegetables are wrapped in salad leaves and dipped in the sauce before being eaten.

Leay Kroeung Trel Chh'or

A sauce made from smoked fish, to be served with fresh fish

This is a very good and subtle sauce, which can be served with, say, groupers (pages 54 to 58) or grey mullet (pages 42 and 43) or bream (page 81). It is also suitable for lobster or spiny lobster.

1 smoked fish of about 350 grams
1 coffeespoonful of shrimp paste (mâmphri phâo)
1 coffeespoonful chopped shallot
1 coffeespoonful chopped fennel bulb
salt, to taste
fish sauce (tuk trey), to taste
palm sugar or ordinary sugar, just a little
1 teaspoonful lemon or lime juice
1 coffeespoonful shredded fresh ginger
1 coffeespoonful shredded lemon grass
1 drop (well, 2 if you wish) makrut lime (krauch soeuch) juice

Grill the smoked fish and let it cool; then remove skin and bones and chop the flesh into little pieces. Pound these in a mortar with the shrimp paste, shallot and fennel. Add a little warm water; salt and fish sauce to taste; the sugar and the lemon or lime juice. Heat the sauce to bind it, but without letting it boil; and stir the ginger and lemon grass into it as it heats. Check the taste (it might need a little more fish sauce, for example). Finally, add the drop of makrut lime juice.

Chhouchhi Trey Thon

Stuffed mackerel

The Khmer title of this recipe might suggest that you have to deal with a whole tunny. Not so; the name trey thon may be applied to small relations, such as fish of the genus *Rastrelliger* and *Auxis*. Buy three such fish, of about 20 to 25 cm in length.

The recipe title provides another puzzle. To stuff something in English means to put something in it. But this recipe does not call for any such operation. The Khmer word for 'to stuff' may, like the French verb 'farcir', mean putting something on something, as in this instance.

3 mackerel (see above)
pork fat for frying
3 stalks lemon grass
3 or 4 cloves garlic   } chopped together
1 small hot chilli pepper
1 makrut lime leaf
fish sauce (tuk trey)
sugar   } to taste
salt
parsley

Gut the mackerel and cut off their pectoral fins. Then fry them briefly (the fish, not the fins) in the pork fat, remove them from the pan, slit them down the side and remove the bones. Take the chopped ingredients and fry them also until they are brown. Remove and reserve them.

Now put the fish back in the pan and finish frying them. When they are done, add the reserved mixture together with the fish sauce, sugar and salt, and let everything simmer together for a few minutes over a low flame. Finally, chop and add the makrut lime leaf.

Now take everything out of the pan. Dispose the fish on a serving dish with the sauce (or 'stuffing', as I suppose one should call it) on top of them and parsley scattered over all.

A refinement is to remove the skin from the bodies of the mackerel after they have been cooked (i.e. strip it off from head to tail, exposing the flesh); and to decorate the dish with 'flowers' made in Cambodian fashion from leek leaves and little serrated discs of carrot.

Chhouchhi Kdam   *Stuffed crabs*

6 to 12 crabs (depending on their size)
3 soupspoonfuls chopped lemon grass
½ soupspoonful chopped fennel root
1 shallot, chopped
4 cloves of garlic, chopped
1 coffeespoonful chopped galingale (romdeng)
1 coffeespoonful peel of makrut lime (krauch soeuch)
2 coffeespoonfuls shrimp paste
1 coconut, to make 1 to 2 cups coconut cream/milk
salt and pepper
fish sauce (nuoc mam)

Cook and prepare the crabs in the usual way, extracting all the meat (and the creamy part) and reserving the carapaces.

Pound together the next seven ingredients, fry the mixture briefly in hot fat until it is golden, then add the crab meat, coconut cream/milk, seasoning and fish sauce. Mix all this together, fill the carapaces with the mixture and put them in the oven for 15 minutes.

Garnish with fennel leaves before serving.

Khyang Samrok Kroeung   *Spiced oysters*

Many people, including myself, believe that oysters are best eaten straight from the shell, with a thread of lemon juice, and that it is a mistake to cook them. However, this attitude requires modification in places where oysters are abundant and reasonably cheap. One may still think that they are at their best au naturel; but one looks for other ways of presenting them. One such is this interesting Khmer recipe.

24 oysters
1 soupspoonful chopped garlic
1 soupspoonful chopped lemon grass (the green part)
½ coffeespoonful chopped galingale
cooking oil
1 soupspoonful peanuts, previously roasted and pounded
a little fish sauce (tuk trey)
1 teaspoonful sugar
a pinch of pepper

Put the oysters briefly in boiling water. When they are open, take them out and remove them from the shells.

Take the chopped garlic, lemon grass and galingale and pound them together. Heat a little cooking oil until it is smoking, then put in the pounded mixture, stir well and add the oysters. When a good aroma arises from all this, add the pounded peanuts, season the mixture with the fish sauce, sugar and pepper, and take the pan off the fire.

Place each oyster, with some of the sauce, in an oyster shell and serve them thus.

Chhâ Yihoeu Sras

A chhâ with cuttlefish

Clean and wash the cuttlefish and cut them into small pieces. Choose a vegetable from the following: cauliflower, onion, green beans or mushrooms. Whichever you choose should be of the best quality. Cut them up too.

Melt some pork fat in a casserole and let some crushed garlic brown in it. Add the pieces of cuttlefish, some fish sauce, sugar and black pepper. Cook all this for about 20 minutes, then add the vegetable and cook for another 15 minutes or so. Finally, put some leaves of coriander (van suy) on top of the dish and serve.

Trey Yuu Hoeu Somhuy

Stuffed cuttlefish

6 cuttlefish
200 grams pork, minced
100 grams pork rind, finely chopped
salt and pepper to taste
a little flour
cooking oil
1 bay leaf

pounded ingredients:
1 fennel bulb
4 cloves garlic
4 shallots

Disengage the bodies of the cuttlefish from heads and tentacles (reserving the tentacles, if you wish, to be chopped small and added to the stuffing). Clean the bodies, rinse thoroughly and dry them. Prepare the pork and pork rind as indicated. Combine the pork rind with the pounded mixture, adding salt and pepper and a little flour. Fry this mixture for a couple of minutes.

Next, stuff the cuttlefish bodies with the pork mixture, taking care not to fill them completely (since the stuffing will expand). Secure them with toothpicks, or sew them up. Fry them lightly until they are golden-brown, then add water (or fish broth, or chicken bouillon) to cover, with the bay leaf, and simmer for an hour or more. Your pot should be covered, and you should turn the cuttlefish from time to time.

Bangkang Chhuoc *Prawn soup*

350 grams prawns
350 grams dried fish
1 large green mango
350 grams 'cornichons' (pickled gherkins)

salt to taste
leaves of sweet basil (chi-neang-vong)
1 or 2 spring onions, chopped

Boil the prawns, peel them, remove the vein from the tail of each and cut the meat into slices. Grill the dried fish, beat them a little to soften them, then pick out the flesh, ensuring that it is free of bones. Cut the mango and cornichons into thin strips.

Strain the broth in which the prawns were cooked and reheat it. Place the pieces of prawn, dried fish, mango and cornichons in a soup bowl and pour the broth over them. Season with salt; and garnish with basil and spring onion.

Recipes from Vietnam

It was not the cuisine of Vietnam which attracted attention to that country in the 1970s, when I was working and travelling in S. E. Asia. Yet, now that the war is long over, the subject may be addressed without any feeling of incongruity; and it is an interesting one.

In visiting both the south of the country and the north, I was impressed by the strength of the indigenous tradition of cookery. Vietnam has been relatively immune to influences from the Asian sub-continent and even to those from China, although the border with the Province of Kwangtung is, like most political boundaries, gastronomically indistinct. French culinary influence seems to me to have been superficial. One could see it in Saigon. One catches echoes of it in Hanoi. But its penetration was never deep and it seems unlikely to persist.

Looking to the future of Vietnamese cookery, I found it particularly interesting to study the recipe books which have been published in Hanoi since 1945. These are mostly out of print and hard to find, but there is a complete collection in the National Library at Hanoi, which was placed at my disposal; and I have included in the anthology which follows a representative selection of fish recipes from these books.

One thing may be prophesied with confidence. The nuoc mam or fish sauce of Vietnam has been supreme in the region and is likely to remain so. It comes in various qualities. The best has no rival.

Canh Chua

Sweet and sour fish soup

This is a recipe from the south of Vietnam, which it is instructive to compare with the Cambodian recipe for samla mchou banlé, an acidulated freshwater fish soup (see page 250). Any good marine fish (except for the tuna and mackerel family which would be too rich) can be used here.

¼ kilo thin slices of sea fish	1 or 2 sticks of celery, chopped
1 litre of chicken bouillon	100 grams soy bean sprouts
12 pods of fresh tamarind	mint leaves, chopped
2 tablespoonfuls or so of sugar	ground chilli pepper (optional)
1 or 2 tomatoes, peeled and sliced	

Steep the tamarind pods in the bouillon for several hours. Then add the fish, fish sauce and sugar, bring it all to the boil and keep it simmering briskly for about 10 minutes.

Next, add the tomato and celery and soy bean sprouts. Continue cooking for 2 or 3 minutes, then put in the mint leaves and the ground chilli pepper, remove from the fire and serve.

Cá Chiên Muôi Xả

Fish with lemon grass

This recipe reminds me of one which I met in Tunisia, where the lemony flavour is provided by quarters of pickled lemon. It has far fewer ingredients than most S. E. Asian recipes, rather a relief after mustering those endless teaspoonfuls of this and that for some of the complex ones.

A fish of the bream family (e.g. those on pages 81 to 84) will do very well for this dish; but any white fish of moderate size and good quality may be used.

1 fish weighing (uncleaned) between ½ and ¾ kilo (see above)
1 stalk of lemon grass, bruised and chopped
1 red chilli pepper, pounded
1 clove of garlic, pounded
1 tablespoonful cooking oil
a little salt

Gut, wash and pat dry the fish. Make slanting cuts in each side, about 2 cm apart. Combine the remaining ingredients and anoint the body of the fish with this mixture, taking care to insert bits of lemon grass into the cuts.

The fish may then be fried in a pan, or baked in an oiled dish in the oven for 25 minutes.

Cá Sào Măng Tuói

Fish fried with bamboo shoots

The quantities given are supposed to be enough for 6 people. The sea fish which are suited to this recipe, anyway according to my North Vietnamese source, are groupers (pages 54 to 58).

½ kilo fish (uncleaned weight)	2 shallots
salt and pepper	100 grams pork fat (or olive oil)
300 grams bamboo shoots	fish sauce (nuoc mam)
25 grams dried mushrooms	spring onion leaves, cut in sections

Clean, skin and bone the fish, so that you are left only with the flesh. Cut it into small pieces and season it.

Cut the bamboo shoots into small pieces, cook them in boiling water and drain them. Soak the mushrooms in water. Cut the shallots up finely.

Heat the pork fat (or olive oil) in a pan, then fry the shallots and the fish in it. Remove them and put in the bamboo shoots and mushrooms with some fish sauce and a little more salt and pepper. After these have cooked briefly, put the fish back in and mix all well together. After a few minutes the dish will be ready to be garnished with the spring onion and served.

Chả Cá Nuóng

A North Vietnamese recipe for fish brochettes

There was a road in Hanoi called Phố hàng chả cá in celebration of this dish; but now it has another name. However, the recipe is still among the most celebrated in North Vietnam. The fish to be used for it may be any sea fish with firm flesh, such as Spanish mackerel (page 110 and 111) or grouper (pages 54 to 58).

¾ kilo fish (see above)	*and for the marinade:*
a slice of larding bacon	3 tablespoonfuls cooking oil
3 tablespoonfuls cooking oil	3 tablespoonfuls fish sauce
a few spring onions, chopped	(nuoc mam)
peanuts, grilled and pounded	2 tablespoonfuls rice spirit
	a pinch of turmeric
	a little rieng (a kind of ginger)
	2 teaspoonfuls of shrimp paste (măm tôm)

Clean the fish, remove bones and skin, and cut the flesh into 3 cm cubes. Marinate these in a mixture of the ingredients in the right hand column for 2 to 3 hours.

Cut the larding bacon into squares of 3 cm. Load skewers with alternating pieces of fish and bacon.

Heat the 3 tablespoonfuls of cooking oil and add the chopped spring onions. Barbecue the brochettes, basting the fish with this mixture. Sprinkle the pounded peanuts over them before serving.

Chả Cá Lão Vong

A speciality from Hanoi

Chả cá lão vong means, literally, 'grilled cut up fish meat of the old fisherman', and is the name of a fish restaurant in Hanoi. 'Dans le temps', as they say, there were four such restaurants in the same street. They were popular eating places for young French officials, especially after the regular Saturday afternoon race meetings. In 1975 only one survived, in the attic of a private house. It had a long history and was the best known of the four, having a reputation for entertaining artistic and intellectual customers, a task in which the lady who ran and was still running it in 1975 was aided by numerous beautiful 'daughters of the house'. After my wife and I had enjoyed a meal there, I wrote:

'The restaurant gives the impression of being quite unchanged since forty or fifty years ago. The old Parisian-café coat rack is still on the wall; the ceiling fan must be almost an antique by now; and the original wooden shutters are still opened to give a view through the windows across the narrow street. The proprietress still serves only one main dish, the "grilled cut up fish meat". It usually suits her to use freshwater catfish, but she readily agreed that the dish could perfectly well be made with sea fish – any species which will yield gobbets of firm white meat. The pieces of fish are first grilled on bamboo skewers, then brought to the table in a pan of pork fat, sizzling over a charcoal brazier. The guests help themselves, adding from side dishes mint leaves (or Chinese parsley) and dill, spring onion, rice vermicelli, peanuts, slivers of chilli pepper and fish sauce. The ladies of the house come up the rickety wooden staircase from time to time with additional supplies of fish. The ceiling fan causes sparks to fly from the brazier on to the plates and persons of those sitting nearest to it. To dine there is, as the Michelin people would say, an experience which warrants making a détour (of, say, one or two thousand kilometres).'

I should add that, when supplies permit this, a rare and costly ingredient is used to give additional flavour to the dish. There is in S. E. Asia a water bug which I have been told is *Lethocerus indicus*, from live specimens of which a few drops of a glandular secretion may be obtained for use as a flavouring agent. It is the custom to serve it from a medicine dropper. This is an expensive ingredient anywhere, and certainly in Hanoi, whither live bugs have to be conveyed from the places where they can be found. The dish with this extravagant addition made to the fish sauce cost 15 dong a head when I had it in 1975.

Cá Kho Tra

Tunny cooked in lotus-flavoured tea

This dish is best made with tunny, but other fish with a relatively high fat content, for example Spanish mackerel, may be used. One effect of the tea is to balance the fat. The tea itself may be ordinary black tea if lotus tea (that is to say, tea containing the little white glands from lotus flowers) is not available.

800 grams tunny, in 4 steaks
cooking oil
lotus tea
100 grams pork, diced (optional)
1 small onion, sliced
1½ soupspoonfuls nuoc mam (fish sauce)
½ teaspoonful black pepper
1½ soupspoonfuls sugar

Heat the oil and cook the tunny steaks in it until they are beginning to turn brown. Reserve them. Meanwhile make a pot of quite strong tea.

Put the fish and the pork in a roomy casserole, pour the tea over them, add all the other ingredients and let the whole mixture simmer over a low flame for 40 minutes (or longer if the steaks are very thick).

Cá Lành Canh Kho

Anchovy balls with tomato

This is one of the 'everyday recipes' in the collection which the Women's Association published at Hanoi in 1961.

Gut and wash ½ kilo of fresh anchovies (probably *Coilia* sp., the long-tailed variety), then mince them with your coupe-coupe (chopping knife), adding a little salt, half a small chilli pepper and a little of the local celery (thià là). When all is well minced, make it into balls the size of a thumb.

Sauté these anchovy balls in some pork fat until they are golden. Cut 3 tomatoes into pieces and put them in the bottom of a casserole, then add the anchovy balls with fish sauce and salt to taste. Pour 2 soupbowlfuls of water over all this and cook it until everything is well done. The resulting dish can be kept for two days.

Cá Kho Rim

A recipe for cooking dried fish

Take a kilo of dried fish and soak it in rice-washing water or ordinary warm water for half an hour in order to make it soft and less salty. Then scale it, wash it well and cut it into pieces the size of a matchbox.

Pound a few cloves of garlic or some dried onion, chop up very finely a piece of ginger. Cut the green part of two spring onions into short sections.

Heat 100 grams of pork fat until it turns golden, then remove it from the pan (i.e. the piece of pork fat, not what has melted). Fry the garlic briefly, then add some fish sauce, sugar, a soupbowlful of water and the pieces of fish. Cover the pot tightly and cook over a low flame until the fish is ready and only about a third of the liquid is left. Add the spring onion and ginger and serve.

This is another recipe which I owe to the publications of the industrious Women's Association of North Vietnam.

Tom Kho Tau

Stir-fried prawns serves 6

You will need 1½ kilos of good-sized prawns. Break each prawn in two where the body joins the tail. Open the body, extract the yellow meat and reserve it. Peel and devein the tail (but leave the tail fin at the end in place).

Heat olive oil in a frying pan. Add a chopped onion and fry this until it turns golden. Add the prawn tails and stir-fry for 20 minutes.

Add 2 tablespoonfuls of tomato ketchup to the meat from the head, with pepper and salt. Pour this mixture over the prawns and give them a good stir to mix it in well. Continue cooking for another 10 minutes then turn off the flame and cover until you are ready to serve.

Serve with rice.

(recipe of Nguyen Thi Tuyen)

Chả Tôm

Prawn pâté

This well-known recipe comes from Nguyen van Tung's book of Vietnamese recipes, which contains 291 recipes for use in North Vietnam.

Peel the prawns. Wash them in salted water and dry them. The author recommends that at this stage you should add a very little alum (phène chua) to the water and wash the prawns again; but treat this procedure as optional. When washing and drying is completed, pound the prawns to a paste, adding just before this task is finished a very small piece of pork fat, salt and pepper and some pounded dried onion, all of which is to be incorporated in the pâté.

Wash and clean well a piece of banana leaf, then brush fat over the upper side of it. Dispose the prawn pâté thereon in balls so that you will be able to make small round packages of 2 cm in diameter. But before the balls are wrapped take the yolk of an egg and a little white wine and beat these well together. Make a tiny brush of 4 or 5 chicken feathers and use this to coat the balls with the egg-yolk mixture, which will give them a golden colour. Then wrap them in banana leaf and steam them for 15 to 20 minutes.

The balls of pâté may be served hot or cold with a sauce made from lemon or lime juice, garlic and chilli pepper.

Cháo Tôm

Unusual lollipops – spiced prawn pâté grilled on sticks of sugar cane

Here is an agreeable and ingenious way of consuming prawns. The Vietnamese deserve credit for inventing it.

What they do is to take sticks of sugar cane about 15 cm long, encase one end of each in a ball of prawn pâté and grill these.

The prawn pâté, which must be quite smooth, is made by mixing thoroughly together:

¾ kilo large prawns, peeled, deveined and pounded
1 soupspoonful oil
1 white of egg
2 cloves garlic, pounded
½ teaspoonful ginger
½ teaspoonful salt
2 teaspoonfuls sugar
1 soupspoonful tapioca flour (or potato flour)
1 soupspoonful rose-perfumed rice spirit (mai kwai loo)

The last of these ingredients is exotic and desirable but may be omitted.

When it comes to eating cháo tôm we have found them very good just as they are. But they may be wrapped in salad leaves (even wrapped again in rice crêpes) and dipped in fish sauce (nuoc mam).

Măng Cua

Crab and Western bamboo soup

Western bamboo is asparagus; and this was our favourite soup in the repertoire of Lee Van Tung, an artful Vietnamese cook who liked nothing better, while working for us, than to produce his native Vietnamese dishes.

meat of 1 large crab, cooked and flaked
1½ litres of chicken bouillon
asparagus tips (probably tinned), cut up in lengths of 1 cm
3 soupspoonfuls of manioc (tapioca) flour (or potato flour)
2 eggs, beaten
a little coriander, chopped (but we preferred parsley)
a little chopped spring onion
salt to taste

There is not much cooking to be done here, since you start with cooked crabmeat. Bring the bouillon to the boil, lower the heat and add the crabmeat and asparagus tips. Thicken the soup with the flour and then add the beaten eggs, stirring well. Season and garnish with the parsley and spring onion before serving.

This soup is to be served hot. People keep telling us that it makes sense to eat hot soups in a hot climate. Although we were never fully converted to this view, we did find that this particular soup always went down well, however hot the day.

Canh Rièu Cua Gach Nãu Vói Dúa

Crab soup with pineapple

1 large crab (with its yellow part)
1 soupspoonful pork fat
50 grams onion, chopped
1 soupspoonful fish sauce (nuoc mam)
½ soupspoonful salt
½ pineapple, cut up finely

several spring onions (the green
**   parts only, cut into sections)**
pepper
parsley, chopped

Clean the crab, discarding the gills. Remove and pound the yellow part of the crab and reserve it for later use. Put the crab in a pot with water, boil it until it is cooked, then take it out and remove all the meat.

Heat the fat in a casserole, cook the onion in it in order to produce a tasty effect, then add the meat of the crab, with a little of the fish sauce. Sauté this mixture, then add to it some of the water in which the crab was cooked with the rest of the fish sauce, the salt and the pineapple. Let all this boil for a minute, then add the pounded yellow part of the crab, remove the casserole from the fire, add the spring onion leaves, pepper and parsley and serve.

This is another Women's Association recipe from Hanoi.

Muc Xao Dua

Squid sauté with pineapple

½ kilo fresh squid
1 pineapple of about ½ kilo
2 spring onions
1 clove garlic, crushed
50 grams pork fat
fish sauce (nuoc mam)
flour
pepper
parsley

for the marinade:
fish sauce (nuoc mam)
salt
pepper
1 piece ginger, pounded

Clean the squid as usual. Wash and dry it, then cut it into small pieces and let these sit in the marinade for at least 10 minutes.

Cut the pineapple into 4 to 6 slices and then cut these into small pieces. Cut the green part of the spring onions into pieces 2 cm long, leaving the bulbs aside.

Put half a soupspoonful of the pork fat in a pan, heat it well, add the garlic and squid and cook over a fierce flame, stirring constantly, until the squid is done. Remove the squid.

Add the rest of the fat to the pan, put in the bulbs of the spring onions and then add the pineapple, with a little fish sauce and some salt. Once the pineapple has absorbed the fat, add another soupspoonful of fish sauce (this time mixed with a little flour). After a couple of minutes add the squid, mix all well together, toss in the green parts of the spring onions and remove from the fire. Serve hot, with pepper and parsley sprinkled over all.

Cha Gio *Vietnamese rolls with crab (or prawn)*

These rolls are delicious. Wherever the Vietnamese go, there you will find them. We have eaten them all over S. E. Asia, and have examined various techniques (varying in detail only – the broad lines of the recipe are immutable) for making them. Nowhere have I found instructions as full and clear as those given by Jill Nhu Huong Miller in her *Vietnamese Cookery*, and it is therefore her recipe which I reproduce almost verbatim below. She prefaces the instructions by observing that the rice paper (bánh tráng) used to wrap these rolls can be bought only in Vietnam (or perhaps in France) and that there is no substitute for it. I would add only that the paper can in fact be bought in some other parts of S. E. Asia where there are substantial numbers of Vietnamese; that in my own heretical view the paper-thin brik pastry of Tunisia and similar products from other Arab countries are a possible substitute, although their use does change the taste; and, finally, that the rolls are just as irresistible if little chunks of prawn are substituted for the crabmeat.

THE STUFFING

Soak a 4-ounce packet of bean thread for about 10 minutes in water to cover. Drain the bean thread and chop it coarsely.

Slice a medium-size Chinese yam (weighing about 1 pound) paper-thin with your vegetable peeler, roughly gather the slices and cut them into fine threads. Finely chop 1 ordinary onion and 5 spring onions.

Now take ½ lb ground pork and add to it successively (mixing well with your hands at each addition) the onions; the bean thread; the yam. The next addition will be the crab meat, of which you may use either 1 can, drained and flaked, or the equivalent amount of fresh crab, cooked and flaked. (As noted above, chopped prawn meat may be used instead.) Finally, add ground black pepper to taste.

THE ROLLING

Take 25 to 30 round sheets of rice paper and cut each in half. Trim off any rough edges which might poke through the paper when it is rolled up later on.

Mix 1 cup water and 1 teaspoonful of either caramelized sugar or dark brown sugar. (The purpose of the sugar in the water is to make the paper turn golden-brown when fried.) Now moisten each half-circle of rice paper by dipping your fingers in the sugared water and then rubbing them gently over the rice paper. Do not make the rice paper too wet. Let each moistened paper sit for a short while (say, while you moisten the next four pieces) before filling it as described below.

Fold the half-circle in half to reinforce it. Put about a teaspoonful of filling near the rounded edge in an oblong shape. Fold the sides over the filling and then roll up, gently but firmly. Put the roll aside, lying on the exposed edge of the paper. If the edge is still hard, this will soften it. See diagram on next page.

THE COOKING

Pour enough cooking oil into a heavy skillet or pot to make the oil about 1½ inches deep. Heat the oil on medium high heat. Slip the roll into the hot oil, the raw edge side first so that the hot oil will seal it onto the roll, then fry until golden brown. Remove to a wire cake cooler or similar rack to drain off the excess oil.

TO SERVE

Serve hot, with leaf lettuce, fresh mint leaves, coriander, thin-sliced cucumbers, and individual small bowls of nuoc mam sauce. (Nuoc mam sauce can be made thus. Crush in a mortar a moderate amount of fresh chilli pepper (seeded) and a clove of garlic with a teaspoonful of sugar. Mash into this mixture the pulp of half a lime. Add a tablespoonful each of vinegar and water and mix well. Finally, add 4 tablespoonfuls of nuoc mam.) To eat, wrap the roll in a lettuce leaf, with mint, coriander and cucumber, and dip in the sauce.

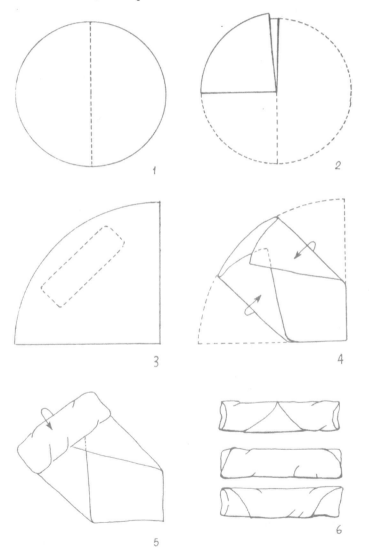

Ca Muc Nhoi Thit

Stuffed squid   serves 4

4 squid (page 181), weighing about 150–200 grams each
½ kilo ground pork
6 large dried mushrooms
10 dried water-lily flowers
¼ cup bean thread
2 cloves garlic, crushed and finely chopped
2 shallots, finely sliced
1 tablespoonful fish sauce (nuoc mam)
a little salt and black pepper
3 tablespoonfuls cooking oil
lettuce leaves

Clean and wash the squid. Cut off and finely chop the tentacles. Combine the ground pork and chopped tentacles in a bowl.

Soak the mushrooms and lily flowers in one lot of warm water, and the bean thread in another lot, for at least 15 minutes. Remove the mushrooms and discard the stems. Take off the hard ends of the stems of the lily flowers. Drain both, chop them finely and add them to the pork. Drain the bean thread and give it the same treatment.

Now add to the stuffing mixture the garlic, shallots, fish sauce, salt and pepper. Stuff the mixture into the squid so that they are almost full and close the openings with toothpicks or slivers of bamboo.

Heat the cooking oil and cook the stuffed squid in it for about 15 minutes, turning them occasionally.

Serve hot, on a bed of lettuce. Suitable accompaniments would be rice and nuoc mam sauce (page 265).

Xoa Xoa

A Vietnamese seaweed recipe, recorded by Gruvel

'Xoa xoa is prepared as follows, using the seaweed known as rau câu, in good Annamite families.

'One soaks the seaweed in rice-water, obtained by washing the rice before cooking it. This sort of soaking lasts about 12 hours. The seaweed is then drained and washed in cold water.

'The seaweed, thus prepared, is then cooked in ordinary water and the whole preparation poured into an earthenware container and allowed to cool. After it has coagulated it is cut into pieces by means of little bamboo knives, sold and eaten with a powdering of sugar. This is the way of preparing the kinds of sugared sweet which are called xoa xoa.'

Recipes from China and Hong Kong

Chinese cookery possesses, in S. E. Asia, something like the prestige accorded to French cuisine in Europe. It is everywhere a noticeable and in some places the dominant influence. Moreover, the southern coast of China falls within the scope of this book as I have defined it. So the cuisine of Canton, at least, must be touched upon. Yet the whole subject of Chinese cookery is so vast, and myself so inexperienced in its subtleties, that I hesitate to open a door which, like the entrance to the Forbidden City in Peking, leads inevitably to further portals and eventually to a maze-like area devoted to specialized subjects in which only the expert can tread with confidence.

The solution which I have adopted is to present a very small selection of recipes from China, especially Canton, and from Hong Kong, accompanied by notes on some kinds of seafood which the Chinese particularly esteem and prefaced by these general remarks. This is superficial treatment; but after all there are many good books in English on Chinese cookery, whereas there are very few for most S. E. Asian countries. (Oddly, there were in the 1970s very few Chinese cookery books in China. A tour of the bookshops in Peking and Canton in the autumn of 1975 produced repeated assurances, which I eventually believed, that no book on Chinese cookery was in print in China at that time.)

For the present edition of the book, I considered doing a radical updating of this chapter, since the situation in 1975 was exceptional and far more has since been published in China about cookery, including fish cookery. However, I decided that the chapter reads quite well as it is, and offers an interesting snapshot of times past.

I referred to the subtleties of Chinese cookery. I have read of a seventeenth-century gourmet who liked to have his rice sprinkled with dew-drops gathered from wild roses (garden roses would not do). Such niceties would seem to have no place in modern China. Yet there are certainly some restaurants, and no doubt some homes, in Peking and Canton where something of this perfectionist spirit survives and where the palate may be perplexed and delighted, as in past centuries, by a blend of tastes which defies analysis by any foreigner. To some extent it is of course a question of different ingredients. For example, Chinese wine (the yellow kind) is often used in cookery. A sweet sherry is habitually recommended as a substitute, but the taste is not the same and nowadays, when authentic Chinese products are available in most of the great cities of the world, it is better to make the effort and obtain the real thing. It is fortunate that most of the essential Chinese ingredients come in cans or bottles (light and dark soy sauce, oyster sauce, Chinese vinegar, etc.) or in dried form (spices, Yunnan ginger, mushrooms and many marine products).

Taste is one thing, texture another. The Chinese take a great interest in texture, which accounts for the care which they lavish on seemingly unpromising ingredients such as fish bladders and lips, jellyfish, shark's fin and their beloved sea-cucumbers. These last we first ate at the Chinese Embassy in Vientiane, far from the sea, and I well remember the circle of interested and smiling faces as we took our initial chopstickfuls and how we only realized later that we had erred in bracing ourselves for a strange taste when we should have been ready to admire a new and exotic texture.

The Chinese also achieve interesting textures by their techniques of preparing food, for example cutting vegetables into matchsticks; and by their methods of cooking, such as stir-frying, in which the cooking time is minimal and the food therefore retains a certain crunchiness which comes as a pleasant surprise to occidental jaws.

Yu Chi

Shark's fin

I begin with this because I suppose that for most people it serves as a symbol of Chinese seafood cookery. Besides, it is a remarkably good dish and usually (but see below) occurs in the form of a soup and would thus come at the beginning of this recipe section, although not necessarily at the beginning of a Chinese dinner. However, I shall not give a full recipe, since this is one of those (few) dishes which in my view are best reserved for preparation by professional cooks. If you wish to do it yourself, properly, consult *Musings of a Chinese Gourmet* by Dr F. T. Cheng, where you will find more than three pages of meticulous and enthusiastic guidance.

Dr Cheng takes one successively through all the stages: the choice of the fin; the three days spent soaking it in cold water; the initial simmering; the cleaning; the second simmering (with ginger, spring onion and Chinese wine); the 3-hour cooking in a double boiler with ¼ pound each of ham and pork, the meat of a fresh chicken, Chinese wine and water; and the further and final 10 minutes of cooking in a concentrated bouillon of chicken and ham, prepared separately (yes, another chicken and another piece of ham are needed for this – 'Economy has no place in the realm of delicacies'); after which a teaspoonful of soy sauce is added and the fin is served in a very hot dish.

This preparation, known as Hung shan, is not a soup. Less good shark's fin is suitable for shark's fin soup, but the finest quality should be prepared as explained above and the greatest care taken throughout to preserve the shape of the fin. On this last requirement Dr Cheng observes that Cantonese cooks enclose the fin in a 'net' of bamboo to keep it intact. However, he comments anxiously, such a device 'might, in the long process of cooking . . . leave, at least psychologically, a trace (however infinitesimal . . .) of the taste of the bamboo. Anyhow, such a net might hinder the juices of the ingredients cooked with the fin from permeating the fin thoroughly. Therefore a net of fine silver wire should be used.'

Yu Sun

Fish lips

Some fish, notably big groupers (pages 55 to 58) have large, fleshy lips. The Chinese preserve these like shark's fin and prepare them as follows.

The dried lips, with bones attached, are first soaked in cold water for at least two days. They are then simmered until the bones can easily be removed, after which the lips are thoroughly cleaned and cut into pieces about 3 or 4 cm square. These are marinated in a mixture of Chinese wine, pepper and finely chopped ginger for a couple of hours, then washed again. (By this time you should also have cooked, slowly, the meat of a chicken and some ham, with 2 or 3 cups of water added, so as to produce a rich gravy as well as the cooked meat.)

Finally, bring 2 tablespoonfuls of peanut oil to the boil in a pan; put the pieces of fish lips in and stir for a few seconds; pour 2 glasses of Chinese wine over them, add the chicken, ham and gravy, a slice of ginger and a few pieces of spring onion; and cook over a low fire for about 1 hour, when the lips will be sufficiently tender. Add pepper and soy sauce to taste. Serve the lips with the gravy only (finding some other use for the chicken and ham!).

Dr Cheng, whose advice I have again distilled above, adds the useful note that 'turtle skirt', i.e. the soft rim of the turtle-shell, sun-dried, may be prepared in similar fashion.

Yu To

Fish bladder

The bladder in question here is an air bladder which, by expanding and contracting, enables a fish to adjust to the different water pressures at different depths. It is a perfectly clean and wholesome apparatus; do not be put off by the alternative name 'fish maw' which is often used!

Fish bladder is sold in dried form, in the shape of a long and very thin balloon (a foot or more in length and an inch or so in diameter). It is cream or stone in colour. It is also available in flat pieces.

Before being eaten, fish bladder must be made spongy and juicy. It has to be soaked in cold water for 2 or 3 hours, weighted down by a plate or something. It must also be squeezed from time to time to expel air bubbles. After the soaking, bring plenty of water to the boil and boil the bladder in it for 10 minutes. Then drain and rinse it and cut it into pieces of about an inch. This completes the preparation. The pieces are ready for use in a dish which will make them even more spongy and juicy, for example a rich soup or a Chinese-style ragoût such as I remember having in an old coaching inn in Peking, when the pieces of bladder were served with an unctuous chicken mixture. The texture was remarkable and the taste strong. Fish bladder is essentially something to add rather than something to eat by itself.

According to the *Nan Shih*, quoted by Read, the Chinese Emperor Ch'i Ming Ti liked to eat fish bladder soaked in honey, of which he would make a meal of several pints at a time.

Smoked Fish

The Chinese, especially in the south, enjoy smoked pomfret, which they serve in various ways, including a kind of salad which is very good. They smoke other fish too (and prawns, as explained on page 275), and similar practices exist in most S. E. Asian countries, where the smoking of fish is carried out either to preserve them or to give them an interesting flavour or for both reasons.

The recipe which I give here is not directly from China but was demonstrated to me in Bangkok in 1973 by Mr Yok Teng, who was completing his fortieth year of service at the house of the British Counsellor there. He was also approaching his 72nd birthday and explained to us that this would mark the beginning of the sixth stage of his life, when he would be in retirement and would be looked after by his family. His sons and daughters were in fact buying a house for him.

Mr Teng came originally from Hainan. Perhaps that is where the recipe too belongs.

Mr Teng had bought a pla kaphong (snapper, see pages 74 to 79), choosing the silver-white kind rather than a red one, of about 1⅓ kilos. He cut off the pectoral fins, removed the gills and gutted the fish through the gill opening (without cutting the belly open). Preparation of the fish was completed by rubbing salt and pepper over the body.

Meanwhile he had a good charcoal fire going, in a container large enough to take the fish's body on top. He sprinkled charcoal ash over the fire, and then a couple of tablespoonfuls of coarse sugar. Smoke billowed up. The fish was then placed on a grid over the fire and left in the smoke for about 10 minutes (5 minutes for each side). Mr Teng found it necessary to sprinkle some more sugar over the fire twice during these 10 minutes, while the skin of the fish crinkled and turned golden-brown.

That completed the smoking of the fish. Mr Teng then skinned it, put it in a greased roasting pan, with a little butter on top of it, and cooked it in a moderate oven for 15 to 20 minutes. (He also added chopped potatoes and mushrooms at some stage, for these were with the fish when it came to table, but we never did discover the details of this last touch, which anyway seemed unimportant, for what really excited us was the engrossingly good taste of the fish itself.)

Sweet and Sour Fish

I confess that the two finest versions of this classic Chinese dish which I have eaten were both done with freshwater fish. One was offered to us by the Deputy Chairman of the Revolutionary Committee of the Mi Yun Dam (who has a wealth of fish at his disposal and gave us no fewer than seven fish dishes in a single lunch). The fish looked like one of those speckled groupers, for the the dark brown sauce which covered it was flecked throughout with tiny pieces of ginger. But it was a carp. And again it was a carp, this time a grass carp, which we ate at the restaurant on the shore of the lake in the Lin Hua Park in Kwangchow, where the fish come straight from lake to kitchen to table and the diner has a pretty view of shimmering water, variegated trees and little bridges, for all the world like a Chinese painting!

However, the recipe is also excellent for seafish, provided that they do not have too strong a marine taste. A really good grey mullet from clean estuarine waters would do very well, as would a pomfret or a snapper.

One of the main constituents of the dish should be a selection of pickled vegetables, shredded into 'matchsticks' or even more thinly. You can make this yourself by selecting suitable vegetables such as cucumber, sweet red pepper, turnip, onion and (essential) ginger, and marinating them for an hour in a mixture of ½ cup vinegar, ½ cup water, 4 teaspoonfuls sugar and 1 teaspoonful salt. But if you have access to a Chinese provision shop it is simpler to buy a jar of Chinese pickles and use them.

1 fish (see above) weighing over 1 kilo (uncleaned weight)
Chinese pickles (see above – if these are not available you will need the ingredients
    for making them)
2 teaspoonfuls cornstarch
1 tablespoonful hoy sien jeung (a red Chinese sauce, the same one as is served with
    Peking roast duck – available in bottles)
salt and pepper
cooking oil
2 cloves garlic

Clean and scale the fish, then either steam, poach or fry it. I recommend frying, to achieve a crisp golden-brown effect. If you are using a sizeable fish, score it diagonally on both sides. (And, if the fish is too big for the number of people who are going to eat it, remember that you can lift the fillets off one side, reserving them for separate use. A fish with one side thus removed will sit very snugly on the platter and in the sauce.)

Make your sauce as follows. Take ½ cup of the liquid from the pickles or ¼ cup vinegar (with 1 to 2 tablespoonfuls sugar) and add enough water to make 2 cups in all. Add to this the hoy sien jeung, the cornstarch (dissolved in a little water) and the seasoning. Heat the cooking oil in a pan, fry the garlic briefly in it, then add the liquid and go on cooking gently.

Place some of the shredded vegetables on top of the cooked fish, pour the sauce over all and serve.

Cha Lau Wong Fa Ue

Fried croaker, Chinese style

In China cooks would choose for this dish the Yellow croaker, *Pseudosciaena crocea* (Richardson), which is plentiful there and of good quality. See page 89. However, any good croaker (see pages 90 to 92) will do.

1 croaker (see above) weighing about ½ kilo
peanut oil
some minced ham
1 onion
3 slices ginger
1 tablespoonful Chinese wine
1 tablespoonful vinegar
a little cornflour
1 tablespoonful soy sauce

Scale and clean the fish thoroughly, and cut off the gills. Make diagonal incisions on each side. Fry it in very hot oil until it is brown all over.

In another pan make a sauce from the remaining ingredients and pour this over the fish before serving it.

Fish Treated by 'Red Cooking'

This is a basic Chinese cooking technique, which may be applied to almost any fish. If you choose one of about 1½ kilos you will need the following further ingredients:

a little flour
oil for frying

3 tablespoonfuls Chinese wine
5 tablespoonfuls soy sauce
5 thick slices ginger
2 shallots, roughly chopped
1 tablespoonful sugar
2 teaspoonfuls salt

Clean the fish and score it deeply on both sides at intervals of about 2 cm. Rub the flour over the skin so that the fish will not stick to the pan and to give the skin additional crispness. Then fry it in a wok, giving each side a minute or two over a fierce flame, then 3 or 4 minutes over a medium flame. Then pour out all the oil, except for 1 tablespoonful or so, and add the ingredients in the right-hand column, with 1½ cups of water. Let the fish cook thus, over a hotter flame, for another 10 minutes before serving.

In describing this recipe in her useful Penguin Handbook on Chinese cookery, Mrs Buwei Yang Chao explains that the fish thus cooked may also be served cold in its jelly.

Steamed Grouper with White of Egg and Crab Sauce

These directions are based on the recipe ascribed to Mr Sawin Wong in the admirable book by Herklots and Lin on *Common Marine Food-fishes of Hong Kong.*

1 very fresh grouper (pages 55 to 58) weighing about 1 kilo (uncleaned)
50 grams crab meat
1 rice bowl of thick soup stock
whites of 3 eggs
1 tablespoonful lard
1 tablespoonful cornflour
salt to taste
a little minced ham

Clean and scale the fish, then steam it until it is just cooked. (This will take 10 to 15 minutes.)

To make the sauce, boil the crab meat in the thick soup for a few minutes. Mix the egg-white, lard, cornflour and salt with a little water, add all this to the soup and let it come back to the boil. Pour this sauce over the steamed fish, sprinkle the minced ham on top and the dish is ready.

Dow See Loong Haah

Cantonese lobster

1 live spiny lobster weighing ¾ kilo
125 grams minced loin of pork
a little oil for cooking
1 clove garlic, finely chopped
2 cups chicken broth
½ tablespoonful cornstarch
2 eggs, beaten

to be mixed together:
1 teaspoonful salt
¼ teaspoonful pepper
1 teaspoonful sugar
½ tablespoonful cornstarch
2 tablespoonfuls black fermented
    beans (dow see)
1 tablespoonful sesame or peanut oil

Kill the lobster. Remove claws and legs, separate them at the joints and crack them. Split the body open, remove all inedible parts and chop it and the tail into pieces (without removing the carapace).

Now take the pork and combine it with the mixture in the right-hand column. Heat a small amount of oil in a pan, fry the garlic in it and then add the pork mixture. After a minute or two add the pieces of lobster, followed a minute later by the (pre-heated) chicken broth. All this should then be simmered until the lobster is sufficiently cooked (say, 12 minutes). The ½ tablespoonful of cornstarch, dissolved in a little water, should then be added to the simmering gravy. Once the gravy has thickened remove the pan from the fire, stir in the beaten eggs and serve.

Prawns with Egg-White

Often, when my wife and I taste a new fish dish, we debate whether it is worth recording; but sometimes our eyes, meeting over the table, register an instant and favourable decision. So it was with this dish, when we first ate it at the Peking Restaurant in Gloucester Road, Hong Kong.

Mr Ng Fook Sun took us behind the scenes to see it being prepared. He pointed out that the furnaces over which the cooking was done were extremely hot, far hotter than an ordinary stove, and that the cooking times which are appropriate in his highly organized inferno, and which I give below, would probably have to be expanded slightly in the less Dantesque conditions of an ordinary kitchen.

10 ounces (peeled weight) of prawns
peanut oil
whites of 6 or 7 eggs
3 tablespoonfuls chicken soup ⎫
1 tablespoonful flour-dissolved-in-water ⎬ combined
20 green peas, already cooked ⎭
2 teaspoonfuls salty Chinese cooked ham, chopped very fine

Fry the peeled prawns in plenty of hot oil for 2–3 minutes, then pour in the egg-whites and stir the mixture around until they set (which will take another 2 minutes or so). Drain the prawns and egg-white in a colander. Then pour the combination of chicken soup and flour-in-water into the wok with the peas and cook for 2 minutes or so. The prawn and egg-white mixture is then returned to the wok, the teaspoonfuls of finely chopped ham sprinkled over all and the dish served. (A little soy sauce may be added when serving.)

The prawns will be swimming, so to speak, in a clear liquid which consists of the chicken soup and the oil which was left on the prawn and egg-white mixture. The pale glassy aspect of this liquid contrasts with the creamy white of the egg-white, the pink prawns and the green peas. (Mr Fook Sun explained to us that colour is important in the dish, and that the peas are indeed added for this reason alone.)

Revolutionary Chinese Recipes for Prawns

Although I could not find any such thing as a contemporary cookery book in the Peoples' Republic of China, whose 7 or 8 hundred million citizens seem to manage very well without, I did discover in the official magazine *China's Foreign Trade* (No. 3 of 1975) several recipes, which evidently bear the imprimatur of the revolutionary authorities, for cooking prawns.

These are simple and clear recipes. I reproduce a pair of them verbatim below as rare examples of recipe-writing in China in the early 1970s. They are prefaced (and rightly so, for the organization of food production and consumption is a fundamental aspect of politics in any country) by a political essay, on then-and-now lines, about Chinese prawn fishermen, an essay which concludes with this pleasing vignette: 'It happened to be a holiday when we visited Shatou Brigade of Chachien Fishery People's Commune in Wudi County. A bunch of vigorous young fishermen were having a rousing game of basketball. In the club, groups of two and three were watching table-tennis or browsing through books in the library. We came to Ma Chang-shan's home. There was a portrait of Chairman Mao on the white wall of this newly built, spacious and bright room. The clock, radio and sewing machine were arranged neatly. Hospitable Ma Chang-shan and his wife warmly welcomed us and cordially chatted about their family life. He said that generations of his family toiled for domineering fishing tyrants in the man-eating old society, but had to flee to beg. Now, all nine members of the family have no worries about food or clothing, and all their needs are met.'

FRIED PRAWNS

1. Shell six prawns, retaining the tail portion; clean and draw out veins; slit lengthwise without severing, and slash lightly. After draining, sprinkle with salt and pepper; dust with 100 g flour and dip in 2 beaten eggs, and coat evenly with breadcrumbs.

2. Heat 0.5 kg cooking oil in a heavy pan until faint blue smoke rises, fry prawns for two minutes, turning several times.

SMOKED PRAWNS

1. Clean six prawns, remove grit and veins, but keep them whole and intact.

2. Pour 5 g cooking wine, a pinch of gourmet powder [monosodium glutamate], scallion, ginger, Japanese pepper and salt to taste into 0.5 kg boiling meat stock. At the same time drop prawns in to boil. As soon as prawns float to surface, take them out and put aside for about 15 minutes.

3. Place prawns on the frames of a smoke cage, side by side, without touching each other.

4. Heat an iron pot until bottom begins to glow red and then add 100 g sugar. As soon as it begins to smoke, place the smoke cage into the pot, replacing lid tightly and leave for five minutes after lowering flame at once to prevent sugar burning which will give a bitter taste.

5. Skim the top off meat stock and mix with 50 g sesame oil. Brush this on the smoked prawns to give them their colour.

Prawn Dumplings

There is a very pleasant tradition in Hong Kong of eating dishes which are collectively known as Dim Sum at lunchtime. There are special Dim Sum restaurants (although not as many as there used to be) and one can enjoy eating up to a dozen different dishes at them while still having what is only a light lunch. I particularly enjoyed prawn dumplings, which are made as follows:

You need what are called egg roll or wun tun wrappers. These can be bought ready made, much the best solution for most people. Otherwise sift ½ lb flour and ½ teaspoonful salt together into a bowl and gradually combine them with ½ pint cold water. When you have a firm, pliable dough, roll it out until it is paper thin, then cut it to the size you need.

egg roll or wun tun wrappers (see above)
2 spring onions, white part only
1 lb uncooked prawns, shelled
4 water chestnuts
1 teaspoonful soy sauce
1 teaspoonful salt
pinch white pepper
3 teaspoonfuls peanut oil

Peel water chestnuts and mince finely. Chop prawns roughly and shred spring onions. Mix together prawns, spring onions, water chestnuts, oil, soy sauce, salt and pepper and allow to stand for 20 minutes. Cut wrappers into 2½" circles. On each piece place a spoonful of the mixture, fold over to form half a circle and seal edges with beaten egg. Place on greaseproof paper in a steamer and steam over boiling water for 10 minutes.

Stir-Fried Squid

1 kilo small squid
4 tablespoonfuls cooking oil
1 shallot, cut up
3 slices ginger
2 tablespoonfuls soy sauce
1 tablespoonful rice wine
1 tablespoonful cornflour

Prepare the squid as usual. Chop the tentacles. Cut the body into squares of about 3 cm.

Heat the oil, put in the pieces of squid, add the shallot and ginger and stir for a minute or so. Add the soy sauce and rice wine and stir for another 2 minutes. Then remove the squid and put them in a serving dish.

Mix the cornflour with 2 tablespoonfuls of water, put it in the pan and cook it until it becomes translucent. Then pour the contents of the pan over the squid and serve.

Bow Yu

Abalone

Abalone is readily available and is often served with an oyster sauce. It is very good so. But Dr F. T. Cheng, whose words are close to being law in our kitchen, declares that this Cantonese mode is to be (mildly) deplored, as tending to obscure the fine intrinsic taste of the abalone. Instead, at his bidding, we proceed thus.

Take ¼ kilo of best-quality dried abalone, wash it with warm water and soak it for 4 days in cold water (to be changed twice daily). Then wash it again and put it in the top of a double boiler with 4 tablespoonfuls of hot water, a few pieces of fat pork, a dessertspoonful of peanut oil and a glass of Chinese wine. Cook it thus, covered, for 5 hours over a medium fire, adding a little more hot water if necessary during this time. Then slice the abalone into pieces and serve it with what little juice remains.

Hoy Sum

Sea cucumber

The sea cucumber (catalogued on page 193) is an animal, so cucumber is not an apt name; but the alternative, sea slug, is off-putting. Whatever you call the creature, be sure to pay close attention to the cleaning. Otherwise the sea cucumber, which is bought in dried form, will not swell properly and will not turn into an efficient vehicle for the rich sauce with which it should be impregnated, indeed saturated.

The process of cleaning has been described as follows. 'Take half a dozen sea cucumber of good size and quality. Soak them in cold water for a few hours, then brush and clean them thoroughly. Boil them for 5 minutes in a fresh lot of water, then remove them from the heat, let them cool, brush and clean them again, take out their stomachs and put them into another lot of fresh water. Carry on thus, cleaning them and changing the water repeatedly, until all impurities have been removed. In practice, it will usually be more convenient to buy the sea cucumbers ready prepared. Then proceed as follows.'

1 tablespoonful rendered pork fat or lard	1 teaspoonful light soy sauce
1 clove garlic, finely chopped	salt to taste
½ teaspoonful minced onion	a dash of dark soy sauce
½ teaspoonful minced ginger	½ teaspoonful cornstarch mixed
½ soupbowl chicken stock	with a little water
1 tablespoonful Chinese wine	

Heat water in a pot and boil the (now immaculate) sea cucumbers in it for a few minutes. Remove from the heat and discard the water.

Heat the pork fat in a pan, fry the garlic, onion and ginger in it briefly, then add the remaining ingredients except for the cornstarch. Simmer the mixture for 10 minutes, then add the cornstarch to thicken it; which achieved, pour the hot sauce over the sea cucumbers and serve them.

Recipes from the Philippines

Filipino cookery is, I suppose, more variegated than that of any other S. E. Asian country. The Spanish influence is strong. It is fascinating to see how many Mediterranean dishes have been adapted for use on the other side of the world. The Americans have left their mark too, at least in the agreeable hubbub which is Manila. Chinese cuisine is prominent; and there are many dishes which have made their way through Indonesia from the Asian sub-continent.

Yet there is also a strong native tradition, which the visitor to Manila may agreeably explore at the Grove Restaurant, where Mr and Mrs Kalaw preside, or used to preside, daily over an array of authentic Filipino food. Thirty-three pans simmer on thirty-three native stoves (plus two very large ones, the first for snails and the second for prawns). There may be seen little moonfish stacked together like silver cardboard cut-outs; triangular banana leaf packets with fresh dilis (anchovy) inside, all set on a bed of tamarind pods; a whole bowl of oysters with tomato, onion, green pepper and whole limes (Kilawen talaba); eels whose flesh has acquired an orange tint in being cooked; a pitch-black dish of squid cooked with its ink; Sinigang mayamaya, the celebrated fish and vegetable stew; and many other marine delicacies.

Sea fishing is highly developed in the Philippines. I remember visiting the market at Navotas, a scene of frenzied activity as amphibious craft ferried in the catch from the fishing fleet, churning their way along a canal of Stygian sludge at one side of the market, while the gaily coloured and fantastically decorated lorries and jeepneys stood ready at the other side to bear the fish away. Variety and quantity were both enormous.

The writing of cookery books is also well developed. The Filipinos are highly communicative people, who have the engaging habit of expressing their sentiments and emotions in all situations. This extends to the writing of cookery books, which are often prefaced by elaborate and sentimental tributes to parents, mentors and others, a habit of which I approve, but from the practice of which I must, as an undemonstrative Scot, remain largely debarred.

Of the Filipino cookery books cited in the bibliography I draw particular attention to those of Maria Y Oroso and of Patricia Arroyo. These are brilliant and arresting works.

More recently, there has been an even larger crop of books which successfully combine scholarship and culinary know-how. Among the numerous authors, Gilda Cordero-Fernando, the late Professor Doreen Fernandez and Edilberto N. Alegre have produced works which are required (and highly enjoyable) reading for anyone seeking to understand the place of food in Filipino culture – or, I should say, cultures, for many co-exist in these fruitful islands.

A Little Lexicon of Filipino Fish Cures

The people of the Philippines have a strong and varied tradition of curing fish, so as to keep it in edible condition for periods ranging from a few days to a month or more. Some of the techniques are native to the islands; others are adaptations from the Old World. Modern techniques are taking their place alongside the traditional ones; but, as happens in so many parts of the world (the British will think of kippers), the traditional methods do not merely result in preservation but also impart special flavours which are well liked and which have so far warranted their survival. Here are summary descriptions of some of these traditional cures.

DAING: Daing is salted, dried fish of any kind. The fish is cut open along one side, lengthways, cleaned, salted and sun-dried.

TINAPA: Tinapa making consists of soaking the fish in strong brine, then boiling in a weak brine and smoking over a mixture of burning sawdust, wood shavings, bagasse, rice hull or coconut husk (depending upon what is available in the locality). Fresh guava leaves are piled on top to avoid flames and to develop a good smoke flavour. The fish are smoked till golden brown. They are not usually dried, hence tinapa have a shelf-life of only a few days. Tinapa-making may be applied to sardines, milkfish and gizzard shad.

ESCABECHE: The method of marinating fish known as escabèche seems to be of Spanish origin. True, it is also well-known in other parts of the Mediterranean (French escabèche, Italian scapece, etc.); but it seems to me significant that in the rest of the world it is found most often in Spanish-speaking countries or countries which have come under Spanish influence. Thus Pescado en escabeche is a familiar dish in Mexico (especially the province of Yucatan) and in other countries of Latin America; and it has been adopted also in the Philippines.

The escabeche technique consists essentially in frying pieces of fish and then marinating them in vinegar, often flavoured with garlic or whatever else is available locally to give an interesting taste.

In the Philippines fish in escabeche may have ginger and red and green peppers incorporated in the sauce, and sugar may be added. The result is fairly close to Paksiw (see below).

Escabeche is not to be confused with ceviche, a term used for the preparation of fish by marinating them in lemon juice or the equivalent. The action of the citrus juice on the fish produces effects like some of those produced by cooking processes. Lime is used instead of lemon in most tropical countries; but in the Philippines calamansi provide the cheapest solution. The recipe for Maria's marinated fish (page 285) is an interesting hybrid between escabeche and ceviche.

PAKSIW: The term Paksiw is applied to either meat or fish which has been pickled with vinegar and salt. Ginger is used too when fish is thus treated; and sugar is a helpful, but optional addition. Various fish are suited to the treatment, for example milkfish, Indian tarpon, grey mullet and apahap (*Lates calcarifer*).

For ½ kilo of fish allow nearly ½ cup of vinegar (which should ideally be coconut vinegar or the milky-white nipa vinegar); 1 piece of ginger, slightly crushed; 1 teaspoonful or so salt; and if you wish 1 teaspoonful of sugar. The cleaned fish, cut into fairly large pieces if necessary, is put in a clay or enamel pot. The other ingredients are added and the whole brought to the boil. Water is then added (but not more than the quantity of vinegar used) and the mixture is brought back to the boil; after which it is simmered until the fish is done. It is to be served cold and may be kept for several days.

PINAKSIW: This is the name for a preparation of sardines in vinegar, which Avery thus describes: 'Fresh sardines are washed in fresh water and placed in a saturated brine for about 2 hours. They are drained and packed in 5-gallon cans or large pots with banana leaves or split-bamboo mats on the bottom to prevent burning. As the fish are put in, each layer is lightly salted. Sliced onion, celery, green pepper, black-pepper berries, and ginger may be added. Nipa or coconut vinegar is poured over the fish until they are submerged. The fish are cooked over a wood fire so that they simmer for 15 to 20 minutes. Sometimes the juice is drained. The produce will keep about 1 week.'

PINANGAT: Pinangat, like Pinaksiw, is a modification of Paksiw. Fish are cooked with salt and a little vinegar, over a low heat, until they are almost dry. The cooking is usually done in the native clay pot called palayok. The fish thus treated include anchovies, which are wrapped in banana leaf, small gobies and sardines. The product will keep for several days, or even, weeks.

PODPOD: This term means a kind of fish cake, with good keeping properties. Cheap fish are used for the purpose. After being steamed or boiled they are cooled on racks and the meat is then separated from the skin and bones. After the meat has been salted and mashed up with young and tender calamansi lime leaves it is formed into cakes which are heavily smoked. They will keep for up to 2 weeks.

SINAING (or SINAENG): This preparation is usually applied to the smallest members of the tunny family, such as *Auxis thazard thazard* (page 110). These fish are apt to be caught in very large quantities and they do not keep well (because they are too bloody, I was told). The problem is solved thus. Take a large new earthenware pot, line the bottom with banana leaf or a piece of woven bamboo or other coarse vegetable fibre. The fish (gutted, scored and rubbed with salt) are put in in layers and water and vinegar are added to the level of the bottom layer. The pot is then well covered and placed on the fire, which should be a low one. When the fish has been cooked in the steam the liquid remaining in the bottom of the pot may or may not be drained off. In either event the pot is sealed and may then be shipped for considerable distances. The sinaing is sold from or indeed in the pot.

TUYO: This is another term for salted and dried fish. Tuyo is a name for small fish thus treated. Tuyo will be fried or grilled when the time comes to eat them, and served with fresh tomatoes. The main difference between Tuyo and Daing (see page 280) is that in making the former one does not cut open or gut the fish. Smaller fish are used for Tuyo than for Daing. The scales of the fish are not removed in either preparation.

Fish Sinigang

A kind of Filipino fish chowder with a distinctive sour taste

Sinigang may be made with meat, or with vegetables only, instead of fish. It is one of those invaluable recipes which can be applied with great versatility and which will always produce a dish which is, with rice, a meal in itself.

Sinigang is one uniquely Filipino dish. It is characterized mainly by its sour broth, brought about by the use of a tart fruit or vegetable, for example unripe tamarind fruit or kamias or calamansi juice. Rhubarb or lemon are suitable substitutes.

This is a moist method of cooking, suitable for lean fish but applicable to others too. Bangos (milkfish) are often used. Talakitok (various carangid fish) are also to be recommended for the dish.

1 fresh bangos, cleaned and cut into slices about 1 inch thick
4 or 5 cups water (rice-cooking water if you have it)
5 or 6 green tamarind pods (or the equivalent amount of kamias, which is *Averrhoa bilimbi*, another sour fruit described on page 213)
2 tomatoes, quartered
2 onions, quartered or sliced
salt
some string beans ⎫
1 eggplant, cut up ⎭ optional, one would suffice
leaves of kangkong (*Ipomoea aquatica*, water spinach, a vegetable widely used in the Philippines)

Boil the tamarind in a little of the rice water until it is soft, then mash it. Add the rest of the rice water, the tomatoes and onions and salt, and the other vegetables. Boil until the vegetables are nearly done, then add the pieces of fish and the kangkong leaves and continue until the fish is done. (Most recipes would have you put the kangkong leaves in with the other vegetables, but Patricia Arroyo argues convincingly that a short cooking time for the leaves results in their being brighter green in colour and pleasantly crisp – see *The Science of Philippine Foods*, page 168. Indeed it may be better to put them in after the fish.)

This makes an excellent lunch dish. What is important is that the fish should be very fresh. And Filipinos would add that the cooking should be done in one of their shallow earthenware pots, if possible. This sort of pot, which is illustrated below, is made of clay and keeps viands cool even in tropical room temperatures.

Filipino Fish Chowder

A recipe of Maria Orosa

enough fish (of any kind) to produce 1 cup when flaked
2 cups coconut milk diluted with an equal amount of water
calamansi juice
2 tablespoonfuls butter
4 slices bacon, cut up small
1 or 2 cloves garlic
1 cup sweet potatoes, previously boiled and cut into small cubes
1 onion chopped
1 teaspoonful salt
½ teaspoonful pepper
5 tablespoonfuls coconut cream

Heat 1 cup of the coconut milk (diluted as indicated above) with the calamansi juice, then simmer the fish in it until it is cooked. Remove the fish, let it cool and then flake it taking care to be rid of all bones.

Fry the bacon in the butter until it is crisp, then the garlic until it is brown. This should be done in a big pan, because the next step is to add the fish, potatoes and onion, with salt and pepper. Fry for another 3 minutes. Add the remainder of the diluted coconut milk and let the whole mixture boil gently for 2 minutes. Finally, add the coconut cream just before serving the chowder, with crackers if you have them.

Pesang Isda

This is one of a number of Filipino fish recipes which call for simmering fish with vegetables. Lean fish are best suited to this sort of moist cookery. The recipe may also be applied to fish heads (cut in half if you use a single large one).

½ kilo fish
1 tablespoonful cooking oil
4 cloves garlic, chopped very fine or pounded
1 small onion, thinly sliced
1 small piece ginger, thinly sliced
2 cups water (rice-cooking water if you have it)
2 cups green papaya or bottle gourd (upo), cut into pieces
1 tablespoonful fish sauce (patis)

Clean the fish (or pieces of fish or fish head). Heat the oil and sauté in it the garlic, onion and ginger.

Add the rice water (or plain water, if necessary). Bring to the boil, then add the green papaya or bottle gourd, followed by the fish. The fish sauce is to be added towards the end of the cooking. When the fish and vegetable are done, check the seasoning and serve hot. (Cooking time should be between 10 and 15 minutes. The papaya or upo will be ready when it becomes transparent. If you are using a fish head, wait for the eyes to turn white and pop out.)

Other vegetables which may be used for or added to Pesa (which is the abbreviated title of the dish) are cabbage, scallions, pechay (Chinese cabbage) and leeks.

Filipino Fish Loaf

Maria Orosa gives two recipes for a fish loaf, of which the one reproduced below is my favourite. It has an interesting flavour and provides a good way of stretching a small quantity of fish. But there would be no harm in increasing the amount of fish, if you have it to spare.

enough fish to provide ½ cup of meat
 when it is flaked
1 cup coconut milk
salt
½ cup breadcrumbs

1 sweet red pepper, chopped
3 eggs, well beaten
1 cup milk
1 tablespoonful lime juice
2 pinches paprika

Simmer the fish in the coconut milk with 1 teaspoonful of salt until it is done. Then flake it, taking care to get rid of all bones and skin. Add the remaining ingredients (first mixing together the beaten eggs and the milk) and a further pinch of salt. Mix everything thoroughly and transfer the mixture to a buttered tin. Bake for 30 minutes in a moderate oven.

Fish and Guava Salad

Here is another recipe of Maria Orosa, in which I slightly alter the proportions to allow more fish than she thought necessary, while acknowledging that less will do and saluting her frugal spirit; a spirit which led her also to suggest making the dish with an inexpensive fish such as dalagang bukid (*Caesio* spp.). These fish are known as Fusiliers in English, for what reason I do not know, although one of them, which has brick-red flanks surmounted by a blackish back, evokes for me those red-faced army officers, wearing black bowlers, who stride bouncily in and out of the Ministry of Defence in London and among whose number may be some who are or were Royal Fusiliers.

enough fish (see above) to provide 1 cup of flaked flesh
salt and pepper
25 ripe guavas
1 orange
3 bananas
½ cup coconut cream

Clean the fish, boil them in a moderate quantity of water with salt and pepper, drain them and remove the flesh in flakes.

Pare 10 of the guavas, open them and remove the seeds, then cut them into small pieces. Peel the orange, divide it into its sections and peel each section. Peel the bananas and cut them into small pieces. Mix the flaked fish and the fruits. Add the coconut cream and chill the mixture.

Cut the tops from the remaining 15 guavas, remove the seeds and fill the guavas with the fish mixture. Replace the tops and serve while the contents are still well chilled.

Maria's Marinated Fish with Mock Artichoke Salad

This recipe, which reflects the hybrid nature of much Filipino cookery, was given to me by Maria Recio.

½ kilo fillets of pompano or snapper or lapu-lapu (grouper) or other good
    white fish
juice of 20 small calamansi
2 tomatoes, peeled and chopped
1 onion, sliced
3 or 4 small hot green chillies
½ cup freshly prepared coconut cream
2 tablespoonfuls vinegar
pinch of oregano (which grows in the Philippines)
salt and pepper

Arrange the fish fillets in a shallow dish and pour the calamansi juice over them. Leave the dish in a cool place for 6 hours or more, turning the fillets once during this time. Then drain them and reserve the juice.

Combine all the other ingredients and mix them with the reserved calamansi juice. Pour the mixture over the fish and keep in a cool place until you are ready to serve it.

Miss Recio is proud of her mock artichoke salad, which is made from banana blossom and is as delicious as it is plausible. It is also simple to prepare.

Buy a large oved (banana blossom, more like a huge phallic bud than a flower), strip off the outer 'petals', cut what is left into four lengthways and then cut the four pieces across into sections about 4 cm long. To 2 cups of water add 2 beef bouillon cubes dissolved in water. Bring this to the boil, then add a teaspoonful of salt, a tablespoonful of vinegar and 2 tablespoonfuls of olive oil (or other oil) and the pieces of banana blossom. Cook as though you were cooking artichoke hearts until the banana blossom is tender, then drain the pieces, let them cool and dress with mayonnaise.

It is well-established that everyone for whom Maria Recio has cooked will, on encountering her again, at once demand this preparation. (Another recipe which calls for banana blossom will be found on page 290.)

Bangos Relleno
Stuffed milkfish

I detect in this recipe a clear echo of Mediterranean techniques for stuffing fish, of which the archetypal version may well be Uskumru dolmasi, the Turkish recipe for stuffed mackerel. Turkish and Levantine influences reached round the coast of North Africa and into Spain; which may account for stuffed-fish recipes which I found in Tunisia and for the enthusiasm with which Spanish cooks prepare Merluza rellena (stuffed hake, the hake being one of their favourite fish). It seems reasonable to suppose that the Filipino practice represents the same tradition applied to the most plentiful and suitable of the Filipino fish.

There are two ways of preparing the fish for being stuffed, difficult and less difficult.

I have already described (in *Mediterranean Seafood*) the difficult method practised in Turkey. Having procured fish of good size, 'the first step is to gut them (through the gills, without opening the belly) and wash them. Then roll each fish backward and forward on a board, to loosen the flesh inside the skin. Without breaking the skin, snap the backbone just short of the tail, and again close to the head. Take hold of the backbone at the head end and work it up and down a little before drawing it out. Put aside any flesh which comes out with it. Squeeze the fish carefully between thumb and forefinger, moving your hand along from tail to head, in order to loosen the flesh a little more. Take out all the loose flesh.'

The less difficult method is as follows. Gut the fish in the ordinary way, taking care not to perforate the abdominal wall. Then make a cut right along the back of the fish, from head to tail, open it carefully, snip the backbone at both ends and lift out all flesh and bones. If you use this technique you will of course have to sew up the back or otherwise secure it in place after stuffing the fish.

1 milkfish of about ¾ kilo
salt
cooking oil
2 cloves garlic, chopped very fine or crushed
1 onion, finely chopped
3 medium tomatoes, finely chopped
1 tablespoonful butter
2 medium potatoes, cubed and fried
2 tablespoonfuls peas, fresh or canned
2 tablespoonfuls raisins
2 eggs, beaten (or the yolks of 3 eggs, beaten)
flour

Prepare the fish according to one of the two methods described above and simmer all the meat from it in a small quantity of salted water. When it is done, finish flaking it and removing all the bones.

Meanwhile heat the cooking oil in a pan and sauté the garlic, onion and toma-toes therein for a few minutes. Add the flaked fish, with seasoning, and continue cooking for another 5 minutes or so. Transfer the cooked mixture to a bowl and add the butter, potatoes, peas, raisins and beaten egg. Mix all well together and then stuff the fish with it.

The stuffed fish is then to be dredged with flour and fried in hot oil until it is well browned. It may be garnished with celery sticks (kinchay) and lemon wedges.

I should add that there are those who recommend that the skin of the fish, after it has been emptied and while it is waiting to be stuffed, should be marinated in a mixture of calamansi juice, soy sauce and pepper.

Bangos en Tocho

Milkfish fried and then simmered in a highly flavoured liquid

1 milkfish (bangos), cleaned and cut into pieces 2 cm thick
1 onion, cut into long thin strips
1 cake toqua (hard soybean cheese), cut into pieces and mashed
2 cloves garlic, finely chopped
2 tablespoonfuls ginger, cut into thin strips
4 to 6 tomatoes, chopped small
2 cakes salted bean curd (tahuri)
2 tablespoonfuls fermented soybean curd (tausi)
2 tablespoonfuls vinegar
sugar to taste
oil or lard for frying

The pieces of fish are to be salted and allowed to stand thus for 20 minutes or so. Then drain and dry them, fry them in the usual way in hot fat or oil until they are just brown, and keep them aside.

The strips of onion and mashed toqua are to be sautéed and then also put aside.

Next, sauté the garlic, ginger and tomatoes. Add the tahuri (dissolved in 1 cup of water), the tausi, the fried toqua and onion. Boil gently for 5 minutes, then add the vinegar with sugar to taste and continue cooking for 5 more minutes. At this point add the pieces of fried fish and let the whole dish simmer for a further 5 minutes.

Bulang-Lang

Milkfish with vegetables

1 bangos (milkfish) of medium size
a little cooking oil or fat
4 cloves garlic, chopped
1 onion, chopped
2 tomatoes, chopped
¼ cup bagoong (salted and fermented shrimp)
1 cup water (rice-cooking water if you have it)

pechay (Chinese cabbage)	moderate quantities of each – or
kangkong (water spinach)	substitute other vegetables, e.g.
green string beans	ampalaya (page 212) or eggplants

Broil the fish and set it aside.

Sauté the garlic, onions and tomatoes with the bagoong in a small quantity of oil or fat. Then add the rice-cooking water (or plain water if necessary) and the vegetables (cut into pieces about 5 cm long) and simmer until the vegetables are done. Meanwhile cut the broiled fish into sections, also of about 5 cm, and when the cooking is nearly complete add these to the dish. Serve hot.

Biya (or Bia) with Coconut Milk: and Suam Na Biya

Maria Orosa recommends buying 1 sizeable biya (flathead goby, page 102) and simmering it for 15 minutes in 1 cup of coconut milk (second extraction) and the juice of 5 calamansi, with ½ teaspoonful of salt. Large anchovies (dilis) may be used instead of gobies.

Once cooked, the fish is removed to a platter, the stock thickened with a table-spoonful of flour and the resulting sauce poured over the fish.

Biya are often available in small size and may then be used to make **Suam Na Biya**, for which the ingredients are 15 to 20 of the little fish and:

2 tablespoonfuls cooking fat	2 tablespoonfuls fish sauce (patis)
1 teaspoonful garlic, minced	4 cups water (rice-cooking water
2 tablespoonfuls onion, sliced	if you have it)
1½ tablespoonfuls ginger,	2 cups sili leaves
cut into strips	1 teaspoonful salt

Sauté the garlic, onion and ginger. Add the patis and rice water (or plain water if necessary). Bring to the boil and add the biya. Cover and cook 5 minutes. Add sili leaves and salt and cook 1 minute. Rice noodles may be added.

Two Filipino Ways with Anchovies

The Spanish influence is evident in some Filipino recipes for dealing with their abundant supply of anchovy (dilis). Malaga is one region of Spain where anchovies are plentiful, and Boquerones a la Malagueña, fans of five anchovies stuck together at their tails and deep-fried, are a popular dish. Dilis fans (but of three rather than five fish) are served in the Philippines, the fish having been seasoned with calamansi juice as well as salt and pepper before being dipped in batter and deep-fried.

However, the first of the two recipes presented here is almost identical (except for the use of calamansi juice instead of lemon juice) with Acciughe al limone, an Italian antipasto which I particularly enjoyed at Boccadasse near Genoa.

DILIS KINILAW

Kinilaw is an uncooked fish dish and therefore requires very fresh fish. For this reason it is popular only in regions bounded by the sea such as the various small southern islands of Samar, Leyte, Bohol, Ceb and Panay. Calamansi juice is the usual acidifying agent, as explained above; but green mango juice, kamias (*Averrhoa bilimbi*, the sour star-fruit) or vinegar may be used. Another option is to use larger fish, filleted before being marinated.

Take 8 or 10 small fresh anchovies, behead and gut them, then set them to marinate for a while in the juice of 4 or 5 calamansi, adding salt and (if you wish) a hot chilli pepper and some thin slices of onion and of green pepper. Serve chilled.

DILIS SINUWAAN

This recipe, in contrast, is a native Filipino one. It comes from Bicol, a coconut-growing region where coconut cream or milk is a staple ingredient in the cookery.

350 grams fresh dilis	3 tablespoonfuls vinegar
6 green peppers, cut into long strips	1 teaspoonful salt
½ cup coconut cream, diluted with 1–1⅔ cups water	2 cloves garlic, chopped fine
leaves of gabi (*Colocasia esculenta*, the taro plant)	1 small piece ginger, crushed

Wrap 2 tablespoonfuls dilis in gabi leaves. Follow the same procedure with the rest of the dilis. Tie the remaining leaves in knots and line them in the bottom of the cooking pan. Add pepper, coconut cream, vinegar, salt, garlic and ginger. Place the wrapped dilis on top and let boil for 45 minutes. The whole contents of the pan are then to be eaten.

Bolador with Ubod

Flying fish with banana blossom   serves 6

This is a recipe from the Cagayan Valley and Batanes, which I reproduce almost exactly as it is given in the admirable *Kitchen-tested Recipes* published by the Food and Nutrition Research Centre of the Philippine National Institute of Science and Technology.

6 fresh flying fish, cleaned	3 tablespoonfuls onion,
1½ teaspoonfuls salt	chopped
2 cups water	1 teaspoonful salt
2 cups sliced banana blossom	1½ cups fish and vegetable broth
2 teaspoonfuls garlic, chopped	½ cup tomatoes, sliced
1½ teaspoonfuls ginger, chopped	banana leaves cut 1" wide

Parboil fish with salt in 2 cups water to facilitate flaking. Remove the fish and boil banana blossom in the fish broth for 2 minutes. Drain and chop finely. Save broth for cooking fish balls. In a bowl, mix together flaked fish, banana blossom, garlic, ginger, onion and salt. Form into balls 2" diameter. Tie with banana leaves. Boil broth and tomatoes in a saucepan. Add fish balls and cook 15 minutes. Serve hot.

Lapu-Lapu with Tausi

Fillets of grouper accompanied by yellow fermented soy beans

500 grams fillets of lapu-lapu (grouper) or other good fish
flour
cooking oil
4 cubes (½") of tokua (soy bean curd)
3 cloves garlic, crushed
1 teaspoonful ginger, chopped
3 onions, sliced
2 tomatoes, sliced
½ cup yellow tausi (fermented soy beans)
½ cup taingang daga ('wood ear' mushroom*), soaked in water
2 tablespoonfuls soy sauce
2 tablespoonfuls cornstarch stirred into 1 tablespoonful water

Roll the fish fillets in flour, then fry them until they are half-cooked. Put them aside. Fry the pieces of tokua and put them aside too.

Sauté the garlic, ginger, onion and tomato, then add to them half the tausi, and a cup of water or so. Add next the fish fillets and the tokua, the rest of the tausi and the soy sauce, and finally the cornstarch for thickening. Cook until done, which will take about 8 to 10 minutes.

*Auricularia auricula. Taingang daga means literally 'ears of mice' which these mushrooms resemble.

Pesca Tagala (or Fish Caldereta)

Grouper with a sauce made from its roe

Mrs Inocencio Ronquillo tells me that this recipe may be used for Apahap (*Lates calcarifer*, page 48) just as well as for Lapu-lapu (various groupers, page 55 to 58). The fish bought must of course be a female with roe. For those who like fresh-water fish, the same dish may be prepared with a female carp (rojo).

1 grouper or sea bass (see above) a foot long
cooking oil
¼ cup margarine
2 cloves garlic, chopped
2 medium onions, chopped
2 medium tomatoes, chopped
1 small can tomato sauce
1 small can liver spread
1 cup grated cheese
1 sweet red pepper (pimiento), cut up finely
hot chilli sauce, as much as you wish, or 2 to 3 hot red chilli peppers
salt and pepper to taste
½ cup American-style sweet-sour mixed pickles

Clean the fish, reserving the roe. Salt the fish and let it stand for 15 minutes, then drain it, wiping off excess salt, and fry it in the cooking oil in a pan until it is done. Set it aside to keep warm while you prepare the sauce.

Sauté the garlic, onions and tomatoes in the margarine in a pan for a few minutes. Then add the fish roes, tomato sauce, liver spread, grated cheese, sweet red pepper and chilli sauce. Stir constantly. Add enough water (about 1 cup) to make the mixture of a sauce-like consistency, with salt and pepper to taste. When the sauce is cooked (which will take 10 to 15 minutes), pour it over the fish.

Garnish the fish with the sweet-sour pickles and serve.

Three Filipino Ways with Crab

The three crabs generally eaten in the Philippines are alimangong palaisdaan, alimasag and talangka, particulars of the first two of which will be found on pages 146 and 148. (The talangka, *Potamon grapsoides*, is a very small crab with two interesting characteristics. The abdominal shell is soft enough to be eaten; and the hard shell covering its back is lined with fat which may be prized off and eaten separately. But it is a river crab and outside the scope of this book.)

The larger crabs may be prepared in all the conventional ways, some of which are susceptible to Filipino variations. Thus **Cangrejos Rellenados**, Stuffed crabs, are made ready in much the same way as they would be on the Mediterranean coast, the crab shells being filled by a mixture of seasoned cooked crab meat with the familiar concoction of garlic, onion and tomato; the whole dipped in beaten egg and breadcrumbs and fried. Possible additions to the stuffing include sweet young peas and raisins.

A more obviously Filipino prescription is that for **Cangrejos Adobo**, Adobo crabs. For this the crabs are cut in half and put in a saucepan with 2 parts vinegar to 1 of water and plenty of crushed garlic. This is brought to the boil and kept cooking until the crabs are just about ready and a lot of the liquid has evaporated. Coconut cream is then added (as much as was used of vinegar) and the cooking continued for a couple of minutes only.

Alimango with Guavas is an interesting combination. A couple of fairly large crabs are carefully cleaned and then cut in two. 4 guavas are peeled and thinly sliced. Half a medium onion and 2 or 3 cloves of garlic are chopped. The procedure is then to sauté the garlic in a little hot oil until it is beginning to turn brown; to add successively the guava slices and the pieces of crab; and to cook all this, covered, over a low heat for several minutes. Finally, add 2½ cups of water, with salt and sugar to taste, bring to the boil and simmer until the crabs are fully cooked.

Shrimp (Prawn) Curry in the Samar Style

The shrimp used in this recipe are what the British would call prawns, of medium size. Peel and devein a kilo of them and place them in a pan with 1 cup coconut milk and a one-inch piece of ginger, crushed. Bring to the boil and cook until the prawns have turned red and are done.

Now take as much coconut cream as you can obtain from 2 coconuts and colour it with a little pounded turmeric. Strain. Add the bright result to the prawns, together with 3 red chilli peppers (seeded and sliced) and salt to taste. Cook a little longer and add a few spring onions, cut into lengths of 2½ cm or so, just before serving.

Pinais Na Hipon

Prawns cooked with a coconut mixture

This is a recipe from Quezon Province, in other words a Southern Tagalog dish.

½ kilo prawns
a little salt
1 cup coconut cream
more salt, about 1 teaspoonful ⎫ combined
4 cloves garlic, finely chopped ⎭
squash or banana leaves for wrapping
coconut milk, between 1 and 1½ cups

Peel the prawns, rub them with a little salt, chop them and combine them with the coconut cream and garlic.

Make packages with the leaves, each containing one sixth of the mixture. Place these in a saucepan with coconut milk to cover and simmer, with the lid on, for half an hour. (Some advise letting the packets become a little burned, asserting that the additional aroma thus created whets the appetite.)

Adobong Pusit

A classic Filipino recipe applied to squid

Adobo is the name of a well-known Filipino dish consisting of pork or chicken (or both) marinated in vinegar with garlic etc, simmered until tender, and finally browned in fat (or coconut milk) before being served. The technique can be and is used for fish (notably in Adobong tulingan, using tuna or bonito) or crab or prawns or, as in this recipe, squid.

1 kilo pusit (squid, page 181) of medium size
8 crushed garlic cloves
¾ cup vinegar
1 small onion, sliced
1 tablespoonful salt (or use soy sauce instead)
1 teaspoonful pepper
cooking oil or fat

Clean the squid in the usual way, (reserving two ink sacs) and set them aside to marinate in the vinegar, with half the garlic, the slices of onion and the salt (or soy sauce) and pepper.

Heat the oil in a pan and sauté the remaining garlic in this until it is brown. Strain it out, reserving the oil, and add it to the squid mixture. Simmer all together until the squid is tender, which will not take long.

Immediately before serving you may use the reserved oil to brown the pieces of squid; and may also add to the mixture the ink from one or two sacs, thus giving to the dish a thoroughly sinister and black appearance.

Calamares Rellenados

Stuffed squid

Squid seem almost to have been designed for stuffing; and there is no end to the different mixtures which can be inserted into them to good effect. The ingredients for stuffing suggested here are only an example; each cook, having grasped the theme, should execute his or her own variations.

4 squid of about ¼ kilo each

for the stuffing:	*for the sauce:*
100 grams minced pork or chicken or ham	cooking oil or lard
100 grams chopped shrimp or prawn or crab	4 cloves garlic, crushed
3 tablespoonfuls breadcrumbs, soaked in milk	2 tomatoes, peeled
1 egg	½ medium onion, chopped
salt and pepper	2 tablespoonfuls vinegar
	1 tablespoonful soy sauce

Clean the squid, discarding the ink sacs and removing the heads and tentacles. Chop up the tentacles (heads too, if you wish, but they are less good).

Combine the ingredients for the stuffing and stuff the result into the bodies of the squid, but without filling them quite full (since room must be left for the stuffing to expand). Sew them up or (easier) fasten them with toothpicks.

Heat the oil (or lard) and gently brown the garlic. Add the tomato and onion and cook gently for a few minutes, then add the remaining ingredients of the sauce and ½ a cup water (or wine, if you have some left over), followed by the stuffed squid. Simmer over a low flame for 20 minutes, adding a little more liquid if necessary. Serve the stuffed squid in the sauce.

Filipino Ways with Mussels (Tahong)

I am privileged to reproduce here three excellent recipes which have been developed by Patricia Arroyo and which she has contributed, with introductory and explanatory remarks, to my book.

Tahong (*Perna viridis*, page 173) is a salt-water mussel with a sea-green shell, commercially cultured in the province of Cavite which is just south of Manila. It also grows in other provinces of Luzon and in other islands of the Philippines though not yet abundantly. It is a good source of shellfish food protein, and a delicious one.

One interesting characteristic of the tahong is that the mantle of the female tahong is red to orange; thus it provides colour to otherwise dull dishes.

The first recipe uses tahong in a rather simple but savoury manner; the others make use of tahong in combination with other shellfish, fish, pork cracklings, rice and/or noodles.

Baked Tahong

1 kilogram tahong mussels, (use large ones, about 50 pieces to a kilo)
4 teaspoonfuls calamansi juice
2 tablespoonfuls butter

1 clove garlic, crushed
pepper to taste
parsley and carrot curls for garnishing

Mix thoroughly the butter, crushed garlic and pepper. Set aside. Wash the mussels, removing the hairy parts, and steam them until they open. Discard one half shell from each mussel. Pour calamansi juice over each mussel, just enough not to make it soggy. Then spread over it the butter-garlic mixture. Bake at 350°F (180°C, gas 4) for about 10 minutes.

Garnish with parsley and carrot curls. (To make carrot curls: peel one carrot and discard skin. Wash. Continue peeling the peeled carrots thus forming carrot curls. Put in iced water.)

Pansit Malabon   serves 12 to 15

Pansit means noodle. In the Philippines, noodles are almost always served during birthday parties since they symbolize long life for the celebrant or honoree. The recipe given is one of rice noodles with seafoods (including tahong) which originated from Malabon, Rizal, a town just north of Manila and known for fine seafoods. It is interesting to note that in this recipe atsuete (annatto) seeds are used as a colouring agent. This is the most widely used food-colouring agent in the Philippines.

400 grams bihon (rice noodles)
1 cup boiled and shucked tahong
1 cup boiled and peeled shrimps
1 cup flaked tinapa (see page 280)
1 cup boiled squid rings (without the ink)
¾ cup ground cicharon (salted pork cracklings)
2 cloves garlic, crushed and fried golden-brown
½ cup minced spring onions
2 hard-cooked eggs

for the sauce:
2 tablespoonfuls atsuete seeds
a small amount of oil
3 cups broth from tahong, shrimps and squid
1 cup strained juice from crushed heads of the shrimps
3 tablespoonfuls patis (fish sauce)
½ teaspoonful pepper
4 tablespoonfuls cornstarch

Soak the noodles in tap water. Set aside until soft. In the meantime, prepare the sauce as follows. Extract colour from the atsuete seeds by heating them in a small amount of oil. Strain into a saucepan and add the broth and shrimp-head juice, the patis and the pepper. Dissolve thoroughly the cornstarch into the mixture and boil it until thick.

Drain the soaked noodles and submerge them in boiling water for about 5 minutes. Drain and set on a platter. Arrange decoratively on top the tahong, shrimps, tinapa flakes and squid rings. Pour over the orange-coloured sauce, sprinkle the ground cicharon and then garnish with the fried garlic, spring onions and hard-cooked egg wedges. Serve with calamansi juice.

Shellfish Bringe (pronounced brin-he)

Bringe is a one-dish meal popular in the province of Pampanga, about 60 kilo-metres from Manila. It is chiefly characterized by its yellow rice, since fresh yellow ginger or turmeric (locally called dilaw) is the colouring agent used. (However dried turmeric powder may be conveniently substituted.) Chicken is the customary meat ingredient but tahong and other shellfish may be used instead. In the latter case, a very colourful dish results. The following is a shellfish Bringe recipe.

For mixture One:

1 cup ordinary rice*, washed

1½ to 2 cups coconut milk (from grated meat of approximately one-half coconut)

For mixture Two:

oil for sautéing
1 clove garlic, crushed
½ bulb white onion, minced
salt and pepper to taste
2 cups boiled tahong in the shell
1 cup boiled squid (without ink)
1 cup tahong broth
1 cup squid broth
1 cup peeled shrimps
1 crab in the shell, boiled
   and cut into quarters

1 cup ordinary rice*, washed
½ cup malagkit (glutinous rice)
1 cup coconut milk (from grated meat of approximately one-half coconut)
½ teaspoonful ground turmeric
1 bay leaf
1 sweet red pepper, cut into strips
red onion rings, thinly sliced, for garnishing

Mixture One. In a small saucepan, boil washed rice in coconut milk and ground turmeric till light and fluffy. Set aside.

Mixture Two. Sauté in a small amount of oil the garlic and white onions. Add salt and pepper, coconut milk, tahong broth and squid broth. Stir in ground turmeric, ordinary rice, malagkit (glutinous rice) and bay leaf. Cover till the rice has absorbed most of the liquid added but make sure the rice does not stick to the skillet. When almost cooked, add the peeled shrimps, squid, crab quarters and tahong and mix thoroughly. Pile on top the red sweet pepper strips. Cover and allow to cook for 1 or 2 minutes or till the red sweet pepper is tender but is still somewhat crisp. Mix thoroughly and test if salt and pepper is enough for one's taste.

Mixtures One and Two. Transfer alternately Mixtures One and Two on to a platter. Garnish with the red onion rings.

With the sea-green tahong, orange shrimps, red crabs, pink squid, yellow rice, red sweet pepper and red onion rings (actually purple), the result should be very colourful indeed!

---

*Ordinary rice in the Philippines is one which is light and fluffy when cooked but is soft enough even when allowed to stand overnight. It is an intermediate amylose rice. See page 49 of *The Science of Philippine Foods* by Patricia Arroyo.

Recipes from Indonesia

I sailed all around and through Indonesia in an aircraft carrier during my youth, but set foot only on the remote island of Morotai, where I ate nothing more excit-ing than the picnic fare provided by the wardroom. Years later I met at The Hague what I thought was Indonesian cuisine, in the form of the rijstafel, which is how-ever a Dutch creation, based on some features of Indonesian cookery and eating habits but expanded and transmuted. It was only in the 1970s, when I visited Indonesia, that I began to receive a correct, although incomplete, impression of how Indonesians in fact cook and eat.

I say incomplete, because Indonesia is a huge and complex country, outdoing in both respects every other in S. E. Asia. From Sumatra in the west (where dishes tend to be hot) through Java (where they are less hot and often include palm sugar) to the Moluccas in the east (where something close to Filipino cookery is practised) there is a bewildering range of cuisines, of which I have been able to study directly only a few. Even so, I have sought, in the collection of recipes which follows, to provide examples from all the main islands, helped by the willingness of Indonesian friends to demonstrate their native dishes.

An Indonesian hostess will not presume to anticipate a liking on the part of her guests for meat, fish or poultry. She will offer all three, accompanied by a dish of rice. She will also ensure that the meal includes a vegetable dish; and something hot, which will almost always take the form of a sambal or sambal goreng; and something crisp, such as prawn crackers (page 311).

A sambal is a small, hot side dish. In its basic form it consists of chilli pepper, shrimp paste (terasi), salt, lime juice and a little sugar. The first three ingredients are ground together. Everything is done just before the meal is served ('like tossing the salad in Europe', as one Indonesian lady explained to me). This basic sambal is uncooked. A sambal goreng usually includes garlic and onion; the mixture is fried in vegetable oil and cooked with coconut milk.

Everything is served at once on an Indonesian table. This principle is most strik-ingly demonstrated in the ubiquitous Padang restaurants (named for the town in Sumatra), where they have the convenient habit of placing dishes of everything available on the table as soon as one sits down. One eats and pays for what one wants and the rest is taken away. For a father who has battled in many a foreign eating-place to elucidate and coordinate the desires of wife and daughters three before ordering the meal for which he himself is over-ready, the system has enor-mous advantages.

With these superficial but enthusiastic remarks I introduce my small selection from the scores of Indonesian seafood recipes. First come general recipes for seafish; then recipes for specific fish; and finally recipes for crustaceans, molluscs and sea turtles.

Arsik

A dish from the north of Sumatra

This recipe comes from Deborah Panggabean, of Batak in North Sumatra. She says that it can be used for freshwater fish as well as for milkfish (bandeng, page 20) and other sea fish suitable for being cooked whole. I suggest using a good-sized fusilier (*Caesio* sp., page 80), which is the right sort of shape and is anyway one of the most abundant and popular fish in Indonesia.

1 fish (see above) of ¾ kilo	*pounded ingredients:*
2 to 3 cups grated coconut	3 cloves garlic
salt to taste	5 small onions or shallots
8 to 10 stalks lemon grass	10 to 15 red chilli peppers
	5 small tomatoes
	1 small piece ginger
	1 small piece galingale
	5 leaves of the small kind of lime
	used for cooking (daun jeruk nipis)

Combine the pounded ingredients with the grated coconut and the salt.

Lay the stalks of lemon grass in the bottom of your wajan or pan (to cover it and keep the fish clear of the hot metal), then add about half of the grated coconut mixture, followed by the fish (cleaned but otherwise whole) and the rest of the grated coconut mixture. Pour 2 to 3 cups of water over all, bring to the boil, then turn the heat down and simmer the preparation until it is dry. It is then ready to serve.

Ikan Santan

Fried fish cooked in coconut milk

1 kilo fish fillets, suitable	*pounded ingredients:*
for frying	2 small onions
salt	4 cloves garlic
peanut oil	6 red chilli peppers
1½ cups coconut milk	6 candlenuts (kemiri)
½ cup coconut cream	1 teaspoonful galingale (laos)
	1 teaspoonful shrimp paste (terasi)
	salt

Wash the fillets and pat them dry. Rub them with salt and fry them in hot oil until they are brown but only half-cooked. Set them aside.

In rather less hot oil, fry the pounded mixture until the onions are soft. Add the coconut cream and cook for another 6 or 7 minutes, stirring the mixture. Then add the fish, turn down the heat and let it all simmer until the mixture has thickened and everything is cooked (about another 10 minutes). Add the coconut cream shortly before the cooking is completed.

Ikan Bumbu Bali

Fried fish with a hot and sweet sauce

1 kilo fish fillets, or small fish suitable for frying whole
salt
coconut or other oil, for frying
and for the sauce:
3 large red chilli peppers, chopped
3 small onions, chopped
4 cloves garlic chopped
½ teaspoonful shrimp paste (terasi)
½ teaspoonful lemon grass, finely chopped
a small piece of ginger, finely chopped
a small piece of galingale, finely chopped
2 teaspoonfuls palm sugar
1 teaspoonful lime peel, grated

juice of half a lemon
2 tablespoonfuls sweetened soy sauce
(ketjap manis: or use ordinary soy
sauce and double the quantity of
palm sugar)

If you are using whole fish, clean them in readiness for being fried; if fish fillets, simply wash them and pat them dry. In either event, rub some salt on the outside of the fish.

Heat the oil and fry the first nine ingredients of the sauce in it until the onions are soft. Then add the remaining ingredients and continue, on a moderate heat, for another 2 or 3 minutes. At this point, add a cup of water, lower the heat and let the sauce simmer until it is fairly thick and quite cooked (about another 5 to 7 minutes).

Meanwhile pan-fry the whole fish or deep-fry the fish fillets until they are cooked through and golden-brown. Then place the fish on a platter and pour the sauce over them.

Ikan Colo-Colo

A recipe for grilled fish from Ambon

This recipe from Ambon is also well-known in the Moluccas as Ikan coco-coco.

Gut and clean the fish, but do not scale it. Then grill it over a charcoal fire until the outside is well browned. Remove it at this stage and put it straight into salt water. Then take it out again, wrap it in banana leaf and continue grilling it until it is cooked through. The banana leaf gives additional flavour.

The fish is served with a sambal consisting of soy sauce to which have been added very thin slices of red chilli pepper and of small onions, lime juice and (so say contemporary Indonesian cookery writers, although the practice cannot be traditional) a little melted margarine, all mixed together. The other accompaniment is a lalap, or mixture of vegetables, which might consist of baked egg-plants, yard-long beans (kacang pajang), lettuce and the kind of Chinese cabbage known as sawi mentah. The lettuce and the Chinese cabbage are not cooked.

To serve the dish, unwrap the grilled fish and place it in the middle of a platter with the vegetables cut up and arrayed around it. The sauce is poured over both fish and vegetables.

Pepes Ikan Jawa Barat

West Javan recipe for steamed fish

I first heard of this dish as a speciality of the famed restaurant Lembur Kuring at Jakarta, where rustic tables are dotted about between large pools in which golden carp of impressive size swish to and fro, whether trying to avoid or to catch the eyes of prospective diners I could not decide. The restaurant and the recipe are for freshwater fish. But on making enquiries I found that the recipe could be and is used for sea fish, particularly those which have no pronounced flavour of their own. I am glad to be able to include it, since it is interesting to compare it with the corresponding Burmese and Thai dishes (see pages 228 and 238).

1 fish (see above) weighing 1 kilo or a little more (uncleaned)
tamarind water, with salt and a little sugar, as a marinade
6 small red onions
6 cloves garlic
a few large red chilli peppers   to be pounded together or
half a dozen very small chilli peppers   finely sliced
1 piece ginger
1 small piece turmeric (kunyit)
3 soupspoonfuls coconut cream
1 stalk lemon grass, bruised and knotted
several makrut lime leaves (daun salam)
banana leaf as wrapping

Clean and scale the fish, make incisions in each side (not deep ones) and anoint it with the marinade. Leave it for 10 minutes or so, while you pound or finely slice the ingredients marked for this treatment.

Arrange the fish on a piece of banana leaf, ready to be made into a package, and add to it the pounded or finely sliced mixture, the coconut cream, the lemon grass and the daun salam. Close the package so that none of this escapes and steam it until the fish is cooked through (30 minutes or so).

Unwrap the package and serve hot or (an alternative which I prefer) let it cool and serve it cold some time later.

The recipe may be made with fewer chilli peppers, or with none at all. If you put them in, remember that the tiny chillis are hottest when pounded, half as hot if only cut up and milder still if left whole.

Ikan Pindang

Sour spiced fish

1 kilo fish or fish steaks (cleaned weight)
banana bark and banana leaf
1 piece turmeric, grilled and ground
tamarind water
a little palm sugar
4 small onions
4 cloves garlic
1 small piece galingale, thinly sliced
1 small piece ginger, thinly sliced
1 stalk lemon grass, bruised and cut into sections
3 large red chilli peppers, seeded and sliced in half
½ teaspoonful shrimp paste (terasi)
3 purut leaves (of the tiny limes used in cooking)
2 makrut lime leaves, torn up

Put banana bark in the bottom of a deep pot. Add the fish, turmeric, tamarind water and sugar; then all the other ingredients. Cover with banana leaf. Bring to the boil and simmer long enough to ensure that the fish are thoroughly cooked. (The time will depend on the size and shape of the fish steaks.) Do not stir while cooking. The banana bark will protect the fish from burning or sticking.

Pengat Asam Pedas

A red fish dish from Padang

This is another recipe which can be applied to almost any fish. It does not require coconut cream or milk. The chilli peppers give it a fine red colour.

¾ kilo fish
tamarind juice
salt to taste
a few leaves of the turmeric
    plant (daun kunyit)
1 soupspoonful coconut oil

pounded ingredients:
10 red chilli peppers
3 small onions or shallots
2 cloves garlic
1 small piece ginger
1 small piece galingale
1 small piece turmeric
3 candlenuts (kemiri) (optional)

Gut and scale the fish wash it and anoint it with the pounded mixture. Place it in your wajan or pan with 2 cups or so of water. Bring to the boil, then lower the heat and simmer for about 10 minutes until the liquid is considerably reduced. Shake the pan if necessary to prevent the fish from sticking, but do not stir it around, lest it break. The tamarind juice, salt and turmeric leaves are now added. After another 5 minutes' cooking put in the coconut oil. Five minutes later the dish will be ready.

Gulai Ikan *A fish and coconut milk stew from Aceh in North Sumatra*

This recipe is often applied to that excellent freshwater fish, the snake-head, but is equally good if made with sea fish. However, choose one with firm flesh, such as Spanish mackerel (tenggiri, pages 110 and 111) or conger pike (pucok nipah or remang, page 34).

1 fish or part of a fish weighing
   ¾ kilo or a little less
coconut or peanut oil for frying
cream and milk of 1 coconut
salt
tamarind water

pounded ingredients:
1 soupspoonful chopped onion
½ soupspoonful chopped garlic
1 soupspoonful dried red chilli
   pepper, chopped
2 fresh bird chilli peppers
1 small piece ginger
1 small piece galingale
1 teaspoonful turmeric
½ teaspoonful coriander and cumin seeds

Clean the fish, soak it in water, then cut it into pieces. Rub the pounded mixture into these.

   Heat the oil and fry the pieces of fish in it until they are golden. Then pour 1 cup of water over them, bring back to simmering point and go on cooking until the water has evaporated. As soon as this has happened, add the coconut milk. When oil separates on top of the coconut milk pour in the coconut cream and bring back to simmering point. Add salt and tamarind water a minute before serving.

Ikan Asap Masak Santan *Smoked fish with coconut cream*

Luwuk is both a region and a city in the Central Celebes, facing eastwards across the Molucca Sea. Mr Tatu Ahadjab, who comes from the village of Lontio in this region, gave me this recipe, which is suitable for any smoked fish. The quantities are large because, as he says, 'we always cook for a lot of people'.

2 kilos smoked fish (cut in chunks)
grated meat of 2 ripe coconuts
½ kilo tomatoes, sliced
¼ kilo small onions, sliced
3 stalks lemon grass
1 dessertspoonful salt
juice of 1 lemon

pounded ingredients:
5 cloves garlic
1 small piece (50 grams)
   turmeric
10 very small chilli peppers
6 white peppercorns

First, soak and squeeze the grated coconut in ½ litre of cold water. Strain and put the resulting coconut cream on one side. Next, soak and squeeze the grated coconut again in 1 litre of cold water. Strain to obtain the coconut milk.

   Put the litre of coconut milk in a large saucepan with all the other ingredients except the lemon juice and simmer this for 45 minutes. Then add coconut cream and lemon juice and continue cooking for another 10 minutes. Serve with plain boiled rice or sago.

Ikan Teri Goreng

Fried and spiced anchovy

Anchovies are more abundant than recipes for preparing them, but here is a good one. The ingredient listed as sambal ulek is a sambal which is bruised or crushed rather than pounded. It is made in an earthenware bowl with a bamboo pestle (the solid end of the bamboo found just below ground level). It is a Javanese condiment and is normally made of chillis, salt, shallots, sugar, garlic and tamarind water. Although a paste, the chilli seeds remain whole and visible.

½ kilo fresh anchovies (scaled, washed and gutted)
2 tablespoonfuls peanut oil
1 medium or several small onions, finely chopped
1 teaspoonful sambal ulek
1 generous teaspoonful salt
½ cup coconut cream
1 tablespoonful tamarind water

Heat the peanut oil in a pan, sauté the onion in this until it is golden, add the sambal ulek and stir. Next add the fish and salt, and continue cooking for a few minutes, stirring frequently to ensure that the fish are fully exposed to the spicy mixture.

Now add the coconut cream and tamarind water. Cover and simmer until all the liquid has been absorbed by the fish. Serve warm, adding fried peanuts as a garnish if you wish.

Panggang Ikan Bawal Jawa

Grilled pomfret, as prepared in Java

1 pomfret (pages 100 and 101)
2 tablespoonfuls Javanese soy sauce (sold under names like Ketjap Manis: it is thick
    and sweet and may be made by adding brown sugar to ordinary dark soy sauce)
2 cloves garlic, finely chopped
4 hot red chilli peppers, finely sliced
juice of ½ lemon
1 more tablespoonful Javanese soy sauce

Clean and scale the fish and marinate it for an hour or more in a mixture of 2 tablespoonfuls of the soy sauce, diluted with 2 tablespoonfuls of water, and the garlic.

Grill the fish over a low charcoal fire, basting with the marinade, until it is cooked through. Remove from the fire. Mix together the last three ingredients and sprinkle this over the fish before serving it.

Other fish may be treated in this way, for example the snapper which we ate one evening in the modest cliff-top restaurant Bayu Amrta at Pelabatun Ratu, to the sound of breakers on the rocks below and with the lights of fishing boats lining a horizon beyond which there was nothing until Antarctica. If one's judgment of a fish dish should take account of the setting, this one was unbeatable.

Rica-Rica Ikan

The Menado way of grilling pomfret

This is one of the recipes expounded in Mrs Latief's charming book on regional cookery in Indonesia.

½ kilo pomfret (page 100)
juice of 1 small lime
¼ cup coconut or peanut oil

ingredients to be ground together:
1½ small onions, sliced
4 red chilli peppers
1 slice ginger
1 stalk lemon grass, chopped
1 teaspoonful salt

Clean the fish, cut it into pieces and dress them with the lime juice. Heat the oil and fry the ground ingredients in it. Then add part of the fried mixture to the fish and let it marinate for an hour.

All that remains to be done is to grill the fish and to serve it with the rest of the fried mixture poured over it as a sauce.

Sepat Banang

An unusual recipe for milkfish from Sumbawa

3 milkfish (bandeng, banang in Sumbawa)
15 small prawns
3 eggplants
2 or 3 tomatoes
2 small onions
3 candlenuts (kemiri)
5 bird chilli peppers

3 unripe mangoes
salt
1 cup coconut cream
juice of ½ lime
basil leaves

Clean the fish and prawns. Prick the eggplants. Then bake them and the other ingredients from the left-hand column in the oven, until the fish are nearly cooked.

Meanwhile peel the mangoes and cut them into small strips like matchsticks. Rub these with salt and squeeze them.

Pound the onions, candlenuts and chilli peppers (having removed them from the oven). Heat the coconut cream and add these ingredients to it, followed by everything else. Continue heating the dish until the coconut cream comes just to boiling point, then serve it with basil leaves sprinkled on top.

Saté Ikan Banten

Fish stuffed as the Banten people do it

The Banten people in the far west of Java are a matrilineal society. The mother of a prospective bridegroom may judge her future daughter-in-law by how well she makes this dish, which is not an easy one.

1 milkfish (ikan bandeng) of about 1 kilo (uncleaned weight)
1 coconut – the white part to be grated, then fried without oil until it is
   golden-brown, then pounded
3 soupspoonfuls margarine (butter could be used)
3 soupspoonfuls of chopped onion which has been fried just enough to turn it
   translucent (not golden, still less brown)
2 soupspoonfuls chopped spring onion
2 soupspoonfuls chopped celery (prei)
2 eggs
salt and pepper to taste
tamarind water (or the juice of 1 lime, or tomato juice)
breadcrumbs

The problem facing the anxious daughter-in-law is to remove the whole inside of the fish without breaking the skin. This is possible if you first beat the fish all over, then gut it through the gill opening, snap the backbone near the tail and again near the head, draw it carefully out from the front and extract similarly all the remaining flesh and bone, squeezing it forward from the tail end.

This feat accomplished, the rest is easy. Sort out the flesh of the fish, taking care to get rid of all the little bones. Mix this prepared flesh with all the remaining ingredients except for the breadcrumbs. Fry the mixture until it is 'half-done'. It must not be too dry. Then mix in the breadcrumbs and stuff the fish with the mixture.

The fish must not be stuffed absolutely full, or it will burst when cooked. Allow space for the stuffing to expand. The actual cooking may be done by steaming, but it is better to wrap the fish in banana leaf and grill it over a charcoal fire for about 20 minutes until it is well browned all over.

Fish of the mackerel family (pages 108 to 111) may be treated in the same way. You then have **Saté Kembung**. You also have an interesting parallel to the dish Uskumru dolması, which is the Turkish way of stuffing mackerel whole (see my *Mediterranean Seafood*).

Ikan Bungbu Acar (or Pesmol Ikan)

A 'pickled' fish dish from West Java

This and the following recipe were kindly demonstrated to me by Mr Hassan Idrus, whose home town is Bogor, 60 kilometres from Djakarta, where flourish the famous Raffles Botanical Gardens, an inoffensive and indeed agreeable reminder of the period of British rule.

Mr Idrus counsels the purchase of a fish which is plump and succulent and bids one take care not to overcook it. (Some snappers dry up rather easily.)

1 snapper (pages 74 to 79) of about 1 kilo to 1¼ (uncleaned weight)
salt
tamarind water } to marinate the fish
oil for frying

to be pounded together:
7 small red onions, peeled and sliced
6 cloves garlic
4 candlenuts (kemiri)
1 generous piece ginger, sliced
1 smaller piece turmeric (kunyit)
1 piece shrimp paste (terasi)
2 teaspoonfuls salt

1 coconut, of which ½ to provide first extraction coconut cream
and ½ to be shredded and fried
⅓ cup vinegar, to which must be added some tiny chilli peppers and tiny onions, also a little sugar
4 leaves daun salam (makrut lime)
1 stalk lemon grass, bruised and tied in a knot
½ soupbowlful chopped spring onion
1 soupspoonful each of white and of palm sugar
6 small red chilli peppers
cherry tomatoes, flowered, for decoration and salad leaves

Clean and scale the fish and score it deeply on both sides. Salt and anoint it with tamarind water and let it stay thus for a short while. Meanwhile bring the oil to the boil in a wok and then fry the fish (whole) until it is of a good golden colour all over. This will take up to 30 minutes.

Next, pound together the ingredients marked for pounding. Heat a little oil in a smaller wok and fry the pounded mixture gently in it for 5 minutes or so until the oil is mostly absorbed and the onion is sufficiently cooked. At this point add half the quantity of the coconut cream which you have made beforehand; and all the fried coconut. The next addition is the ½ cup of vinegar, chillis etc., followed by the daun salam leaves and the lemon grass. Finally, put in the chopped spring onion and the soupspoonfuls of sugar. Taste and add more salt if need be. Carry on cooking the mixture, over a low flame, for a short time, taking care that the spring onion remains white and green (which it will not do if the heat is too great). Then pour the mixture (from which the daun salam leaves and lemon grass are discarded) over the fish on a platter.

A few cherry tomatoes, flowered, may be placed on top of the fish for decoration, and salad leaves around it. Mr Idrus, as considerate as he is skilful, serves the red chilli peppers separately so that only the heat-seekers among his guests will have any. But it would be usual to incorporate them in the pounded mixture.

A Trio of Sulawesi Recipes for Skipjack (Cakalang)

When I first saw Sulawesi, I learned that the strangely-shaped main island and the smaller ones in the group were known as the Celebes. Then, as now, the Skipjack (page 112) was one of the most plentiful and highly prized fish. The people of Sulawesi may be regarded as specialists in its preparation. The first of the three recipes which exemplify this statement comes from Luwuk in the east of the main island, the second from Ujung Pandang (the city which was once Macassar) and the third from Sulawesi as a whole.

Ikan Cakalang Goreng

Skipjack in the Luwuk way

2 kilos skipjack (cakalang) or Spanish
  mackerel
sufficient fresh coconut oil for deep frying
¼ kilo small onions (chopped)
juice of one lemon
½ litre of water for mixing sauce
250 grams white noodles

pounded ingredients:
10 very small red chillis
4 cloves of garlic
50 grams fresh ginger
100 grams turmeric
10 white peppercorns
5 cumin seeds
1 dessertspoonful of salt

Bone the fish and cut it into chunks. Deep fry these in the coconut oil. When well cooked, drain and put them on one side. Drain off most of the oil from the pan leaving only one cup. In this fry the onions until golden, then add the paste of pounded ingredients and continue frying until all is light brown (3 minutes).

At this stage return the fried fish to the pan. After simmering the fish together with the sauce for 5 minutes, add the water, the lemon juice and salt and bring it all to the boil. Then add the noodles and cook until the noodles are done – about 10 minutes.

Serve with plain boiled rice or boiled sweet potatoes.

Pallu Mara Cakalang

Skipjack poached in the style of Ujung Pandang

1 skipjack (cakalang)
2 keluwak nuts (see page 209)
tamarind water
1 teaspoonful salt

2 stalks lemon grass, chopped
2 small onions, sliced
2 slices galingale, chopped
1 small piece turmeric
5 red chilli peppers

Clean and wash the fish, then cut it into pieces, e.g. steaks. Pound the keluwak nuts, mix the result with the tamarind water and salt, and let the pieces of fish marinate in this mixture.

Pound together all the ingredients in the right-hand column, then combine the result with the fish in a suitable pot, add water to cover, bring to the boil and simmer until the fish is cooked.

Ikan Cakalang Rebus

This recipe is suitable for skipjack or any other member of the Spanish mackerel/tuna families (pages 110 to 114).

2 kilos fish (boned and cut into
   large chunks)
½ kilo tomatoes, sliced
200 grams small onions, sliced
a lemon leaf
juice of 1 lemon

pounded ingredients:
1 small piece (50 grams) ginger
10 very small red chilli peppers
5 white peppercorns

Boil all the ingredients except the fish and the lemon juice briskly for 5 minutes in about 1¾ litres of water. Then add the fish and simmer slowly for 40 minutes, adding the lemon juice 15 minutes before serving.

   Serve with boiled green bananas, sweet potatoes, sago or plain boiled rice.

Dabu-Dabu Sesi

A simple recipe from Ambon for mackerel

Buy 2 kembung (*Rastrelliger* sp., pages 108 and 109). Gut and clean them, dress them with salt and lime juice and let them marinate for a quarter of an hour. Then grill them.

   Just before the fish are ready, grill, briefly, 2 or 3 tomatoes, 3 red chilli peppers and a couple of red onions and then place them in a pot and crush them with a spoon. Add the whole fish and sufficient boiling water to cover all the ingredients. Check the seasoning and add more salt if necessary. Place the lid on the pot for 5 minutes or so to steep the contents but do not put on the fire. The dish is now ready and should be served with sago.

Pengat Masin

This recipe is especially suitable for treating a piece of fresh tunny or one of the smaller fish in the same family (see pages 112 to 114).

1 kilo tunny or the like (see above)
2 to 3 cups coconut cream/milk
leaves of the makrut lime
   (daun salam), torn
salt
palm sugar
belimbing asam (the small,
   sour star-fruit), halved
limes, halved

pounded ingredients:
5 small onions
2 cloves garlic
several candlenuts (kemiri)
1 piece ginger
1 piece turmeric
1 stalk lemon grass, bruised
   and chopped

Combine the coconut cream/milk with the pounded ingredients and bring it all to the boil, stirring as you do so. Then add the fish. Let it simmer until cooked. Finally, add the makrut lime leaves, with salt and sugar to taste. The belimbing asam and limes are to be served with the dish.

Udang Nenas

A combination of prawn and pineapple, from Surabaya

Soups do not loom very large in Indonesian cookery. Those which one meets are often of Dutch origin. But this is a liquid dish, which could almost be called a soup.

150–200 grams medium prawns	1½ soupspoonfuls chopped garlic
1 pineapple	1 soupspoonful vinegar
4 red chilli peppers	1 soupspoonful sugar
oil for frying	1 teaspoonful salt

Peel and prepare the prawns. Peel the pineapple, rub it with salt, wash it clean and cut it into small pieces half the size of a thumb. Deseed the red chilli peppers and cut them into sections of about 2 cm.

Heat the oil (you will only need a small quantity) and fry the prawns in it briefly. Remove them and replace them by the garlic, which is to be fried until golden. At this point pour in about 1½ cups of water, stir and bring to the boil. Then put the prawns back in with the red chilli peppers and the other ingredients. Stir assiduously while you bring all this back to the boil, when it will be ready to serve.

Saté Udang

Prawn saté

Prawns of medium size should be bought and prepared in the usual way (i.e. peeled and deveined). They are then skewered on saté sticks, anointed with the paste described below and grilled for several minutes on each side.

1 tablespoonful peanut oil	2 tablespoonfuls ground fried peanuts
1 clove garlic, chopped	½ teaspoonful ground chilli pepper
a little shrimp paste (terasi)	a little salt
½ stalk lemon grass, bruised	1 tablespoonful lime juice
and finely chopped	6 tablespoonfuls coconut cream

Heat the peanut oil, fry the garlic and shrimp paste in it briefly, then add the remaining ingredients and cook gently (without allowing the mixture to boil) for a few minutes until a good aroma arises. You now have the paste with which to anoint the prawns.

The prawns may be served with a peanut sauce which is similar to the paste described above – just subtract the lemon grass and add a little soy sauce.

Udang Sambal Goreng Kedele

Soy beans combined with prawns in a hot dish

Sambal goreng dishes may be prepared with any kind of meat, fowl, seafood or vegetables. What they always contain are coconut cream and hot chilli peppers. The recipe given here provides an interesting and nutritious combination of soy beans with prawns.

The quantities given are relatively small, since in Indonesia a sambal goreng would be presented with a lot of other dishes, and in any case few people would wish to make a meal of something so hot.

300 grams cleaned and peeled prawns	*and for the seasoning mixture:*
	1 large onion, crushed
350 grams soy beans, previously soaked overnight and cooked	4 cloves garlic, crushed
	6 large red chilli peppers, crushed
coconut or other oil, for frying	½ teaspoonful shrimp paste (terasi)
almost ½ litre coconut cream	1 small piece of ginger, finely chopped
2 leaves of daun salam (makrut lime)	salt to taste
2 tomatoes, sliced	

Heat the oil and fry the seasoning mixture all together therein. Once the onion is soft, add the prawns and tomatoes. Continue frying, always on a medium heat, for another 6 minutes or so. Finally, add the soy beans, the coconut cream and the daun salam. Once these last ingredients have heated up, turn the heat down and leave all to simmer until the mixture has thickened and everything is cooked (about another 10 minutes).

Binte Biluhata

Prawns cooked with corn and coconut, as at Gorontalo

1½ to 2 cups medium-sized prawns	3 or 4 small onions
3 to 4 cups corn off the cob (i.e. kernels only – choose young cobs)	4 tomatoes
	15 basil leaves
5 or 6 big chilli peppers	1 cup grated coconut
1 teaspoonful salt	juice of 1 lime

Boil the corn until it is cooked. Meanwhile clean and peel the prawns, slice them thinly and boil them in a little water (say, ½ tablespoonful).

Pound the chilli peppers with the salt. Thinly slice the onions and tomatoes. Chop the basil leaves. Add all these ingredients, and the grated coconut, to the boiled prawns; then add the whole mixture to the corn and continue to cook over a low heat for 5 to 10 minutes more. Finally, add the lime juice and serve hot in a covered tureen.

Kerupuk Udang

Prawn crackers

These crackers, which bear a family resemblance to those of Vietnam and other countries in the region but have a distinctive taste, are so good that I recommend learning how to make them. Cirebon is the place most famous for prawn crackers, but the directions given below are those expounded to me by Mrs Lili Djazuli from Banten in Java.

These crackers are usually made from prawns, but it is possible to make similar ones (which may be smaller and rectangular in shape) from fish such as Spanish mackerel (tenggiri) or Snapper (kakap).

½ to ¾ **kilo prawns**
1 egg
2 to 3 tablespoonfuls sugar
1 kilo tapioca flour (sagu flour in Indonesia)
salt

Clean and peel the prawns as usual and grind the meat.

Beat the egg, mix it with the sugar and add the mixture to the ground prawn meat. Stir. Add the tapioca flour and stir the mixture again, adding salted water as you do so. You will need between 1½ and 2 glasses of water in order to achieve the necessary dough-like consistency.

Shape the dough into a long roll, put a clean piece of cloth such as a table-napkin underneath it and steam it until it is stiff. Then take it out, keep it overnight and cut it on the following day into thin semi-circular slices. Dry these slices in the sun. They will then be ready for use.

To serve the crackers, heat a generous quantity of oil in a wok, then lower the crackers in one at a time, moving each around with a spatula in such a way as to help it expand to 3 or 4 times its original size while remaining flat. Each cracker will be done in a couple of minutes

Mrs Djazuli explained to me that the standard roll shape is subject to innumerable variations. The dough can be worked into all sorts of shapes, for example so that the cut slices resemble flowers; and it is even possible to produce what looks like embroidery!

Bebotok Kepiting Jawa

A Javanese crab dish

Crabs are less prominent than one might expect in Indonesian cookery, since Moslems are not supposed to eat the mangrove crab (*Scylla serrata*, page 146), which is the kepiting in the title of this and the following recipe. They are, however, free to eat crabs of the genus *Portunus* (page 148), of which the name is rajungan.

2 kemiri nuts (candlenuts), grated
1 medium onion, chopped finely
2 cloves garlic, chopped finely
1 tablespoonful terasi (shrimp paste)
½ cup coconut cream
¼ teaspoonful turmeric ⎫
¼ teaspoonful cumin seed ⎬ all in ground form
1 teaspoonful coriander seed ⎭
1 teaspoonful sambal ulek (see page 303)
1 piece lemon grass, finely chopped
2 eggs, slightly beaten
½ kilo crab meat
1 lime leaf

Mix the nuts, onion and garlic in a bowl with the shrimp paste (previously diluted with a little of the coconut cream). Add the remaining ingredients, mixing well as you go, down to and including the crab meat.

Make patties of the mixture, wrap them in leaves or foil and steam them for an hour, adding the lime leaf towards the end of the cooking.

Kare Kepiting *Curried crab in the style of East Java*

3 crabs	*ingredients to be ground:*
¼ coconut	3 red chilli peppers
3 soupspoonfuls coconut oil	2 small onions
1 makrut lime leaf	1 clove garlic
1 piece galingale	2 candlenuts (kemiri)
1 stalk lemon grass	½ slice ginger
1 soupspoonful tamarind water	1 small piece turmeric
	1 teaspoonful shrimp paste
	1 teaspoonful salt

Wash the crabs, take off and crack their claws, and cut the bodies in half horizontally. Use the ¼ coconut to make both coconut cream and coconut milk. Mix these together.

Heat the oil and fry the ground ingredients until they are golden. Add the makrut lime leaf, galingale, lemon grass and tamarind water. Finally, add the coconut cream/milk. Keep stirring the mixture until it comes to the boil. Then put in the pieces of crab, bring it all back to the boil and simmer until the crab is cooked. (Keep stirring throughout.)

Ikan Cumi-Cumi Kalimantan

A recipe for squid from Kalimantan

1 squid weighing ½ kilo	2 tablespoonfuls soy sauce (the
1 teaspoonful salt	sweet kind, ketjap manis)
1 tablespoonful tamarind juice	peanut oil for frying

Clean the squid and cut it into pieces. Dress these with the salt, tamarind juice and soy sauce and let them marinate thus for 10 or 15 minutes.

Heat the oil in a pan and sauté the pieces of squid until they are done, which will take about 4 or 5 minutes only.

In *Resep Lauk Pauk* by Untari there is another interesting recipe for squid, called **Cumi-Cumi Bumbu Rujak**. The squid are cleaned as usual, then stuffed with a mixture of their own chopped tentacles, roasted turmeric, red chilli pepper, ginger, galingale, onion, garlic, salt, shrimp paste, tamarind juice, lemon grass and makrut lime leaves. Saté sticks are used to close the squid after they have been stuffed, and they are then wrapped in banana leaf and either steamed or baked.

Five Balinese Ways with Sea Turtle

In his delightful book *Island of Bali*, Miguel Covarrubias explains that it is always the men who prepare banquet food such as sea-turtle dishes for ceremonial and festive occasions, and that those of Belaluan have a particularly fine reputation. What he wrote is reproduced here for historical interest rather than as an example to follow.

'On the road coming from the seaport of Benua we often met men from Belaluan staggering under the weight of a giant turtle flapping its paddles helplessly in space, and then we knew they were preparing for a feast. For days before the banquet of the bandjar four or five stupefied turtles crawled under the platforms of the bale bandjar awaiting the fateful moment when, in the middle of the night, the kulkul would sound to call the men to the gruesome task of sacrificing them. A sea-turtle possesses a strange reluctance to die and for many hours after the shell is removed and the flaps and head are severed from the body, the viscera continue to pulsate hysterically, the bloody members twitch weirdly on the ground, and the head snaps furiously. The blood of the turtle is carefully collected and thinned with lime juice to prevent coagulation. By dawn the many cooks and assistants are chopping the skin and meat with heavy chopping axes (blakas) on sections of tree-trunks (talanan), are grating coconuts, fanning fires, boiling or steaming great quantities of rice, or mashing spices in clay dishes (tjobek) with wooden pestles (pengulakan).

'The indicated manners of preparing the turtle are [these four styles]:

> lawar: skin and flesh chopped fine and mixed with spices and raw blood;
> getjok: chopped meat with grated coconut and spices;
> urab gadang: same as above, but cooked in tamarind leaves (asam);
> kiman: chopped meat and grated coconut cooked in coconut cream.

'Coconut (nyuh) is an essential element for fine Balinese cooking. Grated coconut meat is mixed with everything, frying is done exclusively in coconut oil, coconut water is the standard drink for one's guests, and a good deal of the food is cooked in rich coconut cream, santen, made by squeezing the grated coconut over and over into a little water until a heavy milk is obtained. Food containing coconut does not keep and must be eaten the same day.

'Santen enters also into the composition of the other delicacy essential to banquets, the saté lembat or leklat. This is a delicious paste of turtle meat and spices, kneaded in coconut cream, with which the end of a thick bamboo stick is covered and which is then roasted over charcoals. The saté lembat is presented with an equal number of ordinary saté, little pieces of meat the size of dice strung on bamboo sticks "en brochette" and roasted over the coals, eaten dry or with a sauce. Rose was always poking around where cooking was going on, and to her I owe the following recipe for preparing the saté lembat given to her by the Belaluan cooks, who warned her, however, that it was a most difficult dish to prepare:

'Take a piece of ripe coconut with the hard brown skin between the shell and the meat and roast it over the coals. The toasted skin is then peeled off and ground in a mortar. Next prepare the sauce: red pepper, garlic, and red onions browned in a frying-pan and then mixed with black pepper, ginger, turmeric, nutmeg, cloves, srá (pungent fermented fish paste), isén and tjekóh (aromatic roots resembling ginger), ketumbah, ginten, and so forth, adding a little salt, all mashed together with the toasted coconut skin, and fry the mixture until half done. Take red turtle meat without fat, chop very fine, and add to the sauce in a bowl, two and a half times as much meat as sauce. Add one whole grated coconut and mix well with enough santen to obtain a consistency that will adhere to the sticks, not too dry or too wet. Knead for an hour and a half as if making bread. Meantime sticks of bamboo of about ten inches long by a half-inch thick should be made ready and rounded at one end. Take a ball of the paste in the fingers and cover the end of the stick with it, beginning at the top and working down gradually, turning it all the time to give it the proper shape, then roast over the coals until done.'

Miguel Covarrubias also mentions Kekalaan, 'a delicious dish . . . made of tender shoots of banana leaves cooked in turtle blood and lime juice'.

Recipes from Malaysia, Brunei and Singapore

To divide up S. E. Asian recipes according to the boundaries of the existing nation states is often an artificial procedure, although a convenient one. So far as Malaysia, Singapore and Brunei are concerned, the division is not even convenient and I have therefore treated the three together, while disclaiming even the faintest implication that their sovereignty and national characteristics are not distinct!

Brunei, where interest in fish and other seafood is symbolized by the magnificent Hassanal Bolkiah Aquarium, is represented by two excellent recipes.

Cosmopolitan Singapore presents a bewildering range of cuisines to the visitor. Among these the Chinese influence is dominant. It is reflected in the traditional Singaporean cuisine known as Nonya, which extends to Penang and to which belong, for example, dishes such as Otak-Otak (page 320) and Ikan asam perkat (page 326); but nonya food is something special which the Straits Chinese have evolved over the centuries and which has always been a family affair. Mrs Lee Chin Koon brings out this aspect of it in the following passages:

'We Straits-born Chinese are known as "Peranakan" – the ladies are called "Nonyas" while the men are called "Babas". We are the descendants of the early Chinese in the Straits Settlement of Penang, Malacca and Singapore. The Peranakan of Malacca and Singapore are more alike in their customs and habits, while their counterparts in Penang have been influenced by the Thais. I am a fourth generation Straits-born Chinese: my grand-children are sixth generation.

'Malay influence, because of mingling and intermarriage, has produced a unique Peranakan culture and set of customs distinct from those of the Chinese community who came from China. Our food, which is basically Malay or Indonesian in method and ingredients, was altered to suit our tastes. It is totally different from Chinese food, though we do use some Chinese ingredients, like pork, which the Malays, who are Muslims, are forbidden to touch or eat . . .

'Our Nonya food is so complicated that it takes years to learn and master. We had to learn to pound our rempah to just the right texture, we had to learn to fry garlic until it was golden brown, light and crispy, we had to learn to combine and measure our spices so that they would harmonize, and we had to learn to fry our dishes so that the gravies would be clear and bright, not dull, in colour. All of these things require training, experience, and skill. In those days, we didn't use recipes and measurements such as tablespoons, and everything was done by agak (estimation). Everything had to be learned by watching and practice.'

Fish cookery in Malaysia, especially West Malaysia, is full of variety, as one would expect in a country so large and containing so many peoples, all with their own cultural traditions. The Malaysian recipes which I give are intended to illustrate this variety, but to direct attention particularly to dishes which are genuinely Malay. Thus only a few recipes represent Chinese and Indian fish cookery in Malaysia. There is anyway no lack of good books on Chinese and Indian cookery; but very little on Malay. Traditional Malay recipes have been handed down the generations by word of mouth rather than written down, partly because Malay cooking has not enjoyed the esteem which it deserves. Indeed it is often difficult to find real Malay cooking in Malaysia; and the food presented in Malaysian restaurants is rarely what you would eat in a Malaysian home.

Malaysian hospitality is justly famous. In one respect, however, it has had an unfortunate effect, namely the risk that the pomfret will virtually disappear from Malaysian waters through ruthless overfishing. The explanation may be given in quasi-syllogistic form. Guests deserve nothing but the best. The best fish are pomfret. Therefore all guests must be served pomfret. Malaysians are loath to serve what they would regard as second-class fish when they have company; while to serve what they rank as low-class fish (a category in which the delicious tuna, sardines and anchovies are surprisingly placed) would be deemed an insult to guests.

It is fortunate that this exaggerated and hierarchical attitude does not apply to dried fish, one of the most common and versatile ingredients in Malaysian cookery. Small dried fish are added liberally to fish dishes to enhance their fishy flavour; or served in their own right, for example fried with peanuts, certain edible leaves and slices of dried red chilli pepper. The bones and heads of larger dried fish are used in the preparation of fish curries. And (turning from fish to crustaceans) it is from dried shrimp that the famous blachan (shrimp paste) is produced. Dried shrimp may also be used for decorative purposes, for example in adding a touch of pink to the colour scheme of a sambal.

Nor is there any snobbery in the Malaysian approach to the humble fish ball, a basic ingredient of fish soups and fish satay. Fish balls may of course be bought ready-made in the markets. Fishermen and their families make them in their spare time. But it is also easy to make them yourself, as I explain below.

Malaysian Fish Balls

To make your own fish balls, Malaysian style, buy some cheap, white-fleshed fish. Gut, skin and bone them. Flake the flesh finely, then put it in a bowl or vat of fresh sea water (heavily salted fresh water will do instead) for a time before pounding and moulding the flaked fish into the desired shapes.

There are two archetypal shapes of fish ball. The first is simply a small round ball with a diameter of about 1½ cm. The second is not really a ball, but a rectangular cake (about 10 cm by 5 cm by 5 cm) which is then cut into thin slices and deep-fried. These slices, floating in a soup, look just like bits of pork crackling.

There are unlimited variations on these two themes. Fish balls may be of any shape, so long as they stick together. They can be stuffed into fresh red chilli peppers or rings of cucumber. They can be hugged by walls of beancurd; or may themselves enclose strips of red and green chilli peppers; or may incorporate finely chopped chilli peppers and herbs.

Fish Ball Soup

This recipe shows how fish ball soup was served in the 1970s when sold from the numerous fish-soup stalls in Penang, which I hope are still pursuing their beneficent trade. For one bowl of soup (i.e. a generous helping for one person) you will need:

fish balls (I suggest 3 or 4 round ones and 7 or 8 slivers from the deep-fried
    rectangular cake variety; see page 316)
2 ladlefuls clear fish broth
a handful of thick rice noodles, already cooked
1 spring onion, finely chopped
1 tablespoonful dark brown sugar (Malaysians would use palm sugar)

To serve the soup, line a large bowl with the noodles, add the fish balls and fish broth, then sprinkle over it the chopped spring onion and brown sugar. Thin soy sauce, to which slivers of fresh red chilli peppers have been added, is served as an accompaniment.

However not all fish ball soups are as simple as this. The Straits Chinese have evolved an extremely elaborate soup which they serve at weddings and birthdays, called 'Heepeow soup'. This consists of fish balls, prawn balls and meat balls floating in a pork bone stock along with fried fish bladder (heepeow), tripe and cabbage.

Soup Ikan

A fish soup from Brunei

600 grams wolf herring (parang,
    page 22), flaked and pounded
white pepper
a little grated nutmeg
300 grams potatoes
2 medium Spanish onions, quartered
4 tomatoes, cut in slices across
5 fresh red chilli peppers, ground

a small handful of so'un, very thin
    Chinese soup vermicelli,
    pre-soaked in water
a knob of butter
salt to taste
chopped spring onion leaves
chopped coriander leaves

Take a pot of suitable size, add water until it is ¼ full and bring the water to simmering point. Put in the white pepper and the nutmeg, followed shortly afterwards by the potatoes, onions and tomatoes.

While this is coming back to the simmering point, start making fish balls by combining the flaked fish with the ground chilli. The balls should be about ¾ inch in diameter. Keep them standing in cold salted water until you use them. Once the pot is simmering again, put in these fish balls, one at a time.

Let the fish balls cook for about 5 minutes, then add the vermicelli, butter and salt. After 2 more minutes, the dish is ready. Before serving, decorate the soup with chopped spring onion and coriander leaves.

Laksa Asam

A popular, thick fish soup with noodles

There is nothing refined about this soup. It is as hearty and pungent as the fish soups which are to be had in Basque, Provençal or Italian fishing villages, although ingredients and flavour are of course different. The dish is well known at Penang and may be met under the name Laksa Penang. The recipe which follows was given to me by Raja Abdullah formerly of the Yazmin Restaurant in Kuala Lumpur, where he worked with infectious enthusiasm and great success to pre-serve and develop the authentic cuisine of the Malay people. (Yazmin, by the way, was the first woman police officer in Malaya before founding the restaurant which bears her name.) The quantities given are for 6 people.

for the soup itself:
6 ikan kembong (mackerel, pages 108
    and 109), gutted, scaled and washed
2 tablespoonfuls coconut oil
10 red chilli peppers, ground
1 thin slice blachan (shrimp
    paste) – about 35 grams
15 to 20 shallots, peeled
1 pint tamarind water
1 pint fish stock (or, failing
    that, water)
1 stalk bungah kantang (i.e. stem
    and pink 'bud' of the ginger plant)
several sprigs of daun kesom
    (*Polygonum odoratum*)
salt and pepper to taste

the noodles:
½ lb spaghetti-type noodles

accompaniments:
1 thin slice patis udang (dark
    shrimp paste) diluted with a
    little water
3 or 4 fresh red chilli peppers,
    cut into thin rounds
4 to 6 more shallots, finely
    chopped
half a cucumber, cut into chunks
3 limes, quartered
5 stalks mint leaves

The soup is made as follows. Heat the coconut oil in a pan, then add the ground chilli (which goes under the attractive name of chilli-bo), the blachan and the shallots. When these ingredients are golden-brown, add the tamarind water and continue cooking for 15 to 20 minutes, stirring all the time.

Next, add the fish stock or water and 3 only of the fish; also the bungah kantang and daun kesom. Boil the whole mixture gently an hour or so, until the fish have completely disintegrated. Season and strain the fish into a periok tanah (a tradi-tional earthenware casserole). The remaining 3 fish have meanwhile had their heads, tails and bones removed and their flesh shredded. This shredded flesh is now added to the broth, which is brought back to simmering point.

The noodles are easy. Prepare as usual in boiling water, strain and place in a tureen.

The accompaniments. Before serving the soup, arrange these on the table together with the tureen of noodles. The diluted patis udang should be in a little bowl; the other items in separate heaps on a platter.

To eat the soup, line your soup bowl generously with noodles, pour in your share of the broth, add what you want of the accompaniments and top the mix-ture off with a small dollop of the diluted shrimp paste.

Laksa Lemak

A distinctive and creamy prawn soup

This coconut-flavoured soup is much more refined (and creamy, which is what lemak means) than the Laksa asam described on the previous page.

600 grams (cleaned weight) medium prawns, peeled, cleaned and deveined
300 grams fish balls, previously made from wolf herring (parang-parang, page 22)
    or Spanish mackerel (tenggiri, more expensive, pages 110 and 111)
oil for frying
2 tablespoonfuls coriander seeds (ketumbar), roasted and ground separately
2 stalks lemon grass (serai), sliced
2 large pieces of galingale (langkuas), sliced
6 candlenuts (buah keras)
12 dried red chilli peppers, seeded and sliced   } pounded together
1 small piece of fresh turmeric
1 slice of shrimp paste (blachan), 2½ by 2½ by ½ cm
2 small red onions, chopped
salt
2 cups coconut milk
2 cups coconut cream

for use when serving:
300 grams cooked rice noodles (beehoon)
300 grams soy bean sprouts (taugeh), scalded and drained
1 cucumber, less skin and seeds, shredded
leaves of daun kesom (*Polygonum odoratum*, page 217), finely shredded
10 fresh red chilli peppers, finely pounded

Fry the pounded ingredients, including the coriander seeds. Add half the prawns. Continue frying for 5 minutes, then add the coconut milk, bring to the boil and add the salt and fish balls. After another 2 minutes' cooking reduce the heat and add the rest of the prawns and the thick coconut cream. Stir continuously to prevent curdling. As soon as the mixture comes back to the boil remove it from the fire; it will be ready.

To serve, place some of the rice noodles and soy bean sprouts in each guest's bowl, pour over these a helping of the prawn soup, and garnish the bowls with the last three ingredients.

Otak-Otak

Highly seasoned fish grilled or steamed in banana leaf

½ kilo (or slightly less; ask for ½ kati if in Malaysia) of any good fish with white flesh
3 or 4 teaspoonfuls coriander seed (ketumbar)
3 or 4 tablespoonfuls grated coconut ⎫
just under 1 cup thick coconut cream ⎬ ½ coconut will yield both
2 tablespoonfuls cooking oil
1 teaspoonful salt
2 teaspoonfuls daun kesom (leaves of *Polygonum odoratum* – see page 217) finely
    chopped
squares of banana leaf (scalded to soften them, and wiped dry)
satay sticks (small wooden skewers – toothpicks would do)

and for the seasoning:
3 stalks lemon grass ⎫
6 small onions
2 cloves garlic   ⎬ chopped first, as appropriate,
6 dried chilli peppers, seeded   and then all pounded together
5 or 6 candlenuts (buah keras)
2 teaspoonfuls turmeric powder ⎭

Wash the fish and cut it into thin slices, discarding any skin and bones.

Toast the coriander seeds.

Lightly fry the grated coconut; and prepare the thick coconut cream.

Prepare the seasoning by pounding together the six ingredients listed. This completes the preliminary work.

Now fry the seasoning mixture until a good aroma arises and it begins to 'separate'. Then add the coconut cream and simmer all together until the mixture is quite thick. Stir in the fried grated coconut and salt and remove from the fire.

When the mixture has cooled, add to it the pieces of fish and the little fragments of daun kesom. You should have enough to make about 8 banana leaf packets. Then pieces of banana leaf (which should be about 1 foot square) are laid glossy side down, the mixture spooned on the middle of each and the packets made up and secured with the satay sticks. The packets may then be grilled over a charcoal fire until they are uniformly browned (10 to 15 minutes); or steamed for 20 minutes, e.g. in a Chinese steamer.

Seafood Satay

This dish provides an interesting example of the fusion which sometimes occurs between Chinese and Malay cuisine. In this case the Malay recipe for satay, which is traditionally made with meat, has been adapted by the Chinese for use with seafood. The following recipe comes from Mrs Winnie Yang, a fifth-generation Chinese, who runs the Happy Garden restaurant along the Jalan Koto sea promenade in Malacca. She emphasizes that a great deal of preparation is required in making the dish. Thus it is only worth preparing if you are giving a large party or own a restaurant.

To make the fish satay it is necessary to prepare a large variety of different kinds of skewered sea food, in enormous quantities. This is because one person alone will usually get through 50 skewers in an evening. (Mrs Yang has known some people to consume 150!)

Cockles, clams, mussels, prawns and cuttle fish all skewer easily, and should be used if available. You should also have lots of skewered fish balls (cf. page 316) of different varieties: plain, wrapped in beancurd, spiced with finely chopped red chilli peppers and herbs, or containing strips of lemon grass, spring onion and red chilli pepper in the middle.*

The gravy-like sauce in which the skewered seafood is cooked is made from a paste containing a large number of pounded or ground ingredients, as follows:

6 stalks lemon grass	8 tablespoonfuls Chinese 'five spices' to
600 grams galingale	give the gravy a rich dark brown colour
15 red chilli peppers	3 tablespoonfuls shrimp paste (blachan)
10 cloves garlic	400 grams dried prawns
20 small red onions	½ kilo peanuts
6 to 8 tablespoonfuls curry powder	plenty of black pepper

Once the above mixture has been prepared, moisten it with peanut oil and fry it in rendered pork fat. Add water, sugar and salt to taste, and the gravy is ready.

The fish satay should be served at a round table holding a vat of bubbling gravy in the centre into which each person dunks his skewers and leaves them to cook for a minute or two. The cooked fish is removed from the skewers and put on a plate with chunks of white bread to mop up the gravy and slices of cucumber to alleviate the spiciness, refreshing the palate for more . . .

*Really high-class balls can be fashioned from prawn or crab meat. To make prawn balls, deep-fry small balls of minced prawn meat mixed with egg yolk and seasoning. To make crabmeat balls, prepare a dough of 2 beaten eggs and 3 tablespoonfuls of plain flour seasoned with salt and pepper and ½ teaspoonful of Chinese 'five spices'. Into this work 150 grams of cooked, flaked crabmeat. Then form the mixture into walnut-sized balls with a little cornstarch, and deep-fry them.

Ikan Panggang Kuali

A recipe from Brunei for cooking pomfret with belimbing fruit

1 kati (catty) (600 grams) pomfret (pages 100 and 101)
pounded ingredients:

1 two-inch piece turmeric	1 tablespoonful coconut oil for frying
1 two-inch piece galingale	½ cup (½ cigarette tin, I was told)
1 two-inch piece ginger	coconut cream
5 cloves garlic	1 cup tamarind water
10 small red onions	6 fresh red chilli peppers, split lengthways
10 dried chilli peppers	4 buah belimbing fruits
1 piece shrimp paste (blachan)	salt to taste
4 stalks lemon grass, bruised and chopped	

Clean the fish. Pound the ingredients to be pounded, heat the oil and fry the pounded mixture briefly. Then add the coconut cream and tamarind water and leave it to simmer for a few minutes.

Next, add the fish and bring back to simmering point. Add the buah belimbing fruits and fresh red chilli peppers. Simmer for another 10 minutes or so, correct the seasoning and serve.

Panggang Ikan Bawal

Barbecued pomfret   serves 4

4 pomfret (pages 100 and 101), each large enough for one person
2 brown onions
4 cloves garlic
8 fresh red chilli peppers, seeded
¼ litre (or so) coconut cream (first extraction)
1 lime or lemon

Clean and scale the fish and make some light incisions in their skins.

Make the marinade by chopping up finely the onions, garlic and chilli peppers and mixing them with the coconut cream. Pour this over the fish and leave them to marinate for several hours.

Remove the fish from the marinade and grill them over a charcoal fire. Keep the marinade warm by the fire and use it to baste the fish, frequently. When the fish are ready, serve them with a squeeze of the lime or lemon juice.

It is interesting to compare this recipe with the Indonesian Panggang Ikan Bawal Jawa (page 303).

Bapsetek Ikan

A recipe collected from Perlis

9 small mackerel (kembong, page 108), cleaned
8 to 10 tablespoonfuls palm oil
8 small red onions
4 cloves garlic
4 potatoes
5 fresh red chilli peppers, split lengthwise
2 tablespoonfuls tomato sauce
2 tablespoonfuls finely powdered sugar
salt to taste

First, fry the fish until they are well browned all over.

Cut up small red onions and the cloves of garlic. Peel the potatoes, and slice them. Fry the potatoes until brown.

Next, fry the onions and garlic until they are golden. Mix the flour with a little water to make a paste and add this to the onions and garlic. Let it simmer briefly before adding the chilli peppers, tomato sauce, sugar and salt. When the mixture has again been brought back to simmering point, add the fried fish and the fried potatoes. Let it all cook for a couple of minutes longer, add a little water, taste and correct the seasoning, and serve.

Pais Ikan

A steamed fish dish which is a speciality of Sarawak

1 snapper (ikan merah or jenehak, pages 74 and 75), weighing about 1 to 1¼ kilo
    before being gutted, scaled and washed
3 candlenuts (buah keras)⎫
9 small red onions   ⎪
10 fresh red chilli peppers ⎬ to be pounded
4 cloves garlic   ⎪
1 one-inch piece galingale ⎭
tamarind water and salt to taste
½ teaspoonful sugar

Leave the fish whole and place it on a bed of banana leaf.

Pound the ingredients to be pounded and mix in the tamarind water and salt, so as to produce a runny paste. Pour this over the fish and then wrap it up in the banana leaf, folding the leaf over carefully so as to cover the fish and prevent juices from escaping. Secure the ends of the leaf with the vein of a coconut-palm leaf (or a toothpick).

When the package has been thus prepared, steam it for about half an hour, until the fish is done. (Were you to use a fish with firmer flesh, such as Spanish mackerel, tenggiri, the steaming would take longer.) Serve the fish in its leafy cover, so that none of the sauce is lost.

Ikan Masak Molek

A recipe for steamed snapper from the Restaurant Yazmin at Kuala Lumpur

However fine the red snapper you buy, this recipe will do full justice to it. Those with whom I tasted the dish at the Restaurant Yazmin were unanimous in saying that they had never had a snapper which was so delicious. Molek, by the way, is a Malay word which, applied to a girl, indicates a multiplicity of attractive features of which physical beauty is only one.

1 whole red snapper (pages 74 to 78) weighing about 1 kilo
½ tablespoonful powdered turmeric (or less for a paler sauce)
coconut cream from 1 whole coconut
200–250 grams shallots, peeled
6 slices ginger, cut into thin strips
2 slices of asam keping (the name for dried slices of asam gelugor, or glugor, a fruit
    of which the scientific name is *Garcinia atroviridis* and to which the English
    name 'apple tamarind' is sometimes given)
salt and pepper to taste
5 fresh red chilli peppers, each partly quartered and turned into a 'flower'

Gut, scale and wash the snapper. Steam it until it is cooked through, which should take about 20 minutes.

Add the turmeric to the coconut cream and heat it gently until it begins to simmer. Then add the shallots, ginger and asam keping. Continue to simmer until the shallots are tender.

Put the steamed fish on a platter with a lettuce leaf as a pillow under its head and pour the sauce over it. Decorate the dish with the chilli 'flowers' and serve it with steamed rice.

Penang Assam

Mrs Chua Thia Eng of Penang kindly provided her recipe, which I reproduce below, for this well-known local dish, thus matching her husband's generosity in helping me with Malaysian fish names.

Ingredients: 1 fish weighing about 1 catty (1¼ lb), 2 stalks bungah kantang (i.e. stem and pink 'bud' of the ginger plant), 15 to 20 small onions, 10 chilli peppers, 5 cloves garlic, 1 one-inch long piece of ginger and a similar piece of turmeric, 1 piece blachan (shrimp paste), 1 round ball of tamarind (assam), 5 to 7 candlenuts (buah keras), salt, sugar and cooking oil.

Method: (1) slice the fish into pieces about 1 inch thick; (2) slice the bungah kantang very finely; (3) mix the tamarind with 2 cups of water, blending well and discarding the seeds: (4) grind the small onions, red chilli peppers, garlic, ginger, turmeric, blachan and candlenuts until fine; (5) heat about 4 tablespoonfuls of cooking oil in your kuali (wok), add the ground ingredients and fry them; (6) add the sliced bungah kantang, tamarind water and salt bring to the boil and add sugar to taste; (7) add the fish slices and continue boiling for a few minutes until they are cooked; (8) serve with rice.

Ikan Masak Puteh

A dish from Negri Sembilan

½ catty (300 grams, cleaned weight) Spanish mackerel (pages 110, 111)
1 one-inch piece ginger, pounded ⎫
1 teaspoonful ground black pepper ⎬ mixed together
salt to taste ⎭
2 carrots, sliced   *and for the sauce:*
2 or 3 spring onions, sliced   5 red chilli peppers
a few coriander leaves   3 cloves garlic
lettuce or other salad leaves   oil for frying
½ catty (300 grams) fried potato slices   1 cup coconut cream
10 small red onions, sliced and fried   a little vinegar
                                           sugar to taste

Rub the fish with the pounded mixture. Add the carrots, spring onions and coriander leaves. Steam the fish, thus prepared, until it is cooked, then arrange it on a bed of lettuce and surround it with the fried potato and onion.

The sauce may either be served separately or poured over the the fish mixture. It is easily made. Pound together the red chilli peppers and the garlic, fry the pounded mixture briefly then add the coconut cream and vinegar together with the sugar and a little of the liquid from the steamed fish. Cook this for a short time. The sauce may need a little salt, but take care not to make it too salty.

Ikan Masak Asam

A spicy fish and vegetable dish

The directions given below provide for using eggplants as the vegetable. I think that this is the best choice, but other vegetables, for example yard-long beans cut into pieces of 3 cm, may be used successfully.

300 grams (cleaned weight) fish,
    cut into small pieces
oil for frying
2 cups tamarind water
salt to taste
2 or 3 eggplants (brinjal) cut into
    pieces of 5 cm, which must be
    soaked for a long time before-
    hand and drained before use

pounded ingredients:
5 candlenuts (buah keras)
6 slices galingale (langkuas)
2 stalks lemon grass (serai), sliced
1 dessertspoonful peppercorns
1 small piece of fresh turmeric
3 small onions, chopped
30 grams red chilli peppers
1 piece shrimp paste (blachan),
    2 by 1 by ½ cm

Fry the pounded mixture until it starts to brown. Then add a little of the tamarind water and the salt and cook for about 5 minutes more, letting it all come to a gentle boil. Next, add the rest of the tamarind water and continue to simmer until the mixture comes back to the boil, at which time the pieces of eggplant are to be added. When the eggplant is nearly cooked, add the fish. Continue simmering until the fish is cooked and the oil rises to the top. (When it is ready, this dish should have plenty of liquid left in it – well over 1 cup.)

It is possible to make this dish with a much larger quantity of chilli peppers (60 grams, or even more). It would then be called Ikan masak asam pedas, the last word meaning 'hot for the tongue'.

Ikan Asam Perkat

Fish in a tamarind and turmeric gravy

½ kilo or a little more fish (e.g. tenggiri, Spanish mackerel, pages 110 and 111,
    cleaned and cut into small pieces
tamarind water made from 6 tablespoonfuls tamarind pulp
1 stalk lemon grass, crushed
1½ tablespoonfuls salt
4 shallots ⎫
a small piece of turmeric ⎬ pounded ingredients
1½ tablespoonfuls shrimp paste ⎭
6 fresh red chilli peppers, slit lengthwise
6 fresh green chilli peppers, slit in the same way
1 tablespoonful oil

Strain the tamarind water into a deep pot. Add the lemon grass, sugar, salt and pounded ingredients and bring the mixture to the boil. Add the fish and chilli peppers and simmer for 5 minutes or so, until the fish is cooked. Just before serving add the tablespoonful of oil to the dish, which should be served hot.

Achar Ikan *Pickled fish*

A popular Malaysian dish which will keep for up to a week. The version which I first tasted was prepared by Mrs Brobiah Ismail on the following lines, using red snapper (pages 74 to 77).

a fish weighing about 600 grams
    suitable for cutting into steaks
salt
ground turmeric
coconut oil for frying (several
    tablespoonfuls at least)
5 or 6 small red onions

2 cloves garlic
1 one-inch piece ginger
3 green chilli peppers
a dozen or so one-inch pieces
    of cucumber, cut lengthways,
    free of peel and seeds
vinegar to taste
more salt to taste

Clean the fish and cut it into steaks about 2 cm thick, then let these dry in the sun. Later, rub salt and turmeric into them. Then fry them.

The small onions, cloves of garlic and ginger are sliced (not finely – if the onions and cloves of garlic are very small they may even be left whole, but peeled). The green chilli peppers are sliced lengthways into two, as far as the stem. Fry the onions until they are golden, then add the fish, chilli peppers, cucumber, vinegar and salt. Let it simmer for a while (5 minutes or more). Serve hot or cold. (I like it cold.)

Rendang Ikan *A speciality of Sarawak*

1 fish of about ¾ kilo
    (uncleaned weight)
2 coconuts
6 tomatoes, quartered
2 green chilli peppers, pounded
oil for frying
3 or 4 small onions
tamarind water to taste
coriander leaves
salt to taste

ingredients to be pounded:
6 or 7 small onions, sliced
4 cloves garlic
1 stalk lemon grass, bruised and chopped
1 piece galingale, sliced finely
1 teaspoonful white cumin seed
    (kintan halus)
1 teaspoonful aniseed (jintan kasar or
    jintan manis)

First extract the coconut water from both coconuts and boil it until it is reduced to a 'cake' of palm sugar. Then use one of the coconuts to make both coconut cream and coconut milk in the usual way.

Heat the oil and put the fish (cleaned and scaled, and scored on the sides if necessary) in it. Leave there until it is half cooked, no more. Then add the 3 or 4 onions, halved or sliced, and let them turn golden. At this point add the pounded ingredients. When the pounded ingredients have been fried briefly add the coconut cream and coconut milk, palm sugar and tamarind water. Let the whole mixture simmer until the liquid is greatly reduced (it should have almost dried up) and then put in the tomatoes and the coriander leaves. Add salt to taste and serve.

Gulai Ikan

A basic Malay fish curry

Almost any fish will do for this recipe. Threadfin (pages 44 and 45) would be one possibility; snappers or croakers would be others.

1 kilo (cleaned weight) of fish (see above) cut into small pieces
6 small red onions (or 1½ Spanish onions), finely chopped
4 cloves garlic, chopped
2 small pieces fresh ginger, smashed
6 dried red chilli peppers, seeded and sliced finely
2 stalks lemon grass, finely chopped

2 cups coconut milk	*pounded ingredients:*
2 cups coconut cream	3 teaspoonfuls coriander seeds
3 pieces asam keping (dried apple tamarind)	2 teaspoonfuls fennel seeds
	1 teaspoonful cumin seeds
salt to taste	1 teaspoonful turmeric powder

Combine the onions, garlic, ginger, chilli peppers, lemon grass and all the pounded ingredients with coconut milk to produce a paste.

Heat the paste, bring it to the boil and let it simmer for 10 minutes. Then add the asam keping and the coconut cream, allowing the curry sauce to simmer for a further 10 minutes and finally add the fish with salt to taste. Continue to cook the dish gently until the pieces of fish are cooked through (10 minutes or so, according to their size).

Ikan Pudichchi

As Harvey Day points out, when giving a version of this recipe in his *Third Book of Curries*, this is one of the few Oriental dishes in its category which does not require the use of fat or oil. The dish is of Indian origin and is popular in Indian Moslem families in Malaysia.

1 kilo (dressed weight) of a substantial fish such as a large snapper (page 74 and 75), cut into eight steaks or slices
2 cups coconut cream

1 tablespoonful finely sliced onion	8 red chilli peppers, pounded
4 cloves garlic, chopped	1 teaspoonful turmeric powder
3 1-inch slices of fresh ginger, chopped	1 sprig curry leaves (daun kari)
1 tablespoonful rempah (curry paste)	½ teaspoonful fenugreek
½ stalk lemon grass, chopped	1 stick of cinnamon
salt to taste	juice of 1 lime or lemon

Place the pieces of fish in a thick pan (or, better, a fireproof earthenware pot) and add all the other ingredients except the lemon juice. Bring to the boil and cook gently for 15 minutes or so until the fish is nearly done. Then add the lemon juice and finish cooking. Discard the curry leaves and cinnamon before serving.

Fish Moolie

This dish illustrates the connection between the cooking of Southern India and that of Malaya. The Tamils of Southern India have a traditional series of curries which they call Moli and which are in turn related to a Ceylon curry which (according to 'Wyvern', the learned author of *Culinary Jottings for Madras*, who described it in great detail) was known sometimes as the Malay curry. Whatever the origins of the dish, it is a good one in both the Indian and Malay versions.

6 steaks of threadfin (ikan kurau or senangin, page 45) or snapper (ikan merah, page 75)
2 large Spanish or 8 small red onions, sliced
4 slices of ginger, cut into strips
2 red chilli peppers, seeded and cut into halves
oil for frying
1 stalk lemon grass (serai) ⎫
3 slices galingale (langkuas) ⎪
4 candlenuts (buah keras) ⎬ pounded together
1 small piece of fresh turmeric (kunyit) ⎭
salt to taste
1 cup (first extraction) coconut cream
1 cup (second extraction) coconut milk

for the garnishing:
1 red chilli pepper, seeded and sliced
1 green chilli pepper, seeded and sliced
2 small red onions, finely chopped and fried
several long thin strips of ginger, fried

First, fry the onions, ginger and chilli peppers until they are soft but not brown. Add the pounded ingredients and continue frying for another minute. Then remove the pan from the heat.

Pour into the pan all the coconut milk and half only of the coconut cream. Return the pan to a low flame and bring the mixture slowly to the boiling point, taking care that it does not curdle. Let it simmer for a couple of minutes, then add the salt and the fish steaks and continue cooking, still on a low flame, for 15 to 20 minutes, until the fish is done.

Just before serving the dish, pour in the remaining coconut cream. Add the garnishings and serve with cooked rice.

Sambal Udang

Curried prawns

A Sambal is traditionally and usually a side dish. But recently Malaysians have started to treat some of them, such as this one, as a main dish.

300 grams prawns, washed but left whole
oil for frying
the juice of 2 limes, added to
    ½ litre water
1 tablespoonful sugar
salt
coriander leaves, chopped

ground ingredients:
8 small red onions
10 dried red chilli peppers, previously
    soaked
3 fresh red chilli peppers
2 candlenuts (buah keras)
2 teaspoonfuls turmeric powder

Fry the ground ingredients until they give off a fragrant aroma (5 to 10 minutes). Pour on the diluted lime juice and add the sugar and salt. Bring to the boil, add the prawns and cook rapidly for a minute or two before lowering the heat and simmering them for 15 minutes. Sprinkle them with the coriander leaves and serve.

Sambal Tumis Ikan Bilis

A sambal made with dried anchovies

250 grams anchovies, bought after being steamed and dried whole (or, if you
    prefer, the same quantity of dried shrimp or fresh squid)
2 tablespoonfuls coconut oil
10 dried red chilli peppers, ground
1 slice shrimp paste (blachan) of about 35 grams
1 cup tamarind water
4 large onions, cut into rings
salt and pepper to taste

Behead and gut the anchovies (a double operation which can be effected by a single movement, since the gut will come away with the head), fry them in coconut oil until they are crisp and set them aside to drain. (If dried shrimp are used, they need only be washed and drained; if squid, clean them as usual and slice them finely.)

Next, fry the ground chilli and shrimp paste in the coconut oil until they are brown. Add the tamarind water gradually. When it has all been put in and has come to the boil, add the onion rings and simmer them until they are soft. Finally, add the prepared fish with the seasoning. The dish should continue to simmer, uncovered, for a further 20 to 30 minutes, if you like a fairly liquid sambal, or for 40 minutes if you prefer it to be almost dry.

The sambal should be served with well salted rice cooked in coconut milk.

Kerabu Paku

This is a delicious side dish. The delicate flavour of the shrimp and leaves is best set off by coconut-flavoured rice.

100 grams dried shrimp
½ kilo daun paku (an edible fern)
200 grams shredded dried coconut, fried until golden brown
5 or 6 fresh red chilli peppers, seeded and cut into thin strips
½ litre coconut cream seasoned with salt and pepper
juice of 1 lime

Trim the daun paku so that the thick stalks are discarded and you are left with the tender young shoots only. Cut these into 4 cm strips and soften them for 3 minutes in water which has just come off the boil.

Mix the shredded fried coconut, shrimp and chilli peppers in a wooden bowl. Then add the drained leaves and the coconut cream, taking care that the mixture does not become too watery (which it will not be if the leaves have been well drained and the coconut cream is thick). Finally, sprinkle the lime juice over the dish.

Fried Kway Teow

In her neat little book on Malaysian recipes Mrs Linda Quo explains that this sort of hawker-style fried Kway teow is a common sight in market areas, 'five-foot paths' and night stores in Malaysia.

2 slices kway teow (white sheets of rice noodle)
4 tablespoonfuls lard (with a few bits of pork fat)
5 cloves garlic
20 sprigs of Chinese chives (kochai)
1 handful bean sprouts
1 tablespoonful thick black sauce
4 tablespoonfuls chilli paste
salted water
½ cup shucked cockles or clams
1 egg (optional)

Open the kway teow and cut each into about ½ inch sections. Heat the lard and bits of pork fat in a wok, then fry in it the garlic, kway teow, chives and bean sprouts. Add the sauce, chilli paste and salted water. Go on frying for a short time, then add the cockles or clams. If you wish to incorporate an egg, push the kway teow mixture to one side of the wok, put in a little more lard and break the egg over this. When it sets, stir it into the kway teow.

Udang Masak Lemak

Prawns in coconut cream

10 to 12 medium-sized prawns
½ coconut
1 large onion
2 teaspoonfuls coconut oil
¼ teaspoonful turmeric powder

Peel, devein and wash the prawns. Use the coconut to prepare 1 cup coconut cream.

Peel the onion and slice it thinly. Heat the oil and fry in it, for a minute or so, the sliced onion and the turmeric. Then add the coconut cream and the prawns and simmer the mixture for 15 to 20 minutes, by which time the liquid will have thickened satisfactorily. Rice is served separately with this dish.

Baked Crab

400 grams cooked crab meat
4 crab shells
oil for frying
4 small red onions, finely chopped
1 tablespoonful chilli sauce

2 spring onions, finely chopped
4 tablespoonfuls grated coconut
salt and pepper to taste
2 egg whites, stiffly beaten

Fry the onions until they are golden brown. Put them in a mixing bowl and add the chilli sauce, spring onions, crab meat, grated coconut, and seasoning, stirring thoroughly. Spoon this mixture into the crab shells and coat each one with the beaten egg white. Fry the stuffed shells in plenty of very hot oil for about 3 minutes, or until the tops are golden.

Curried Cuttlefish

400 grams small cuttlefish (page 180)
coconut oil for frying
½ litre coconut milk
1 tablespoonful fennel seeds
6 curry leaves (or use sweet basil)
1 stalk lemon grass, bruised
salt to taste

ground ingredients:
1 tablespoonful poppy seeds
1 piece of fresh ginger, shredded
4 red chilli peppers
2 tablespoonfuls curry powder
4 cloves garlic, chopped
4 small red onions, chopped

Remove the head, gut and ink sac from each cuttlefish and skin them. Cut the prepared cuttlefish into small pieces; wash and drain them. Fry the ground ingredients gently for about 4 minutes until brown or until a fragrance is given off. Add the coconut milk and bring to simmering point before adding the cuttle-fish, fennel seeds, curry leaves, lemon grass and salt. Simmer gently for 30 minutes.

Nasi Goreng

Malaysian Fried Rice

This dish, one of the most common in Malaysia, always includes prawns, which give it a strong marine flavour. In other respects it is subject to small variations, both in ingredients and in presentation. The Chinese make it with pork, decorate it elaborately with slivers of omelette, chopped spring onion, fried onion, red chilli peppers and parsley, and serve it with a thick chilli sauce. The Malay people, on the other hand, use beef as the meat, adding onions and sometimes green peas. They present the dish in a neat mould, surrounded by shredded lettuce; decorate it with flowered chilli peppers and a single fried egg on top; and serve with it soy sauce containing thin slices of chilli pepper. Europeans living in Malaysia have their own variations too; in one such household the nasi goreng is garnished with croûtons, an addition which adds a pleasurable crunch to the dish.

The basic recipe which follows provides what many Malaysians would regard as generous quantities of prawn and meat. Less may be used. I should explain also that, although the combination of prawn and meat is what one meets in almost all restaurants and most homes, there does exist in coastal villages a nasi goreng which has fish in place of meat. This is naturally even more marine in flavour than the standard versions, and I recommend trying it by substituting 150 grams of chopped fish for the 150 grams of meat listed in the ingredients below.

150 grams prawns (peeled weight)
150 grams pork or beef, trimmed
  of fat and finely chopped
1 cup rice
oil for frying
1 clove garlic, finely chopped
5 small onions, finely chopped
  (optional)
1 tablespoonful sultanas
1 tablespoonful light soy sauce

suggestions for garnishing:
4 small red onions, sliced or chopped
  and fried
4 lettuce leaves, shredded
2 fresh red chilli peppers, seeded and cut
  into slivers
3 spring onions, finely chopped
a one-egg omelette, rolled up like a
  pancake and cut into strips,
  OR a fried egg
a tablespoonful of chopped parsley
croûtons

After preparing the prawns and meat, boil the rice. Then prepare the garnishings you have chosen and set them aside.

Next, fry the prawns and meat with the garlic and onions until brown. Then stir in the cooked rice, sultanas and soy sauce and continue to fry gently until the mixture is thoroughly heated and evenly browned.

Garnish the dish and serve it with chilli sauce or soy sauce.

Bibliography

Part One. Catalogues.

ABBOTT, R. TUCKER (ed.): *Indo-Pacific Mollusca*: a collection of monographs published as a continuing series by the Department of Mollusks, Academy of Natural Sciences, Philadelphia.

Academia Sinica: *Commercial Marine Fishes of China* (in Chinese): Peking, 1964.

Academia Sinica: *Crabs of China* (in Chinese): Peking, 1964.

ALLEN, G.R.: *Snappers of the World*: Vol 6, FAO Species Catalogue, FAO, Rome, 1985.

AVERY, ARTHUR C.: *Fish Processing Handbook for the Philippines*: Research Report 26 of the Fish and Wildlife Service of the United States Department of the Interior: Washington, D.C., 1950.

BAGNIS, R., MAZELLIER, P., BENNETT, JACK and CHRISTIAN, ERWIN: *Poissons de Polynésie*: Les Editions du Pacifique (Papeete, Tahiti) et Les Editions Albin Michel (Paris), troisième édition 1974.

BANAPOST, THIEN and WONGRATANA, THOSAPORN: *A Check List of Fishes in the Reference Collection maintained at the Marine Fisheries Laboratory*: Contribution No 7, Marine Fisheries Laboratory, Department of Fisheries, Bangkok, December, 1967.

BIANCHI, GABRIELLA: *Field Guide to the Commercial Marine and Brackish-Water Species of Pakistan*: FAO, Rome, 1985.

BIRKENMEIER, ELMAR: *Notes on some 'Coral Fishes' in Brunei Waters*: reprinted from the *Brunei Museum Journal*, Vol. 2, No. 1, 1970.

BURKILL, I.H.: *A Dictionary of the Economic Products of the Malay Peninsula*: 2 volumes, Crown Agents for the Colonies, London, 1935 (and reprinted for the Governments of Malaysia and Singapore, Kuala Lumpur, 1966).

BUSTARD, ROBERT: *Sea Turtles*: Collins, Sydney, 1972.

CANTOR, T.E.: *Catalogue of Malayan Fishes*: reprinted from the *Journal of the Asiatic Society of Bengal*, Volume XVIII, Part 2, 1849: Asher, Amsterdam, 1966.

CARPENTER, KENT, E.: *Fusilier Fishes of the World* – Volume 8, FAO Species Catalogue, FAO, Rome, 1988.

CARPENTER, KENT E. and ALLEN, GERALD R.: *Emperor Fishes and Large-Eye Breams of the World* – Volume 9, FAO Species Catalogue, FAO, Rome, 1989.

CARPENTER, KENT E. and NIEM, VOLKER H.: *The Living Marine Resources of the Western Central Pacific - Volume 1 Seaweeds, corals, bivalves and gastropods*: FAO, Rome, 1998.

CARPENTER, KENT E. and NIEM, VOLKER H.: *The Living Marine Resources of the*

Western Central Pacific - Volume 2 Cephalopods, crustaceans, holothurians and sharks: FAO, Rome, 1998.

CARPENTER, KENT E. and NIEM, VOLKER H.: *The Living Marine Resources of the Western Central Pacific - Volume 3 Batoid fishes, chimaeras and bony fishes part 1*: FAO, Rome, 1999.

CARPENTER, KENT E. and NIEM, VOLKER H.: *The Living Marine Resources of the Western Central Pacific - Volume 4 Bony fishes part 2*: FAO, Rome, 1999.

CHAN, W.L.: *Marine Fishes of Hong Kong*, Part I: Government Press, Hong Kong, 1968.

CHEVEY, P.: *Poissons des campagnes du 'de Lanessan' (1925-29)*: Travaux de l'Institut Océanographique de l'Indochine, 4ème Mémoire: Gouvernement Général de l'Indochine, Saigon, 1932.

CHUANG, S.H.: *On Malayan Shores*: a Log Cabin Book published by Muwu Shosa, Singapore, 1961.

CHUANG, S.H. (ed): *Animal Life and Nature in Singapore*: Singapore University Press, Singapore, 1973.

COLLETTE, BRUCE B., and NAUEN, CORNELIA E.: *Scombrids of the World*: Volume 2, FAO Species Catalogue, FAO, Rome, 1983.

COMMISSION OF RESEARCH ON THE FISH OF THE WESTERN PACIFIC: *Illustrated Dictionary of the Names of Fish of Commercial Importance of the Western Pacific* (introduction in Russian, names given in Russian, Chinese, Korean, Vietnamese, Mongolian, Japanese and English): Peking, 1964.

DAVIDSON, ALAN: *Fish and Fish Dishes of Laos*: the author, Vientiane, 1975 and Prospect Books, Totnes, 2003.

DAVIDSON, ALAN: *Mediterranean Seafood* (new edn): Ten Speed Press and Prospect Books, Berkeley and Totnes, 2002.

DAVIDSON, ALAN: *The Oxford Companion to Food*: Oxford University Press, Oxford, 1999 (and as *The Penguin Companion to Food*, Penguin Books, London, 2002).

DAY, FRANCIS: *The Fishes of India, being a natural history of the fishes known to inhabit the sea and fresh water of India, Burma and Ceylon*: Dawson, London, in 2 volumes (1875-78) and with a Supplement (1888) – also available in a facsimile reprint from Today and Tomorrow's Book Agency, New Delhi, 1971.

DAY, FRANCIS: Fishes, Vols 1 and 2, in *The Fauna of British India Including Ceylon and Burma* (a series edited by W.T. Blanford): London, Calcutta and Bombay, 1889 – also available in facsimile reprint by the Government of India Press, 1963.

DE BRUIN, GEORGE H.P., RUSSELL, BARRY C., BOGUSCH, ANDRÉ: *The Marine Fishery Resources of Sri Lanka*: FAO, Rome, 1994.

Department of Fisheries, Ministry of Agriculture, Bangkok: *Seafood for Thai People* (in Thai): Ministry of Agriculture, Bangkok, 1969.

DWIPANGGA, A.: *Ikan Laut Indonesia* (in Indonesian – the title means Indonesian Sea Fish): Lembaga Penelitian Perikanan Laut (Marine Fisheries Research Institute), Jakarta, 1973.

FAUSTINO, see under TALAVERA.

Fish Marketing Organisation, Hong Kong: *50 Important Food Fishes and the Fishing Industry In Hong Kong*: Government Printer, Hong Kong, 1972.

Fish Marketing Organisation, Hong Kong: *Sea Life Around Hong Kong:* annual volumes each containing material on 12 species: Hong Kong Government, 1969/70 onwards.

GRABAU, A.W. and KING, G.S.: *Shells of Peitaiho:* 2nd edition, Peking 1928.

GREY, D.L., DALL, W., BAKER, A.: *A Guide to the Australian Penaeid Prawns:* Department of Primary Production of the Northern Territory, Darwin, 1983.

GRUVEL, A: *L'Indochine – Ses Richesses Marines et Fluviales:* Paris, 1925.

GUILBERT: *La Pêche dans le Golfe du Tonkin* [publication details not available].

GUINOT, DANIELE: *Les crabes comestibles de l'Indo-Pacifique:* Fondation Signer-Polignac, Paris, 1966.

HEEMSTRA, PHILLIP C. AND RANDALL, JOHN E.: *Groupers of the World:* Vol 16, FAO Species Catalogue, FAO, Rome, 1993.

HERKLOTS, G.A.C. and LIN, S.Y.: *Common Marine Food-fishes of Hong Kong:* South China Morning Post, 3rd enlarged edition, undated but ? early 1960s.

HERRE, ALBERT W.: *Check List of Philippine Fishes:* Research Report 20 of the Fish and Wildlife Service of the United States Department of the Interior: Washington, D.C.. 1953.

HERRE, ALBERT W. and UMALI, AGUSTIN F.: *English and Local Common Names of Philippine Fishes:* Circular 14 of the Fish and Wildlife Service, US Department of the Interior: Washington, D.C., 1948.

HOLTHUIS, L.B.: *Shrimps and Prawns of the World:* Vol 1, FAO Species Catalogue, FAO, Rome, 1980.

HOLTHUIS, L. B.: *Marine Lobsters of the World:* Vol 13, FAO Species Catalogue, FAO, Rome, 1991.

HORNELL, J.: *Fishing in Many Waters:* London, 1950.

HOSKING, RICHARD: *A Dictionary of Japanese Food:* Charles E. Tuttle, Rutland, Vermont, 1996.

Inspection Générale des Pêches de l'Indochine: *Principaux poissons comestibles d'Indochine:* a booklet also described as a production of the Institut Océanographique at Nhatrang-Annam and of the Service de la Marine Marchande, under the auspices of the Commissariat de France pour l'Indochine: Léon Feuillet, Saigon, 1945.

KIRA, TETSUAKI and HABE, TADASHIGE: *Shells of the Western Pacific in Colour,* Vols. 1 and 2: Hoikusha Publishing Co., Osaka, 1962.

KREUZER, RUDOLF (ed.): *Fishery Products:* Fishing News (Books) Ltd, West Byfleet, by arrangement with the FAO, 1974.

KURONUMA, KATSUZO: *A Check List of Fishes of Vietnam:* United States Operations Mission to Vietnam, 1961.

LANE, FRANK W.: *Kingdom of the Octopus:* Jarrolds, London, 1957.

LEE, DING-AN and YU HSIANG-PING: *The Penaeid Shrimps of Taiwan:* Joint Commission on Rural Reconstruction, Taipei, Taiwan, 1977.

Lembaga Oceanologi Nasional (National Institute of Oceanography): *Bahan Makanan Dari Laut* (in Indonesian – the title means Seafood, but the contents are restricted to species which are not commercially important): Jakarta, 1973.

'LE NESTOUR': *La pêche en Cochinchine:* printed at Tandinh, undated but? about 1922 (an inscription on the copy in the Bibliothèque Nationale at Hanoi suggests that only 100 copies of this booklet were printed).

LOVETT, DONALD L: *A Guide to the Shrimps, Prawns, Lobsters, and Crabs of Malaysia and Singapore:* Faculty of Fisheries and Marine Science – Occasional Publication No 2, University of Pertanian Malaysia, Selangor, 1981.

MARQUEZ, M. RENÉ: *Sea Turtles of the World,* Vol 11, FAO Species Catalogue, FAO, Rome, 1990.

MAUNG AUNG MYINT: *Edible Molluscs of the Mergui Area:* term paper, Arts and Science University, Rangoon, 1966-67.

MAXWELL, C.N.: *Malayan Fishes:* Singapore, 1921.

MUNRO, IAN S.R.: *The Marine and Fresh Water Fishes of Ceylon:* Department of External Affairs, Canberra, 1955.

NAKAMURA, IZUMI: *Billfishes of the World:* Vol 5, FAO Species Catalogue, FAO, Rome, 1885.

NEWTON, LILY: *Seaweed Utilisation:* Sampson Low, London 1951.

OMMANNEY, F. D.: *A Draught of Fishes:* Longman, London, 1965.

PAVILLON, JEAN-FRANCOIS and BRULHET, JACQUES: *Principaux poissons comestibles des côtes du Cambodge,* Volume 1 (all published): published under the auspices of the Institut Oceanographique de Kompong-Som and the Museum National d'Histoire Naturelle de Paris by the Services de Coopération Technique de l'Ambassade de France, Phnom Penh, 1970.

People's Pearl and Fishery Corporation (of Burma): *The Commercial Fishes of Burmese Coastal Waters:* unpublished document of the Planning and Research Department of the Corporation, Rangoon, 1972.

PETILLOT, LOYS: *Une richesse de Cambodge – La pêche et les poissons:* Paris, 1911.

PUNPOKA, SUPAP: *A Review of the Flatfishes (Pleuronectiformes – Heterosomata) of the Gulf of Thailand . . .:* Kasetsart University Fisheries Research Bulletin No 1, 1964.

RACEK, A.A.: *Indo-West Pacific Penaeid Prawn Species of Commercial Importance:* Document No. IPFC/C70/SYM/3 of the Indo-Pacific Fisheries Council, 14th session, Bangkok, 1970.

RAO, G.N. SUBBA, ed.: *Boiling Fish for Short Term Preservation:* Indo-Pacific Fisheries Council, Regional Study No. 1: FAO Regional office, Bangkok, 1965.

RAO, G.N. SUBBA: *Use of Seaweeds Directly as Human Food:* Indo-Pacific Fisheries Council Regional Study No. 2, FAO Regional Office, Bangkok, 1965.

RAU, NORBERT and RAU, ANKE: *Commercial Fishes of the Philippines:* German Agency for Technical Cooperation, Eschborn, 1980.

READ, BERNARD E.: *Common Food Fishes of Shanghai:* Southern Materials Centre, Taipei, 1977.

READ, BERNARD, E.: *Chinese Materia Medica: Fish Drugs:* Southern Materials Centre, Taipei, (1939 and 1982).

Research Section, Fishery Department, Bangkok: *Sat Thaleh Thi Ben Pai She-wit* (in Thai, a book on dangerous sea animals) Bangkok, 1968.

ROBERTS, JOE and SEN, COLLEEN TAYLOR: 'A Carp Wearing Lipstick: The Role of Fish in Bengali Cuisine and Culture' in *Fish – Food from the Waters*, Proceedings of the Oxford Symposium on Food and Cookery, 1997, (ed. Harlan Walker): Prospect Books, Totnes, 1998.

ROFEN, ROBERT R.: *Handbook of the Food Fishes of the Gulf of Thailand:* George Vanderbilt Foundation and University of California, Scripps Institution of Oceanography, La Jolla, California, 1963 (not complete when published).

ROPER, CLYDE F.E., SWEENEY, MICHAEL J. and NAUEN, CORNELIA E.: *Cephalopods of the World*, Vol 3, FAO Species Catalogue, FAO, Rome, 1984.

ROUGHLEY, T.C.: *Fishes and Fisheries of Australia:* Angus and Robertson, Sydney, revised edition 1966.

SAANIN, HASANUDDIN: *Taksonoml dan Kuntji Identifikasi Ikan* (in Indonesian – the title means Taxonomy and Key for the Identification of Fish): volumes 1 and 2: Binatjipta, 1968.

SAUL, MARY: *Shells:* Country Life, London 1974.

SAWADA, TOSIZO: *A Dictionary of Fish in Indonesia*: Japan International Cooperation, 1977.

SCHROEDER, ROBERT E: *Philippine Shore Fishes of the Western Sulu Sea*: National Media Production Center, Manila, Philippines, 1980.

SCHUSTER, W.H. and RUSTAMI DJAJADIREDJA: *Local Common Names of Indonesian Fishes:* N.V. Penerbit W. van Hoeve-Bandung, The Hague, 1952.

SCOTT, J.S.: *An Introduction to the Sea Fishes of Malaya:* Ministry of Agriculture, Federation of Malaya, Kuala Lumpur, 1959.

SEALE, ALVIN: *Notes on Philippine Edible Molluscs:* in No 4 of Vol VII of the *Philippine Journal of Science*, 1912.

SMITH, J.L.B.: *The Sea Fishes of Southern Africa:* Central News Agency Ltd, South Africa, 1949.

SOPHER, DAVID E.: *The Sea Nomads:* in Memoirs of the National Museum of Singapore, No. 5, 1965.

SUVATTI, CHOTE: *Molluscs of Thailand* (in Thai): Kasetsart University, Bangkok, 1966.

SUVATI, CHOTE: *Fishes of Thailand*: Royal Institute of Thailand, Thailand, 1981.

TALAVERA, FLORENCIO and FAUSTINO, LEOPOLDO A.: *Edible Mollusks of Manila:* reprinted from the *Philippine Journal of Science*, Vol. 50, No. 1, Bureau of Printing, Manila, 1933.

TALAVERA, FLORENCIO and FAUSTINO, LEOPOLDO A.: *Industrial Shells of the Philippines:* reprinted from the *Philippine Journal of Science*, Vol. 45, No. 3, Bureau of Printing, Manila, 1931.

THIEMMEDH, JINDA: *Edible Molluscs of Bangkok* (in Thai): Kasetsart University, Bangkok, 1960.

TIN TIN SOE: *A Systematic Study of the Prawns Found in the Rangoon Markets:* thesis, Arts and Science University, Rangoon, 1972.

TIRANT, G.: *Mémoire sur les poissons de la rivière de Hué:* Saigon, 1883.

TIRANT, G.: *Notes sur les poissons de la Basse-Cochinchine et du Cambodge,* in *Excursions et Reconnaissances*, Vols IX and X, Saigon, 1885.

TRAN-NGOC-LOI and NGUYEN-CHAU, de l'Institut Océanographique de Nhatrang: *Les poissons d'importance commerciale au Vietnam:* in *Bulletin de la Société des Etudes Indochinoises,* NS Tome XXXIX, No. 3, 3ème trimestre 1964.

TRONO, GAVINO C. JR. and GANZON-FORTES, EDNA T.: *An Illustrated Seaweed Flora of Calatagan, Batangas, Philippines*: University of Philippines, Manila, 1980.

TWEEDIE, M.W.F. and HARRISON, J.L: *Malayan Animal Life*: Longman Malaysia, Singapore, 1970.

U KHIN: *Fisheries In Burma:* Government Printing and Stationery Office, Rangoon, 1948.

UMALI, AGUSTIN F.: *Edible Fishes of Manila:* Department of Agriculture and Commonwealth of the Philippines, my copy undated.

U TINT HLANG: *A Classified List of Fishes of Burma:* paper read at the Third Burma Research Congress on 19 March 1968.

Vien Nghien Cuu Bien (Institute of Marine Research): *Cá Kinh Tế Vịnh Bắc Bộ* (Fish of Economic Importance in the Gulf of Tonkin): Hanoi, 1971.

VOSS, G.L.: *Cephalopods of the Philippine Island:* Bulletin No. 234 of the United States National Museum, Washington, D.C., 1963.

VOSS, G.L. and WILLIAMSON, G.: *Cephalopods of Hong Kong:* Government Press, Hong Kong, 1971.

WENG, CHUA CHONG: *Commercial Prawns of Peninsular Malaysia*: Ministry of Agriculture Malaysia, Kuala Lumpur, 1978.

WHITEHEAD, P.J.P.: *A Synopsis of the Clupeoid Fishes of India:* reprinted from the *Journal of the Marine Biological Association of India,* Vol. 14, No. 1, pp. 160-256, 1972: Madras, 1973.

WHITEHEAD, PETER J.P.: *Clupeoid Fishes of the World*: Vol 7, Part 1 FAO Species Catalogue, FAO, Rome, 1985.

WHITEHEAD, PETER J.P., NELSON, GARETH J. and WONGRATANA, THOSAPORN: *Clupeoid Fishes of the World:* Vol 7, Part 2, FAO Species Catalogue, FAO, Rome, 1985.

WONGRATANA, THOSAPORN: *Sea Fishes of Commercial Importance of Thailand:* unpublished paper prepared for the Indo-Pacific Fisheries Council: Bangkok, 1967.

YANG, HUNG-CHIA and CHEN, TUNG-PAI: *Common Food Fishes of Taiwan*: Joint Commission on Rural Reconstruction, Taipei, Taiwan, 1971.

YULE, COL. HENRY and BURNELL, A.C.: *Hobson-Jobson*, ed. William Crooke (1st edn published John Murray, London, 1903), New Delhi, 1979.

ZANEVELD, J.S.: *Economic Marine Algae of Tropical South and East Asia and their Utilization:* Special Publication No. 3 of the Indo-Pacific Fisheries Council, FAO Regional Office, Bangkok, 1955.

Part Two: Cookery Section

ALEGRE, EDILBERTO N. and FERNANDEZ, DOREEN G.: *Kinilaw – A Philippine Cuisine of Freshness*: Bookmark, Manila, 1991.

ARROYO, P.T.: *The Science of Philippine Foods:* Quezon City, 1974 (and re-issued in 1982, the author's surname now given as Staub).

AVERY, ARTHUR C.: *Cosmopolitan Fish Cookery for the Philippines:* a mimeograph booklet published by USIS, Manila, undated but? about 1950.

BRACKMAN, AGNES DE KEIJZER: *The Art of Indonesian Cooking:* Asia Pacific Press, Singapore, 1970.

BRENNAN, JENNIFER: *Encyclopaedia of Chinese & Oriental Cookery*: Black Cat, London, 1988 (first published by Macdonald, London, 1984).

BRISSENDEN, ROSEMARY: *South East Asian Food:* Penguin, London, 1969.

CAMARA-GUMBAN, INDAY: '*What's Cooking?':* Cebu City, 1974.

CHAANMAATRA, S., CHARIYA and SUPAVATNA: *Tam-ra Arhaan Kao-waan 775 Chanit* (in Thai – 775 Thai dishes and sweets): Pittayakaan Publications, Bangkok, 1967.

CHAO, MRS. BUWEI YANG: *How to Cook and Eat in Chinese:* Penguin, London, 1962.

CHOW, DOLLY (MRS. C.T. WANG): *Chow! Secrets of Chinese Cooking:* Charles E. Tuttle Company, Tokyo, 1952.

CORDERO-FERNANDO, GILDA (ed): *The Culinary Culture of the Philippines*: Bancom, Philippines, 1976.

Cremation Cookery Books, various (see Thai recipe section).

DAVID-PEREZ, ENRIQUETA: *Recipes of the Philippines:* 19th printing, National Book Store, Manila, 1973.

DAVIDSON, ALAN: *A Kipper With My Tea*: Macmillan, London, 1988.

DAW KHIN THAN WAY: *Chat-ni pyote-ni hnint moint-myo sone-lote ni* (in Burmese – the title means Cooking Methods and Boiling Methods and Recipes for Various Foods): Rangoon, 1974.

DAW MAY KHINE: *Padatha chat-al pyote ni* (in Burmese – the title means The Padatha Book of Cooking and Boiling Methods): Rangoon, 1972.

DAY, HARVEY, 'Third Book of Curries' in *The Complete Book of Curries:* revised edition, London, 1970.

DAZA, NORA V.: *Let's Cook with Nora:* improved edition, ? Manila, 1969.

Departemen Pertanian (Department of Agriculture of the Government of Indonesia): *Mustikarasa* (in Indonesian – the title means mystical stone of taste): Djakarta, 1967.

DEVI, E. MAHESWARI: *Handy Rice Recipes:* MPH Publications, Singapore, 1971.

FENG, DOREEN YEN HUNG: *The Joy of Chinese Cooking:* Faber and Faber, London, 1952.

FERNANDEZ, DOREEN G. and ALEGRE, EDILBERTO N.: *Sarap – Essays on Philippine Food:* Mr. and Mrs., Manila, 1988.

FERNANDEZ, RAFI: *Malaysian Cookery*: Century Publishing, London, 1985.

GRIGSON, JANE and KNOX, CHARLOTTE: *Exotic Fruits & Vegetables*: Jonathan Cape, London, 1986.

HANDY, ELLICE: *My Favourite Recipes:* fourth revised edition, MPH Publications. Singapore, 1974.

HELLEI, PROFESSOR ANDRAS: *Les coutumes alimentaires Khmères:* No. 3 of the Etudes Statistiques of the Institut National de la Statistique et des Recherches Economiques Phnom Penh, 1973.

HERKLOTS, G.A.C.: *Vegetables In South-East Asia:* George Allen and Unwin, London, 1972.

HITCHCOCK, JOHN (ed.): *The Flavour of Malaysia:* Four Corners Publishing Co, Hong Kong, 1974.

HOANG THI FAN and others: *Day Nâu An Và Trang Trí:* Hanoi, 1972.

JACQUAT, CHRISTINE and BERTOSSI, GIANNI: *Plants from the Markets of Thailand*: Editions Duang Kamol, Bangkok, 1990.

JOHNS, YOHANNI: *Dishes from Indonesia:* Chilton Book Company and Thomas Nelson (Australia), 1971.

KHAING, MI MI: *Cook and Entertain the Burmese Way*: Karoma Publishers, Ann Arbor, 1978.

KOMOLTHITI, CHITSAMAAN: *Tam-ta Arhaan:* (in Thai – the title means Everyday Thai Dishes): Kaona Publications, Bangkok, 1973.

KOON, MRS. LEE CHIN: *Mrs Lee's Cookbook:* Singapore, 1974.

'KULAWEE': *Tam-ra Arhaan Kao-waan 1208 Chanit* (in Thai – 1208 Thai dishes and sweets): Pittayakaan Publications, Bangkok, 1970.

LANE, LILIAN: *Malayan Cookery Recipes:* University of London Press, 1964.

LATIEF, NY. TUTY: *Resep Masakan Daerad* (in Indonesian – the title means Regional Food Recipes): Pt. Bina Ilmu, Surabaya, 1975.

LECOURT, H.: *La cuisine chinoise:* Peking, 1925 (and reprinted in facsimile by Robert Laffont, Paris, 1968).

LIN, MISS CHAN SOW: *Chinese Restaurant Dishes, Indonesian and Nonya Dishes:* 6th edition, Kuala Lumpur, 1974.

LIN, HSIANG JU and LIN, TSUIFENG: *Chinese Gastronomy:* Hastings House, New York, 1969.

MA, MRS NANCY CHIH: *Mrs Ma's Chinese Cookbook:* Charles E. Tuttle Company, Tokyo, 1960.

MASEFIELD, G.B., WALLIS, M. and NICHOLSON, B.E.: *The Oxford Book of Food Plants:* Oxford University Press, 1969.

MEYNELL, ELIZABETH: *Kuala Lumpur Cookery* (only a few Malay recipes, but the glossary is comprehensive and valuable): Kuala Lumpur, undated but 1970s.

MILLER, JILL NHU HUONG: *Vietnamese Cookery:* Charles E. Tuttle Company, Tokyo, 1968.

MONAROENG, ARAMSRI and MONTRIVEJBOL, BUSRAKOM: *Tam-ra Kapkao* (in Thai – the title means Thai Dishes): Rungvithya Publications, Bangkok, 1969.

NGUYEN VAN TUNG: *Nâu Cóm Viêt-nam* (in Vietnamese – the title means Food in Vietnam and the book contains a collection of 291 recipes): Hanoi, date not noted but probably in the 1960s.

Nha Xuat Ban Phu Nu (Women's Publishing House in North Vietnam): *Huong Dan Nau An* (in Vietnamese – the title means, roughly, Cookery Manual): Hanoi, 1974.

Nha Xuat Ban Phu Nu (Women's Publishing House in North Vietnam): *Món An Thường Thúc* (in Vietnamese – the title means Usual Dishes): Hanoi, 1961.

OROSA DEL ROSARIO, HELEN (ed.): *Maria Y. Orosa, Her Life and Work* (with 700 recipes): 1st edition, ? Quezon City, 1970.

ORPIN, JACKI: *The Flavour of Hong Kong:* Four Corners Publishing Co., Hong Kong, 1974.

OWEN, SRI: *Indonesian Food and Cookery*, 3rd edn: Prospect Books, London, 1986.

OWEN, SRI: *Indonesian Regional Food & Cookery*: Transworld Publishers [first published Doubleday], London, 1994.

PONG PANGAN, SOMCHIT and POOBRASERT, SUPARB: *Edible and Poisonous Plants In Thai Forests:* Science Society of Thailand, Bangkok, ? 1974.

QUO, LINDA: *A Wide Selection of Local Recipes:* Petaling Jaya, Malaysia, 1974.

RICE, BILL: *Far Flung Food:* Siam Communications, Bangkok, 1974.

RIKS, DOLF: *A list of Spices, Herbs, Condiments etc used in Southeast Asian Cookery:* typescript of a book which was to be published if Mr Riks had time to finish it.

RIKS, DOLF: *Southeast Asian Cookery* – (1) Herbs and Spices, (2) Fruits and Seeds, (3) Condiments and Flavourings: in *Sawaddi* magazine, issues of March/April, June/July, August/September, 1972.

ROBEAU, ALEC: *Cooking the Indonesian Way:* Drake Publishers, New York, 1973.

ROUTIER, NICOLE: *Foods of Vietnam*: Stewart, Tabori & Chang, New York, 1989.

SAUNT, JAMES: *Citrus Varieties of the World*: Sinclair Int, Norwich, 1990.

SIMMONDS, PETER LUND: *Curiosities of Food*: London, 1859 (and reissued as a facsimile reprint by Ten Speed Press, Berkeley, 2001).

SO, YAN-KIT: *Classic Food of China*: Macmillan, London, 1992.

SOBHANA, S.A.R. LA PRINCESSE RASMI: *Le Guide Culinaire Cambodgien:* published for the American Women's Club of Cambodia by USIS, Phnom Penh, 1963.

SOLOMON, CHARMAINE: *Encyclopaedia of Asian Food*: William Heinemann, Victoria, Australia, 1996.

SONAKUL, SIBPAN: *Everyday Siamese Dishes:* sixth publication, Bangkok, 1971.

TAN, CECILIA: *Penang –Nyonya Cooking*: Eastern Universities Press, Singapore, 1983.

TENG, UNG: *Les aliments usuels au Cambodge:* thesis published by the Université Royale, Phnom Penh, 1967.

UNTARI, S.: *Resep Lauk Pauk* (in Indonesian, a book of recipes for dishes with rice): P.T. Bina Ilmu, Surabaya, undated but ? 1970s.

U SAN KHIN: *Some Medicinal and Useful Plants, both Indigenous and Exotic, of Burma:* Rangoon, 1970.

VAN DER MEIJDEN, MEVR. J.M.J. CATENIUS: *Groot Nieuw Volledig Indisch Kookboek:* 7th edition, undated (originally published in the 1920s ?), van Goor Zonen, Den Haag.

VILLACORTA-ALVAREZ, HERMINIA: *Philippine Cookery and Household Hints:* revised edition, Manila, 1973.

Women's Society of Christian Service of the Methodist English Church: *Rangoon International Cookbook:* Rangoon, 3rd edition, 1962.

'WYVERN': *Culinary Jottings for Madras:* 5th edition, Higginbotham and Co., Madras, 1885.

YWCA: *Asian Cook Book:* Bangkok, 1972.

YWCA: *1974 Asian Cook Book:* Bangkok, 1974.

ZAINU' DDIN, A.G.: *How To Cook Indonesian Food:* Australian-Indonesian Association of Victoria (Australia), revised edition, 1967.

ZAINUDDIN-MORO, SITTI NUR: *Nasi dan Sambal-sambalan* (Indonesian – the title means Rice and Sambals): P.T. Dian Rakjat, 1970.

Index

Part One. Names of Fish, Crustaceans, etc. in the Catalogues

This index has been designed to combine maximum convenience with minimum size. It does not include obsolete names or names of purely local significance. Nor does it contain names of species which are mentioned only incidentally in the catalogues. Otherwise, it covers all the names which are in the catalogues.

In revising this index for the present edition, priority has been given to pragmatic considerations, such as make it more user-friendly, rather than to strict consistency of presentation.

Part Two. Recipes

This index contains the recipe titles in their original languages and also, where appropriate, in English. It also contains the English and scientific (but not the local) names of ingredients which are described in the book. As a further aid to finding recipes, the reader is reminded that within each recipe section the normal order of recipes is fish soups, general recipes for fish, recipes for specific fish, recipes for crustaceans and, finally, recipes for molluscs. Many of the entries in the catalogues which constitute the first half of the book contain references to recipes suitable for the species in question.

Tables of Weights and Measures

Measurements of Volume/Liquid Measures

Liquids and powders and finely chopped things can conveniently be measured by volume. The measures most often employed are spoons, glasses and cups for any of these; and litres, pints etc. for liquids only.

Spoons may be measuring spoons, which are exact; or they may be the spoons in everyday use, which vary slightly in capacity. So far as I am concerned, either will do. I recommend the Chinese soupspoon (shown at the foot of the page) as a useful instrument to have in the kitchen. It is pleasant to wield, and its capacity is almost exactly equal to that of the dessertspoons and soupspoons issued by the British Government for use by Her Majesty's Representatives abroad (which are presumably the most official British spoons available).

Glasses, for example wineglasses and water glasses, can be useful measures in some parts of the world; but they are not much used in S. E. Asia, where indeed one is more apt to find a recipe referring to a cigarette tin or something like that.

Cups may be breakfast cups, teacups or coffee cups, all of which vary in size to an inconvenient extent; or measuring cups, which are exact but come in two versions, American and British. The American measuring cup (like the American pint) is distinctly smaller than its British counterpart. (Never mind. Use whichever you have. It will not normally matter. But the tables show the differences if you wish to take account of them. References in the recipes are to American cups.)

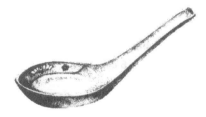

TABLE 1: MAINLY ABOUT SPOONFULS

a pinch	very little, just what you can pick up between thumb and forefinger
1 coffeespoonful	⅓ to ½ teaspoonful
1½ teaspoonfuls	1 dessertspoonful
1 dessertspoonful	1 soupspoonful
3 teaspoonfuls	1 tablespoonful
2 dessertspoonfuls	1 tablespoonful
4 tablespoonfuls	¼ cup (American)
5 tablespoonfuls	¼ cup (British)

TABLE 2: IN WHICH FLUID OUNCES ARE MATCHED TO THE METRIC SYSTEM AND TO BRITISH AND AMERICAN PINTS AND MEASURING CUPS

fluid oz	metric	British	American
½		1 tablespoonful	1 tablespoonful
1		2 tablespoonfuls	2 tablespoonfuls
2		4 tablespoonfuls	¼ cup
2½		¼ cup	5 tablespoonfuls
3½	100 ml	7 tablespoonfuls	7 tablespoonfuls
4	just over 100 ml	8 tablespoonfuls	¼ pint / ½ cup
5	nearly 150 ml	¼ pint / ½ cup	½ cup + 2 tbs
8	just under ¼ litre	¾ cup + 1 tbs	½ pint / 1 cup
8¾	¼ litre	just under 1 cup	just over 1 cup
10	nearly 300 ml	½ pint / 1 cup	1¼ cups
16	just under ½ litre	1½ cups + 2 tbs	1 pint / 2 cups
17½	½ litre	1¾ cups	just over 2 cups
20	nearly 600 ml	1 pint / 2 cups	2½ cups
35	1 litre	3½ cups	just over 4 cups

It may be useful to add that the French cuillère à bouche and cuillère à soupe are both equivalent to a tablespoon; and that their cuillère à pot, which is what we would call a small soup ladle, has a capacity of 4 tablespoonfuls. If a French recipe refers to a verre à liqueur, take this to mean 1 tablespoonful; if to a tasse à café, about 5 tablespoonfuls.

The standard size of tablespoons is subject to some variation. The American tablespoon is a little smaller than the British one; the Australian is larger.

TABLE 3: MEASUREMENTS OF WEIGHT, METRIC AND NON-METRIC

50 grams	just under 2 oz
100 grams	just under ¼ lb
¼ kilo (250 grams)	just over ½ lb
½ kilo (500 grams)	1 lb 1½ oz
¾ kilo (750 grams)	just over 1 lb 10 oz
1 kilo	2 lbs 3 oz
1½ kilos	3 lbs 5 oz
2 kilos	4 lbs 6 oz
1 oz	just under 30 grams
2 oz	just over 55 grams
3 oz	85 grams
¼ lb	nearly 115 grams
½ lb	just over 225 grams
¾ lb	nearly 350 grams
1 lb	454 grams
1½ lbs	680 grams
2 lbs	just over 900 grams

TABLE 4: MEASUREMENTS OF LENGTH, METRIC AND NON-METRIC

1 cm	⅜ inch
2 cm	¾ inch
2.5 cm	1 inch
5 cm	almost 2 inches
10 cm	almost 4 inches
15 cm	almost 6 inches
20 cm	7⅞ inches
25 cm	9⅞ inches
30 cm	just over 11¾ inches
30.5 cm	12 inches (1 foot)
35 cm	just over 13¾ inches
40 cm	15¾ inches
45 cm	almost 17¾ inches
50 cm	19¾ inches
60 cm	almost 23¾ inches (almost 2 feet)
70 cm	just over 27½ inches
80 cm	just over 31½ inches
90 cm	about 35½ inches
91.4 cm	3 feet (1 yard)
1 metre	3 feet 3⅜ inches

Everyone agrees that most solid foods are best measured by weight, unless they are regular in size and can be counted (like eggs and some vegetables). But American cookery writers and those who follow them have a habit of using measurements of volume for some solids like butter. This perverse practice is matched by cookery writers elsewhere who use weights to measure liquids such as cooking oil! And there are various foods which may be measured either by weight or by number. So I provide some miscellaneous equivalences below, intended to cover at least some of these points, for the benefit of readers who are using other books in conjunction with this one.

TABLE 5: MISCELLANEOUS EQUIVALENCES

cooking oil	7½ oz	1 cup
butter	2 oz	¼ cup (or 4 tablespoonfuls)
flour	4 oz	1 cup
noodles	¼ kilo	2½ cups (cooked and drained)
rice	1 lb	2 cups (uncooked), 6 cups (cooked)
cake of bean curd	4 oz	⅔ cup (in chunks)
garlic	nearly 1 oz (or 25 grams)	5 cloves (of S. E. Asian, i.e. rather small, garlic)
onions	¼ lb	4 small red ones or 1 medium Spanish (brown) one
dried mushrooms	2½ oz	¾ cup
Chinese cabbage	1 lb	4 cups (shredded)
shrimp, dried	3 oz	1 cup
prawns, medium	½ lb	1 cup (peeled, whole) or ¾ cup (diced)
crab meat	½ lb	1⅓ cup
fish fillets	¼ lb	½ cup (flaked)

TABLE 6: SOME LOCAL MEASURES

Burma
1 viss = 100 ticals = 3½ lbs
½ viss = 50 ticals = 1¾ lbs
¼ viss = 25 ticals = 14 oz
10 ticals = 5½ oz

Malaysia
1 tahil = 1⅓ oz: nearly 40 grams
16 tahil = 1 kati
1 kati = 1⅓ lbs: about 600 grams
1 ricebowl = ½ pint (British)
1 chupak = 2 pints (British)
1 cigarette tin rice = 5 oz

A Chinese ricebowl, matching
the Chinese soupspoon on page 365